→ See Hunsley + LeFebre ('90) – 15-20% estimated

Professional Psychology in Canada

List of Participants

Editors

Dr. Keith S. Dobson
Department of Psychology
University of Calgary
2500 University Drive N.W.
Calgary, Alberta
T2N 1N4

Dr. Deborah J. G. Dobson
Division of Psychology
Foothills Hospital
1403 – 29th Street N.W.
Calgary, Alberta
T2N 2T9

Contributors

Dr. Ken Craig
Department of Psychology
University of British Columbia
Vancouver, British Columbia
V6T 1W5

Dr. Steven Cronshaw
Department of Psychology
University of Guelph
Guelph, Ontario
N1G 2W1

Dr. Anna-Beth Doyle
Department of Psychology
Concordia University
1455 Demaisonneuve Blvd. West
Montreal, Quebec
H3G 1M8

Dr. Larry Eberlin
Department of Psychology
University of Alberta
6-102 Education North
Edmonton, Alberta
T6G 2G5

Dr. Henry Edwards
School of Psychology
University of Ottawa
Ottawa, Ontario
K1N 6N5

Dr. David Evans
Department of Psychology
University of Western Ontario
London, Ontario
N6A 5C2

Dr. Luc Granger
858 Davaar
Outremont, Quebec
H2V 3B5

Dr. Lee Handy
University Counselling Services
University of Calgary
2500 University Drive N.W.
Calgary, Alberta
T2N 1N4

Dr. Marg Hearn
Department of Psychology
University Hospital
London, Ontario
N6A 5C2

Dr. Bryan Hiebert
Department of Educational Psychology
University of Calgary
2500 University Drive N.W.
Calgary, Alberta
T2N 1N4

Dr. Barbara Holmes
Department of Educational Psychology
University of British Columbia
Vancouver, British Columbia
V7T 1Y7

Dr. Pierre Ritchie
Canadian Psychological Association
Chemin Vincent Road
Old Chelsea, Quebec
J0X 2N0

Dr. Bob Robinson
Department of Psychology
Alberta Children's Hospital
1820 Richmond Rd. S.W.
Calgary, Alberta
T2T 5C7

Dr. Carole Sinclair
The Dellcrest Children's Centre
1645 Shephard Avenue
Downsview, Ontario
M3M 2X4

Dr. Max Uhlemann
Department of Psychology
Foundations in Education
University of Victoria
Victoria, British Columbia
V8W 2Y2

Dr. Barbara Wand
Ontario Board of Examiners in Psychology
101 Davenport Road
Toronto, Ontario
M5R 1H5

Dr. Chris Webster
Clarke Institute of Psychology
250 College Street
Toronto, Ontario
M5T 1R8

Dr. Stan Whittsett
Department of Psychology
Alberta Children's Hospital
1820 Richmond Road S.W.
Calgary, Alberta
T2T 5C7

Dr. Robert Wilson
Wilson, Banwell & Associates
Suite 1610, Marine Building
355 Burrard Street
Vancouver, British Columbia
V6C 2G8

Keith S. Dobson & Deborah J. G. Dobson
Editors

Professional Psychology in Canada

Hogrefe & Huber Publishers

Library of Congress Cataloging-in-Publication Data
is available via the Library of Congress Marc Database under the
LC Catalog Card Number 93-078173.

National Library of Canada Cataloguing in Publication Data

Main entry under title:

Professional psychology in Canada

Includes bibliographical references and index.
ISBN 0-88937-043-5

1. Psychology — Canada. 2. Psychology — Study and teaching (Higher) — Canada. I. Dobson, Keith Stephen, 1954– . II. Dobson, Deborah J. G. (Deborah June Gora), 1954– .

BF108 C3P7 1993 150'971 C93-094142-X

ISBN 0-88937-043-5
Hogrefe & Huber Publishers, Seattle • Toronto

ISBN 3-8017-0444-0
Hogrefe, Göttingen • Bern

USA: P.O. Box 2487, Kirkland, WA 98083-2487
CANADA: 12–14 Bruce Park Ave., Toronto, Ontario M4P 2S3
GERMANY: Rohnsweg 25, D-3400 Göttingen, Phone +49-551-496090, Fax +49-551-4960988
SWITZERLAND: Länggass-Strasse 76, CH-3000 Bern 9, Phone +41-31-242533, Fax +41-31-243380

Printed in USA

Preface

This book is intended to achieve two major goals. The first is a documentary function: to identify and describe the major areas in which professional psychology has developed within the Canadian context. We believe profoundly that this country is a unique environment within the world of nations and have been unhappy that no comprehensive source is available detailing the history or current status of professional psychology in Canada. We hope this book will begin to fill this void.

Our second aim is to be aspirational: to have this book serve as a pivotal point of reference for future human service applications of psychology. Even if that is a somewhat grandiose goal, we hope that this volume will become a part of the professional library of most psychologists and psychologists-in-training in Canada. Through the reader's encounter with the description of professional psychology, as elaborated in this text, we wish to give psychologists a sense of pride in their accomplishments to date – and a sense of the possible. With a positive vision for the future of the profession, we trust that psychologists will strive to ensure that the future of the profession is at least as brave and successful as the past.

We feel this book achieves our major goals. There are undoubtedly some areas where it could have been strengthened, but as the first volume in this area we believe it is an important book. The text has been developed to educate and stimulate, and we look forward to the comments and reviews of our colleagues.

This book could not have been produced without support from a number of people. We want to thank Dr. Christine Hogrefe for encouraging the development of the book and Dr. Thomas Tabasz for the management of the publication. Our contributors have borne the long process from an idea through writing to publication with grace, and we certainly appreciate their good will in the eventual release of this volume. We thank our children, Chris and Beth, for their years of having to put up with a two-psychologist family. As we watch our children mature, we are struck by the preciousness of life, and are thankful for the happy and secure lives we share. Knowing that others are not as fortunate as we have been, our wish is that this book will provide an impetus for the further development and application of psychological knowledge, so that the lives of those who receive psychological services may benefit.

Keith and Deborah Dobson
Calgary, Alberta, Canada
March, 1993

Table of Contents

I

Overview of the Field of Professional Psychology

Psychology). Relevant publications for professional psychology in Canada include the proceedings from the Couchiching conference (Webster, 1967) and the Opinicon II State of the Discipline review (Ritchie, Hogan & Hogan, 1988). These documents tend to be written from the viewpoint of the national organization of psychologists, and do not address multiple practice areas, nor do they purport to review the scope of the profession.

The current volume seeks not only to define professional psychology in Canada, but also to describe, besides regulatory and practice issues, current training models and programmes, some of the areas of practice and some of the settings in which psychologists work in this country. Because there are no nationally agreed upon definitions of what a professional psychologist is (or if they do exist, all do not agree), and because the boundaries between differing areas are not always clear cut, there are some differences and overlap among the chapters. Some topics are covered from various differing "angles". We hope the occasional overlap will in fact add to the depth and richness of the reviews.

This volume does not pretend to examine all areas of professional psychology (for example, we have not included separate chapters on neuropsychology or psychosocial oncology). It is not a historical document, but rather a snapshot or cross-section of the profession at this point in time. For the sake of understanding and completeness, however, some chapters do provide an overview of historical trends and issues.

The Definition and Scope of Professional Psychology

> I think the only psychologist who is not a professional is one without a job – and I don't know very many of them (Myers, from Webster, 1967, p. 18)
>
> ... there is a tendency to view clinical psychology as if it were all of professional psychology (ibid, p 24).

The first tongue-in-cheek statement notwithstanding, there remains a tendency to equate professional psychology with clinical psychology. However, the following chapters amply demonstrate the falsity underlying that statement – professional psychology in Canada exists in a diverse range of work settings, practice areas and work activities.

In some ways, the struggles within professional psychology for identity parallel those of the entire country; psychology is still a young profession, sometimes struggling for independence from other professional groups or from the American (or to a lesser extent, British) influence. It has sometimes been defined more by what it is *not* than by what it uniquely *is* (e.g. not medicine or psychiatry, not academia or teaching, not counselling or social work). Psychology has struggled internally as well (e.g. scientist vs. practitioner, M.A. vs. Ph.D., provincial vs. national organizations). There have been developmental struggles, with psychologists organizing into various groups, finding their ways in traditional or nontraditional work settings and advocating for the profession. Through these experiences, those of us in the profession have (hopefully) begun to develop a confident "sense of self". This and the other chapters in this volume seek to define professional psychology according to what it uniquely is. Ready or not, national accreditation standards, provincial licensure acts and increased public exposure and expectations have conspired to put psychologists into a position of societal trust, with concomitant rights and responsibilities. It is incumbent upon professional psychologists to be able to state clearly who they are and what it is they do.

In order to define professional psychology, it is necessary first to define a profession (see also Sinclair, this volume). Typically, distinguishing features of a profession include a unique body of knowledge and set of skills, a code of conduct, self-regulation and disciplinary procedures for its members. Hogan (1979) states that "the construction of a professional code of ethics will be one of the first and most important tasks of the profession, as will be the task of building a strong professional association" (pp. 220–221). Canadian psychology has a set of skills and knowledge, its own code of ethics (CPA, 1991) and guidelines for practice (CPA, 1989), as well as self-regulatory acts in all provinces (though not in the Yukon or North West Territories). Thus, it meets the formal criteria for a profession in this country.

Yet, it is clear that psychology is still a new and developing field. Many of the provincial acts governing its activities are relatively recent. Barber (1965, from Hogan, 1979) notes several characteristics of a newly emerging (or marginal) profession:

> Typically, its members have widely differing backgrounds in their levels of education and community orientation. Attempts at licensure will often take place in order to add prestige, but such attempts will usually be resisted by the less professional members. Attempts will be made to establish or strengthen university professional schools. An effort will be made to inform the public about the services that the profession has to offer (pp.220–221).

The history of Canadian professional psychology shows there is some truth to these statements, and today there remains some diversity of opinion regarding such issues as the appropriate training and qualifications for psychologists.

While professional psychology is in some ways still emerging, increasingly it has reached an "emerged" status: All provinces now have psychology acts that protect the title "psychologist". As a point of clarification, various provinces have acts that "register", "charter" or "certify" psychologists. Essentially, these are all *title acts*, that is, laws requiring professionals to meet certain minimal standards to gain use of the title, but not restricting the right of others to actually practise in that particular area. In other words, only those who meet the standards are allowed to call themselves a psychologist, though other professionals may engage in similar practices. In contrast, laws that forbid the practice of a profession without a licence as well as prescribe certain minimal standards are termed *practice acts* (Hogan, 1979) (e.g. engaging in the practice of medicine without a licence is not permitted according to most medical acts). There is not yet consistency across the provinces or territories as to the required minimal acceptable credentials to be eligible to use the title psychologist.

Another aspect of the increasing standardization and regulation of professional psychology lies in the area of training. Since 1984, the CPA has accredited university and professional training (internship) programmes that follow certain, agreed upon minimal standards (see Doyle, Edwards & Robinson, this volume). These standards are very similar to those accepted by the American Psychological Association (APA), and a number of programmes have now been accredited by both organizations. Benefits of accreditation include assurances to both the prospective trainee and the public served that recognized training standards have been achieved, and that the programme is reviewed and regularly evaluated by professionals both internally and externally.

Increasingly, minimal training standards are being ensured both through provincial registration and national accreditation; however, these changes may also restrict the availability of services (both to trainees and ultimately to the public) in some areas or to some populations. As regions of Canada are far flung and culturally very diverse, the appropriateness of these standards and the ability to follow them has been identified as a problem in some jurisdictions, especially in the North and/or in rural areas. Some provinces have yet to develop accredited training programmes, and standards do not exist or are only now being developed in some practice areas. It is beyond the scope of this chapter to review the impact of professional regulation on training and practice, but it is important to note that there are both advantages and disadvantages to both the profession and the public it serves posed by regulation (see also Dobson & Dobson, this volume; Doyle et al., this volume; Hogan, 1979). Certainly, there are some limits to regulation, as certification at present does not ensure competence, which is difficult to define in practice. As well, there are only regulations for entry into the profession, but no requirements for upgrading or continuing education (see Handy & Whitsett, this volume).

The ability to be self-regulating ensures that psychology is an independent profession, thought to be sufficiently mature to act in the best interests of the public, rather than of the profession. Checks and balances have been inserted into provincial regulatory bodies by having members of the public sit on Councils or Boards.

Napoli (1981) argued that psychology is a unique profession in that it is the only occupational group with academic origins. While all Canadian training programmes are in university academic departments and endorse the scientist-practitioner model (see Dobson & Dobson, this volume), this practice is no longer always the case in the United States, with many professional schools existing outside departments of psychology and even outside universities altogether. It remains to be seen whether or not such schools will develop in Canada as well.

In addition to having a unique body of academic and applied knowledge, Fox, Barclay and Rodgers (1982) have argued, to be a profession psychology must be able to identify the unique field of *need* being served. To that end, they consider a psychologist to be "that professional which is concerned with enhancing the effectiveness of human functioning" (p. 307) and psychology is "the only profession that consistently focuses its efforts in solving problems through alterations in patterns of behavioral coping" (p. 308). Webster (1967) defines the professional psychologist as synonymous with an applied psychologist. This definition assumes that the professional psychologist applies the unique body of knowledge (psychology) to the unique field of need (solving human problems) within the boundaries formed by regulation, ethics and standards of practice. This definition includes such practice areas as counselling and clinical psychology, school psychology, industrial-organization psychology and human factors psychology. The "client" can be an individual or a group of individuals (family, classroom or work group), or a system or organization. Work settings are diverse in professional psychology and include clinics, counselling centres and hospitals, as well as schools, private practice, group practice, business, the military and large corporations. The practice can be "traditional" assessment, therapy or counselling, or can be consultation, programme implementation and evaluation and/or research. Certainly, with its academic roots and scientist-practitioner model, research is important to most psychologists and is a distinguishing feature of the profession (Webster, 1967).

Perhaps one of the least well researched aspects of professional psychology is its economic base. Although funding sources and levels of funding clearly help to shape how professions develop and grow, it appears that few studies exist on the economics of psychology. Sources of funds have increased over time in scope and include governmental institutions, third-party carriers and insurance companies, businesses, individuals and employers (see also Wilson, this volume). Funding sources and work settings differ regionally to some degree and between urban/rural settings. Canada's national health-care system, while not directly including payments to psychologists, has certainly had an indirect impact on the profession (Ritchie et al., 1988).

Summary

Psychology in Canada has developed considerably as a profession over the past few decades and has utilized an academic body of knowledge as well as an applied set of skills. Psychologists have worked hard in provincial bodies, in the CPA and in special interest groups to develop further organization; these structures are described in the following chapter (Craig). Training issues facing psychologists (e.g. graduate education, internship practice and continuing education) and the concomitant issues that have arisen in their evolution are detailed in the next section of chapters (Dobson & Dobson; Holmes; Doyle et al.). Regulatory issues and requirements for psychologists entering the profession (Wand) and for those already practising are highlighted in terms of ethics, standards of practice (Sinclair; Eberlin) and distinctions between the provinces are described in a number of contexts (e.g. Granger). The historical development of the CPA's unique code of ethics is also described (Sinclair). The latter section of the text demonstrates the ways in which such training, professional standards and skills are put into practice in various work settings, both traditionally in medical settings, counselling centres and schools, and less traditionally in industrial-organization settings, corporations and forensic settings. These applications of professional psychology are a sample that is hopefully representative of the diversity and scope of the practice of psychology in Canada.

References

Barber, B. (1965). Some problems in the sociology of the professions. In K.S. Lynn and the Editors of Daedalus (Eds.), *The professions in America.* Boston: Houghton Mifflin.

Canadian Psychological Association (1989). *Practice guidelines for providers of psychological services.* Old Chelsea, Quebec: Author.

Canadian Psychological Association (1991). *Code of ethics.* Old Chelsea, Quebec: Author.

Dobson, K.S., & Dobson, D.J.G. (1993). Graduate programmes in professional psychology. In K.S. Dobson & D.J.G. Dobson (Eds.), *Professional psychology in Canada.* Toronto: Hogrefe & Huber.

Doyle, A., Edwards H., & Robinson, R. (1993). Psychology programmes and internship accreditation. In K.S. Dobson & D.J.G. Dobson (Eds.), *Professional psychology in Canada.* Toronto: Hogrefe & Huber.

Ferguson, G. (1977). *Report on the Vancouver Conference on the organization and representation of psychology in Canada.* Unpublished paper.

Fox, R.E., Barclay, A.G., & Rodgers, D.A. (1982). The foundations of professional psychology. *American Psychologist, 37,* 306–312.

Fretz, B.R., & Mills, D.H. (1980). *Licensing and certification of psychologists and counselors.* San Francisco, CA: Jossey-Bass.

Handy, L., & Whitsett, S. (1993). Continuing education and retraining in professional psychology. In K.S. Dobson & D.J.G. Dobson (Eds.), *Professional psychology in Canada.* Toronto: Hogrefe & Huber.

Hogan, D.B. (1979). *The regulation of psychotherapists* (Vol. I–III). Cambridge, MA: Ballinger

Napoli, D.S. (1981). *Architects of adjustment: The history of the psychological profession in the United States.* Port Washington, NY: Kennikat Press.

Pryzwansky, W.B., & Wendt, R.N. (1987). *Psychology as a profession: Foundations of practice.* New York: Pergamon Press.

Ritchie, P., Hogan, T.P., & Hogan, T.V. (Eds.). (1988). *Psychology in Canada: The state of the discipline, 1984.* Old Chelsea, Quebec: Canadian Psychological Association.

Sinclair, C. (1993). Codes of ethics and standards of practice. In K.S. Dobson & D.J.G. Dobson (Eds.), *Professional psychology in Canada.* Toronto: Hogrefe & Huber.

Webster, E.C. (Ed.). (1967). *The Couchiching Conference on professional psychology.* Ottawa: Canadian Psychological Association.

Wilson, R.F.W. (1993). Non-traditional applications of professional psychology. In K.S. Dobson & D.J.G. Dobson (Eds.), *Professional psychology in Canada.* Toronto: Hogrefe & Huber.

Wright, M., & Myers, C.R. (1982). *History of academic psychology in Canada.* Toronto: C.J. Hogrefe.

2

The Organization of Professional Psychology in Canada

Kenneth D. Craig
Department of Psychology, University of British Columbia

Psychologists have long recognized that group action is an effective means of producing societal change, professional development and achievement of individual goals. Recent decades have seen rapid growth in Canada of organizations committed to enhancing the scientific and professional interests of psychologists and their impact on the community. A relatively large and growing network of lively, vigorous, sometimes fractious and often very productive organizations has evolved. While heated debate and contentious issues are often on the agenda, these organizations appear to be robust and healthy, perhaps reflecting the growing strength of the discipline of psychology. In recent years, there has been a proliferation of roles for psychologists in research, education and service delivery, dictating both larger, more complex organizations and new, specialized organizations. Many successes in achieving objectives have been recorded, and the organizations have gained in stature and confidence. Thus, the issues confronting organized psychology in Canada are readily seen as exciting, challenging and full of potential.

Geographical, Legislative and Cultural Determinants

The growing number and the complexity of organizations have resulted from many factors, particularly numerous societal influences, including the demands for psychological services in the community, the requirements of various levels of government and the pressures of working with other professions. In addition, important features of geography of Canada and its societal structure have dictated diversity and unique characteristics for Canadian organizations.

It seems inevitable that a country stretching more than 6000 kilometres wide and 4500 kilometres deep would have organizations representing regional interests. The vast size and cultural complexity of Canada were recognized in the 1867 British North America Act and the 1982 Canadian Constitution Act, broad rights and responsibilities for education, health, judicial systems and control of the professions being assigned to the Provinces and Territories. The different regions have exercised, sometimes very aggressively, their unique needs, identity and independence, often contributing to organizational stress within the field of psychology. While there are many similarities in the structures developed by psychological organizations across Canada and in the issues addressed, important differences do exist. For example, as provincial powers include control of professional certification, different standards have been imposed in different regions. All Provinces and Territories, save the Yukon, now have, in one form or another, statutory requirements for professional registration, yet educational requirements for entry into the profession vary by region between the doctoral and master's degrees, as do other standards. Thus, while registration or certification provides consumers with confidence concerning the competence and ethical standards of the psychologist, the definition of a psychologist varies across the country.

A further example of regional disparity in legal and regulatory standards would be the barriers provincial laws potentially represent to the incorporation of psychological interventions in the health-care delivery system (Lacroix, 1987). In some Provinces and Territories, a psychologist might be violating a Medical Act by engaging in such conventional activities as making a diagnosis, using biofeedback equipment, assuming the title "Dr." or other activities that could be construed as "medical". While prosecutions under medical acts focus upon nonregulated practitioners, and the dearth of psychological services in health delivery systems is the product of many more complex historical factors, anomalous laws and regulations persist. This lack of uniformity in regulations also has created difficulties for national organizations attempting to establish comparable ethical codes and standards of practice, professional certification credentials that would enjoy reciprocity across different jurisdictions in Canada and high standards for graduate education programmes in professional psychology (Conway, 1984; Davidson, 1971).

Canadians also live in a multicultural and multiracial society characterized by linguistic, cultural and ethnic diversity. Organized psychology has endeavoured to respect this basic feature of Canadian culture. Of great importance has been the two dominant and official languages, and the different traditions relating to the language differences. For example, graduate education in applied psychology in Quebec has been more practitioner oriented (Granger, 1984; Pinard, 1964); elsewhere the scientist/practitioner model has dominated (Conway, 1984). Canada's bilingual character also has dictated that either French or English be the dominant language in the operation of different regional organizations, and that the business of the major national organizations be conducted in both languages. Just as important in the Canadian cultural mosaic as the two dominant languages would be the substantial "allophone" community – that rich cultural mix of peoples whose language roots are in other than the two official languages. These people may speak neither French nor English well enough to receive services in these languages.

Relations Between Canada and the United States

Given the substantial physical and psychological proximity of Canada to the United States, it should not be surprising that American organizations have had a considerable influence on Canadian organizations. There has been a tendency in Canada to use organizational structures and quality assurance standards pioneered by American organizations as models. To varying degrees, these have been adapted to reflect the distinctive Canadian culture. Adaptations are necessary, as there are crucial differences in the linguistic mix, ethnocultural make-up, patterns of professional practice as well as the health, educational, judicial and political systems of the two nations. Yet, there have been criticisms of the tendency of Canadian psychologists to support American intellectual traditions and organizations rather than to commit themselves to strong national, provincial and local organizations (Gibson, 1971, 1974; Hebb, 1960; Wright, 1969). While mutual support is desirable and each should benefit from the developments of the other, tension continues as needs for autonomy persist. Fortunately, there has been a history of collaboration, including a joint fee agreement between the Canadian Psychological Association (CPA) and the American Psychological Association (APA), substantially reducing membership costs for those who wish to belong to both organizations. As well, a memorandum of understanding establishes procedures for ensuring cooperation on projects of mutual interest. Provincial organizations have benefited from an association with the American Association of State Psychology Boards, formed in 1961 to discuss legal, regulatory and licensure issues common to individual state boards so that high standards of practice could be attained.

The Variety of Organizations

The national and provincial organizations referred to above do not represent all of the organizational commitments of psychologists in Canada. Any given psychologist could hardly belong to all organizations, but few belong to none. Statutory requirements to register and the potential for developing the profession dictate membership in certain organizations for practitioners, while academics and scientists have the professional responsibility to belong to organizations concerned with scholarship and education. Psychologists also often participate in the activities of multidisciplinary organizations, including those of international importance. Thus, practitioners are likely to belong to the Association for the Advancement of Behavior Therapy, the Society for Psychotherapy Research or the Society of Behavioral Medicine, among others; and scientists often belong to the American Association for the Advancement of Science, Sigma Xi (The Scientific Research Society) or the Society for Neuroscience. The French-language community of psychologists enjoys the benefits of l'Association canadienne-francaise pour l'avancement des sciences, la Société québécoise de recherche en psychologie and l'Association de psychologie scientifique de langue Francaise.

A large number of smaller organizations have also developed. Pressures for specialization have come from increased sophistication of the discipline as well as outside forces, including the market demand of individual consumers, government agencies and health-insurance organizations. There is interest in identifying psychologists with specialty credentials in clinical, educational, industrial/organizational, health, forensic and clinical neuropsychology, and subdisciplines can be expected to continue to emerge (Service et al., 1989). Examining only one of the areas of focus, the field of education, one finds numerous organizations focussing upon such themes as counselling psychology, special education, school psychology and educational psychology. Specialty groups in the field of women's studies have been particularly lively. Canadian psychologists have exercised considerable leadership in both understanding and advancing the interests and rights of women, given evidence of systemic bias towards professional women and increasing numbers of women psychologists (Canadian Psychological Association Task Force on the Status of Women in Canadian Psychology, 1977). Prominent groups within the CPA are the Section on Women and Psychology and the Committee on the Status of Women. Canadian psychologists have also been prominent in the Canadian Research Institute for the Advancement of Women.

Other organizations that attract attention include the Canadian Council of Clinical Psychology Programmes, Heads of Western University Psychology Departments and the Canadian Society for Brain, Behaviour and Cognitive Science. These organizations, and others, periodically exert substantial influence upon psychology in Canada. For example, the CPA has recognized the National Research Council (NRC) as the suitable authority for international representation of Canadian psychology. The NRC National Committee for Psychology is a member of the International Union of Psychological Sciences and is presently organizing the 1996 XXVI International Congress of Psychology to be held in Montreal.

Psychologists also have been very active in large professional and lay public service organizations addressing issues of mental health, physical well-being, education and social welfare. For example, the predecessor organization of The Canadian Mental Health Association was established in 1913 under the direction of Clarence Hincks, a psychologist and physician (Wright & Myers, 1982). William Line, a psychology professor at the University of Toronto, was elected President of the World Federation for Mental Health in 1951. Through these and other organizations, psychologists have been remarkably successful in influencing community development and services (Babarik, 1979).

Historical Development of Canadian Organizations in Psychology

Rapid development of the discipline and profession in Canada has meant that the history of its organizations is relatively recent. The first formal organizations of psychologists in Canada were the departments of psychology that became rooted in the universities primarily throughout the first half of the 20th century (Wright & Myers, 1982). Often initially appointed to university departments of philosophy, psychologists established experimental laboratories and worked toward institutionalizing independent departments of psychology, the first being established at McGill in 1924 and at the University of Toronto in 1926 (Wright & Myers,

1982). Since then, there has been a flourishing of departments as psychology has established itself as a basic discipline and thus been in great demand as a course of study. Departments of psychology will undoubtedly remain important organizational entities for psychologists across Canada, not only in the universities and colleges, but also in hospitals and other health service agencies, schools, independent consulting firms, correctional institutions, counselling centres, businesses, research institutes, government departments and agencies and other organizations.

The founding of provincial and national organizations appears to have been the result of an awareness of the potential for applied psychology as well as the challenges of World War II and postwar realities. Prior to that time, Canadian psychologists participated substantially in the American Psychological Association; noteworthy examples are Professor James Baldwin of the University of Toronto, who was a founding member of the APA in 1892 and served as its sixth President in 1897 (Meyers, 1982), and Donald Hebb, who served as President in 1960. The APA was initially founded as a "continental" organization (Wright, 1974), but it rapidly became a national organization as issues that were unique to the legislative and social systems of the United States captured its attention and resources.

National Organizations

The major national organization representing psychologists in Canada since 1939 has been the Canadian Psychological Association. The 38 founding members represented a substantial proportion of the 53 psychologists scattered across Canada in that era (Wright, 1974). The demands for psychological services during a time of war (e.g. classification and selection, training, psychological disability and rehabilitation, development of child-care resources) provided early incentives, vitality and major accomplishments. During the postwar period, energies were devoted to establishing funds for psychological research and to the development of standards for professional services (Wright, 1974). Its history reflects an ongoing concern with the mutual, but often perceived to be disparate interests of professional and scientific psychologists.

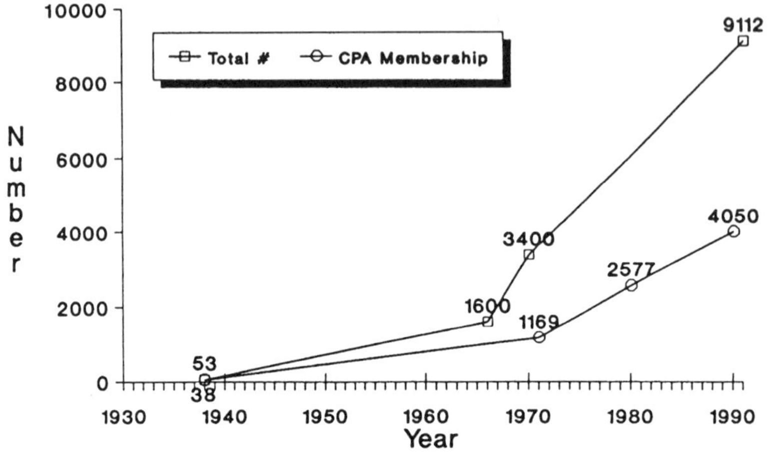

Figure 1. Estimates of the number of psychologists in Canada and membership in the Canadian Psychological Association.

Since World War II, there has been dramatic growth in the number of psychologists in Canada (see Figure 1). In 1966, there were some 1600 psychologists and in 1970 better than 3400, a remarkable doubling in the total estimated number (Wright, 1971 a). As Table 1 indicates, the total number of psychologists presently registered by Provinces and Territories is about 9,112. This underestimates the total number of active psychologists as many – most often provincial and federal employees and university professors – are exempt from registration requirements. As well, many professionals operating under nonpsychologist occupational titles were educated as psychologists.

The CPA has not enjoyed the benefit of the contributions of all Canadian psychologists over its years, although it has increased its membership substantially. There was a total of 1169 members recorded in 1971, 2577 in 1980 (Adair, 1981; Wright, 1969) and 4335 members in 1990 (3205 excluding student memberships). In a recent random poll of 800 members of the CPA and provincial organizations, it was found that 66% of the responding CPA members were also members of a provincial association, whereas only 35% of the provincial sample belonged to the CPA (Service et al., 1989). This creates a substantial diminution of the voice of all psychologists at the national level. Some of the national interests of members of provincial organizations are represented alternatively in the Council of Provincial Associations of Psychologists (CPAP).

According to Gibson (1974) and Wand (1990), inspiration for the CPAP dates to a meeting of the CPA Committee on Regional Associations in 1967, when there was discussion "about the problems of finding national expression for provincial concerns in psychology" (Berry, Davidson & Gibson, 1968, p. 368). A meeting of the CPAP's predecessor, the Advisory Council of Provincial Associations of Psychologists (ACPAP), was held in Montreal in 1968, apparently representing a convergence of enthusiasm in the CPA and provincial and territorial organizations for communication and collaboration. The CPAP presently counts as members provincial and territorial associations of psychologists and regulatory bodies, as well as the CPA as an *ex officio* member. The CPAP has indicated that it will serve the purposes of professional psychology in Canada, by providing information and sharing resources, developing briefs and coordinating provincial lobbying efforts concerning important legislation, including those relating to regulation of the profession, identifying opposing actions inimical to the profession (e.g. nonpsychologist or administrative supervision of psychologist service delivery), enhancing the quality of consumer access to professional services (e.g. confidentiality, record-keeping, access to information), promoting professional development through education and training, and coordinating conjoint action to promote, market and improve access to psychological services. Continuing evolution of psychological organizations in Canada is illustrated by the entrance in January 1990, of two new organizations as members of the CPAP: the Manitoba Psychological Society and the Newfoundland Board of Examiners in Psychology. For the first time, the CPAP was able to claim that it represented all provincial organizations of psychologists in Canada.

While there were early efforts to establish national standards and to provide a professional credential for psychologists across Canada (Hogan, Hogan & Gupton, 1982; Meyers, 1965), only recently has this been successful. The most recently founded national organization of psychologists, the Canadian Register of Health Service Providers in Psychology (CRHSPP), arose from this perceived need for a credential recognizing achievement of a high level of professional standards that would be uniform across Canada, yet still recognized provincial rights to register and regulate members of the profession (Wand, 1990). The CRHSPP provides a voluntary listing of well-qualified psychological health service providers which is increasingly being recognized by governments, insurance companies and quality assurance agencies.

Provincial Organizations

The first provincial organization of psychologists was the British Columbia Psychological Association, founded in 1938 (Wright, 1971 b). This predating of the founding of CPA perhaps reflects the importance of regional associations to psychologists in our far-flung country. In succeeding years, all Provinces and Territories set up similar organizations (see Table 1). The subsequent growth of the profession, enabling legislation, and the command of substantial human and financial resources led to substantial and powerful organizations in most regions.

Two important forms of provincial organizations emerged: First were those pursuing societal goals, primarily advancement of the profession; second were organizations responsible for statutory regulation of psychologists delivering services to the public. The first regulatory board was established in Ontario in 1960, and the last one was established in Prince Edward Island in 1990. The interests of the different types of organizations (see below) were recognized as compatible as each would benefit from high standards in the delivery of services.

Coordination of Organizational Efforts

There have been efforts to coordinate and integrate the activities of the many regional and national organizations, in the interests of greater efficiency and harmony (Hogan, 1988). At the 1977 Vancouver Conference on Representation and the Organization of Canadian Psychology (Ferguson, 1977), Berry noted, "It is ludicrous that 5000 psychologists in Canada would require 17 as-

Table 1. Provincial Organizations of Psychologists*

	Members	Revenue ($)
Regulatory Bodies:		
Psychological Association of Manitoba	150	50,000
Nova Scotia Board of Examiners in Psychology	254	58,093
Ontario Board of Examiners in Psychology	1617	590,304
Saskatchewan Psychological Association	85	10,059
Newfoundland Board of Examiners in Psychology	110	17,000
Prince Edward Island Psychologists Registration Board	13	1,800
Joint Regulatory and Societal Organizations (Registrations)		
Psychologists Association of Alberta	1486	346,000
College of Psychologists of British Columbia	804	317,352
College of Psychologists of New Brunswick/ Collège des psychologues du Nouveau-Brunswick	261	54,256
Association of Psychologists of the Northwest Territories	20	1,000
Corporation professionnelle des psychologues du Québec	4313	1,387,222
Societies (nonregulatory)		
Manitoba Psychological Society	135	8,302
Association of Newfoundland Psychologists	102	6,708
Association of Psychologists of Nova Scotia	144	18,055
Ontario Psychological Association	1110	461,112
Psychological Association of Prince Edward Island	39	4,101
Psychological Society of Saskatchewan	109	
Canadian Psychological Association	4335	1,016,911

*Information was provided by the organization within the six months prior to 1 May 1991, and refers to documents dated in both 1990 and 1991.

sociations, several divisions and untold numbers of special interest groups to meet their needs" (p. 14). The complexity of the organizational structure was seen as "incredibly expensive and inefficient" (p. 14). The Conference was convened because professional psychologists were concerned that the CPA was not sufficiently attentive to applied issues. Even though the Vancouver Conference was held at a time of considerable dissatisfaction among practitioner psychologists with the services rendered by the CPA, it concluded in ringing terms with the resolution "that it be recognized that the Canadian Psychological Association under its federal charter speaks for Canadian Psychology, and that it has both a mandate and an obligation to do so" (Ferguson, 1977). Hogan (1988) has commented that the Vancouver Conference averted the establishment of a national association of professional psychologists.

The development of psychologists' organizations in Canada has rarely been a fully consensual and harmonious process. In addition to disparate, external formative pressures, lack of consensus concerning objectives occasionally has led to internal conflict and tension. Achieving a balance among different priorities of psychologists has long posed a problem for organizations that would attempt to unify the profession and represent all interests, with the different perspectives of scientists and practitioners creating particular difficulties. Twenty years ago, Virginia Douglas articulated the organizational challenge as follows:

> The Board of Directors of the CPA has been very much aware of how shackled we have been in taking action on behalf of psychology. If we do something that looks as if it is in support of the 'rat' men, then the applied psychologists feel that the CPA only represents 'rat' men. If, on the other hand, we go 'gung ho' for something for the clinicians, or we start talking about community psychology, then the 'rat' men say, 'Well it has finally happened. The clinicians have taken over. We might as well pull out. It costs $45.00 anyway, and that is far too much. We'll go off and form our own tight little society where we can stay very pure. (Myers, 1971, p. 19–20)

Conflict in priorities among psychologists remains an important issue for organizations that would represent them. Recent efforts to promote unitary action and harmony do not appear sufficient. In part, special interests, expertise and backgrounds are represented in the CPA organizational structure by Sections, some 26 in 1990 (see Table 2). These now have substantial powers and responsibilities. In a further effort to ensure broad representation on the Board of Directors, the CPA changed its by-laws in 1989 to create six new positions: Two Directors now represent each of the categories of Scientist, Scientist/Practitioner and Practitioner. However, a number of psychologists recently have charged that the CPA is overly preoccupied with practitioner issues and neg-

Table 2. CPA Section Membership (including students).

	Membership (1992)
Brain and Behaviour	113
Social Responsibility	70
Community Psychology	62
Criminal Justice Systems	137
Developmental Psychology	195
Educational Psychology	119
Environmental Psychology	24
Health Psychology	166
Industrial/Organizational	159
International and Cross-Cultural	85
Programme Evaluation	58
Psychology of Sport and Exercise	36
Psychopharmacology	25
Social Psychology	151
Teaching of Psychology	49
Women and Psychology	254
Adult Development and Aging	93
Psychology and Religion	53
Behavioural Science and Applications in the Military	55
Students in Psychology	71
Psychophysiology	38
Evolutionary Psychology	9
Clinical Neuropsychology	184
Counselling Psychology	159
History and Philosophy of Psychology	64
Clinical Psychology	352
Perception, Learning and Cognition	59
Family Psychology	82

lects scientific and academic concerns. Given that there is a disproportionate number of practitioners relative to scientists and academics in psychology, omnibus organizations are prone to becoming preoccupied with professional, social or political issues rather than theoretical, empirical or methodological issues. As well, fees have been characterized by some as excessive and overly committed to nonscientific pursuits. The wax and wane of opinion that the CPA overemphasizes particular issues undoubtedly will continue.

A further example of organizational strain was evident when long-neglected womens' issues surfaced in the mid-1970s and it became evident that discriminatory practices did exist. Most conspicuous was the substantial time-lag between the dramatic increase in the number of women psychologists and their participation as senior scientists, professionals and administrators (Canadian Psychological Association Task Force on the Status of Women in Canadian Psychology, 1977). While many major discriminatory practices have been addressed, many challenges remain (Williams, Zabrack & Harrison, 1980).

Organizational Objectives

Organized psychology is extremely diverse in character and cannot be treated as a monolithic entity. The diversity is reflected in the many explicit and implicit purposes of the various organizations. To varying degrees all organizations of psychologists in Canada have interests in (a) the creation of knowledge concerning the behaviour of organisms, (b) the development of services designed to enhance human functioning and to relieve human suffering and (c) the educational process of imparting systematic knowledge to students of the discipline, of all types.

Research Issues

A major source of strength of contemporary psychology has been the recognition of its roots in the knowledge base of the discipline. It has adhered to the fundamental principle that understanding any natural phenomenon and applications of this knowledge are the product of systematic inquiry. To this end, organized psychology has argued extensively that respect and vigorous support for the contributions of psychological science have major societal implications.

Research psychologists tend to work independently or in well-defined collaborative relationships when pursuing their scientific interests. But it is increasingly obvious that scientists must become professionally organized if they are to obtain external support for their scientific endeavours. Membership in networks of scientists and professional organizations serves two major goals: First, it provides the means to exchange and disseminate information and, second, it allows collective interests and concerns to become known and action to be taken to advance these interests.

The process of scientific information exchange is complex and beyond the scope of this analysis, but an important feature would be the informal and formal organizations that promote information dissemination. Most scientists have informal networks of colleagues and memberships in both specialized and broad-scope disciplinary and multidisciplinary organizations to fulfil their personal needs. The development of electronic communication systems and the tendency toward providing external support for networks of scientists will further reduce the isolation of individual scientists and lead to improved understanding of shared concerns.

The CPA has long enjoyed recognition as the major national vehicle serving scientific interests from both the majority of psychologists in Canada and agencies external to psychology. A major question continuously under review has been: "Is the CPA visible and meaningful in the formulation of public policy in support of research in psychology?" Through its Scientific Affairs Committee, the CPA has monitored and attempted to influence decision-makers, including federal departments engaged in research and those federal agencies that have commitments to the research enterprise, primarily the Social Sciences and Humanities Research Council, the Natural Sciences and Engineering Research Council and the Medical Research Council. Even though there has been a continuing need to monitor, influence and support the actions of these agencies and councils, their policies and programmes generally support psychological research. Stable patterns of awards for operating grants, equipment grants and student support are evident, and there generally have been positive attitudes toward the psychology community. The problems psychologists encounter in their efforts to finance their research programmes derive primarily from the inadequate external support these Councils receive, leading to unfortunate competition with other scientific disciplines, and inadequate support for scientific research in Canada as a whole (National Consortium of Scientific and Educational Societies, 1990). For example, since the creation of the Social Sciences and Humanities Research Council in 1978, the volume of demand for research grants has increased by more than 150%, although in real terms the Council's budget has remained essentially unchanged during this span of time. Among other unfortunate consequences, success rates for applicants of operating grants have fallen from 77% to 37% (Leduc, 1990).

Maintaining a bridge with other scientific disciplines and engaging in joint collaborative projects has been an important responsibility for the CPA. Membership in the Social Science Federation of Canada, the major national organization representing the collective needs of the social science disciplines, provides a mechanism for establishing and maintaining a liaison with other groups of scientists. In 1990, 25 disciplinary-based organizations and 65 universities and colleges comprised its membership. Lobbying for the interests of social scientists is the primary objective. The CPA also maintains a role in the Canadian Federation of Biological Sciences through participation in its committee structure. Finally, the CPA is a member of the National Consortium of Scientific and Educational Societies, an informal coalition of 35 national organizations, representing some 55,000 researchers and educators in various disciplines and 400,000 students, that endeavours to lobby for improved educational and scientific services in Canada.

Professional Issues

Recognition of psychology as a vital and autonomous profession has been long sought, and often achieved, with practitioner-based organizations providing the major resources to achieve this end. Growing evidence of enhanced professional status and greater opportunities for psychologists is evident in public decisions in various jurisdictions favouring professional certification, third-party insurance coverage, expert witness standing in courts, equal professional liability with medicine and, most recently in several States, hospital privileges.

There is a continuing tradeoff between enhanced status as a profession and duties to ensure that services are delivered in a responsible and competent manner. Conflict is ordinarily resolved by placing public over guild interests. While enhancement of the profession is often construed by professional organizations as being in the best interests of the public, purposeful planning and action are still necessary to ensure the balance is achieved. Policy statements of the CPA concerning important issues such as universal health care, sexual harassment, discrimination on the basis of sex, marital or parental status and sexual orientation, child care and capital punishment reflect efforts to ensure commitments are made to public interests (CPA, 1988).

In the interests of achieving commitments to social development and values, the CPA endeavours to act proactively and maintains liaison with other national organizations working on the resolution of important national issues. For example, a coalition of organizations known as the National Associations Active in Criminal Justice has been working on an "Interdisciplinary Project on Domestic Violence" to provide information to the federal Minister of Justice concerning the deficiencies and need for revisions to the Young Offenders Act. The CPA is also represented on the Professional Advisory Committee of the Correctional Services of Canada, to provide policy concerning psychological services and programmes for inmates in correctional institutions.

Promulgating, monitoring and adjudicating professional standards and codes of ethics provides the primary means of ensuring that psychologists engage in responsible conduct. Codes and standards encompass the full range of professional services, research and education. There are numerous constituencies, including society in general, individual clients, groups and organizations to whom services are delivered. As Ross (1982) notes, ethical standards as espoused and exercised by professional organizations control only those who are sensitive to the opinions of their colleagues, those who are members of the organization and those who value continued membership. Countercontrol also represents a possibility as directors and ethics committees of professional associations bear a risk of countersuit by accused practitioners.

Unfortunately, a consensus has not emerged across Canada on ethical standards for psychologists. After a substantial period of development, in 1986 the CPA adopted a Canadian Code of Ethics for Psychologists (CPA, 1988; Pettifor & Sinclair, 1991). While the Code also has been adopted by the majority of provincial organizations, there has not been universal endorsement. For example, the Corporation professionnelle des psychologues du Quebec (CPPQ) uses a separate "Code of Ethics of Psychologists" in the form of Regulations approved by the Quebec government through Order in Council in 1983. The College of Psychologists in British Columbia revised and adopted a version of the American Psychological Association's 1981 Ethical Principles of Psychologists, and in 1990 the Ontario Board of Examiners in Psychology also adopted the APA's 1981 Code, again with variations. Similar practices and traditions within other provincial organizations also have prevented widespread adoption of the CPA Practice Guidelines for Providers of Psychological Services. Variation in ethical codes and professional standards in different jurisdictions across Canada poses a difficult problem for psychology: How is the public to have confidence in psychologists when it sees that they have not been able to agree as to what constitutes ethical behaviour?

Educational Issues

The quality of science and service delivery is only as good as the education and training in the knowledge base and technical skills of the discipline. Most organizations in psychology share an interest in the design and delivery of instructional programmes. In 1984, the CPA "State of the Discipline" review (Ritchie, Hogan & Hogan, 1988) identified education as an ongoing focal concern of Canadian psychology (Craig & Melanson, 1988). Interests and issues range from relatively conventional concerns for undergraduate education and graduate programmes in the diverse fields of psychology through emergent issues concerning mid-career education for psychologists with masters degrees who wish to return for doctoral work, to whether continuing education for practitioners should be mandatory or voluntary.

Professional organizations represent a source of community influence upon education and training policies and practices. A significant recent example would be the impact of the Accreditation Criteria for Doctoral Programmes and Internships in Professional Psychology, as developed and adopted by the Canadian Psychological Association in 1984. These standards address the quality of institutional resources and practices, faculty and staff qualifications, graduate student or intern selection and development, curriculum, practical and internship experiences and many other issues. As originally conceived, the criteria were designed for graduate programmes and internships in clinical psychology, but since have been extended to include counselling psychology and clinical neuropsychology. The CPA Accreditation Panel which administers this programme had, by March 1991, approved ten doctoral programmes and 16 internships. A number of universities and internship facilities have employed the standards in the development of their programmes in clinical psychology, so that the standards appear to have been positively received and integrate the diverse interests present in Canadian psychology (cf. Gibson, 1974).

One of the more divisive professional issues in Canada at the present time concerns whether the master's degree in psychology constitutes a sufficient educational credential for independent practice of psychology. While the majority of statutory registration bodies require the doctorate, several do not, and some graduate students in psychology seek professional recognition after terminating their studies with the master's degree.

Psychologists have not neglected their responsibilities to ensure public awareness of the discipline and profession. The public must come to understand the contributions that psychologists make as scientists and be informed about the educational and practical requirements for competent professional practice. Banwell (1989) describes the latter objective well when describing plans for the College of Psychologists in British Columbia. He observes:

> We will be clearly distinguished as a regulated, responsible profession in the Province and one which the public, including government and other professions, respects and recognizes as a key contributor to human welfare.

Structure

Governance structures, operational strategies and mechanisms for accomplishing work often dictate organizational effectiveness. These features of the policy and management of psychologists' organizations differ primarily with the size of the organization as well as idiosyncratic conventions and traditions. Membership organizations ordinarily are required by federal and provincial statutes to have by-laws, proposed by the membership but subject to governmental ratification. These usually address the mission and objectives of the organization, its membership, the election and duties of directors and officers, dues and budgets, the relationships maintained with external agencies and committee structure (Kerr & King, 1984). Ultimately, the authority for the actions of membership organizations derives from decisions of the members, with annual or special meetings representing the common means for establishing and authorizing policy development and the commitment of financial and human resources.

The larger organizations (e. g. CPA, CPPQ, CRHSPP, the Ontario Psychological Association and the College of Psychologists in British Columbia) have the financial resources to employ professional and administrative staffs to work on programmes and projects under the management of an executive director in accordance with policy decisions of an elected Board of Directors. Many of the smaller organizations have part-time Registrars, Executive Directors or occasional and contracted support staff, as financial circumstances permit, but primarily rely upon the time volunteered by their members.

The development of policy and – in the vast majority of cases – the maintenance of programmes is largely dependent upon the commitment and donated services of members. With exceptions, a committee structure which includes standing committees, ad hoc committees and task forces is used to accomplish the work. While elected boards and membership meetings are responsible for decisions, the quality of the policies, work done and the momentum sustained is ultimately dependent upon the commitment and efforts of individual members and the teamwork they display.

Financing these organizations is a serious problem, given the finite resources available. Most of the organizations described here rely primarily upon self-imposed taxes, including membership and registration fees, although grants (e. g. an administrative grant from the Social Sciences and Humanities Research Council of Canada to the CPA) and sales receipts (e. g. from member and library journal subscription fees) often are a source of additional revenue. The CPAP operates on a cost-sharing agreement that taxes constituent organizations on the basis of the size of their membership. Table 3 summarizes recent reports of revenues re-

Table 3. Financial status of selected Canadian psychological organizations in 1989.

	Revenue ($)
Canadian Psychological Association	1,016,911
Saskatchewan Psychological Association (1988–89)	10,059
Corporation professionnelle des Psychologues du Quebec (1989)	1,387,222
Association of Newfoundland Psychologists	???
Newfoundland Board of Examiners in Psychology	???
Manitoba Psychological Society (89–90) (General & Institute Accounts)	8,302
College of Psychologists of New Brunswick	???
Ontario Board of Examiners in Psychology (1989)	590,304

ceived by the majority of the major organizations of psychologists in Canada, indicating that more than $4,450,000 was earned to meet the objectives of Canadian organizations in psychology in their most recent fiscal year. Beyond staff costs, travel costs often represent a substantial expenditure item for Canadian organizations, given this country's vast size. Geographical representation is important given regional variation in needs and interests. Reflecting this, the CPA Board of Directors is required by a by-law to have a broad geographical dispersion across Canada, and the CPPQ Board is representative of the different regions of Quebec.

As with all voluntary organizations, leadership is an intriguing though poorly understood subject. At any given time, only a small committed group of people is given control through democratic processes. The same individuals are often nominated, elected or commissioned to undertake leadership and executive roles in different organizations. With time, there is a turnover in those given senior responsibilities. The roles are diverse and include executive positions, chairing and participating in task forces, committees and board meetings, acting as representatives and ambassadors for psychology in the community and promoting the goals and values of the organization. Psychologists who contribute their time and professional effort to these organizations appear to derive considerable satisfaction from it. Such benefits must compensate for loss of work opportunities and occasional considerable frustrations deriving from limited resources, lack of agreement on priorities and the often slow process of achieving objectives. However, active volunteers come to recognize that they are in fact able to influence the governance structures, policies and practices of their profession; that they have the opportunity to develop and apply a wide range of organizational, administrative and political skills; and that they work for worthwhile scientific and social causes and enjoy opportunities to work closely with respected colleagues. Organizations would do well to commit sufficient resources to leadership development: The broader the base of expertise and informed participation in their affairs, the more effective the organization becomes.

The return for membership in these organizations varies from the tangible and concrete to the abstract and ambiguous. For most psychologists, registration with a provincial regulatory body represents a requirement for earning one's livelihood; hence, the benefits can be measured in financial gain. Membership benefits from societal organizations, on the other hand, are less tangible. In addition to opportunities to participate in the affairs of the organization, there may be a range of member benefits, including access to practitioner opportunities that would otherwise not be available, conferences and workshops, publications and subscriptions to journals free or at reduced rates, access to professional liability insurance and financial benefits through reduced insurance, hotel or travel costs. Societies also may confer Fellow status upon members who have made distinguished contributions to the advancement of the science or profession of psychology or who have given exceptional service to their organization, and recognize life-long contributions by conferring Distinguished Life Member status upon long-serving, retired members.

Types of Organizations

The various organizations of Canadian psychologists differ in their mandates as to whether they promote the interests of individuals, the profession or the community. An obvious distinction (made above) would be between organizations focussing upon practitioner interests and those advocating scientific advancement. Omnibus organizations attempt to represent all scientific, practitioner and scientist/practitioner issues, but inevitably suffer organizational strain because of conflict between competing sectors of the organization.

A further major distinction can be made between regulatory and societal organizations: Regulatory organizations operate under provincial statutes to govern the practice of the profession, including entry and discipline; societal organizations primarily operate to promote development of the profession itself. In several regions (Alberta, British Columbia, New Brunswick, the Northwest Territories and Quebec), a single organization fulfils the responsibilities of both a regulatory board and a societal organization. These organizations attempt to resolve potential conflict of interest by giving regulatory functions precedence over societal organizational objectives. The distinction may not always be easily made. For example, some jurisdictions permit hiring generic mental-health workers. While these employees may be of great value to the community, they preclude employment opportunities for psychologists, which may lead to opposition from psychologists. One unfortunate consequence of organizations combining regulatory and societal functions has been that membership becomes comprised exclusively of registered psychologists. This excludes a range of potential members, despite substantial interest and talent, including those who are exempt, or do not choose to register, or who are ineligible for registration for a variety of reasons, including academics and students.

Societal Organizations

Societal organizations are primarily oriented toward promotion of the development and interests of the profession, under the supposition that the profession will act in the best interests of the community at large. They are most often incorporated as nonprofit societies under provincial or federal statute. They tend to focus upon providing membership services, collegial support, and promoting a sense of professional identity and collective pride. Provision of educational services for members, usually through an annual convention, fulfils responsibilities to professional development.

Participation in the affairs of these organizations, whether through membership support or contributing time to the organization, is entirely voluntary. The membership tends to be more representative of the psychological community than in regulatory bodies since the society is not restricted to those who are delivering psychological services in the community. For example, full membership in the CPA is available to anyone with a master's or a doctoral degree from a recognized graduate school. Thus, societal membership rolls include academics, scientists and practitioners (including those who may not satisfy standards for registration), as well as students planning careers as psychologists and interested members from other disciplines. Mandates of societal organizations extend substantially beyond the regulatory activities of registration boards and permit the commitment of resources to the development of the science and profession of psychology in a manner that may be opposed by governments.

While not as powerful as statutory organizations in their immediate impact on the lives of individual psychologists, societal organizations can have a considerable long-term impact. Societal organizations first sought registration acts, and they continue to monitor and influence legislation regulating psychology and other professions. For example, in Nova Scotia licensure legislation is now being proposed for the profession of "Speech-Language Pathologist/Audiologist", which could preclude the delivery of certain services by psychologists; intensive lobbying has been necessary to ensure that this will not become reality (Byrne, 1990). As a further example, standards documents are often developed by societies, including those describing the values and constraining scientific and professional practice of psychologists across Canada developed and promulgated by the CPA. The most prominent standards would be "A Canadian Code of Ethics for Psychologists" (1986) and "Practice Guidelines for Providers of Psychological Services" (1989). As a further example, the CPA adopted minimum standards defining a core educational programme in psychology in 1986. This document now provides published criteria for judgments by registration boards as to whether university graduate degrees can be described fairly as in the field of psychology. Failure to demonstrate a programme of studies in psychology comparable to the CPA core programme can lead to denial of registration or licensure as a psychologist.

Statutory Organizations

Professional regulation of psychology is maintained primarily through provincial registration boards. They were created as instruments of the government to ensure competent, responsible delivery of service. As with other statutory professional organizations in medicine, law and other professions, regulatory boards are primarily comprised of representatives of the profession, though in many instances include representatives of the lay public, in the interest of community participation. Provincial legislators have endowed these boards with statutory powers to control entry into the profession, determine professional standards and enforce standards of practice. In many instances, the impetus was the abuse of clients by incompetent or unscrupulous frauds who were free to misrepresent themselves as psychologists in the absence of control over the title. The term "psychologist" and related titles and terms are now restricted to qualified persons.

Over the past 30 years, entry into professional practice has become increasingly difficult as statutory organizations have imposed strict educational and experiential certification standards and restrictive title requirements. Title protection has been favoured by legislators over the more restrictive licensure acts, which limit the offering of defined services to practitioners who are licensed, because of the overlap in professional practices between psychology and those of other professions. Strong title protection is generally believed to be in the best interests of the public, and registration boards are usually able to impose severe penalties for contravention. Otherwise, people who have neither qualifications nor ethical commitments might claim to offer services to the public as psychologists or argue that they "practise psychology" or provide "psychological services". Ross (1982) has observed that regulatory boards represent only one of a range of methods available to ensure the responsible practice of psychology in Canada. Others include criminal and civil law, professional peer control, federal regulations and civil malpractice litigation.

While very powerful in their mandate to protect the public, regulatory boards tend to be limited in their activities to setting qualifications for admission to registered status, and to prescribing and assuring adherence to ethical guidelines and standards of practice. Discipline, usually involving professional misconduct, negligence or incompetence, consumes substantial financial and human resources of the regulatory bodies. Dealing with a psychologist who violates the regulations or professional standards is a very serious matter. The process requires systems to monitor adherence to standards, investigate complaints and exercise discipline through reprimand, or restriction or revoking of registration. All have proven to be expensive undertakings, in part because they represent legal and judicial proceedings. The costs of operating regulatory bodies are invariably paid for by psychologists' registration fees. Complaints are not infrequent. For example, Wand (1991) reports the following: In 1988, the Ontario Board of Examiners in Psychology had 1610 psychologists on its permanent register. In the 14-month period ending December 31, 1989, 77 complaints against psychologists were received. Although relatively few complaints have the substance to lead to disciplinary action, they must all be investigated seriously. Of the 77 complaints Wand (1991) describes, 30 (37%) were believed to give cause for concern, but formal hearings were held in only three cases (4%). Adjudicating complaints makes extraordinary demands on a regulatory board member's time and personal resources. In Ontario, there is now provision for per diem stipends to board members in lieu of engaging in paid work.

Ensuring the competence of registered psychologists may extend beyond the processes of registration, continuing education and ethical scrutiny. In its statutory regulations the CPPQ has provision for a professional inspection committee of psychologists whose supervize the profession and provide appraisals of the competence of psychologists. Special enquiries into the competence of psychologists are authorized, and recommendations concerning further education, including refresher courses, or restricted practice can be made. The Psychological Association of Alberta also has adopted a programme for review of professional practices.

Activities

The broad range of organizations engage in complex activities that largely defy summary. Nevertheless, certain consistencies emerge.

External Relations

The decisions and policies of external agencies often influence the development of psychology as a science and as an autonomous profession. Communication or liaison must be reciprocal. Psychological organizations must have ready access to information for planning purposes, and psychologists need to make known their needs, concerns and real and potential contributions. A close watch must be kept on population trends and the actions of external agencies. This includes monitoring impending legislation, the activities of other professional organizations, and the policies of funding agencies and research divisions of government departments.

Psychologists' organizations are increasingly engaged in active lobbying and representation in the interests of influencing public policy. A variety of strategies has been developed to maintain ties and to achieve external influence, all of which demand substantial management and leadership. Most often task forces and executive committees are charged with developing policies and influencing external decisions. Some organizations have established political networks wherein psychologists become responsible for maintaining ongoing contact with elected officials. The OPA has an active lobby programme of this type, and the CPA is presently pursuing the possibility. Grass-roots, constituency-based contacts and collaborative relationships with politicians permit long-term mutual nurturance. In Quebec, the CPPQ has joined a coalition of agencies concerned with psychological and social well-being to lobby the provincial government to improve mental-health care.

Efforts to influence external organizations can have a dramatic impact upon opportunities for psychology in Canada. For example, a strong collaborative campaign, coordinated by the CPA and the CPAP, to have health services provided by CRHSPP-registered psychologists exempt from the federal Goods and Services Tax mobilized the discipline to engage in active lobbying of federal politicians and was successful in meeting its objective (Sabourin, 1991). Similarly, in 1990 there was a nationally orchestrated lobby of the Canadian Council for Health Facilities Accreditation (CCHFA) to provide a strong endorsement of the role of psychologists in health-care institutions. The CCHFA is the national body that oversees development of quality assurance standards in health-care facilities, including general hospitals, rehabilitation centres and mental-health facilities. There was considerable satisfaction in seeing revised standards that endorsed psychology departments as independent, administrative units, the participation of psychologists in senior, decision-making bodies of the institutions, and the expectation that psychologists should be registered with the CRHSPP.

Relationships with other disciplines and professions sharing the interests of psychologists need to be nurtured. Action on behalf of psychology may not be perceived as advantageous or benign by members of other professions. For example, social workers perceived the efforts to include psychologists' health services as GST exempt as threatening to them. In the United States, major lobbying efforts by the American Psychological Association and other organizations have led to a number of valuable changes in service delivery. Federal legislation was introduced to include psychological services in Medicare. A favourable decision in an antitrust suit against psychoanalytic institutes ended the exclusion of psychologists from psychoanalytic training. As well, a California Supreme Court decision revised long-standing hospital practices by granting psychologists the authority to serve as primary-care providers of inpatient mental-health services, including the right to diagnose and treat patients without supervision or prior approval by a physician and the right to admit and discharge patients. These satisfying developments could not have been accomplished without the cooperation of many members of other health-care professions, and were not favourably endorsed by many others.

Other representation for Canadian psychologists is provided by the CPA to the Working Group on Multicultural Health established by the federal Minister of Health and Welfare, the International Test Commission and the United Nations Congress on Prevention of Crime and Treatment of Offenders, and the International Union for Health Education. These behind-the-scenes activities can be very important for both the profession and the community at large.

Internal Relations

Activities in this sphere attempt to enhance development of the Canadian professional and scientific community. A broad range of activities again can be observed. The organization may be devoted to no more than providing a forum in the form of conventions, workshops or seminars where ideas and strategies can be exchanged or learned. Facilitating communications within the community of psychologists is also accomplished through newsletters and journals. The CPAP maintains a database on provincial organizations and regularly exchanges information on issues of mutual interest. Studies are often initiated that may be so broad as to examine the state of the discipline (Ritchie, Hogan & Hogan, 1988), but more often are restricted to limited issues such as the mid-career education for master's-level psychologists, the credentialing of practitioner specialties (Service et al., 1989) or the funding of health services (Ritchie et al., 1988).

The development of standards represents a valuable contribution to the profession. Throughout the 1980s, the CPA was involved in the development of ethical codes, practice standards, guidelines for the development and use of psychological tests, standards for health-care facilities, standards for animal-care facilities, accreditation standards for graduate programmes and internships in professional psychology and accreditation standards for continuing education programmes.

Recognizing emergent interests and promoting the development of special interest groups may also become an important role. For example, the CPA provided a home to the various interest groups that became its Sections (see Table 2) and played a role with other organizations in the development of the CPAP, the Canadian Council of Clinical Psychology Programmes and the CRHSPP. Other member services of note include professional liability insurance provided at a substantially reduced cost over that provided by independent brokers.

Various agendas are likely to be acted upon in the relatively near future. The further development of Provincial Registration Acts and other credentialing of psychologists can be expected (Conway, 1984), given that provincial organizations are now debating whether systems of specialty designation should be developed (forensic, neuropsychology, paediatrics, etc.).

Research Communications

Organizations differ in their commitment to science advocacy. Provincial organizations have largely relegated this focus to a secondary place in favour of practitioner issues. While the CPA has recognized the importance of the scientific bases of contemporary psychology and attached priority to scientific issues since its inception, it became clear in the latter part of the 1980s that a large segment of the scientific community of psychologists was not participating in its affairs. In 1989, a CPA Task Force was given the mandate to make recommendations concerning the role of the CPA as an advocate of scientific support from industry and government and its role in the promotion of an effective national collaboration between research-based psychologists and the CPA.

The major programmes of the CPA in support of the research community have been carried out with governmental and other research agencies in the area of research communications and science advocacy. Advocacy efforts largely focus upon promoting the availability of resources (human, material, financial) and enhancing the quality of education. Through its Scientific Affairs Committee, the CPA maintains an active lobby with the federal granting councils (NSERC, MRC and SSHRC) and the Department of National Health and Welfare research programme, the National Health Research Development Programme. As well, it attempts to influence government ministries and federal politicians.

Disseminating the products of research has largely been facilitated through sponsorship of scientific meetings, for the most part the annual convention and the journals programme. The most prominent Canadian journals in psychology are published by the CPA, namely the *Canadian Journal of Experimental Psychology*, *Canadian Psychology* and the *Canadian Journal of Behavioural Science*.

Public Awareness and Information

There are ongoing efforts to foster a greater and more positive public understanding of the contributions of psychology to Canadian society. This may be partly accomplished when psychological organizations act as an information resource for the community at large. There is considerable expertise within the community of psychologists on most behavioural and social problems. They are able to speak effectively to the communications media and general public, and are in a position to develop proactive positions on matters of public importance. Organizations have established various mechanisms to ensure a regular flow of information. In some provinces, the services of commercial organizations have been contracted to increase public awareness of the contributions of psychologists.

Conclusion

There can be little doubt that organized psychology in Canada will continue to be very active. Indeed, competition in the marketplace among the various sciences and professions makes it imperative that psychologists marshal their resources and act in strength with a unified, coherent perspective and organized strategies. The issues range from those of international importance to detailed problems of local or regional concern. Psychology has a great deal to say about issues of international conflict and cooperation, and it must pursue research and engage in advocacy on issues of peace and social action. Global issues concerning the environment are effectively the actions of individuals and their collectives, thereby demanding the attention of psychologists, as well. On a national level, Canadian science policy, support for psychological research and relationships with other scientific disciplines all require careful attention and the commitment of resources. Psychology as a science must be made more visible and the contributions better understood. Concerning practitioner issues, we must address the lack of agreement on entry standards into the profession, ethical standards for psychologists and standards for competent practice.

Chronic underfunding of psychological services, education and research must be highlighted. Continuing leadership in egalitarian reforms is important for many subgroups in Canadian society, including women and cultural minorities. The design of services for Canada's native peoples is particularly important. Federal legislation must be monitored and influenced. For example, revisions to the Young Offender's Act are needed, as are reforms in the provincial legislation providing mental-health services for women. At the provincial level, legislation concerning the professions, including psychology, must be continuously monitored and influenced. Continuing education is widely recognized as imperative, yet it is not clear how the profession can ensure this. Improved access to psychological services will undoubtedly remain an issue: If we assume universal access to health care, then one must question why psychological services are not universally available and how this can be accomplished – while also ensuring that the costs of psychological services to consumers do not represent personal burdens. Public information services must be designed to help the public understand the importance of psychological well-being and the availability of psychological services. Promoting high levels of competence and ethical responsibility in professional activities will remain a primary task, as will the financial and human resource costs of maintaining disciplinary systems. Increasingly, the emphasis appears to be on rehabilitation of psychologists who have been reprimanded; but guidelines for the regulation and assistance of impaired psychologists are also needed. All these issues must be dealt with, though the list is by no means comprehensive. One of the more interesting features of involvement with organized psychology in Canada is that one cannot predict what tomorrow's demands will be.

Acknowledgements

I am indebted to the following psychologists for providing valuable information; Carl von Baeyer, David Belanger, Ruth Berman, Jane Bow, Jim Browne, Gordon Butler, Joseph M. Byrne, Beverley Cater-Gauthier, Robert Colby, Rene Corriveau, Lois Edmund, John Garland, Luc Granger, Marlene Harper, Lee Klas, Andrew Langford, Wolfgang Linden, Juanita Mureika, James Newton,

Patrick O'Neill, Elizabeth Percival, Carole Pond, Pierre Ritchie, Philip Smith, Barbara Wand, Patricia Wilensky and Sandra Wolfe. Often the information provided was in the form of official documents and minutes recording the activities of the various organizations of psychologists they represent. The opinions expressed here are those of the author.

References

Adair, J.G. (1971). Canadian psychology as a profession and discipline: Developments, issues and trends in the Seventies. *Canadian Psychology, 22*, 163–173

Babarik, P. (1979). The buried Canadian roots of community psychology. *Journal of Community Psychology, 7*, 362–367.

Banwell, G.T. (1989). *Life in the valley: Paradox and the development of professionalism.* British Columbia Psychological Association.

Berry, R.G., Davidson, P.O., & Gibson, D. (1969). Advisory Council of Provincial of Associations of Psychologists. *Canadian Psychologist, 15*, 368–375.

Byrne, J.M. (1990). Personal communication, July 12, 1990.

Canadian Psychological Association (1977). Report of the Task Force on the Status of Women in Canadian Psychology. *Canadian Psychological Review, 18*, 3–18.

Canadian Psychological Association (1988). Policy statements.

Conway, J.B. (1984). Clinical psychology training in Canada: Its development, current status and the prospects for accreditation. *Canadian Psychology, 25*, 177–191. Responses to Conway, 192–231.

Craig, K.D., & Melanson, D. (1988). Education and training. In Ritchie, R.L-J., Hogan, T.P., & Hogan, T.V. (Eds.), *Psychology in Canada: The state of the discipline, 1984.* Old Chelsea, Quebec: Canadian Psychological Association.

Davidson, P.O. (1971). *Graduate training and research funding in clinical psychology in Canada* (Special Report to the Science Council of Canada, 1970). Reprinted in *Canadian Psychologist, 12*, 141–175.

Ferguson, G.A. (1977). *Report of the Vancouver Conference on the organization and representation in Canada.* Toronto: Canadian Psychological Association.

Gibson, D. (1971). On tub thumping. *Canadian Psychologist, 12*, 1–2.

Gibson, D. (1974). Enculturation stress in Canadian psychology. *Canadian Psychologist, 15*, 151.

Granger, L. (1984). Comment on Conway, 1984. *Canadian Psychology, 25*, 205.

Hebb, D. O. (1960). The American revolution. *American Psychologist, 15*, 735–745.

Hogan, T.V. (1988). From Opinicon I to Opinicon II. In R. L-J., Hogan, T.P. Hogan, & T.V. Hogan (Eds.), *Psychology in Canada: The state of the discipline, 1984*. Old Chelsea, Quebec: Canadian Psychological Association.

Hogan, T.P., Hogan, T.V., & Gupton, T.W. (1982). Credentialing in Canada: The Zimet Conference. *Canadian Psychology*, *23*, 38–40.

Kerr, M.K., & Kerr, H.W. (1984). *Procedures for meetings and organizations*. Ottawa: Carswell Legal Publications.

Lacroix, R. (1987). Stumbling blocks to the practice of health psychology: A Canadian perspective. *Canadian Psychology*, *28*, 280–284.

Leduc, P. (1990). *Address at the Conference on Scholarly Publishing*. Social Sciences and Humanities Research Council.

Myers, C.R. (1965). Notes on the history of psychology in Canada. *Canadian Psychologist*, 4–19.

Myers, C.R. (1971). Research funding for psychologists in Canada: A symposium. *Canadian Psychologist*, *12*, 3–24.

Myers, C.R. (1982). Psychology of Toronto. In M.J. Wright & C.R. Myers (Eds.), *History of academic psychology in Canada* (pp. 68–99). Toronto: Hogrefe.

National Consortium of Scientific and Educational Societies. (1990). *Towards a coherent educational and scientific research policy for Canada*. Ottawa: Author.

Pettifor, J., & Sinclair, C.M. (1991). Enhancing fairness and justice in the ethical complaint process. *Canadian Psychology*, *32*, 63–71.

Pinard, A. (1964). Le Modele Scientiste-Professionnel: Synthese ou Prothese. *Canadian Psychologist*, *5*, 187–208.

Quarrington, B. (1989). The freedom of information and protection of privacy act. *Bulletin of the Ontario Board of Examiners in Psychology*, *15*(4), 1–6.

Ritchie, R.L-J., Hogan, T.P., & Hogan, T.V. (Eds.). (1988). *Psychology in Canada: The state of the discipline, 1984*. Old Chelsea, Quebec: Canadian Psychological Association.

Ritchie, P.L.J., Wilson, R.F., Berry, R., Boulay, M., King, M., & Sabourin, M. (1988). The funding of psychological health care services. *Canadian Psychology*, *29*, 187–205.

Ross, C.F.J. (1982). The governance of psychological practice. *Canadian Psychology*, 229–234.

Sabourin, M. E. (1991). Faire reconnaître la psychologie sur la scène politique: L'approche TPS (Tractations, Planification, Stratégie). *Canadian Psychology, 32*, 3–15.

Service, J., Sabourin, M., Catano, V.M., Day, V., Hayes, C., & MacDonald, G.W. (1989). *Report of the CPA/CPAP task force on specialty designation*. Canadian Psychological Association.

Wand, B. (1990). *The Council of Provincial Associations of Psychologists: 1967–1990*. Unpublished manuscript.

Wand, B. (1991). Informal natural justice. *Canadian Psychology, 32*, 77–78.

Webster, E.C. (Ed.). (1967). *The Couchiching Conference on professional psychology in Canada*. Montreal: Canadian Psychological Association.

Williams, T.M., Zabrack, M.L., & Harrison, L.F. (1980). Some factors affecting women's participation in psychology in Canada. *Canadian Psychology, 21*, 97–108.

Wright, M.J. (1969). Canadian psychology comes of age. *Canadian Psychologist, 10*, 229–253.

Wright, M.J. (1971 a). Number of psychologists is Canada: 1970 estimate. *Canadian Psychologist, 12*, 66–67.

Wright, M.J. (1971 b). The psychological organizations of Canada. *Canadian Psychologist, 12*, 420–431.

Wright, M.J. (1974). CPA: The first ten years. *Canadian Psychologist, 15*, 112–131.

Wright, M.J., & Meyers, C.R. (1982). *History of academic psychology in Canada*. Toronto: Hogrefe.

II

Training Issues in Professional Psychology

3

Graduate Education in Professional Psychology in Canada

Keith S. Dobson
University of Calgary

Deborah J. G. Dobson
Foothills Hospital & University of Calgary

One of the first "rights of passage" on an individual's journey to obtaining professional status is graduate education. Graduate education lies prior to licensing examinations or any of the various forms of specialty recognition in modern professional psychology. It is appropriate, therefore, that one of the first chapters in this volume be devoted to the topic of graduate education of psychologists in training.

Here, we highlight some of the issues facing graduate educators in psychology, such as the connection between education and licensing requirements and education and accreditation programmes. Further, we examine some of the issues inherent in the development of specialty designation and how graduate programmes affect such designation systems. After reviewing the above issues, we turn to a description of Canadian programmes in professional psychology and offer some comments about how well these programmes meet the needs for education. Finally, we conclude with some suggestions for further research and programme development.

The Need for Graduate Education

Two dominant and intersecting forces conspire to require advanced education for all professions. One is the public demand for highly trained and competent service providers – individuals who possess greater than ordinary expertise in their respective service area. The second force is the guild interests of members of a profession to ensure that standards are set and maintained so as to ensure public respect, professional autonomy and market protection.

Ensuring Competence

It is generally recognized that advanced education, in whatever profession, is valuable when there is a unique body of knowledge and set of skills to master. Psychology has for some time been recognized as having a body of knowledge unique in the natural and social sciences as well as in applied aspects of the field. This is reflected in the independent departmental status of psychology throughout different colleges and universities, the existence of autonomous psychological scientific organizations, journals and research publications, and the large number of specialty courses offered in the field.

Establishing a unique set of skills for the profession of psychology is perhaps more difficult than establishing a body of knowledge. Although psychologists are typically trained in a number of skills that, in the aggregate, make them a unique type of professional, many composite skills comprising that aggregate are shared with other professions (Pryzwansky & Wendt, 1987). Psychologists share with psychiatrists the ability to diagnose, with special education teachers the assessment of childhood disability, with social workers martial and family therapy, with graduates of organizational behaviour programmes business management analyses and interventions, and with a number of specialty counselling groups counselling services, to name but a few examples.

The unique body of knowledge inherent in the practice of professional psychology has been recognized for some time in legal statutes. In that a licensing or credentialing system authorized by the State reflects general societal acceptance of the independent status of a profession, it can be said that every state in the United States has enjoyed such recognition since 1977. In Canada, the development of provincial acts to enable the independent regulation of professional psychology has been somewhat slower than in the United States, but with the establishment of a regulatory body in Prince Edward Island in 1990, every province can now boast statutory professional autonomy.

In summary, there exists the combination of scientific principles and findings, professional skills and competencies, and regulatory autonomy converging to establish the independent existence of the profession of psychology. The competence to practise as a professional psychologist is ostensibly garnered through the combination of incorporating that body of knowledge and set of skills through graduate education, and subsequently having the relevant regulatory body for psychology recognize that type and level of training.

The Guild Interest

In contrast to the competencies established through graduate training, relatively less has been written about the salutary effect that the defining, maintaining and enhancing standards of training has for the status and power of professions. As has been pointed out (Hogan, 1979), however, high standards create a type of specialized profession that may have several negative effects upon the service area in question. These potential negative effects include (relatively) fewer service providers, higher costs to obtain service and training and credentialing processes remote from the societal needs. To Hogan's list we would add the *potential* dangers of undue respect and/or awe of practitioners, the difficulty of new service providers entering the market, the difficulty in upgrading service providers already in the profession but trained at a time when entry requirements were lower, the stifling of creative alternative methods for providing some areas of service within the broad umbrella of the profession (Davidson, 1970) and an insular sense of elitism among the members of the profession.

In the development of any profession there is a dynamic balancing between the need to meet societal needs for expertise and trained professionals and the need for the profession to define its own service areas and competencies (and, by implication, those groups that will *not* share this part of the service market). As the profession of psychology grows, it will be an ongoing task to ensure that the optimal balance is struck between these potentially conflicting interests.

Controversies of Type and Level of Training for Professional Psychology

Throughout the relatively short history of professional psychology, two major controversies have arisen: the appropriate type or model of training given to emerging professionals, and the appropriate level of graduate training for entry into the profession.

Science and Practice in Professional Psychology

Two models of training for professional psychologists dominate the graduate domain in contemporary psychology. The model with the longest history is the scientist-practitioner model, sometimes also referred to as the Boulder model, from its inception at the Boulder, Colorado, conference on clinical psychology training (Raimy, 1950). The Boulder conference was held in response to the need for some common standards for the training of clinical psychologists and was precipitated by the fact that at the conclusion of the Second World War the Veterans Administration in the

United States was prepared to fund the development of graduate clinical psychology programmes if some type of standardization and quality of training could be achieved. The Boulder conference took as its working document a report written by an APA committee (Shakow, 1947) and adopted that report in large measure.

The essential aspect of the scientist-practitioner model is its acceptance that, in addition to the development of skills and competencies necessary to practise as a professional, clinical psychologists should have a level of training in research and scientific methods comparable to that in any other area of psychology. In graduate programmes, this is typically translated to mean that clinical psychology students must meet the research requirements made of all students in the graduate programmes. It also means that at the termination of their graduate training these students should have the same research skills as any other graduate in order to enter an active research career.

After the scientist-practitioner model was embraced as the major model for training clinical psychologists and funds to develop programmes based upon this model became available, a number of American universities quickly moved to establish such programmes. The APA accreditation programme (see Doyle, Edwards & Robinson, this volume), established in 1949, further strengthened the importance of this model. With the subsequent review and accreditation of programmes that subscribed to this regimen, and with the gradual establishment of preferential employment opportunities for graduates of such programmes, this training model profoundly influenced the training of clinical psychologists in the United States.

Somewhat unusual in the context of the models for graduate training is the "ripple effect" of the scientist-practitioner model for clinical psychology. It is entirely conceivable that other areas of professional psychology might have expressed the need for other models of graduate training and in fact might have developed alternative programme structures. But when other areas of professional psychology sought to develop accreditation programmes through the Office of Accreditation in the APA, the scientist-practitioner model was applied to these other areas as well. Even though the last American conference on general graduate education in psychology was in 1958 (Roe, Gustad, Moore, Ross & Shodak, 1959), it is clear that the scientist-practitioner model continues to dominate the training of professional psychologists in that country (Pryzwansky & Wendt, 1987).

The other ripple effect of the APA adoption of the scientist-practitioner model was felt in Canadian psychology. At the first Opinicon conference on Canadian psychology, sponsored in 1960 by the Canadian Psychological Association, the issue of training of clinical and other "applied" psychologists was addressed (Bernhardt, 1961). Two recommendations emerging from that conference are of relevance here. One of these related to clinical psychology in particular and stated:

> As the scientist-professional model of the clinical psychologists at the Ph. D. level has been accepted, it is necessary to educate the student preparing for an applied role in basically the same way as other graduate students in psychology. Though the *primary emphasis should be on research* in the Ph. D. clinical programme, *part of the training programme should be devoted to the teaching of clinical skills* such as diagnostics and psychotherapy. (Bernhardt, 1961, p. 42; emphases added)

The other relevant recommendation related more broadly to applied psychology and stated, in part:

> Whenever a university department of psychology embarks on a programme of training psychologists in an applied area, such training should be firmly rooted in a basic research orientation. (Bernhardt, 1961, p. 42)

It thus appears that from an early point in time Canadian graduate education in professional psychology had an even stronger research component than was reflected in the Boulder scientist-practitioner model.

The stronger support given to research training in Canadian programmes relative to those in the United States is understandable from the perspective that there was not analogous pressure to that created by the U.S. Veterans Administration to evolve professional training within graduate departments of psychology. Thus, professional or applied training was adopted within the Canadian context as part of an evolution of graduate departments from their traditional base as trainers of research-oriented doctoral graduates to graduates with a firm rooting in the research tradition of psychology, but with applied professional skills as well.

Even though the Opinicon conference strongly endorsed the need for research training in professional psychology, the general sentiment in the psychological community may not have been as firm in its position. In anticipation of the 1965 Couchiching conference on professional psychology in Canada (Webster, 1967) a survey of 429 Canadian psychologists (Sydiaha, 1966) was conducted. Included in the survey was the statement "All University courses in psychology (including applied psychology) should have a research emphasis". Survey respondents demonstrated a remarkable lack of agreement on this item, with 50.2% either agreeing or strongly agreeing and 44.3% either disagreeing or strongly disagreeing with that statement. This split in opinion was present, even though almost all respondents agreed that research experience should be required. For example, in response to the statement "All graduate students (including master's students) should be required to do a research thesis", fully 71.5% agreed or strongly agreed, while only 23.1% disagreed or strongly disagreed. While research training was thus seen as a necessary part of graduate training, it was not perceived to be the primary focus of that training.

The scientist-practitioner model was endorsed at the Couchiching conference:

> The professional psychologist, therefore, should receive his training within the scientist-professional model and should be a competent research producer. (Webster, 1967, p. 119)

Yet the emphasis of the programme had shifted slightly: Rather than focusing primarily on research, the model now produces a person capable of producing research. Such a definition left considerable room for the development of programmes with equal weight given to research and professional training, and indeed several such programmes were then developed.

The scientist-practitioner model continues to be the dominant model of graduate education in Canadian psychology. The teaching group at the 1984 Opinicon II conference (Ritchie, Hogan & Hogan, 1988) reaffirmed this position, with the following statement: "It is recognized that the scientist-professional model is the generally accepted model for the graduate training of professional psychologists in Canada". Further, with the establishment of the

CPA system in 1984 for accreditation and the incorporation of the scientist-practitioner model into that accreditation system, this training model will surely be dominant for some time to come.

The adoption of the scientist-practitioner model in Canadian psychology, and its gradual evolution to an equally balanced type of programme accreditation, took place from roughly the mid-1960s to the mid-1980s. In the United States, the comparable process roughly occurred from 1949–1965. By the middle of the 1960s, however, it had become clear in the United States that there was opposition to the Boulder model within several quarters. Predicated upon the position that professional psychologists did not need to be competent at producing research – even if they needed to be competent to be research consumers – and further given that most graduates of professional programmes were not in fact engaged in ongoing research, the argument was made for the need for a nonresearch, or *professional* model of training.

The professional model of training, also referred to as the Psy. D. model, was first endorsed at the Vail conference (Korman, 1976). This endorsement reflected the fact that a number of such programmes had already been established, but it also perpetuated the development of other such programmes. The establishment of professional schools was further stimulated by the accreditation of several training programmes, which "legitimized" their existence from the perspective that a scientist-practitioner model could train research consumers (Fox, Barclay & Rodgers, 1982; Peterson, 1976).

The current graduate training situation for professional psychology in the United States is more complex than at any previous point in history. There are university-based Ph. D. programmes, university-based Psy. D. programmes and free-standing private Psy. D. institutions and programmes. Although the number of accredited programmes is still somewhat higher in university-based Ph. D. programmes than in professional schools, there are also many accredited Psy. D. programmes. And since many professional schools admit and graduate many more students that Ph. D. programmes, professional psychology in the United States is being increasingly influenced by the professional training model.

Every graduate programme in professional psychology in Canada is grounded in a university context. Despite some diversity among programmes in terms of the extent of their research emphasis, all provide some type of training and experience in research as well as applied training. To date, efforts to establish professional training programmes for Canadian psychologists outside the university context have been unsuccessful, although it can be only a matter of time until such programmes emerge on the Canadian landscape.

Doctoral Training

In contrast to the often heated debate over the value of research training in professional psychology and the type of training model best suited to this domain, there has been remarkably little debate over the *level of training*. In 1949, the Boulder conference endorsed the Raimy committee's recommendation to adopt the doctoral degree in psychology as the appropriate entry degree into independent practice. A clear statement of the position of the APA was made on this issue in 1977, when it passed a resolution that included the following declaration:

> ... the APA takes a position and makes part of its policy that the use of the title "Professional Psychologist" and its variations such as "Clinical Psychologist", "Counselling Psychologist", "School Psychologist" and "Industrial Psychologist" are reserved for those who have completed a Doctoral Training Programme in Psychology in a university, college or professional school of psychology that is APA or regionally accredited.

In summary, the doctoral degree has been widely promoted as the appropriate level of training throughout the United States and is the dominant degree obtained, be it the Ph. D., Psy. D. or Ed. D. (Brickman, 1985). The availability of doctoral training through professional schools has clearly advanced the ability of American professional psychology to train the numbers of psychologists necessary to need societal needs.

The situation in Canada is in some ways analogous to that of the United States. The 1960 Opinicon conference endorsed the Ph. D. as the "desirable" degree for psychologists working in applied settings. It has been the position of the Canadian Psychological Association since that doctoral training is required for the development of appropriate competencies to practise psychology. In contrast to the United States, however, where opposition to doctoral requirements have been relatively minimal, in Canada there has clearly been an evolution of opinion regarding the doctoral requirement.

In the period of the early to mid-1960s there was the tendency in the psychological community to recognize master's-level training as appropriate for the entry into professional practice. The survey conducted by Sydiaha (1966) asked two questions relevant to this issue. On one – "A doctoral degree should be the minimum academic qualification for professional work in psychology" – fully 57.4% of the respondents either disagreed or strongly disagreed, while only 32.2% agreed or strongly agreed. The other relevant question – "A two year terminal professional degree (master's level) should be the minimum academic qualification for professional work in psychology" – was agreed or strongly agreed to by 59.7% of the respondents, with only 31.5% of the respondents disagreeing or strongly disagreeing.

At the Couchiching conference (Webster, 1967), it became clear that a consensus on the need for doctoral training was not complete. The report indicates that speakers often stressed the need for doctoral training in order to have the person in question use the title "psychologist". At the same time, the resolution "Be it resolved, however he [sic] be trained or qualified in scientific or professional terms, the psychologist must merit and possess a Ph. D. degree in Psychology" was soundly defeated (35 against, 5 for, 5 abstentions). Resolutions were passed which endorsed the "D. Psychology degree" as "an acceptable way of recognizing successful completion of a professional training programme at the doctoral level", and for recognizing "the principle of certifying the professional competence of persons below the doctoral level", but a number of specific recommendations related to recognition of master's-level trained personnel and training programmes for subdoctoral personnel failed to achieve a majority of votes. As such, while the Couchiching conference re-endorsed the doctoral requirement for psychologists, it was novel for supporting a professional model of training and for its lack of consistency on the issue of training and credentialing of subdoctoral individuals.

In the wake of the Couchiching conference, the Science Council of Canada initiated a report on "Graduate Training and Research Funding for Clinical Psychology in Canada" (Davidson, 1970).

This report reflected upon the large number of doctoral graduates from experimental psychology programmes emerging at the time, but also offered the opinion that "To the extent that the clinical psychologist is seen as a front-line worker spending any amount of his time on individual testing and therapy, a manpower shortage for the next ten years would be crucial and universities in Canada could not begin to turn out the number of people trained to the Ph. D. to meet this need" (Davidson, 1970, p. 112). Davidson recommended the creation of psychology technologist training programmes, either in universities or postsecondary colleges, further suggesting that a pyramid of service providers be created with three levels of training: "The one or two year trained technician or psychological assistant trained at the junior college, the four year technologist and the seven year Ph. D. researcher-consultant" (Davidson, 1970, p. 116).

It appears the Davidson's suggestions, however creative and with whatever potential they had for meeting personnel needs (see also Albee, 1965), were not acted upon; rather, the focus on doctoral training continued. The period of the late 1960s appears to have been a time of differing opinions on the professionalization of psychology at the national level. It should also be noted that this was a time during which the recognition of psychology as a profession was increasing, as evidenced by the rise in the number of provinces given statutory control over the profession of psychology. The Advisory Council of Provincial Associations of Psychology (ACPAP), established in 1968 as a communication vehicle among the developing regulatory and societal bodies of psychology, began to argue that increased national discussion of professional issues was warranted, and that this issue was not being adequately pursued by the Canadian Psychological Association. There were preliminary discussions about the formation of a "National Association of Professional Psychologists".

In 1977, the Vancouver conference was held in order to deal with some of the concerns raised by the ACPAP as well as the general issues related to professional psychology (Ferguson, 1977). In general, the conference accepted the need for a re-orientation of Canadian psychology and had a number of specific outcomes, including the acceptance by the CPA to address issues of professional psychology, to develop a Canadian Code of Ethics, to begin national lobbying on professional issues, to begin to establish accreditation standards for clinical psychology programmes, and generally to become more responsive to professional issues. Most importantly, perhaps, the formation of a separate national professional organization was averted.

By 1984, the CPA had established accreditation criteria for doctoral programmes in clinical psychology (see Doyle et al., this volume), the Canadian Code of Ethics was in development (see Sinclair, this volume) and several other initiatives were under way. The Opinicon II State of the Discipline review, conducted in the same year (Ritchie, Hogan & Hogan, 1988), further advanced professional issues at the national level. Most relevant here, the recommendations of the Teaching Group at the conference restated the support for doctoral training:

> The Canadian Psychological Association should continue to provide leadership in promoting the doctoral degree as the appropriate educational requirement for statutory recognition as a psychologist. (Ritchie et al., 1988, p. 131)

Further specific recommendations to meet the above general recommendation were also elaborated.

Despite the long history of support for doctoral entry into psychology in Canada, this principle is still not universally embraced. There are several jurisdictions in Canada where the doctoral requirement to practise psychology has yet to be established in law. Further, there continue to be some disagreements within the profession by some service providers about the necessity of doctoral training. This issue of subdoctoral training is nowhere more clear than in the area of school psychology (see Holmes, this volume). Many educators in the area of school psychology, as well as the National Association of School Psychology (NASP, U.S.) and the Canadian Association of School Psychology (CASP) continue to debate the need for doctoral training, and both the NASP and CASP currently endorse the master's degree as the appropriate minimum educational graduate degree for entry in the practice of school psychology.

In summary, despite some initial hesitations and with some limited jurisdictions and areas of practice continuing to resist this development, the recognition of the doctoral requirement for training professional psychologists has been established in Canada. A safe prediction is that as doctoral programmes establish themselves in those provinces where they currently do not exist to meet personnel requirements, the doctoral requirement will be adopted on a national level. Whether school psychology will adopt the doctoral requirement is a more complex issue, as there are sound academic and service-related arguments for subdoctoral entry into the practice of school psychology (see Holmes, this volume).

Graduate Education and Licensing

In a mature profession, the type of graduate education provided matches the entry requirements for licensing in the profession. Ideally, graduates are prepared for licensing upon graduation (or, perhaps, after some limited supervised experience, but no further formal education), but they will not have been required to undertake educational requirements for the degree that are superfluous to licensing requirements. Within professional psychology, the meshing of graduate education and licensing requirements is sought through the processes of programme accreditation and designation.

Graduate education and the Accreditation Process

Accreditation is a process by which graduate programmes voluntarily submit to a review by the accrediting body, in order to determine if the programmes meet the type and quality of training promoted. Since 1984, the Canadian Psychological Association has maintained an Accreditation Panel, which stipulates both the general nature as well as the specific course content of doctoral programmes and internships in clinical psychology striving to meet accreditation criteria. The CPA accreditation programme for clinical programmes was supplemented by comparable programmes for counselling and clinical neuropsychology programmes, and the Accreditation Panel now refers to itself as the Accreditation Panel in Professional Psychology (see Doyle et al., this volume).

The accreditation standards set by the CPA are largely consistent with those of the APA, and CPA and APA have formulated an agreement for joint review by both organizations for those programmes that seek accreditation by both CPA and APA (although not the formal decision to accredit or not, which is retained by both the CPA and the APA). In general, these criteria stipulate training in professional issues and ethics, statistics and research, several areas of broad exposure to psychology, as well as training specific to the practice area being trained (e.g. clinical vs. counselling psychology).

Graduate programmes are not obliged to submit to accreditation: it is a voluntary activity. In the professional community, and increasingly among educated potential "consumers" of graduate programmes, however, there is certainly the feeling that accredited programmes offer a certain security of quality of training not given by nonaccredited programmes. It is not surprising, therefore, that applicants to graduate programmes prefer admission to accredited programmes. This force drives many universities to work toward meeting accreditation criteria. Further, because of the ability to attract and train stronger applicants, and because of the security of the level of training provided, accredited programmes have little difficulty obtaining good positions for their graduates. Indeed, the practice of preferential hiring of accredited programme graduates is well established in the United States, and there are early signs of this practice beginning in Canada.

In summary, despite the voluntary aspect of the accreditation process, there are sound pedagogical and practical reasons for graduate programmes to work toward accreditation status. As the next section makes clear, there are benefits to graduates of accredited programmes related to licensing as well as in the job market.

Designation of Graduate Programmes

One of the typical statements found have in the registration process of licensing bodies in psychology is that the applicant must possess "a doctoral degree in psychology or its equivalent" (in some provinces, the requirement is still the master's degree). As a result of the combination of (1) the large numbers of psychology programmes, (2) the diverse range of these programmes, (3) the presence of applicants from foreign programmes where standards of training may be different than in Canada and (4) the unfortunate, but likely unpreventable, fact that if there is a market for doctoral degrees, institutions or groups will try to meet that market demand by offering minimal (or even less than minimal) programmes, it has become necessary for regulatory bodies of psychology to determine some mechanism for recognizing a doctoral programme or its equivalent. In the United States, the American Association of State Psychology Boards (AASPB) and National Register of Health Services Providers in Psychology (NRHSPP) have established a system for the "Designation of Graduate Programmes". This system establishes a set of criteria that can be used to identify known programmes or to evaluate an individual's programme of studies if not from a known programme. Not surprisingly, the criteria adopted by the AASPB/NRHSPP are very similar to the accreditation criteria promoted by the APA's accreditation panel. As many states have adopted the designation criteria, there is a good fit between the requirements of accreditation and the training requirements for licensing in these jurisdictions.

One of the recommendations of the 1984 Opinicon II conference was that the CPA, in conjunction with the Council of Provincial Associations of Psychology (CPAP; formerly the Advisory Council of Provincial Associations of Psychology), establish a system for designating programmes in psychology. The CPA/CPAP Task Force on Designation reviewed the AASPB/NRHSPP criteria, and with appropriate revisions for the Canadian context recommended the adoption of the criteria for Canada (Dobson & Wand, 1987). Both the CPA and the CPAP have subsequently adopted these recommendations, and several Canadian jurisdictions have moved to implement this designation system. As in the United States, Canadian programmes accredited by the CPA or the APA are automatically assumed to meet the designation criteria.

In summary, the designation of programmes of psychology has now moved to a point where there can be the linkage between graduate programmes, accreditation of these programmes and the recognition of these programmes for licensing that is a mark of a mature profession. It is hoped that in the succeeding years, further linkage among these processes will occur in those jurisdictions where it does not yet exist.

Generic and Specialty Programmes

Graduate training in medicine can be distinguished from training in psychology in that medicine first requires of all physicians a generic training programme before they specialize, whereas in psychology this is not the case. Although almost all graduate psychology programmes now require the applicant to have earned an undergraduate degree in psychology or its equivalent, those undergraduate degrees vary in terms of their coverage of the domain of psychology and in the required number of courses. Further, students apply and are selected for specialty graduate programmes based in part on the appropriateness of their undergraduate course selection for the graduate programme they are applying to enter. The net result of these processes is that students enter graduate programmes in psychology with differing types of undergraduate training.

In a typical Department of Psychology, the only course graduate students share is statistics and research methodology. Students in accredited graduate programmes may also take breadth courses in basic areas of psychology with other students, but the nature of the courses taken as well as their number vary from student to student, based upon his or her research and training interests. Specialty areas in the student's area of training (e.g. clinical psychology, industrial/organizational psychology) will be shared primarily with colleagues in that training programme. Indeed, in some graduate programmes training courses are not open to students who are not formally admitted to the training programme.

One of the consequences of providing only specialized graduate programmes is that the profession has no equivalent to the General Practitioner in medicine. Although graduates of psychology programmes may have several sets of overlapping skills, they typically identify themselves as a specialist in a particular practice area. Such specialized identification is further fostered through the accreditation process, which recognizes specialized programmes of studies. Finally, the requirements of many regulatory bodies to stipulate one's area of practice when becoming licensed (and then restricting practice to that area) further exacerbates psychologists' tendencies to view themselves as specialists without a general or common training background.

Although this is not the appropriate place to debate the merits of graduate generic training and specialization in psychology, it is appropriate to acknowledge that the general issue of statutory recognition of specialties in psychology does bear a relationship to graduate education. It is a fact that all psychology acts in Canada are generic in form; that is, they are intended to regulate all aspects of professional psychology equally. No province has yet established and attempted to enforce specializations that not only define who may practise in those areas, but also exclude other practitioners who do not possess the requisite training. Reasons for this lack of development are several, but principally include the fact that specialties in psychology cannot be uniquely defined in terms of practice skills or competencies, as several specialties include overlapping practices. Specialties in psychology are therefore best viewed as "fuzzy sets" of skills, some overlapping and some distinct. Nor can specialties be uniquely identified by virtue of the training offered, as training programmes offer some degree of overlap with other professional areas.

The consequence of the above conundrum is that while graduate programmes in psychology claim specialized training, this training does not uniformly rest upon a definite base set of knowledge (i. e. an undergraduate degree in psychology with required content); and the training they provide offers skills and competencies that overlap with other practice areas, both at the level of graduate education and practice. To the extent that this is perceived as a problem, and to the extent that formal statutory recognition of specialties is deemed important to advance the profession (Service, Sabourin, Catano, Day, Hayes & MacDonald, 1989), it is suggested that the overlap among areas of professional psychology will need to be reduced and graduate programmes will need to focus their energy on truly specialized areas of skills and competencies.

Canadian Programmes of Professional Psychology

Having reviewed the above issues related to graduate programmes, we are now in a position to examine the graduate training in psychology offered in Canada. Appendix 1 at the back of this book lists all graduate programmes in professional psychology that could be identified by the authors, using the titles of the programmes as offered in the documentation created by the programme. Table 1 provides a breakdown of programmes by type and degree offered, although only the highest earnable degree for each programme is enumerated in Table 1. Almost every doctoral programme also offers the master's degree, so the *total* number

Table 1. A profile of Canadian graduate programmes in professional psychology.

Program Type	Degrees offered					
	M. Ed.	M. A./M. Sc.	M. Ps.	Ph. D.	Ed. D.	Total
Clinical	0	3	3	19	0	25
Educational	8	1	0	5	1	15
Counselling	6	0	0	5	1	12
Applied Social	0	3	0	4	0	7
School	0	1	0	5	1	7
Ind./Organizational	0	1	1	3	0	5
Neuropsychology	0	0	0	5	0	5
Applied Community	0	1	0	2	0	3
Applied Child	0	2	0	0	0	2
Environmental	0	0	0	1	0	1
Forensic	0	0	0	1	0	1
Psychopathology	0	0	0	1	0	1
Special Education	0	0	0	1	0	1
Rehabilitation	0	0	0	1	0	1
Beh. Modification	0	0	0	1	0	1
Guidance Counselling	1	0	0	0	0	1
Totals	15	12	4	54	3	88

Index: M. Ed. – Master's of Education; M. A. – Master's of Arts; M. Sc. – Master's of Science; M. Ps. – Master's of Psychology (offered only in Quebec); Ph. D. – Doctorate of Philosophy, Ed. D. – Doctorate of Education
Note: For a complete list of programmes that contributed to the above table, see Appendix A.

of master's degree programmes offered is higher than the numbers depicted in Table 1. By simply tabulating the programmes listed in this table, however, it can be seen that there are 88 distinct graduate programmes of psychology in Canada.

The single most frequent type of programme in professional psychology is in clinical psychology, the most common type of training programme being doctoral. Only six terminal master's programmes in clinical psychology exist in Canada, three of which are in Quebec, which recognizes the master's degree as the entry level to practise psychology.

The next two most available programme types are those in educational and counselling psychology. In both instances, approximately half of the Canadian programmes offer a terminal master's degree, while the other half are doctoral. As many of these programmes are offered within Departments of Educational Psychology, it is not surprising that many of the degrees are Education degrees.

Several programme areas have in the range of three to seven programmes in Canada, including applied social psychology, school psychology, industrial/organizational psychology, neuropsychology and applied community psychology. The majority of these programmes are doctoral in nature, with the exception of applied social psychology, which has a number of terminal master's programmes.

Finally, there are eight programme areas that have only one or two programmes in Canada. Six of these are doctoral: environmental, forensic, psychopathology, special education, rehabilitation and behaviour modification, while guidance counselling and applied child are master's-level programmes.

Table 1 offers some interesting insights into graduate education in psychology in Canada. It appears that of the various areas of training, clinical psychology is the most developed. Not only does it have the largest number of clinical programmes, most of those programmes have accepted the doctoral standard espoused by the CPA and reflected in the CPA Accreditation criteria. One could easily speculate that there is resistance to doctoral training in the areas of educational and counselling psychology, as fully half of the programmes offer terminal master's training. Other programme areas, while less common in numbers, seem to have adopted the doctoral degree requirement.

Another speculation emerging from Table 1 relates to the issue of specialties: As can readily be seen, there are several unique programme areas (e.g. psychopathology, special education) as well as several programme areas that appear with sufficient frequency to be able to be claimed as specialties, possessing unique knowledge bases and sets of skills and therefore requiring specialized training programmes. Within the Canadian context, Table 1 suggests that these areas are clinical, educational, counselling, applied social, school, industrial/organizational and neuropsychology. At present, three of these areas (clinical, counselling and neuropsychology) are recognized by the accreditation process as unique areas. One might postulate that these others areas might also qualify as specialties.

Finally, the list of programmes comprising Appendix 1 offers some insights into the regional availability of graduate education in psychology in Canada. Table 2 presents a breakdown of the graduate programmes, by province or regional area. In most areas of Canada, the proportion of master's to doctoral programmes is about 1:3, with the clear exception of Atlantic Canada, where that ratio is almost reversed. Clearly, the development of doctoral level programmes in Atlantic Canada has lagged behind that in other areas of the country.

In summary, there are a large number of graduate programmes of psychology in Canada, and about two-thirds of these are doctoral in nature. These programmes cover a wide range of areas of professional psychology, although the most frequent types of programmes are in clinical, educational and counselling psychology. The exact number of graduates emerging from the professional

Table 2. Regional breakdown of Canadian graduate programmes in professional psychology.

Province/Region	Degrees offered: Master's level	Degrees offered: Doctoral	Total
British Columbia	3	8	11
Prairie Region	4	14	18
Ontario	8	18	26
Quebec	5	15	20
Maritime Region	10	3	13
Totals:	30	58	88

programmes in Canada each year is not known, though this information would be useful to obtain. Finally, there are regional disparities in programme development, with the Atlantic provinces of Canada being less well developed than other parts of the country.

Future Issues in Graduate Education

As this chapter has argued, graduate education in psychology has become an increasingly complex issue. Presumed to rest upon the need for protection of the public, graduate programmes have been established to train qualified personnel to meet society's psychological services needs. In this final section, we offer some suggestions about future trends for graduate training in professional psychology.

Continued Programme Development

It is difficult at present to establish the relationship of the production of psychology graduates with the societal need for those graduates. Although the common wisdom amongst psychology educators is that graduates are able to obtain positions, we know of no recent survey establishing either the employment rates of recent psychology graduates or the personnel needs of psychology employers in relation to their ability to hire appropriately trained personnel. It would appear, at face value, that although there may be some regional shortages, there is neither a national glut nor shortage of Canadian psychologists. Data on this issue are clearly worth collecting.

Assuming the above conclusion about the adequacy of trained psychologists is accurate, and given the financial constraints that most postsecondary institutions find themselves in at this point in history, the next few years will most likely not see any dramatic increase in the number of graduate programmes in psychology. Although in some regions provincial governments may devote specialized attention to graduate psychology programmes (e.g.

the Atlantic provinces), and some departments of psychology or universities may redeploy existing funds into establishing specialized programmes as a means to attract higher calibre students, the number of programmes so created is likely to be modest in relation to the existing number.

What may occur – in contrast to a burgeoning number of programmes – is that existing programmes increase in quality. The number of clinical psychology programmes accredited in Canada since 1984 has risen sharply, and many nonaccredited programmes are working to be able to meet those criteria. Some counselling psychology programmes are working toward meeting accreditation criteria, which may set off a new round of increasing standards in that training area. One might expect, for example, that several of the currently terminal master's programmes establish doctoral programmes to complement the existing programmes. Clinical neuropsychology, a recently adopted area of accreditation, may well see an increase in number and quality enhancement. Thus, it is expected that the quality of existing programmes will increase despite the lack of large new sums of money for establishing programmes, and that there will be a marginal increase in number and level of programmes in less-developed areas.

Research Training in Graduate Programmes

The traditional attitude toward research training in graduate psychology programmes is that graduates of professional programmes should have no less formal education and experience in research than other graduates. This attitude has been expressed in most surveys assessing this question (Sydiaha, 1965; Webster, 1967), although recent data are not available. It is almost certain that the Ph. D. or Ed. D. models of training, with its doctoral dissertation requirement, fosters the attitude that doctoral psychologists should be producers of research, capable of assuming a research position as well as a professional position on graduation.

In contrast to the doctoral training model which states that graduates should be able to produce research, it has been argued that the necessary skill for trained professionals is to be able to consume (i. e. read, keep current with) research, rather than produce it (Fox et al., 1982; Rodgers, 1964; Stricker, 1975). Most professional schools of psychology adopting the scientist-practitioner model of training educate students in research design and statistics, but do not have a formal research requirement. The type of training experience inherent in a professional school of psychology, as well as the length of training associated with producing original research, is significantly different than traditional doctoral training. This model of training has had a remarkable impact on the type of professional training, not to mention the number of psychology graduates, in the United States.

Although no professional schools of psychology yet exist in Canada, this area of graduate training is rife with potential. The Couchiching conference (Webster, 1967) endorsed the D. Psychology degree as a means for professional training, and there have been some efforts to establish professional programmes. At present, it is difficult to anticipate what will happen with respect to the issue of professional schools of psychology in Canada. The strong influence of governmental Ministries of Advanced Education or Universities (as they are called from province to province), coupled with the strong interprovincial influences in advanced education fostered by the federal transfer payment programme, suggest that it is unlikely that other than established programme models will emerge in the near future. Further, Canada's limited experience with private educational institutions make it unlikely that a private institution granting doctoral degrees will be soon developed. If, on the other hand, federal transfer payments are curtailed to the point where national considerations begin to be mitigated in educational planning, the establishment of provincially based professional training may emerge. If so, it is predicted that a single occurrence of a professional psychology programme in Canada is likely to have a powerful "domino effect", with other provinces examining and adopting this training model.

Funding Issues in Graduate Education

Little has been said in this chapter on the issue of funding in graduate education. Reviews and recommendations related to the institutional support for professional psychology have been infrequent (for exceptions, see Davidson, 1970 and Berlyne, Black, Berry & Douglas, 1971). Judging by the slow and steady development of programmes, it appears that funds exist for the creation and maintenance of graduate programmes (see Appendix 1). Formal review of this conclusion would be a useful exercise.

At the individual level, it is unclear whether financial support matches the need for funding. A recent CPA/CPAP Task Force on mid-career training (see Whitsett & Handy, this volume) suggests that a major problem for individuals with existing master's degree who wish to return to the university for doctoral studies is financial. It is unclear whether this financial difficulty is also manifest for individuals just entering the graduate training sequence. To our knowledge, there are no current data on the number of students taking graduate training who either receive limited funding support, earn scholarships or take out personal loans to finance their education. Nor, to our knowledge, is information available on the debt load of a typical beginning professional psychologist. Such information would be useful to determine whether the financial support offered to our future generation of professionals is adequate.

Integrating Training, Accreditation and Licensing

It has already been argued that one sign of a mature profession is that graduate programmes meet the accreditation standards set by the profession, and that these accreditation standards naturally dovetail with licensing requirements so that graduates move directly through the licensing procedure (Fretz & Mills, 1980). An examination of the training programmes and accreditation and licensing procedures in Canada does not support the conclusion that professional psychology is a mature profession. Many programmes do not meet the licensing requirement set in other provinces (for example, terminal master's programmes do not entitle one to practise in provinces with doctoral entry into the profession). Accreditation is available only for a limited number of areas of professional psychology and has only been attained by a limited number of programmes within those few areas. Licensing requirements are set provincially and vary dramatically across the country, with some provincial entry requirements being substantially lower than the training requirements adopted elsewhere in the country.

Considerable effort continues to be needed to establish national linkages between training, accreditation and licensing. Although the CPA and the CPAP have worked in some limited arenas (for example, the CPA/CPAP Task Force on Programme Designation), efforts to establish national criteria for training and licensing have been limited, at best. This issue needs further consideration, both by provincial regulatory bodies and by the national organizations for professional psychology.

Specialty Training

Although graduate education and professional identification arises through the process of specialization, and although professional psychologists recognize several *de facto* specialties, it has been argued that the implications of formal statutory recognition of specialization has not been fully explored. Further, even though accreditation of programmes has become an established mechanism for doing so, the criteria by which a training programme in a specialized area should be identified are yet to be formally established. A clear implication of this state of affairs is that consideration of the criteria for recognizing specialties in Canada needs to occur in the near future.

The pressing need for consideration of specialties has been recognized by both the CPA and CPAP: Both have endorsed in principle the need to formally recognize specialties in professional psychology. This area will become a matter of vital activity in the impending years, and the effects of whatever decisions are made will have profound implications for graduate education of professional psychologists into the 21st century.

Concluding Comments

Graduate education in psychology is the bedrock upon which professional practice is founded. It is hardly surprising, therefore, that much debate has gone into the evolution of ideas and practice in the area of graduate education. Issues such as the need for doctoral training and the requirement for research training have warranted and received untold amounts of attention in past decades. The debate about graduate education will continue, although the substance of the debate may alter. We predict, for example, that issues of accreditation, linking training with licensing and specialization will become the dominant issues in the training of professional psychologists in the next two decades.

As the trends toward increasing complexity and specialization expand in professional psychology, one issue psychology educators will need to address is whether or not there is (or should be) a stable core to training in psychology. For example, if specialization is to continue at the graduate level, then increased uniformity of undergraduate training may be required in order to assure some common basis of knowledge among psychologists of all professional proclivities.

In general, a number of emerging issues facing professional psychology have implications for graduate education, just as developments in graduate education have implications for the future of professional psychology. One of the concerns the authors have is that these issues receiving the kind or degree of informed discussion that is likely to be optimal. The last formal conference on professional issues in psychology was held in 1977 in Vancouver (Ferguson, 1977). Although education and professional issues were certainly dealt with at the 1984 Opinicon II conference (Ritchie et al., 1988), much has happened in professional psychology in the ensuing years. We suggest that it may now be a propitious time for the next Canadian conference on professional psychology.

References

Albee, G.W. (1965). Manpower needs for mental health and the role of psychology. *Canadian Psychologist*, 6, 82–92.

American Psychological Association (1990). *Graduate study in psychology and associated fields*. Washington, D.C.: Author.

Association of Universities and Colleges of Canada (1986). *Directory of Canadian universities*. Ottawa: Author.

Berlyne, D.E., Black, A.H., Berry, R.G., & Douglas, V.I. (1971). *The future of Canadian psychology: A report prepared by the Canadian Psychological Association for the Science Council of Canada.* Ottawa: Science Council of Canada.

Bernhardt, K.S. (Ed.). (1961). *Training for research in psychology.* Toronto: University of Toronto Press.

Brickman, L.B. (Ed.). (1985). *Issues and concerns: Graduate education in psychology.* Washington, D.C.: American Psychological Association.

Davidson, P.O. (1970). Graduate training and research funding for clinical psychology in Canada. *Canadian Psychologist, 11*, 101–127.

Dobson, K.S., & Wand, B. (1987). *Report of the CPA-CPAP Task Force report on designation.* Old Chelsea, Quebec: Canadian Psychological Association.

Ferguson, G. (Ed.). (1977). *Report on the Vancouver conference on the organization and representation of psychology in Canada.* Ottawa: Canadian Psychological Association.

Fox, R.E., Barclay, A.G., & Rodgers, D.A. (1982). The foundations of professional psychology. *American Psychologist, 37*, 306–312.

Fretz, B.R., & Mills, D.H. (1980). *Licensing and certification of psychologists and counsellors.* San Francisco: Jossey-Bass.

Hogan, D.B. (1979). *The regulation of psychotherapists; Volumes I to IV.* Cambridge, MA: Ballinger.

Korman, M. (Ed.). (1976). *Levels and patterns of professional training in psychology.* Washington, D.C.: American Psychological Association.

Peterson, D.R. (1976). Is psychology a profession? *American Psychologist, 31*, 572–581.

Pryzwansky, W.B., & Wendt, R.N. (1987). *Psychology as a profession: Foundations of practice.* New York: Pergamon Press.

Raimy, V.C. (Ed.). (1950). *Training in clinical psychology.* Englewood Cliffs, NJ: Prentice-Hall.

Ritchie, P., Hogan, T. P., & Hogan, T.V. (Eds.). (1988). *Psychology in Canada: The state of the discipline, 1984.* Old Chelsea, Quebec: Canadian Psychological Association.

Rodgers, D.A. (1964). In favor of separation of academic and professional training. *American Psychologist, 19*, 675–680.

Roe, A., Gustad, J.W., Moore, B.W., Ross, S., & Shodak, M. (Eds.). (1959). *Graduate education in psychology.* Washington, D.C.: American Psychological Association.

Service, J., Sabourin, M., Catano, V.M., Day, V., Hayes, C., & MacDonald, G.W. (1989). *Report of the CPA-CPAP Task Force on Specialty Designation.* Old Chelsea, Quebec: Canadian Psychological Association.

Shakow, D. (Ed.). (1947). *Recommended graduate training programme in clinical psychology.* Washington, D.C.: American Psychological Association.

Stricker, G. (1975). On professional schools and professional degrees. *American Psychologist, 30,* 1062–1066.

Sydiaha, D. (1966). A survey of psychologists in Canada. *Canadian Psychologist, 7,* 413–485.

Webster, E.C. (Ed.). (1967). *The Couchiching conference on professional psychology.* Montreal, Quebec: Eagle Pub. Co.

4

Accreditation of Doctoral Training Programmes and Internships in Professional Psychology

Anna Beth Doyle
Concordia University

Henry Edwards
University of Ottawa

Robert W. Robinson
Alberta Children's Hospital

Though accreditation of professional training in psychology has been operative nationally in Canada for a relatively short time, it has a long history. As early as 1965, delegates at the Couchiching Conference on Professional Psychology strongly recommended that a national, peer-administered accreditation programme be created by the Canadian Psychological Association (Webster,

1967). CPA implemented this recommendation nearly 20 years later, in 1983. The nature of accreditation in Canada today, its historical roots, significance and future directions are the subjects of this chapter.

The Concept and Value of Accreditation

In academic and professional settings, the term "accreditation" typically refers to a system of evaluation of educational or service programmes that train students for a profession[1]. Programmes are evaluated in terms of a set of criteria which are widely accepted by the profession as indicators of quality. Thus, accreditation concerns programmes as wholes, and is distinct from certification or licensing, which is concerned with the qualifications of the individual professional. Moreover, it is the training programme *per se* which is accredited, rather than a department or its individual students.

The overriding purpose of programme accreditation is to ensure the quality of training (Fretz & Mills, 1980), with the inherent goal of promoting excellence. To this end, a set of training goals and minimum training standards, and a mechanism for peer review of training programmes seeking accreditation, are agreed upon by a representative group of the profession. Training programmes voluntarily accept the accreditation process they undergo. An additional essential feature is periodic review and consensual revalidation of the accreditation standards.

---

1 Accreditation is also used more broadly to signify that an entire institution (for example, a university or a hospital) meets an established set of standards and is therefore a legitimate institution. Thus, in the United States, universities are accredited by the Council on Post-secondary Accreditation (COPA). In Canada, doctoral training programmes are all housed in universities whose legitimacy is recognized through founding provinical charters and by membership in the Association of Universities and Colleges of Canada (AUCC). Hospitals are accredited by the Canadian Council on Health Facilities Accreditation (CCHFA).

Intrinsically, the acceptance and promulgation of explicit written standards for training promote quality. That is, the periodic processes of self-study by individual programmes and subsequent external peer review foster their continuing evolution. Moreover, accreditation has the potential to reduce the number of students who graduate without adequate training and thereby promotes the provision of competent professional services for the general public. In terms of extrinsic value, accreditation enables the student or professional to identify programmes of recognized quality. For accredited programmes, the quality and number of applications for admission and employment, and the ability to obtain additional resources from the institutions in which the programmes are located, may be enhanced. In addition, when the accreditation process is well established and its intrinsic value widely accepted, graduation from an accredited programme tends to facilitate licensure and job opportunities. Increased credibility within the community of academic or training programmes may also result. Not surprisingly, programme accreditation has gained wide acceptance in the established professions in North America.

Nevertheless, at the time the Canadian accreditation programme for psychology was initiated there was considerable concern about possible negative consequences, for example, loss of programme autonomy. The pros and cons of this programme, as well as current issues relevant to its future integrity and viability will be examined in this chapter.

Milestones in the History of Canadian Accreditation

In 1966, in response to the recommendation of the Couchiching conference, CPA proposed that accreditation be handled by a National Council of Training Boards in Psychology comprising chairs of provincial boards. This structure was suggested ostensibly because educational and professional matters were constitutionally under the jurisdiction of the provinces and, hence, the provincial psychological associations (Wright, 1969, 243 ff.). Another reason may have been that CPA then viewed itself primarily as a scientific society (Gibson, 1974). The provinces, however, were not sufficiently interested in cooperating with each other or with CPA, and in 1967 rejected the idea of a council of training boards.

Nevertheless, considerable interest in accreditation remained. In 1969, the Ontario Psychological Association (OPA) adopted its own accreditation standards and procedures. By 1980, OPA had accredited six doctoral training programmes, all but one in clinical psychology – York, Waterloo, Queen's, Windsor, Ontario Institute for Studies in Education and Ottawa – and six clinical internship settings – the Clarke Institute of Psychiatry, Royal Ottawa Hospital, Kitchener/Waterloo Hospital, Children's Hospital of Eastern Ontario, Thistletown Regional Hospital and the Royal Ottawa Rehabilitation Centre. Moreover, several Canadian programmes sought accreditation from the American Psychological Association. By 1980, four doctoral clinical training programmes – Manitoba, McGill, Saskatchewan and Waterloo – and one internship programme – the Behavioural Sciences Section of the University of Manitoba Health Sciences Centre – were APA-accredited. This resort to accreditation from across the border was in response to the lack of an equivalent Canadian programme, to a desire to attract well-qualified American graduate students and faculty, and to a desire to help Canadians enter the US job market (Poser, 1984). The OPA and APA systems of accreditation differed in several ways, including the accreditation of specialties, the specificity of the criteria for internship programmes, and several specific doctoral criteria. For example, the OPA criteria were designed to accredit a broad range of training programmes in applied psychology without differentiation as to specialty, whereas APA accredits specialities (e.g. clinical, counselling and school), separately under the same generic criteria, with the largest number of accredited programmes being in clinical psychology.

Momentum towards a national system of accreditation was regained at the 1980 annual meeting of the Canadian Council of Clinical Psychology Programme Directors (Schallow, 1984). The CCCPPD was a loose organization of directors of clinical training in psychology at university and service settings, founded in 1977 by Park Davidson of the University of British Columbia. An informal CCCPPD working group, chaired by John Schallow of the University of Manitoba, took on the task of drafting accreditation criteria for clinical training programmes in Canada. Its work was encouraged by the CPA Committee on Professional Affairs through the creation of a subcommittee on accreditation, chaired by Ken Craig of UBC. Draft accreditation criteria, modelled on but not identical to those of the American Psychological Association, were circulated in 1981. Over the next two years, these were debated heatedly, in particular by the CCCPPD which became more organized in the process. In 1983, the revised and refined *Accreditation Criteria for Clinical Psychology Programmes and Internships* (1984) were strongly endorsed by the CCCPPD and adopted by the CPA Board. Thus, agreement on CPA standards was achieved in just three short years. Increasing public interest in things psychological, demand for psychological services by individuals and institutions, pressure from students wishing careers in clinical psychology and the expansion of applied job opportunities at a time when academic jobs were relatively few, all played a role in creating an environment responsive to individual efforts (Adair, 1981; Martin, 1984). The success of the Ontario Psychological Association accreditation programme was no doubt also a factor, though some OPA members opposed the CPA programme because of specific differences in the two sets of criteria (Inglis & Marshall, 1984).

After 1983, the Canadian Accreditation Programme developed rapidly (see Table 1). CPA adopted accreditation procedures in 1984, and appointed a nine- member Accreditation Panel to implement the programme. This first Panel was chaired by Ken Craig and included the authors of this chapter. The Panel was struck so as to be representative of Canadian doctoral and internship training programmes culturally, geographically and in programme orientation. With volunteer professional help and makeshift secretarial services, they developed application documents and guidelines for both doctoral and internship training programmes in both official languages. The programme was publicized, procedures refined and fees set for site visits and annual renewal of accreditation. A representative roster of Canadian psychologists was constituted to carry out site visits. In addition, discussions with both the Ontario and the American Psychological Associations were initiated with the aim of establishing mutual recognition of equivalency in standards, co operation on dual applications, joint site visits and fee sharing.

Table 1. Major events in the development of Canadian accreditation.

Event	Date
Couchiching Conference on Professional Psychology	1961
Ontario Psychological Association establishes Accreditation Council	1969
Canadian Council of Clinical Psychology Programme Directors undertakes to draft accreditation standards	1980
CPA Professional Affairs Committee creates subcommittee on accreditation	1980
Accreditation Criteria for Clinical Psychology endorsed by CCCPPD and adopted by the CPA Board	1983
Accreditation Procedures adopted and Accreditation Panel constituted	1984
First programmes accredited (without site-visit)	1985
First site visit	1986
Memorandum of Understanding on Accreditation between CPA and the Ontario Psychological Association	1987
First CPA/APA joint site visit	1988
Memorandum of Understanding between CPA and the American Psychological Association	1989
First review of the CPA Accreditation Criteria	1989
Programme name changed to "Accreditation of Doctoral and Internship Training Programmes in *Professional* Psychology"	1989
Criteria extended to counselling psychology as a specialty	1989
Criteria adopted for clinical neuropsychology as a specialty	1991

Applications were first solicited early in 1985. Because of the similarity between the APA and CPA criteria, programmes holding APA accreditation were initially accredited by CPA without a site visit. Programmes holding OPA accreditation could be similarly accredited with the approval of the Panel. By 1986, six programmes were accredited by CPA, site visitor training workshops were held annually and some secretarial aspects of the programme were handled by the CPA Head Office.

In 1987, a Memorandum of Understanding between CPA and OPA to facilitate concurrent accreditation by both organizations through joint site visits and fee-sharing was approved. Subsequently, OPA has referred inquiries from interested programmes to CPA and in March, 1991, passed a resolution to cease the functioning of its Accreditation Council. In 1989, a similar Memorandum of Understanding between CPA and APA was ap-

Table 2. CPA-accredited doctoral and internship training programmes[1,2].

Doctoral Programmes	Date accredited
McGill University[3]	1985
Concordia University[3]	1985
Simon Fraser University[3]	1985
University of Ottawa[3,4]	1986
University of British Columbia[3]	1987
University of Manitoba[3]	1987
University of Western Ontario[3]	1987
University of Waterloo[3,4]	1989
University of Windsor[3,4]	1989
University of Saskatchewan[3]	1990
York University[4]	1992

Internship Programmes	Date accredited
Manitoba Health Sciences Centre[3]	1986
Kitchener-Waterloo Hospital[3,4]	1986
University Hospital, Saskatoon	1986
Alberta Hospital, Edmonton	1987
Alberta Children's Hospital	1987
University Hospital, UBC[3]	1988
Calgary General Hospital	1988
Chedoke McMaster Hospitals	1988
Credit Valley Hospital	1990
Calgary District Hospital Group	1990
Children's Hospital of Eastern Ontario[4]	1990
Clarke Institute of Psychiatry[4]	1991
Royal Ottawa Health Care Group[4]	1991
Foothills Medical Centre Consortium	1992
University Hospital — London	1992
University of Ottawa Psychological Services	1991
Victoria Hospital — London	1991
University of Manitoba Counselling Service	1992
Windsor Western Hospital Centre	1992
Workers Compensation Board — Edmonton	1992

[1]As of March 1993

[2]All are clinical psychology programmes, except for the University of Manitoba Counselling Service

[3]Prior accreditation by APA

[4]Prior accreditation by OPA

proved. Besides providing a mechanism for fee-sharing and for the conduct of joint applications and site visits, the agreement included mutual recognition of similarity of standards. The CPA-APA agreement preserves independent decision-making on accreditation by each organization.

In 1989, the Accreditation Panel completed the first mandatory five-year review of its criteria, with input from clinical training programmes, provincial associations and regulatory bodies, and site visitors. These groups and individuals evaluated the *Criteria* and their applicability to Canadian programmes quite positively, deeming only a few minor changes necessary. In the same year, in response to the desire of professional specialties other than clinical psychology to be accredited, psychologists specializing in counselling and neuropsychology were appointed to the Panel and the scope of the Programme expanded to include the "accreditation of doctoral programmes and internships in *professional* psychology". The door was thus opened for separate accreditation, under the current generic *Accreditation Criteria*, for specialties designated by CPA as outlined in the *Report of the CPA/CPAP Task Force on Specialty Designation* (1989). Accreditation of counselling psychology was approved by the CPA Board in 1989, and for clinical neuropsychology in 1991.

It is remarkable that in nine short years the CPA Accreditation Programme has become firmly established, with 12 doctoral and 20 internship clinical programmes accredited (see Table 2). Following is a summary of the *Criteria* and the operation of the Programme.

The CPA Accreditation Criteria and Their Specific Aims

In this section, our intent is not to enumerate the published *Criteria* (1989), but rather to summarize their most salient aims and features. To avoid undue repetition, criteria that are applicable to both doctoral and internship training programmes are noted under doctoral programmes with an asterisk (*).

Accreditation Criteria for Doctoral Programmes in Professional Psychology

- *I. Institutional settings.* The current practice in Canada, of locating professional psychology training programmes in university departments of psychology or educational psychology, thus encouraging the highest standards of scholarship and teaching, is endorsed.
- *II. General eligibility for accreditation.* These criteria require: doctoral training by documentably legitimate universities, supportive of professional education, with adequate resources to implement the programme; clear identification of the programme as a doctoral programme in professional psychology; an integrated, broad and complete plan of study, including predoctoral internship and research training; programme staffing by faculty who are identifiable, assume responsibility for it, and have visible leadership(*); and an identifiable student body.
- *III. Cultural and individual differences.* In recognition of the cultural diversity of Canada, sensitivity to and respect for cultural and individual differences must be reflected in all facets of the programme's composition and operation (*).
- *IV. Training models and curricula.* The following are considered basic to sound training in professional psychology: Theory, research and practice must be integrated early in the training programme. The faculty should serve as professional role models, have a close working relationship with their students (*), and facilitate students' early identification with the profession. Programmes implement this criterion according to two distinct models. In some, the full-time faculty responsible for clinical training are themselves part-time practitioners and practicum supervisors. In others, the full-time faculty serve primarily as scholarly role models, and professional role modelling is provided by adjunct staff responsible for practicum supervision. The curriculum must encompass at least three years of full-time resident graduate study (typically one at the master's level and two more at the doctoral level), and include a sound education in general psychology as a prerequisite to professional training, accomplished by graduate instruction and/or demonstration of competence. Training in professional psychology must include psychological assessment, individual and group in-

terventions, consultation, programme development and programme evaluation. While respecting the fact that individual programmes may have dominant theoretical or applied emphases, students' familiarity with a diversity of perspectives is expected (*). The importance of teaching scientific and professional responsibility, in particular as adopted by the Canadian Psychological Association (*), and the need to provide access to instruction in related disciplines, where appropriate, are emphasized. Research training on topics and methodology appropriate to professional psychology, and in applied or natural settings, should be an integral part of any programme, although methodologies may vary across programmes. Such training not only leads to new knowledge and practices but helps to develop problem solving skills that will be useful in professional practice. An explicit comprehensive system for evaluating the competence of students to practise is required (*). Such evaluations should be relevant to the skills emphasized by the training programme, and/or required for licensure or registration by the relevant provincial board. The training programme curriculum is evaluated on the extent to which it promotes its stated aims effectively. Though the scientist-practitioner model leading to the Ph.D. degree in psychology is most common in Canada, other models (e.g. the PsyD or DPs) may be acceptable for accreditation.

- *V. Faculty*. This criterion emphasizes the importance of highly qualified faculty to ensure that students are exposed to the knowledge and skills they require. The core faculty, on aggregate, should be experienced, productive and devoted to the programme as their major career commitment. They must have relevant professional background and experience, reflected in registration/licensure, and keep abreast of new professional developments, e.g. through continuing education (*). Senior, tenured, licensed/registered psychologists should be administratively responsible for the programme, since they must serve as key role models and leaders (*). The faculty should reflect and be sensitive to cultural, lifestyle and other individual differences.
- *VI. Students*. This criterion notes that good students are the hallmark of a good programme. An honours baccalaureate in psychology or equivalent is required, to ensure a general under-

standing of psychology and a pre-existing commitment to it. An academically talented, culturally diverse and socially sensitive student body provides the appropriate environment in which to foster development of professional skills. To foster an appropriate match between programme and student, each programme is required to inform prospective students of its unique goals, style, training resources available, and other details (*). Finally, ongoing evaluation practices and explicit procedures for dealing with grievances and ensuring due process in relation to student problems or complaints are required (*).

- *VII. Facilities.* A range of instructional and service resources appropriate to high quality training in clinical psychology are required (*).
- *VIII. Practicum and internship training.* Systematic field training in the application of psychological principles and skills to human problems is required in the form of practica, and an internship in field settings providing psychological services. Practicum training should begin early in the training sequence, should be integrated into it, may be given on or off campus. It is prerequisite to the predoctoral internship(*), and entails lesser responsibility for care. Practicum training is designed to facilitate commitment to professional psychology, conceptualization of human problems, awareness of human diversity and self-understanding, as well as to provide training of appropriate breadth in specific professional skills such as interviewing, testing and psychotherapy (*). Practicum training consists minimally of 600 hours, of which at least 250 must be in direct service experience and 125 in formally scheduled supervision.

A predoctoral internship is required of every student. It should take place in an accredited internship setting whose programme is consonant with the graduate programme's training model and with which the doctoral training programme maintains close liaison for the purposes of evaluation (*).

Criteria for CPA Accreditation of Internship Programmes in Professional Psychology

The internship represents an essential, supervised immersion in a professional service setting prior to the granting of the doctoral degree. Currently, a full-time experience for a full year, or half-time experience over two years, in either case comprising a minimum of 1600 hours, is required.

- *I. Administrative issues.* All internships are accredited separately from doctoral programmes, whether they are associated with university settings or free-standing programmes in other institutions. The training setting should conform to all applicable CPA guidelines for ethical professional practice, and demonstrate respect for human dignity and for the exercise of civil rights. The setting should be committed to a training mission, and the training activities of internship staff should be endorsed and rewarded. There must be adequate and stable resources available to the programme, including financial support for interns.
- *II. Professional psychology staff.* The training staff should be part of a formal, stable organization of professional psychologists reporting to a chief psychologist. As role models with the primary training responsibility, they should be registered/licensed psychologists with doctorates in professional psychology. Their own training should have included a one-year internship, preferably from an accredited programme, although, in fact, because of the initially small mass of accredited doctoral programmes in Canada, and an even more skeletal network of accredited internships, this aspect of the staff profile has not always been present. As the accreditation movement has taken root in Canada, however, graduates from accredited programmes are becoming supervisory staff and assuming leadership positions in internship programmes. There also should be opportunities for the interns to collaborate with members of other disciplines.
- *III. Interns.* The interns should be selected systematically from students in accredited doctoral programmes who have completed relevant coursework and practica, or from applicants certified by a director of training of an accredited programme as having equivalent qualifications (as for supervisory staff,

there has been an increase since the inception of CPA accreditation in the proportion of interns emanating from accredited doctoral programmes). In order to develop a sense of collegiality and shared learning among trainees, there must be at least two interns, preferably more (smaller internships within a geographic locale have jointly offered a seminar series to facilitate collegiality, and others have combined training experiences with other disciplines within their own facility). The role of interns as service providers must not conflict with their primary role as professionals-in-training.

- *IV. Programme.* To protect the applicants' right of free choice among alternative internship offers, the internship programme must comply with the methods and procedures for notifying applicants outlined by the Association of Psychology Internship Centres (APIC). The programme should include an organized and coherent sequence of experiences, including opportunities for research, providing both depth and breadth of training. Supervision is expected to be formally scheduled, individual and intensive, totalling a minimum of four hours per week. In addition to interns being informed regularly of their progress, supervisors and the programme's effectiveness should be appraised systematically with input from the interns. The facilities for internship training must be adequate for professional practice. Moreover, both client records and the working files of the programme must be organized and appropriately protected for confidentiality.
- *V. Consortia.* For a group of smaller internships, the *Criteria* provide the option of combining resources, training opportunities and training faculty to support a substantially more comprehensive internship than any single unit could manage; the key requirement is that the constituent members enter into a formal contract to offer a programme that functions as an integrated whole.

In summary, the CPA *Accreditation Criteria* for doctoral and internship programmes in professional psychology represent a widely accepted model for training in which theory, research and practice are considered essential components, and in which the process of socialization into the profession takes place throughout the programme in a collegial and intellectually challenging environment.

The particular focus of the internship is to integrate theory and practice within a service setting providing contact with a variety of client populations and problems, to allow for progressively increased responsibility and autonomy for the intern, with appropriate supervisory and didactic support for professional growth and development.

The Accreditation Process

Impetus and Programme Self-Study

The impetus to initiate an application for accreditation arises from the programme and institution itself. The programme first examines the degree to which it meets the tenets and criteria of Accreditation as set out in the *Canadian Psychological Association Accreditation Manual* (1990).

Pre-Application Consultation Visit

The Canadian Psychological Association maintains a roster of experienced site visitors including former Panel Members who may be invited by the programme for a pre-application visit. Prior to this site visit "dress rehearsal", the programme prepares a thorough self-study including all necessary documentation, and an appropriate interview schedule is negotiated. Typically, the consultant will thereafter provide an oral and written report to the programme to use in refining its own objectives and operation. The advantage of the consultation is that a confidential, supportive opinion is offered in an atmosphere unencumbered by formal appraisal.

Programme Application

In the process of formally applying for application, the burden of proof of compliance to the criteria rests with the programme. The paper application is designed to answer questions which are keyed to the standard criteria while permitting the distinctive strengths and attributes of the programme to be described. The curriculum vitae of the faculty, programme and institutional brochures, and other appended material should assist in creating an image which is both impressive and accurate. The process of submitting the application for public peer review itself represents a significant developmental milestone for most programmes.

Application Review

Upon receipt of the application, the Accreditation Registrar verifies that the materials are sufficiently thorough and complete for Panel review. On the basis of a review of the complete paper application, two or more Accreditation Panel members render an initial opinion of the applicant's conformity to fundamental criteria for accreditation, thus, assisting the Panel with the decision as to whether a site visit should be approved or denied. In actual practice to date, applying programmes have been sufficiently well advised and thoroughly prepared to enable virtually all formal applications to move to a site visit. The Registrar then plays a vital role in assisting the programme with preparations for the site visit.

Site Visit Preparation

Since accreditation is a voluntary process, the senior executive officer of the sponsoring organization issues a letter of invitation for delegates of the Accreditation Panel to visit the facility at a mutually agreed date. Delegate selection is a negotiated process in which lists of approved site visitors are forwarded to the training director for consideration. The applicant programme chooses a two person site visit team for internship, and/or a three person team for doctoral programmes, constrained by guidelines for the team Chair to be a Panel or former Panel member, for regional balance, for university and internship association, and for capacity to properly conduct interviews and generate a professional report in the official language of the programme. For joint CPA-APA visits, regional and other requirements are relaxed to permit balance between visitors drawn from the CPA and APA rosters. The Registrar ratifies the team selection and delegates the responsibility for forwarding the application materials, arranging the logistics of the visit and establishing a precise schedule, to the training director, who works in consultation with the chair of the site visit team.

While the team reviews the materials, the programme gears its senior administration, faculty and student body for the site visit. Despite the contrast between the evaluative duties and obligations of the site visitors, and the burden of self-disclosure for the applying programmes, they have a common task: to provide the Accreditation Panel with a picture of the three major facets of the programme: the training curriculum, the faculty and the student body.

Site Visit

On the eve of the site visit the team typically organizes itself to maximize the functionality of the visit. What are the shared impressions? Are there key questions? How might the various interviews elicit information critical to an overall recommendation? The next morning, the team typically meets initially with the training director and head of psychology to overview the history, operation and leadership objectives of the training programme. It is an opportunity to set the real agenda for the visit and to establish a participatory climate. Most CPA visitors are themselves associated with accredited training programmes, and programme representatives may themselves be trained site visitors; thus there is solid ground for mutual respect and understanding of their reciprocal roles.

Individualized meetings with core faculty follow the preliminary meeting. Their interests, actual involvement, professional and scientific attitudes and competencies, and career activities that may vitalize the training programme and shape its character are communicated. The students'/interns' transactions with faculty, through which knowledge is assimilated, skills are learned, and professional values and identity emerge, are described. The visitors have to restrain the temptation for excessive collegial exchange and interaction and to maintain the focus to the key objective of ascertaining the actual contributions of faculty and their role in the programme.

If the faculty meetings are prone to collegiality, interviews with trainees are prone to ambivalence. On the one hand, those being educated and trained know the programme on the inside, blemishes included; on the other hand their careers will be significantly enhanced by graduating from an accredited professional training programme. In some ways they are the key informants, yet they also have the most at risk. This dilemma is usually adressed by interviewing students and interns as a group, assuring them anonymity, explaining the dual processes of accreditation as programme enhancement as well as evaluation, and acknowledging the very special position that interns and students hold during the site visit process.

In contrast, the ambience in interviews with senior administrators is typically laden with the greatest formality and structure. The master plan for the organization, and the role of psychology within it, are the focus. How is psychology perceived, and how is the education and training of scientist-practitioners valued within the facility? Beyond generalities, what are the actual resources and the institutional commitments, present and future, that will be invested in achieving and maintaining an accredited training programme in psychology? These are crucial components for developing an enduring infrastructure for the programme. From the training programme's perspective, interviews with senior administration are typically the most unpredictable, and consequently they await feedback with interest.

Other interviews place the training programme in a community and/or multidisciplinary context. For doctoral programmes there is typically an on-site training facility and/or a network of practicum settings. University-based supervisors and adjunct faculty portray the professionalization process for students. The orientation and preparation for field-based training is often a significant test of the scientist- practitioner model espoused by the programme. Moreover, practicum experiences are formative to successful internship placement and functioning. Thus, interviews with field supervisors, though not extensive, reveal very important evidence of integrated training and of the relations among programme and adjunct faculty. Within internships there is a parallel set of collegial dynamics that are tapped through ancillary interviews, namely that of the construction and functioning of the multidisciplinary team. To what extent do psychologists make a unique contribution in service, education and research to the facility; and how reciprocally receptive is the department of psychology and training programme to the allied expertise of other professions? These contextual questions are fundamental to appraising the professional socialization processes to which students and interns are exposed.

Once the extensive sequence of interviews has been completed, covering most of two days, the site visit team deliberates. They need to corroborate impressions, weigh the self-study and interview data against the criteria, and make a professional judgement in offering a firm recommendation for the consideration of the Panel. For newly applying programmes three options are available: No Accreditation, Provisional Accreditation or Full Accreditation. In the case of previously accredited programmes the alternatives are: Revocation, Probation or Full Accreditation. Thus the site visit team meets its charge to serve as the "eyes and ears" of the Panel and forwards a recommendation for its debate and final decision-making.

Before the site visit team leaves the facility it structures an outline for the site visit report and delegates authorship. Finally, a feedback session is conducted with the training director, head of psychology and any other key participants in the process they may wish to invite. Though the specific recommendation for accreditation is not disclosed at this session, major substantive impressions are conveyed which should be consistent with, and supportive of the recommendation. It is an opportunity for the programme and site visitors to verify the accuracy of impressions.

The site visit report is submitted within 30 days and forwarded to the applying programme for reaction and comment. It in turn has 30 days to prepare a response for the Panel, in which it is important to correct or corroborate factual information and react to the substance of the report. The Panel must evaluate all the information set before it: the self-study, site visit report and programme's response, decide the programme's merits and what category of accreditation, if any, should be considered. Through formal voting procedures at the next regularly scheduled Panel meeting, currently held twice yearly, this decision is made, and a term of accreditation between one and five years is attached. The decision, along with points for development to which the programme's attention is drawn, is then conveyed to the programme subject to their agreement or appeal.

Once accredited, all programmes file a brief report of progress on an annual basis. During the year in which their term of accreditation expires, they file a more extensive report, a self-study which once again forms the basis of a site visit. Thus, the accreditation process is regenerative.

The Debate About Accreditation

During the initial development of the programme, some serious reservations were expressed about the likelihood that the Accreditation Programme would enhance the quality of clinical training. A main reservation was that the criteria intrude upon programme autonomy, flexibility and creativity through the specificity of requirements (Agnew, 1984; Coons, 1967, 1974, 1990). There was concern that this specificity regarding such issues as practicum and internship structure and particular courses, would stifle experimentation, inhibit new developments in clinical training and lead to increased conservatism around a single model of training. For example, Payne (1984), wondered whether the Accreditation Panel could handle diversity of the sort where one programme trained students to administer the Rorschach and another denounced it as scientifically invalid. The emphasis on a single set of standards with quantifiable criteria has been called "the nemesis of a progressive psychology which must rely on its free spirits to point the way to advancement" (Coons, 1990, p. 144). Many Canadian psychologists share the perception that uniformity among U.S. programmes has increased and feel that the greater diversity of clinical training in Canada is worth preserving (Conway, 1984).

Another objection was that the *Criteria* emphasize practice rather than research, thus impeding programmes from successfully implementing the scientist-practitioner model. Moreover, the CPA programme was said to be "Made in USA" (Inglis & Marshall, 1984), and the *Criteria* were seen by some as failing to reflect our distinctly Canadian cultural values and institutions (e.g. Catano, 1984; Brooker, 1984; Gibson, 1984). In a similar vein, it was feared that an accreditation programme would exacerbate inequitable resources, to the detriment of those programmes located in disadvantaged regions of the country without the capacity to mount accreditable doctoral training programmes and/or without provincial legislation requiring doctoral training, further reducing their ability to attract students (Inglis & Marshall, 1984; Poser, 1984). In contrast, Wright (1984) worried that a CPA accreditation programme might respond *too* much to regional differences, on the basis of personal ties, local limitations or biases and, thus, would not be impartial and rigorous enough to be of benefit. The similarity of the CPA Criteria to the APA Criteria led to questioning the very need for a separate Canadian programme of accreditation (Poser, 1984).

Five years after the first programmes were accredited, the impact of the CPA Accreditation Programme was empirically evaluated. In September, 1990, directors of training in university and internship clinical and applied programmes with membership in the Canadian Council of Clinical Psychology Programmes[2] were surveyed concerning their perceptions of the impact of CPA Accreditation on their programme and on the diversity of training programmes in Canada. Preliminary responses are summarized in Table 3, separately for doctoral clinical (n=13) and internship (n=33) clinical programmes, accredited, newly accredited and nonaccredited respectively. Responses were also received from five nonclinical masters and doctoral programmes, but these were too few in number for their responses to be presented. Albeit limited, these data provide a fascinating sketch to be delineated more clearly with further empirical study.

One of the aims of the accreditation programme is to add impetus to programme development. When the Accreditation Panel began its work in 1984, they estimated that there were approximately 20 doctoral training programmes and 20 predoctoral internship programmes in clinical psychology in Canada. To date, one new doctoral programme has been established (at Dalhousie),

2 The name was changed from the Canadian Council of Clinical Psychology Programme Directors in June, 1990.

Table 3. Impact of the CPA Accreditation Programme on training programmes: Percent of programmes reporting increases and attributing these to CPA accreditation (percent noting increase / percent attributing increase to CPA accreditation).

	Doctoral programmes		Internships			
	Accred. prior to 1889–90	Not accred.	Accred. prior to 1989–90	Newly accred	Not accred	Total
N	6	7	0	4	19	51
1. Curriculum changes	50/100	57/100	60/83	75/67	63/92	51/90
2. Programme autonomy	17/100	29/100	30/100	0	11/50	18/71
3. Emphasis on practice	17/100	43/100	30/67	0	21/50	24/63
4. Diversity of doctoral programmes	67/25	57/25	20/100	50/100	37/14	41/43
5. Diversity of internships	100/50	86/33	70/43	50/100	58/9	69/33
6. Number of applicants	17/100	14/100	30/67	75/100	37/43	33/69
7. Quality of applicants	33/100	29/50	50/100	75/100	21/75	35/82
8. Availability of resources	33/50	43/33	40/100	50/0	63/50	50/54
9. Quality of graduates	50/67	14/0	50/100	50/50	21/50	33/55

and fully 39 internship programmes are listed in the CCCPP *Survey of Canadian Internship Settings* (1990). More than half (61%) of the clinical programmes surveyed for this chapter, encompassing all categories, have revised their curriculum and procedures in ways largely guided by the *Accreditation Criteria* (see Table 3). Thus, both in terms of numbers of programmes and programme content, CPA accreditation has had a developmental influence.

With reference to accreditation's impact on programme autonomy, some loss is inherent in adhering, albeit voluntarily, to any set of accreditation criteria. It requires care by accrediting bodies to keep intrusions on autonomy from increasing over time. Nevertheless, some accredited programmes (25%) reported *increased* autonomy, in particular in their dealings with the institutional administration, and attributed this to accreditation. Only two of the 51 responding programmes, an accredited doctoral programme and an internship programme preparing to apply for accreditation, reported some felt loss of autonomy.

Concerning accreditation's effects on programme innovation, it should be noted that it is not the responsibility of accreditation to stimulate innovation, nor does accreditation aim to stifle it. Programmes are free to choose the manner in which they fulfil the criteria, which provide considerable room for creativity and for diversity of content and focus. That is, the overriding principle by which programmes are evaluated is the degree to which they fulfil their stated aims for training, meeting or exceeding the minimum conditions set out in the *Criteria*. The wish to meet the *Criteria* and to simultaneously attain other programme goals may also serve, therefore, to stimulate creative, innovative and diverse approaches to training. With respect to survey respondents' opinions on this issue, fully 41% perceived *increased* diversity in doctoral training programmes. Moreover, most doctoral programmes (92%) and, to a lesser extent, internship programmes (61%) perceived an increase in the diversity of internship programmes. Whereas doctoral programmes and nonaccredited or newly accredited internship programmes rarely (18%) attributed this increased diversity to CPA accreditation, accredited internship programmes uniformly did (only one doctoral and one internship programme reported any decrease in diversity, though they did attribute it to the accreditation programme). The 1990 CCCPPD internship survey indicates that internships established to date are housed in a variety of settings, serve a wide range of client populations, and offer different intervention models, all of which represent a cross-section of professional psychology.

The *Criteria* are relatively more specific on practice issues than on research, but are neutral on the balance between the two. A major principle of accreditation is that the stated aims of the programme regarding this balance be achieved within the context of high quality training. Few (24%) of the programmes surveyed perceived an increased in emphasis on practice (see Table 3). There was some tendency for nonaccredited doctoral programmes to exceed accredited doctoral programmes (43% vs. 17%) in this perception, and all of these attributed the perceived increase to accreditation. Internships were lower on both counts. Moreover, two nonaccredited internship programmes commented spontaneously that research emphasis had increased in their settings. This is perhaps due to the hiring of new staff members trained in the scientist-practitioner model. The scientist-practitioner model is overwhelmingly the model endorsed by Canadian doctoral training programmes, which are uniformly located within university departments of psychology or educational psychology. Though this training model is viewed as the hardest to implement successfully, the CPA Accreditation Programme and Canadian training programmes may be uniquely qualified to foster high quality research training in professional programmes.

Concerning the view that the CPA criteria are clones of the APA criteria, the parallels should not *de facto* engender rejection. In developing the CPA criteria, the CCCPPD and CPA retained some features of the APA Criteria and adapted other aspects to fit the Canadian context, including our distinctive minority cultures and cultural mosaic, the undergraduate honours background of our students and our more lengthy practicum and internship training. The resulting criteria were seen as being the best minimum training standards for Canada. It merits reemphasizing that the criteria may be met in diverse and even regionally specific ways. Though several critics bemoaned the failure of the CPA criteria to reflect the distinct cultural values and institutions of Canada, few of these critics proposed standards which better reflected those values. With reference to the question of whether a separate Canadian Accreditation Programme is needed at all, despite the similarity of many CPA and APA criteria, the two accreditation programmes also differ greatly in the pool of site visitors they use, and in the composition of the committee/panel which makes the ultimate decisions. The CPA Accreditation Programme appears to have achieved a healthy balance between impartial evaluation which maintains training standards and an informed perspective on diverse national and regional issues, e. g. language, minorities and federal and provincial funding. The CPA-APA joint site visit procedure appears to have further enhanced this healthy balance. Currently, all 10 CPA- accredited doctoral programmes and four of the 11 CPA-accredited internship programmes are also accredited by the APA.

With reference to the concern that the Accreditation Programme would further disenfranchise the "have nots" in disadvantaged and less populated areas of the country, our survey respondents were not numerous enough to break down by geographical area. Nevertheless, only 12% of the 26 nonaccredited doctoral and internship programme respondents reported a decrease in numbers of applicants, and only one of these perceived the quality of applicants or the availability of resources to have decreased. On the contrary, 75% of newly accredited internship programmes and, on average, 29% of other clinical programmes saw an increase in the number and quality of applicants. Most (82%) of these attributed the increase to the inception of the Accreditation Programme. Somewhat fewer but a substantial number (50%) of programmes saw an increase in the availability of resources (see Table 3), increases which 51% attributed in part to the existence of the Accreditation Programme.

A final objection to accreditation is that it focuses on the actions of a programme, e.g., numbers of hours, etc., rather than on the products, i.e. graduate psychologists who are knowledgeable, ethical and competent (Day, 1984, Coons, 1990). It is important to reiterate that accreditation deals with the evaluation and enhancement of the training programme as a whole, not with the evaluation of the individual graduates. Evaluation of the effectiveness of a training programme, however, in terms of the *overall* quality of its graduates, is a much neglected aspect of accreditation programmes both in Canada and the US, and one which is receiving attention currently as a direction for development. In our survey, 50% of accredited programmes perceived an increase in the calibre of their graduates and 80% attributed these increases to effects engendered by CPA accreditation. Only 19% of nonaccredited programmes reported increases in the calibre of graduates; no programmes reported decreases. Thus, programme characteristics are important determinants of programme effectiveness, and should be recognized as such and not as rigid requirements. The overall quality of graduates is ultimately enhanced by the the features of the programmes in which they train.

In summary, evidence suggests that the fears voiced at the inception of the CPA Accreditation Programme have not been validated and, for the most part, accreditation has had a positive effect on the quality of training programmes. Though more study of the actual impact of the Programme is clearly needed, these initial findings are encouraging. It appears that the aim of the Accreditation Programme to encourage the development of high quality, accreditable doctoral training and internship programmes in Canada, has been successful.

Current and Future Issues in Canadian Accreditation

An accreditation programme is constantly evolving, responding to both internal and external tensions. One current tension for the CPA Accreditation Programme is between continued coordination with APA to develop a continental system of accreditation, with resultant economy of scale and mobility of trainees and graduates, vs. promotion of criteria responsive to our unique Canadian situation. The APA Accreditation Program is currently under review, and changes may or may not be in a direction consistent with our own evolving needs. For example, in the US there is pressure from state licensing boards, VA hospitals and third-party insurers to maintain or even enhance the prescriptive nature of the APA criteria, and to require graduation from APA-accredited programmes for licensing, employment and third party payments. This position was evident in the discussions surrounding the Model Licensing Act for States, adopted by APA in 1989. Canadian licensing standards and third-party reimbursement criteria are currently much less restrictive than in the United States, to the liking of most Canadian training programmes. If the APA criteria evolve in the direction of greater prescriptiveness, and CPA chooses not to follow suit, the feasibility of joint site visits and the viability of mutual recognition and fee-sharing, for the 70% of CPA-Accredited programmes which are concurrently accredited by APA, are at risk. Fortunately, the final report of the APA Task Force on the Scope of Accreditation (1989) rejects prescriptive criteria in favour of a conceptual framework which encourages ongoing, explicit programme evaluation. This report has been circulated for comment to APA boards and committees and to many non-APA bodies, including the CPA and accredited programmes, but in the past year no further movement to revise the

APA accreditation criteria has been announced. Instead, the structure of the APA Committee on Accreditation has been revised to include representatives from several non-APA groups, including the Council of Graduate Departments of Psychology, the Council of University Directors of Clinical Psychology and the Association of Psychology Internship Centers. The outcome of the debate in the United States will have important implications for the CPA Accreditation Programme.

Another tension which pressures the CPA Accreditation Programme is the applicability of the criteria to new and emerging specialities. The pressure to maintain the existing criteria vs. the pressure to adapt to the characteristics of new specialities is intense. In 1991, CPA adopted separate *Criteria for the Accreditation of Doctoral and Internship Programmes in Clinical Neuropsychology*, which differ primarily in the content of core scientific and clinical training required. This development in the CPA Accreditation Programme marks a divergence from the APA, which does not accredit clinical neuropsychology as a specialty and which considers all specialties under the same generic criteria. To date, however, it does not appear that this new venture poses any problem for the CPA/APA dual accreditation process, which would continue to apply to and only to clinical and counselling programmes. Expansion of the scope of accreditation is an exciting challenge for the Programme, marking its maturity and leading role in the development of professional training.

Another related issue confronting the CPA Accreditation Programme is the capacity to mount the resources needed to maintain an operation of high quality which will earn the respect of both participating programmes and cooperating organizations. The financial outlay to mount and participate in the Programme is large. At this time, site visit fees to training programmes range from $1920 to $2880, and annual fees from $950 to $1050. Funding of the Programme came initially from CPA, and subsequently by CPA and by fees from accredited programmes, with the hope of self- sufficiency by 1989. However, the relatively small number of training programmes in Canada has led to the realization that self-sufficiency for the Accreditation programme is unlikely. It is envisioned that up to 25% of the Accreditation Programme budget will continue to be contributed from CPA general funds. This funding arrangement is similar to that of APA's Accreditation Programme, which obtains 10%–25% of its budget from APA general funds. Stability of staff is another resource issue. In the six years since programme inception, there have been four Registrars and five Panel Chairs. While it is traditional and appropriate for committee chairs to change yearly, with committee continuity ensured by members' three-year staggered terms, a stable professional office staff is essential to ensure an equitable, impartial, timely public and professional process. It is a credit to the commitment of the CPA to the accreditation programme that this year the Registrar's position has been made paid and part-time. Nevertheless, any expansion of the scope of accreditation signals a significant increase, however, in both the conceptual and administrative complexity of the Programme. It will necessitate the careful consideration, breadth of perspective and coordination of resources that characterized the initial development of the Programme.

Summary

From a developmental perspective, it is apparent that national accreditation of professional training was conceived relatively recently in the life of organized psychology in Canada, long after the desire for such offspring was expressed. However, gestation was short and delivery not unduly difficult, in part due to a healthy constitution and the supervision of many talented and dedicated parental figures. Despite a sometimes exhausting and demanding infancy and toddler period, aggravated by the primiparous parents' inexperience and lack of resources, a sense of autonomy and initiative has been fostered. Growth has been steady, and the developmental challenges of middle childhood and adolescence have been met successfully, including cooperating with peers, developing a coherent sense of identity and individuating. The achievements of the Accreditation Programme to date augur well for its future and for the future of professional psychology in Canada.

References

Adair, J. (1981). Canadian psychology as a profession and discipline. *Canadian Psychologist*, 22, 163–172.

Canadian Psychological Association (1984). *Accreditation criteria for clinical psychology programmes and internships and accreditation procedures.* Ottawa: Author.

Canadian Psychological Association (1989). *Accreditation criteria for professional psychology programmemes and internships and accreditation procedures.* Ottawa: Author.

Canadian Psychological Association (1990). *Accreditation Manual.* Ottawa: Author.

Canadian Psychological Association (1989). *Report of the CPA/CPAP Task Force on Specialty Designation.* Ottawa: Author.

Catano, V. (1984). Reply to Conway. *Canadian Psychology*, *25*, 208–210.

Conway, J. (1984). Clinical psychology training in Canada. Its development, current status and chances for accreditation. *Canadian Psychology*, *25*, 177–191.

Coons, W. (1967). Training in professional psychology: The keynote address to the Couchiching Conference on Professional Psychology. In E.C. Webster (Ed.), *The Couchiching conference on professional psychology.* Montreal: Industrial Relations Centre, McGill University.

Coons, W.H. (1974). Accreditation and graduate education in psychology. *Ontario Psychologist*, *6*, 41–43.

Coons, W. (1990). The crooked path. *Canadian Psychology*, *31*, 138–145.

Day, H. (1984). Reply to Conway. *Canadian Psychology*, *25*, 224.

Fretz, B.R., & Mills, D.H. (1980). *Licensing and certification of psychologist and counsellors.* San Francisco: Jossey Bass.

Gibson, D. (1974). Enculturation stress in Canadian psychology. *Canadian Psychologist*, *15*, 145–151.

Gibson, D. (1984). Reply to Conway. *Canadian Psychology*, *25*, 212–213.

Inglis, J. & Marshall, W.L. (1984). Reply to Conway. *Canadian Psychology*, *25*, 202–204.

Martin, R. (1984). Reply to Conway. *Canadian Psychology*, *25*, 227–228.

Payne, R.W. (1984). Reply to Conway. *Canadian Psychology*, *25*, 201–202.

Poser, E. (1984). Reply to Conway. *Canadian Psychology*, *25*, 219–220.

Schallow, J. (1984). Reply to Conway. *Canadian Psychology*, *25*, 228–229.

Task Force on the Scope and Criteria of Accreditation (1989). *Draft Standards and Categories of Accreditation.* Washington, D.C.: American Psychological Association.

Webster, E.C. (1967). *The Couchiching conference on professional psychology*. Montreal: Industrial Relations Centre, McGill University.

Wright, M.J. (1969). Canadian psychology comes of age. *Canadian Psychologist*, *10*, 229–253.

Wright, M.W. (1984). Reply to Conway. *Canadian Psychology*, *25*, 220–221.

5

Continuing Education for Professional Psychologists in Canada

L. Handy and S. Whittsett
University of Calgary/Alberta Children's Hospital

Continuing education (CE) for professional psychologists in Canada has historically represented a challenging dilemma for the discipline, and this challenge continues today. The dilemma arises, in particular, from two perspectives concerning CE. On the one hand, there is consistent and consensual agreement that CE is desirable for the ongoing professional activity and development of psychologists. On the other, many diverse and often conflicting views regarding the degree to which CE should be organized and regulated by the psychology profession exist.

The consensual validation of desirability of CE appears to be growing among professional psychologists. It would be surprising, in fact, to find any recognized psychological association or individual proposing otherwise. Dubin's (1972) conclusion that the half-life of psychologists' professional training is approximately

10–12 years provides a sobering argument in favour of CE. Dubin has also noted that we may expect this half-life to steadily decrease over the years due to the accelerating expansion of knowledge and technology in the field. Thus, we might currently estimate the half-life of a professional psychologist's repertoire of knowledge and skills to be significantly less than the original 10–12 years. Though estimation of the actual decay of psychological knowledge is recognized to be a difficult issue (cf. McMamara & Flanders, 1985), Dubin's point remains one of concern when addressing the need for CE for psychologists practising in the field.

Rationale for Continuing Education

It is our belief that the positive value of CE may be better understood and addressed by a more explicit examination of the goals of such endeavours that extend beyond maintenance or currency of knowledge and skill. Based upon the authors' communications with colleagues throughout North America, and a review of the content of both the literature and professional conference programs, we suggest the following as goals for professionally comprehensive CE programs. In our view there are at last six areas of potential emphasis within CE for psychologists. Though these are clearly not mutually exclusive, we would suggest that each area represents a degree of unique emphasis which warrants individual consideration. The six areas are listed in Table 1, and described below.

1. As already mentioned, *professional psychologists must maintain awareness of advances in psychological knowledge and skill.* Keeping abreast of the growing body of professional knowledge and professional skills is perhaps the easiest area of CE for most to recognize. That the body of knowledge and skills is constantly evolving, and therefore requires ongoing evaluation and refurbishing, is a point which, though widely accepted, may not be attended to by individual psychologists. As maintaining the currency of knowledge and skill is both an ethical and professional responsibility, its importance is paramount to CE endeavours.

Table 1. Proposed goals and objectives for continuing education endeavours for psychologists.

1. To maintain awareness of advances in psychological knowledge and skill.
2. To maintain an understanding of the nature of clientele seeking psychological services.
3. To obtain relevant contextual knowledge and attitudes.
4. To gain opportunities for personal and professional self-maturation and development.
5. To gain opportunities for professional socialization, collegial interaction, and professional networking.
6. To gain and maintain motivation for individual personal and professional development.

2. The professional *psychologists must maintain a clear understanding of the nature of the clientele* seeking psychological services. The diverse nature of our clientele places demands on the individual psychologist to be acutely aware of the specific needs and life circumstances of the population served. This observation follows naturally from the overdue recognition that much of traditional psychological knowledge was developed within cultural- and gender-bound contexts. Psychological practice, on the other hand, is deliberately involved in engaging an ever expanding variety of recognizably distinctive cultures and subcultures.
   Furthermore, the "client" for psychological services has become increasingly complex over the years. It is common in psychological practice that the client is not simply an individual, but rather a member of a couple, a family or extended family, a work group, an organization, an institution, or in some cases samples of entire cultures or subcultures. Adequately addressing the concerns of the "client" may potentially require a different set of knowledge and skills in each case.
3. Highly related to issues concerning the nature of our clientele is the view that *CE should provide the psychologist with relevant contextual knowledge and attitudes*. Most similar to the issue raised in point 2 above are attitudes and specific information related to the various cultures and subcultures which are crucial to understanding the psychological functioning of indi-

viduals within these groups. In addition, for many psychologists a knowledge of relevant legislative and legal statutes is necessary for the appropriate delivery of services to individuals on whom those statutes have impact. For example, psychologists delivering services to couples undergoing separation or divorce need to understand divorce proceedings and custody and access statutes. Those dealing with incarcerated or paroled clients may well require knowledge specific to legislation regarding these situations.

4. The needs of the psychologist may also be served more directly in that *CE may provide opportunities for personal and professional self-maturation and development.* Although much of this function may be seen to be part of the above mentioned goals, in that acquisition of knowledge and skill, awareness of the characteristics of the client, etc., contribute to professional development, personal and professional growth may be addressed as an independent function of CE.
   Within and after formal psychoanalytic training, for example, the practioner's own analysis is usually seen as a crucial component of the preparation of a competent therapist. While not implying that CE performs a function totally synonymous with formal analytic training, we are suggesting that attention to the personal professional integration and growth of psychologists can and should be enhanced through CE activities.

5. Again, in relation to the individual needs of the psychologist, *CE often provides an opportunity for professional socialization, collegial interaction, and professional networking.* The value of professional socialization, especially for new members to the profession of psychology is, in our view, an often unrecognized, yet specific and desirable aspect of CE. Much of what is to be constructively gained from experience may be accelerated through interactions with, if not explicit learning from, those with broader and more extensive professional experience. Collegial interactions and resulting professional networking will in most cases greatly increase the probability of a psychologist becoming aware of new issues relevant to the maintenance or increase of competent functioning and increased awareness of appropriate referral sources and resources.

6. Finally, we recognize the important function of CE to *provide motivation for individual development* through exposure to broader horizons and new challenges. CE opportunities which expose psychologists to the work of others, our peers and students, as well as the "superstars" of the profession, provides the conscientious psychologist with the stimulation of new ideas and questions. Many of these will translate into new research and practice, or equally important, increased commitment to one's work. The deliberate seeking of situations where one's concepts and procedures are both challenged and affirmed is an admirable characteristic of the psychologist who wishes to maintain a high level of practice and motivation. Though this function may be served through other activities – such as consultative supervision and peer evaluation – the CE format seems an especially important one for doing so, in that it allows both the presenting psychologist and other participants an opportunity to reflect upon and challenge their respective positions.

The Status of Continuing Education for Psychologists in Canada

If one accepts that CE serves a number of vital functions for the professional development of psychologists, one might anticipate that the professional psychological associations would take a lead in the development and establishment of CE opportunities. Furthermore, given the apparent "consensual agreement" as to the importance of CE, it might also be anticipated that CE would become embodied in the regulation of the profession. These assumptions, according to our research, are only partially verified. Though it is the case that most of the provincial psychological associations have made efforts to provide opportunities for CE for their members, and many have worked toward the development of regulatory guidelines for CE, only one of the regulatory bodies has in fact established any requirements for CE. The status of CE in each of the provincial organizations is shown in Table 2. This

Table 2. Regulations, guidelines and opportunities for continuing professional education provided by provincial psychological organizations. (Data provided in response to a survey conducted in April, 1991.)

Provincial organization	Regulations governing CE	Guidelines for CE	Provide CE opportunities
College of Psychologists of British Columbia	No	Yes	Yes – A variety of programs during year
Psychologists Association of Alberta	No	No	Yes – Annual conference plus professional issues workshops during year
Saskatchewan Psychological Association	No	No	Yes – Annual, 2 day institutes. Cosponsor other CE events during year
Psychological Society of Saskatchewan	No	No	Yes – Annual, 2 day institutes. Cosponsor other CE events during year
Psychological Association of Manitoba	No	No	
Manitoba Psychological Society	No	No	Yes – Two or more institutes per year. Cosponsor other CE events during year
Ontario Board of Examiners in Psychology	No	No	Yes – Workshops at O.P.A. conference
Ontario Psychological Association	No	Yes – Based on APA guidelines for approval of sponsors of CE	Yes – Annual conference and workshops during year

Table 2 continued

Provincial organization	Regulations governing CE	Guidelines for CE	Provide CE opportunities
Ontario Psychological Association	No	Yes – Based on APA guidelines for approval of sponsors of CE	Yes – Annual conference and workshops during year
Corporation professionelle des psychologues du Quebec	No	No	Yes – Annual conference plus 1–2 other CE activities during year
College of Psychologists of New Brunswick	No	No	Yes – Annual conference and workshops
P.E.I. Psychologists Registration Board	Yes – Renewal of registration requires demonstration of variety of CE activities	Yes – Specify types of CE activity for renewal of registration	No
Psychological Association of P.E.I.	No	No	Yes – Annual CE workshop and others during year
Nova Scotia Board of Examiners in Psychology	No	No	Yes – Occasional workshops during year
Association of Psychologists of Nova Scotia	No	Yes – Voluntary & anonymous listing of CE activities	Yes – 1–3 workshops during year
Newfoundland Board of Examiners in Psychology			
Association of Newfoundland Psychologists			

table, unfortunately, does not reflect efforts by many of the provincial associations to develop CE guidelines or regulations in recent years. Most report that they have done so, and many have developed extensive models describing minimum standards for CE pursuits on the part of their members. All of these associations have, obviously, met with difficulties in implementing these models.

The PEI Psychologists Registration Board, on the other hand, in its recently proclaimed regulations, has instigated a very flexible requirement for CE as part of application for renewal of a certificate. This requirement places responsibility on the individual psychologist to "demonstrate (that they have) maintained familiarity with current practice and endeavoured to enhance professional competency." A broad range of CE activities is acceptable, including reading of professional journals, consultative supervision, and attendance of lectures and courses. The psychologists are required simply to demonstrate to the Board that they have engaged in any of these CE activities for a total of at least 40 hours during the year prior to their application for renewal. Other associations and boards have made efforts to establish guidelines for CE, which recommend, but do not require, CE activities. The Association of Psychologists of Nova Scotia (APNS), for example, though not a regulatory body, has demonstrated support for CE activities of its membership by establishing a voluntary (and anonymous) registration of CE activities.

At the national level, the Canadian Psychological Association has recently rejuvenated efforts by its CE committee to support CE through the accreditation of CE programs and activities. The committee (Continuing Education Committee, CPA, 1990), through the board of the CPA, has "established a system for viewing and approving sponsors of formal CE programs and activities, such as universities, clinics, professional associations, specialty groups, and consulting firms." This system is based closely on a similar one developed by the American Psychological Association. At the time of this writing it is described in the manuscript entitled "Criteria, Standards and Procedures: Approval of Sponsors of Continuing Education for Canadian Psychologists," available from the CPA office.

Difficulties in the Development of Continuing Education Guidelines

Given the longstanding, mostly undocumented history of its development, the specific reasons for the absence of formal requirements and recommendations for CE in psychology can probably never be fully described. However, the major obstacles to this development appear to have arisen from three concerns. First is the recognition that CE requirements do not provide absolute insurance of enhancement of skill or knowledge. Second is the discomfort that many psychologists have with efforts to further develop the profession through regulatory rather than collegial functions. These two points will be discussed independently in turn. The third is more pragmatic and arises from the logistics and costs of providing and accessing CE in Canada.

There has been considerable research on the value of CE for various professional groups. Given the more abstract nature of psychological knowledge, and the difficulty in precisely defining outcome measures in the field, research on CE in psychology is more difficult to conduct than in some of the other health professions. For this reason, a larger portion of the literature on professional CE has focused on studies conducted within the field of medicine. Despite the recognized differences between medicine and psychology, the format and outcome of medical CE research seem applicable here.

Whether in psychology or medicine, the majority of the studies have suggested that the benefit of CE is to some extent dependent on the outcome which is evaluated. Those studies which have examined merely attendance at CE activities have found that guidelines and requirements for CE have increased the level of attendance. Following the institution of mandatory CE requirements for psychologists in Maryland in 1978, for example, (Brown, Leichtman, Blass & Fleisher, 1982), it was found that there was a significant increase in attendance at courses and workshops, both of which were activities specifically required by the Maryland regulations. These increases, somewhat surprisingly, though significant, were small. This same study also revealed that psychologists in that area tended to spend "a substantial number of hours in continuing professional development," regardless of regulations.

More importantly, studies that have evaluated knowledge have shown that increased attendance at CE programs also leads to at least short-term increases in knowledge regarding the content area provided in the program. Pre–post tests of changes in level of knowledge have shown almost uniform increases immediately following attendance at various programs, while those studies which have looked at more long-term follow-up have shown more modest changes in knowledge base.

The goal of CE must be one of influencing practice and, in turn, the impact of that practice on competency levels and patient outcomes. Unfortunately, these outcomes have been the most difficult areas to examine, and the literature, particularly with regard to psychology, is notably lacking. Studies in medicine (many of which were reviewed by Haynes et al., 1984) have found discouragingly limited impact of CE on patient care.

For psychologists and other health care professionals, the question remains, then, as to whether the absence of evidence for the impact of CE on matters of patient care should be construed as the equivalent of evidence of absence of impact of any positive nature. Clearly, further efforts are necessary to document the demonstrable efforts of CE.

The second point frequently raised by psychologists in opposition to the requirement of CE, while overlapping with the first, stems more from a sense that regulation is not necessary for professional development. The previously cited study by Brown et al. (1982) would seem to support this contention in its finding that the requirement for CE did not greatly increase the mean number of hours in which psychologists were engaged in CE activities. That study suggested that it was the "availability" of CE opportunities, rather than the requirement for such, which seemed to have the greatest impact on CE activities. Likewise, the respondents to the survey utilized in that study found that many of the activities prescribed by CE regulations – namely workshops and courses – were less valued than other activities that allowed for pursuit of more specialized interests.

The third, more pragmatic issue confronting the development of CE, stems from the difficulties of access to and delivery of CE in Canada. For example, it has been difficult to provide CE to outlying and rural areas or, conversely, for psychologists in rural areas to take advantage of CE opportunities in the urban centers. In such situations the existing incentives associated with voluntary CE activities may not offset the costs.

What has not been addressed is the often voiced concern that when CE is voluntary, it is those professionals who least need to participate who take advantage of such opportunities. Though unsubstantiated by empirical evidence, it might be argued that mandatory CE would at least partially remedy this perceived dilemma.

Future Directions for Continuing Education

Despite the difficulties encountered in the development of formal mechanisms for requiring, recommending, and recognizing CE activities, there are many areas in which development is proceeding. CPA's reestablishment of a procedure for reviewing and formally approving sponsors of CE is one such endeavor. This process will provide guidance to psychologists in their independent pursuit of CE activities, regardless of whether those activities occur on a voluntary or mandatory basis. In addition, it provides a more visible recognition by CPA of the importance of continued development and enhancement of professional knowledge and skill through CE activities.

It is interesting to note that, in the United States, mandatory CE has been adopted by approximately half of the state psychology boards at this time (1991). This is almost certainly a reflection of the APA position supporting "the principle that State licensing boards mandate CE as a requirement for re-license of licensed psychologists ...."

It is our impression that much of the resistance to a greater degree of structure within Canadian psychology's approach to CE results from attempts to move too quickly from the current situation to what proponents see as the ideal. Perhaps a little more attention to the efficacy of shaping of behavior is warranted. Such an approach would allow psychologists to experience the benefits of moving in the direction of increased CE activity, so that organizational decisions implementing greater structure might be made on the basis of psychologists' own expectations that CE will be both personally and professionally valuable. Such a stance of course challenges us all to provide CE which leads to such expectations. Quality control of and enhanced accessibility to CE activities are major concerns which immediately become relevant. An example of a jurisdiction moving constructively in this manner is the CE Committee of the College of Psychologists of British Columbia (Continuing Education Committee, 1990). This group has identified and recommended a "phased sequential implementation" covering six steps from identifying goals to implementation of mandatory CE standards. These include:

1. Becoming more involved in the provision and distribution of CE services.
2. Identifying voluntary standards of adequate levels of CE.
3. Developing incentives to enhance motivation towards regular CE participation.
4. Developing a more convenient and sophisticated system of keeping track of members' CE activities.
5. Providing a "CE info" service to members that would offer information on CE opportunities.
6. Phasing in mandatory CE standards.

Prince Edward Island's requirement for 40 hours of self-monitored CE mentioned earlier might also be seen as a step in this direction.

A Look at Retraining and Additional Degrees

While retraining and respecialization are often thought of as synonymous with CE, there are some noteworthy differences. For those who are seeking additional and/or advanced degrees it is suggested that these differences take on increased importance. For psychologists wishing to develop new specialities, change career paths, or gain an additional or advanced degree, the short (maximum 2–3 days) seminar or workshop, as well as other brief formats, found in most CE activities is simply not adequate (McNamara & Flanders, 1985). In these cases the presence of a coherent body of knowledge and skills presented within an integrated educational program is required. It is with respect to the provision of opportunities for developing new competencies or gaining new degrees that the questions which have been raised regarding the nature of professional psychological training become quite relevant. Of particular importance are issues such as those raised by Stern (1984), on the distinctions between the Boulder model of education and the professional model of training, or the Psy.D.

Opportunities for upgrading will continue to be of interest to Canadian psychologists. At the Opinicon II conference on the state of discipline (1984), a joint CPA–CPAP Task Force on Mid Career Training was mandated to explore issues related to upgrading (CPA–CPAP, 1991). Part of a survey conducted by that Task Force indicates that a significant percentage (40%) of Master's level psychologists within Canada express an interest in obtaining doctoral level training. Impetus in this direction no doubt comes not only from the fact that a majority of provinces either have in place or have clearly stated aims of requiring doctoral-level work for entry into the profession, but also that psychologists have had in place since 1985 the Canadian Register of Health Service Providers in Psychology (CRHSPP). This, while including a very generous grandfathering period (15 years), has from its inception built in the doctoral degree as the ultimate requirement for registration.

Relevant to those seeking any type of retraining as well as advanced degrees, psychological codes of ethics make it very clear that to engage in professional activity for which one is not trained is unacceptable. Therefore, further education becomes a necessity for those psychologists venturing into new areas of practice. Clearly, those Master's-level psychologists currently practising could continue to do so without pursuing advanced degrees. Yet, as noted above, a significant number indicate an interest in doing so.

Stern's (1984, p. 235) distinction between genotypic competence ("the ability to do a particular job well") and phenotypic competence ("the generic knowledge and skills that enable one to learn to do many jobs well and to continuously improve one's professional effectiveness") and his accompanying discussion highlight a concern that currently has no profession-wide resolution. If Canadian degree-granting institutions continue to favor the phenotypic (Boulder model) approach, while those wishing retraining or advanced degrees lean toward a genotypic preference, frustration and the seeking of training elsewhere is to be expected. It is reasonable to anticipate that a practicing psychologist who has developed an interest in new areas will in fact wish to focus on those areas in their further education. While all doctorate-granting programs within Canada currently indicate a willingness to recognize and give credit for Master's degree training for applicants to their programs, it appears very safe to say that current educational opportunities are not readily available which allow the practitioner to add a particular area of expertise to existing training.

There are additional factors reflected in the CPA–CPAP survey which will influence participation in further education. It is clear at this point in time that there is not the degree of flexibility regarding residency requirements, diversity in the locations of offerings, and the degree of financial assistance that many of those looking toward advanced degrees would desire. Such issues obviously raise the importance of exploring alternative methods of providing high-quality further education. For both retraining and ongoing CE activities which go beyond workshops, courses, and conferences in major population centers, the utilization of technology for distance education such as that described by Turkat (1983) may well offer further opportunities. Courses and workshops utilizing teleconferencing, cable television, electronic mail, and other computer innovations are all worth exploring as mediums of both more accessible and, at the same time, interactive CE which is more likely to address the specific needs and interests of the individual psychologist.

References

Abrahamson, S. (1984). Evaluation of continuing education in the health professions: The state of the art. *Evaluation and the Health Professions, 7,* 3–23.

Brown, R.A., Leichtman, S.R., Blass, T., & Fleisher, E. (1982). Mandated continuing education: Impact on Maryland psychologists. *Professional Psychology: Research and Practice, 13,* 404–411.

Continuing Education Committee (B.C.). (1990). The continuing education committee: Policy options for continuing education. Footnotes, September, 2–4.

Continuing Education Committee, CPA. (1990). Approval for sponsors of continuing education. *Psynopsis, 12,* 9.

CPA–CPAP. (1991). Report of the Task Force on Midcareer Training. In preparation. (Contact authors of present article for further information.)

McNamara, J.R. & Flanders, P.A. (1985). Continuing education for psychologists: A reexamination. *Clinical Psychologist, 38,* 32–34.

Stern, S. (1984). Professional training and professional competence: A critique of current thinking. *Professional Psychology: Research and Practice, 15,* 230–243.

Turkat, D. (1983). Cable television and psychology: Bringing peace to the planet. *Clinical Psychologist, 36,* 40–43.

6

Issues in Training and Credentialing in School Psychology

Barbara Holmes
School District No. 36 (Surrey), British Columbia

Canadian readers of publications in school psychology are familiar with the dominance of American writers, American models, American issues and American developments in this professional area. The field has been so completely driven by the American experience that we in Canada have learned to predict our future on the basis of the American past gauging a 10- to 15-year interval between developments there and here.

This experience of the predictive relationship is no less borne out today in training and credentialing issues than it has been in other aspects of professional development and practice. Many articles published recently in two mini-series issues of the journal of the National Association of School Psychologists (NASP) (*School Psychology Review*, 1989, *18*(1) and *18*(2)) focus on trends in training, credentialing and the debate over entry-level credentials for school psychology practice. In one of these volumes, Curtis and Zins (1989) report that:

> Prior to mid-1970, graduate study in many school psychology programs did not reflect systematic preparation for a defined profession, as much as it represented the pursuit of additional employment opportunities for education personnel ... Furthermore, the completion of requirements that led to certification usually was accomplished through programmes in related fields such as guidance and counselling, clinical psychology, or special education. Study was rarely attained through a *school psychology* program. (p. 183)

A second article noted that by 1969, 80% of the states had credentialing standards, and these were independently defined by each state department of education. Because of this, "there existed in 1969 an extremely wide range of academic and experience requirements necessary to attain credentialing in school psychology. The range varied from only one or two academic courses and teaching experience to the equivalent of a complete specialization in school psychology" (Batsche, Knoff & Peterson, 1989, p. 194).

The issue of doctoral vs. nondoctoral training as the entry-level requirement for credentialing in school psychology is one which has driven the structure of professional affiliation bodies in the United States. The opposing positions of the American Psychological Association (APA) and the National Association of School Psychologists (NASP) have provided conflict and debate since the inception of the latter organization in 1969 (Bardon, 1979, 1983; Fagan, 1986; Trachtman, 1981). The following comments clarify this duality:

> The American Psychological Association (APA) and the NASP have worked unsuccessfully to achieve joint resolution on entry-level and title issues ... (Fagan, 1986, p. 851).
> ... school psychology has become organizationally fixed at two different levels .... The two groups, the National Association of School Psychologists (NASP) and the American Psychological Association (APA), by and large represent two different constituencies holding different views about the nature of practice, the appropriate level for independent practice and the relationship of school psychology to other areas of psychology (Bardon, 1983, p. 186).
> A network of state-level representations has developed, and this network

is usually separate from the APA-affiliate state association network (Fagan, 1986, p. 853).

School psychologists seem to be rather unified on the issue of entry level. A national survey found an overwhelming preference for a nondoctoral entry level with the two-year master's level gaining the most support ... (Trachtman, 1981, p. 163).

It is the purpose of this chapter to delineate training and credentialing issues in school psychology both as they inevitably reflect those in the United States and as they represent situations unique to Canada. Throughout the discussion, there is reference to situations across this country. I have purposefully, however, refrained from descriptions of specific training programme criteria since many of these programmes are currently known to be in a state of flux. While this omission may be frustrating in an attempt to chronicle the status of the profession, it provides first-hand awareness of the dynamics occurring in many provinces. School psychology is changing, and it is changing as a result of many and diverse forces, ranging from internal political and guild-related issues to the more externally imposed need to respond to changes within the education system itself.

History of Training Programs

In a brief statement published in *The Canadian Psychologist* in April 1962, Bowers (1962) quotes a statement about the growing demand for trained psychologists in applied settings in Canada and the attendant concern that this situation will result in the hiring of inadequately prepared personnel. She concludes her comments with the plea: "It is hoped that the staffs of university departments of psychology will keep the training of school psychologists 'continually under review' " (p. 52). Despite this apparent reference to school psychology training, Stein (1964), reporting from the results of a national survey conducted in March 1962, claimed that, "School psychological personnel have no specific university preparation or psychological experience. Teaching experience is common. All workers do have qualifications and experience that are related somewhat to school psychology" (p. 12).

Table 1. Training programs in school psychology.

Province	Institution and Department	Training focus	Degrees granted
British Columbia	University of British Columbia, Department of Educational Psychology and Special Education	School Psychology	M.Ed. M.A. Ed.D
Alberta	University of Alberta, Department of Educational Psychology	School Psychology	M.Ed. Ph.D.
	University of Calgary, Department of Educational Psychology	Clinical, School and Community Psychology	M.Ed. M.Sc. Ph.D.
Saskatchewan	University of Saskatchewan, Department of Educational Psychology and Special Education	Counselling	M.Ed. M.A. Ed.D. M.Ed.
	University of Regina, Department of Educational Psychology	Counselling	
Manitoba	University of Manitoba, Department of Educational Psychology	School Psychology	M.Ed. Ph.D
Ontario	Ontario Institute for Studies in Education, Department of Applied Psychology	School Psychology	M.A. Ph.D. M.Ed. M.A.
	University of Ottawa, Department of Educational Studies		
Quebec	McGill University, Educational Psychology and Counselling	Clinical Psychology	M.A. M.Ed. Ph.D. D.Ed.
	Université de Montréal, Departement de Psychologie, Psychologie de l'Education	Clinical Psychology	M.Ps. M.Sc. D.Ps. Ph.D.

Province	Institution and Department	Training focus	Degrees granted
New Brunswick	Université de Monctón, Departement de Psychologie	Assessment and Counselling	M.A.
Nova Scotia	Dalhousie University, Department of Education Mount Saint Vincent University, Psychology and Education		M.Ed. M.A. Ph.D. M.A.S.P.
Prince Edward Island			
Newfoundland	Memorial University, Department of Educational Psychology	School Psychology	M.Ed.

In an article published three years later, McMurray (1967) advised that "to this day no Canadian psychology departments have graduated students with a specific specialty in school psychology" (p. 208). He did note, however, that a Ph. D. school psychology programme was currently in its first year of operation within the Division of Applied Psychology at the Ontario Institute for Studies in Education. By 1971, Arthur (1971) had documented four school psychology training programmes in Canada, at the Universities of Alberta, Calgary and Montreal, and at the Ontario Institute for Studies in Education.

Five years later, Schmidt (1976), then Chair of the Department of Educational Psychology at the University of Alberta, complained about the dearth of Canadian applicants for positions in educational fields.

> As far as I can ascertain, there is no university offering doctoral programs in educational psychology in the whole of the Maritimes. There is OISE in Toronto, Calgary and UBC [in addition to the U. of A.]. While there is some excellent training relevant to educational psychologists in departments of psychology throughout Canada, the educational and practice-oriented focus of the training is usually lacking. (p. 5)

The Canadian Association of School Psychologists (CASP) recently published a *Directory of School Psychology Programmes in Canada*. The first edition (1989) lists programmes in 13 institutions from 8 provinces, but acknowledges that it is not an exhaustive compilation. The writer of this chapter, as guest editor of a special issue of the *Canadian Journal of School Psychology* (1990) which reviewed the "state of the art" of school psychology across Canada, identified 14 training programmes spanning all of the provinces except Prince Edward Island. For the sake of documentation, these are listed in Table 1. As stated earlier, however, the list is published with the cautionary note that the situation is changing, and any attempt at specification is outdated almost as soon as it is published.

Such an attempt at definition must be issued with a qualification that is critical in the field of school psychology in Canada, both historically and currently: The providers of psychological services in schools, and the graduate training programmes from which they derive their academic credentials, carry what Sweet (1990) has termed a "bewildering array of titles" (p. 2). As a result, it is often difficult to designate a training programme as one which produces "qualified" school psychologists when departmental affiliations range from Educational Psychology to Applied Psychology to Educational Studies, and when areas of specialization include such diverse offerings as testing, psychopathology, guidance and counselling and communication disorders. As will become increasingly clear in the sections to follow, any actuarial efforts in this field are hampered by nomenclature diversity, which is specifically attributed to the lack of consistency in training programmes and provincial variations in credentialing resulting from title restrictions.

Traditional Training Focus

It would be impossible to discuss school psychology without acknowledging the long-standing dominance of its liaison with special education and the service role it has provided of testing for the purpose of classification of students within that system (e.g.

Sarason, 1977, p. 27). The designation of the school psychologist as "gatekeeper for special education" is so common that its origin is no longer traceable. The earliest references to the provision of school psychology services refer to this assessment function. For example, Perkins (1990) dates the earliest psychological services in Ontario schools to 1919 when the Toronto Department of Public Health hired psychologists to test students with the purpose of identifying and ultimately placing those found to be mentally defective in special classes. Bartell (1990) documents the hiring, in 1935, of the first "psychologist" by the Winnipeg School District. At that time, a special education teacher with mental testing qualifications was charged with the task of identifying mental retardation problems within that district. The results of Stein's (1964) survey showed that school psychologists spent 50% or more of their time in direct testing activities. This focus of role activity has persisted throughout our history (e. g. Bardon, 1976; Goh, Teslow & Fuller, 1981; Holmes, 1980, 1986) and has determined the content of training programmes. Regardless of the additional components of a training programme they all include – in fact, focus on – the training of psychoeducational test administration and interpretation. It is this particular aspect that provides the single common denominator across training and practice in school psychology and allows for identification despite variations in programme and job titles.

Traditionally, the training focus has been on the standardized, individually administered IQ test. In addition, school psychologists are typically trained in the use of tests of academic achievement, perceptual-motor functioning, adaptive behaviour, personality, aptitude and interest. Some programmes allow for training in projective techniques and neuropsychology batteries. Despite long-standing objections to the narrowness of the role definition engendered by this training pattern (see, for example, Siegel & Cole, 1990), it persists to the present day (*Canadian Journal of School Psychology*, Special Issue, 1990; Wilson & Humphries, 1986). French (1991) argues that the focus on a limited range of assessment techniques has "ill prepared many school psychologists for practice in the schools" (p. 3). I would contend, however, that the demands within the school system drive the training programmes, and the need for IQ-based labels for deviancy to support funding of special-education programmes has rendered the limited testing function not only acceptable but desirable. With changes in the philosophy of special education placements (Reschly, 1988; Wilson & Humphries, 1986); in the nature of assessment strategies (Bateson, 1989; Bountiogianni & Pratt, 1990; Tindal & Marston, 1986); and in the shift to collaborative consultation (Anserello & Sweet, 1990), it is predicted that a major change will be seen in the transcripts from school psychology training programmes. Such a change will incorporate an emphasis on counselling and preventive intervention strategies in place of the current emphasis on identification and categorization.

Training in School Psychology

As noted previously, school psychology training programmes in Canada exist under a variety of departmental affiliations and with an array of areas of specialization. Some programmes have a specific school psychology specialization (e.g. the Universities of Alberta, British Columbia and Manitoba), while others focus on counselling psychology (Universities of Regina and Saskatchewan) or clinical psychology (McGill University and Université de Montreal). Those listed in Table 1 at least lay claim to specific training in this area and to graduating students with academic preparation to offer psychological services in school settings.

Bleak as this reality may be for those wishing to see a higher degree of professional regulation and consistency, it is worth repeating that an identical situation existed in the United States prior to the formation of the NASP in 1969. Although there has been tremendous progress since then toward national definition of role and training criteria, there still exist "large variations in professional practice and development ... from state to state" (Fagan, 1989b, p. 3).

The descriptor "bewildering array," formerly applied to titles, is no less appropriate for training sources. The Curtis and Zins (1989) quote presented above characterizes training in Canada at present. While it is common for school providers of psychological services to hold a master's degree, the programme source of the degree varies tremendously as a result of students broadening their professional base by adding to their transcript a course or two in testing. Thus, many, if not in fact most, practitioners in Canada are graduates of programmes with a major focus in some other specialty area. For example, for many years there has been a summer session programme in the Department of School Psychology at U.B. C. offering credit coursework in testing. The courses were in great demand and systematically drew students from several provinces and a variety of graduate programmes. Given that the functional base of psychology in schools is eclectic in nature, such training may not be seen as detrimental for practice. Where it does have an impact, though, is in credentialing, as will be addressed in the next section.

Before leaving a discussion of training, it should be noted that it is in the areas of in-service training and continuing education that the greatest needs for growth and change will be evidenced (Drake, 1991). It is the practitioner, now facing the need to provide services beyond those acquired in assessment-oriented graduate coursework, often 10–20 years ago, who will provide the challenge for training. In the process, it is anticipated that formal training institutions will, at least initially, be supplanted by the efforts of local school districts and provincial certification bodies (as noted by Fagan, 1989 a), which can be more immediately responsive to the needs of the field. One such example is seen in the commitment of the Vancouver School District to Feuerstein's *Learning Potential Assessment Device* (Harris, 1991) and the provision of extensive in-service to their school psychologists and other special service personnel who were formerly untrained in this area.

Credentialing in School Psychology

In this chapter the term "credentialing" has been adopted for its generic connotation and is used with reference to licensing or certification or any comparable procedure that, following the completion of formal training, serves to validate the right of a person to adopt a specific title and/or to work in a specific pro-

Table 2 Regulation and credentialing for school psychologists.

Province	Regulatory Body	Entry-Level Requirement	Jurisdiction	School Psychologists' Affiliative Body	Jurisdiction	Use of Title
British Columbia	College of Psychologists of British Columbia	doctorate	– restricted use of title "psychologist" or any affix or prefix or abbreviation of the title to Registered Psychologists – exempted: government agencies, universities and schools	British Columbia Association of School Psychologists	– voluntary collegial and regulatory body – certification of school psychologists at master's level	– "School Psychologist" for registered or exempted practitioners
Alberta	Psychologists' Association of Alberta (PAA)	master's	– restricted use of title "Chartered Psychologist"	Alberta Association of School Psychologists (AASP)	– collegial body – full membership status requires being a Chartered Psychologist	"Chartered Psychologist"
Saskatchewan	Saskatchewan Psychological Association (SPA)	doctorate		Saskatchewan Educational Psychology Association (SEPA)	– collegial body	
	Provincial Government, Department of Education	master's	– delineates qualifications to conduct assessments in special education			– "Educational Psychologist" "School Psychologist"

Province	Regulatory Body	Entry-Level Requirement	Jurisdiction	School Psychologists' Affiliative Body	Jurisdiction	Use of Title
Manitoba	Psychological Association of Manitoba	doctorate	– restricted use of title "Certified Psychologist" – exempted: school, hospital and university settings – provides "Psychology Associate" at master's level – must be supervised by a C.Psych. – certification for all practising school psychologists under title "School Clinician (Psychology)"	Manitoba Association of School Psychologists (MASP)	– collegial body	
	Board of Teacher Education and Certification	master's				"School Clinician (Psychology)"

Province	Regulatory Body	Entry-Level Requirement	Jurisdiction	School Psychologists' Affiliative Body	Jurisdiction	Use of Title
Ontario	Ontario Board of Examiners in Psychology	doctorate	– restricted use of title to Registered Psychologists – limits provision of psychological services in schools to registered psychologists or those supervised by registered psychologists	Ontario Association of Consultants, Counsellors, Psychometrists and Psychotherapists (OACCPP)	– collegial body – master's level entry	"Psychoeducational Consultant" "Psychometrist" "Teacher Diagnostician"
Quebec	Corporation Professionnelle des Psychologues du Québec	master's	– restricted use of title or any abbreviation of title	Groupe d'intérêt en psychologie scolaire (GIPS)	– collegial body – psychologists working in elementary schools	"Counsellor in Reeducation"
New Brunswick	College of Psychologists of New Brunswick	master's	– restricted use of title to "Accredited Psychologists"			"Psychometrist"

Province	Regulatory Body	Entry-Level Require-ment	Jurisdiction	School Psycholo-gists' Affiliative Body	Jurisdiction	Use of Title
Nova Scotia	Nova Scotia Board of Examiners in Psychology	master's	– restricted use of title to registered psychologists	School Psychology Committee (standing committee of the Association of Psychologists of Nova Scotia		"Psychometrist" "Educational Assesser"
Prince Edward Island	Psychological Association of P.E.I.	master's (doctorate after July 1993)	– restricted use of title "Certified Psychologist" – exemptions: government, hospitals, schools, universities			
Newfound-land	Association of Newfoundland Psychologists Provincial Department of Education	master's plus eligi-bility for teacher cer-tification	– regulation for practice as a school psychologist			

fessional capacity. School psychology, as a profession, is potentially regulated by two sources as a result of its dual affiliation with education and psychology. As will be seen in the following descriptions, the regulatory bodies governing the use of titles are most commonly those that govern psychology in general. Although it is operationalized only in Saskatchewan, Manitoba and Prince Edward Island (the respective provincial government certifies school psychologists in Manitoba and has set standards of qualification in Saskatchewan and Prince Edward Island), it is understood that some degree of regulation also exists within the school system. For example, in B. C., most school psychologists hold teacher qualifications and are hired under teacher contracts which automatically bind them to the regulatory powers of the B. C. Teachers' Federation.

In all provinces, training at the master's level is accepted for the practice of psychology in the schools, and with the exception of Ontario, there is no status differential between nondoctoral and doctoral practitioners. In Ontario, psychological services must be either provided by or supervised by a registered (i. e. doctoral-level) psychologist. Perkins (1990) points out that the result of this constraint is that only a small proportion of actual psychological service providers in Ontario schools are registered psychologists, since many hold supervisory positions. Even in the absence of this type of regulation, all provinces report the general standard for practitioners to be a master's degree. It is additionally clear that some psychological services, for example, testing, may be provided by persons with less than master's level qualifications. Again in Ontario, the title "psychometrist" is used, though not exclusively, for persons who provide assessment services and whose training was at the undergraduate level. The term "teacher diagnostician" designates a person with a background in special education and additional training in assessment. Accounts from Quebec (Gagne & Boivin, 1990) and Nova Scotia (Haverstock & Millman, 1990) also make reference to alternate title designations for practitioners who fail to meet master's-level qualifications.

Table 2 represents an attempt to summarize both the regulatory bodies and the professional affiliation bodies relevant to school psychology at the provincial level. Most noteworthy is the restriction on use of title in all provinces to persons who have met the entry requirements of the provincial regulatory body for psychologists. In only four of the ten provinces – B. C., Saskatchewan, Manitoba and Ontario – is this currently restricted to the doctoral level. As a result, access to credentialing as a psychologist is available to master's-level providers of school psychological services in most provinces. In the provinces holding doctoral-level registration restrictions, there are alternate provisions for school practitioners. In Saskatchewan, a variety of collegial bodies exist representing practitioners trained in areas related to the practice of psychology, with the Saskatchewan Educational Psychology Association (SEPA) specifically oriented toward educational and/or school psychologists. To date, SEPA has assumed no certification role, although this is an ongoing issue for debate within the association (Saklofske & Grainger, 1990). In Manitoba, school employees are exempt from the restrictions of the *Psychologists Registration Act* and are instead certified by the Board of Teacher Education and Certification of the provincial Department of Education. That body certifies six groups of "School Clinicians" with one of them designated "School Clinician (Psychologist)". Requirements for permanent certification include a master's degree in school psychology or an equivalent area plus an internship and two years of clinical experience (Bartell, 1990). The situation in Ontario has already been discussed to some extent. Perkins (1990) points out that, "Because, except for the title 'psychologist', there is no provincial guideline regulating the use of particular titles for providers of psychological services in schools, it is not possible to equate title with a specific level of training" (p. 34). The master's-level-trained personnel who would carry the title "school psychologist" are elsewhere designated "psychoeducational consultants" and generally assume a broader range of responsibilities than assessment. Two other titles used for assessment service providers are "psychometrist" and "teacher diagnostician". Persons in these roles generally do not hold master's degrees.

British Columbia is unique in that there is a specific certification procedure available for school psychologists which is governed by their own provincial association rather than by either the College of Psychologists of B. C. or the Ministry of Education. The British Columbia Association of School Psychologists (BCASP) was incorporated as a society in 1990 and has implemented voluntary certification for practitioners employed by school boards. The following definition of a school psychologist was adopted by this organization:

> A school psychologist provides, or is qualified to provide, psychological services and consultation for students, parents and teachers in order to address learning, behavioral and emotional concerns, and has training in, and provides psychoeducational assessments when necessary in order to address these concerns. (BCASP Bylaws, 2.1)

To be a "Certified School Psychologist", a person must hold a master's or a doctoral degree in school psychology or a related field, provide evidence of supervised experience, undergo a criminal record check and be refereed by two professionals who can attest to the suitability of the applicant to work in this capacity. To date, certification as a school psychologist is voluntary and school districts may hire persons under the title "school psychologist" without restrictions. Many districts are, however, requesting that their personnel be "Certified School Psychologists", and it is expected that this will become the norm. In the meantime, it is known that there are persons performing school psychology services, particularly in more rural areas, who are neither certified nor would qualify for certification.

School Psychology in the Nonschool Sector

It is in the nonschool sector that the credentialed vs. noncredentialed status is most keenly felt by master's-level providers of psychological services. The private sector is the area of dominion for the provincial regulatory bodies in psychology. As noted earlier, use of the title "psychologist" is restricted in all provinces by the local psychologists' association. Since school psychology is primarily represented by a master's-level body of professionals, an obvious issue has to do with access to private practice. The situation is actually very straightforward. Since registration in the majority of provinces is at the master's level, this credential is potentially available to most school psychologists. In the provinces with doctoral-level registration requirements, only school psychologists meeting this standard may use this professional title for private practice. In many cases (e.g., B. C.) there is a substantial number of master's-level registered school psychologists who achieved that status prior to the imposition of the doctorate-only standard. Since there is no differentiation between doctoral and nondoctoral *registered* psychologists, these persons may practise outside the school system. Note, however, that the licence to practise under special title or as the result of an employment-specific exemption in legislation regulating psychology does not include practice in the private sector.

In actual fact, this situation is not as exclusionary as it sounds, since persons may work privately under a title other than the restricted one. Where it does become an issue is in cases where persons qualified by training are hired to provide psychological services in nonschool settings and are ineligible for any professional affiliation. This anomaly has been brought to attention in B. C., where graduates from the school psychology training programme at the master's level accept employment in other than a school district. Such graduates cannot be registered because of doctoral-level entry requirements, nor can they be certified as school psychologists – although all training and experience criteria are met – because certification is restricted to public school employees. Consequently, school psychologists by training are not school psychologists by professional designation if they work in a hospital, college, or other agency. In this province, in addition, use of any affix or prefix or abbreviation of "psychologist" is restricted with the result that what is perceived as a qualitatively inferior title, such as "educational diagnostician" or "consultant", must be assumed in other settings, while a peer (or less) in a school system may use the more prestigious term "psychologist".

National Credentialing in School Psychology

In 1988, the NASP implemented the National School Psychology Certification System (NSPCS) in an effort to promote uniform credentialing standards for American school psychologists

(Batsche, Knoff & Peterson, 1989). Adoption of the examination component of the system is voluntary, but many states have done so and it is hoped that more will follow. Many Canadian school psychologists have sought NASP certification both in the absence of a comparable standard for demonstration of competence – and in the hope that provincial organizations may endorse it. At the time of writing, it is not known that any such recognition has occurred in Canada.

The Canadian Association of School Psychologists (CASP) was established in 1985 and incorporated under the Canada Corporation Act in 1989. To date, it is adamantly a collegial rather than a regulatory association, although its commitment to the development of national standards and ethical principals for Canadian school psychologists may ultimately have an impact on both training and credentialing.

Directions

This chapter began by drawing on the American experience as predictive of the Canadian situation in the field of school psychology, and perhaps it is fitting that it end using the same sources to identify directions and summarize issues. Tom Fagan, twice president of the NASP and the acknowledged archivist of American school psychology, speaking to the Alberta Association of School Psychologists in 1985, noted that "Canada is at a critical juncture in the history of school psychology and I suspect the decisions of the next few years will set your direction for at least the next fifty years" (Fagan, 1985, p. 5). In that context, he predicted the growth and strengthening of provincial school psychology bodies and of the CASP because of the need to protect and develop training and credentialing levels in school psychology. He anticipated:

> a fully functioning Canadian Association of School Psychologists by 1990 with provincial affiliates in more than half the provinces; and by the year 2000, the existence of two major professional psychology camps – the CPA and its affiliates and the CASP and its affiliates. Separate standards for practice, accreditation, training and all the other things that help to give professional identity will also be forthcoming (Fagan, 1985, p. 5).

In later addresses in Winnipeg (1987) and Vancouver (1989 b), he drew parallels between the United States and Canada and offered the following needs related to training issues:

> – The distribution [of training programmes] does not match well with school enrollment projections and seems foreboding for the continued development of quality services to rural areas (Fagan, 1989 b, p. 3).
> – There is a need for existing and new programs to raise enrollments to meet replacement and new position demands (Fagan, 1989 b, p. 4).
> – There is an especially strong need to improve the availability and quality of field experiences in training and credentialing requirements" (Fagan, 1989 b, p. 4).

Trachtman (1981), outlined a series of needs for the 1980s in the United States which forecast some issues in Canada in the 1990s:

> – We should support training for a predoctoral level ... (p. 175).
> – We should support a broad definition of school psychology that centers on the application of psychology to education in *or out* [italics added] of the schools (p. 175).
> – Unified school psychology organizations must define the [level of] entry for independent practice in and out of the schools and for the use of the title 'school psychologist' (p. 175).

Drawing on the American statements and the contents of the chapter, the following three major problem areas are identified and briefly summarized.

Identity and Focus in Training Programs

While it is unrealistic, and possibly also undesirable, to call for a high level of consistency across training programmes, the current absence of a cohesive standard for title and content is seen as detrimental. The possibilities for regulation of programmes are to adopt American structures (school psychology programmes are accredited by the National Council for Accreditation of Teacher Education or by the American Psychological Association) or to develop new Canadian formats. Regardless of which route Canadian training institutions adopt, the further issue in training is to recognize the needs for a broad base of skill development exceeding the testing function, and for a competency-based field experience or internship that will adequately prepare graduates to assume the full range of roles expected of them in their work. This statement is not intended to imply that such training and supervised practice does not occur; rather, it does not occur *systematically* across programmes. The onus of responsibility in this arena must rest on the Canadian Association of School Psychologists as the only body presently able to claim to represent the profession both in terms of membership and expertise.

Master's Level Credentialing

There is clearly a need for recognition and credentialing of school psychology at the master's level. The history of the NASP in the United States and its parallel, the CASP, in Canada as well as several provincial associations attests to the inevitability of fragmentation within professional psychology when this need is not recognized. Whether the kind of separation that has occurred in the United States will result in Canada in the long-term, or whether new relationships will be forged aimed at keeping school psychology within the working framework of psychology in general, remains to be seen. Two points, however, are certain and will likely hold throughout Fagan's 50-year prediction: School psychology will remain largely a nondoctoral profession, and school psychologists will not accept exclusionary solutions. The drive for identity and the related drives for affiliation and professional validation through the implementation of specific and appropriate credentialing standards will no doubt create conflict. It is hoped that good will and creative solutions will carry the day.

Right to Practise

Perhaps not as prominent currently, but certainly anticipated, is the issue of nonschool practice for school psychologists. It is unrealistic to assume that all persons trained in school psychology programmes, especially given the expected increase in the breadth of those programmes, will seek employment in schools. As organized groups of school psychologists continue to develop and grow at both the provincial and national levels, so will the advocacy of those groups for the total profession and all of its practitioners. It is in this larger arena that there is a major contact point with the existent regulatory bodies for psychology which is guaranteed to challenge the coexistence of professional affiliatory groups. It is hoped that the – by then – accumulated experience of American psychology and school psychology will be instructive in easing our way in Canada.

Final Word

In closing, it is worth reiterating that school psychology is now experiencing its adolescent growth spurt and the attendant maturation dilemmas of that developmental period. The existence of the CASP and its affiliation with provincial associations, the publication the *Canadian Journal of School Psychology* and the success of independently functioning professional bodies such as the B. C. Association of School Psychologists and the Saskatchewan Educational Psychology Association herald a period of change unprecedented in this profession in this country. To call it exciting is an understatement. Guessing the outcome in the next decade or two is impossible, except that it will be in the direction of continued expansion and change. Imagine it will not be dramatic is ill-informed. To draw once again on Tom Fagan's (1986) comments, the following applies perfectly to the Canadian situation in 1991:

> To the outside observer, it may appear that school psychology is at a crisis point, lacking the professional vitality that resolution and unification might provide. On the contrary, the field is enjoying a strength uncharacteristic of any previous period in its history (p. 851).

References

Anserello, C., & Sweet, T. (1990). Integrating consultation into school psychological services. In E. Cole & J.A. Siegel (Eds.), *Effective consultation in school psychology* (pp. 173–199). Toronto: C.J. Hogrefe Publishers.

Arthur, A.Z. (1971). Applied training programmes of psychology in Canada: A survey. *Canadian Psychologist, 12*, 46–65.

Bardon, J.I. (1979). Debate: Will the real school psychologist please stand up? Part 1: How best to establish the identity of professional school psychology. *School Psychology Digest, 8*, 162–167.

Bardon, J.I. (1983). Psychology applied to education. A specialty in search of an identity. *American Psychologist, 38*, 185–196.

Bardon, J.I. (1976). The state of the art (and science) of school psychology. *American Psychologist, 31*, 785–791.

Bartell, R. (1990). School psychology in Canada: The state of the art in Manitoba. *Canadian Journal of School Psychology, 6*(1), 23–31.

Bateson, D.J. (1989). A psychometric refresher. *Canadian Journal of School Psychology, 5*(1), 23–30.

Batsche, G.M., Knoff, H.M., & Peterson, D.W. (1989). Trends in credentialing and practice standards. *School Psychology Review, 18*, 193–202.

Bountrogianni, M., & Pratt, M. (1990). Dynamic assessment: Implications for classroom consultation, peer tutoring and parent education. In E. Cole & J.A. Siegel (Eds.), *Effective consultation in school psychology* (pp. 129–140). Toronto: C. J. Hogrefe Publishers.

Bowers, J.E. (1962). Wanted – trained psychologists for employment in school systems. *Canadian Psychologist, 3a*, 51–52.

Canadian Association of School Psychologists. (1989). *Directory of school psychology programmes in Canada*. B.C.: Author.

Canadian Journal of School Psychology (1990). Special issue: The state of the art of school psychology in Canada, 6(1).

Curtis, M.J., & Zins, J.E. (1989). Trends in training and accreditation. *School Psychology Review, 8*, 182–192.

Drake, S. (1991). The changing role of the psychologist in consultation, assessment and program evaluation. *Nova Scotia Psychologist, 6*(3), 12–14.

Fagan, T.K. (1989a). Guest editor's commentary on the entry level debate. *School Psychology Review, 18*, 34–36.

Fagan, T.K. (1985, June). On the unification of school psychologists in Canada. *Alberta School Psychologist*, 5–6.

Fagan, T.K. (1986). School psychology's dilemma. Reappraising solutions and directing attention to the future. *American Psychologist*, *41*, 851–861.

Fagan, T.K. (1989 b). School psychology: Where next. *Canadian Journal of School Psychology*, *5*(1), 1–7.

Fagan, T.K. (1987, June). Trends in the development of American school psychology with implications for Canadian school psychology. First Annual Convention, Canadian Association of School Psychologists, Winnipeg, Manitoba.

French, F. (1991). Introduction to the special issue on school psychology: Nature and prospects. *Nova Scotia Psychologist*, *6*(3), 3–6.

Gagne, N., & Boivin, G. (1990). The situation of Quebec school psychology services in 1989. *Canadian Journal of School Psychology*, *6*(1), 39–45.

Goh, D.S., Teslow, C.J., & Fuller, G.B. (1981). The practice of psychological assessment among school psychologists. *Professional Psychology*, *12*, 696–706.

Harris, L. (1991). Personal communication.

Haverstock, C., & Millman, E. (1990). School psychology in Nova Scotia—1990. *Canadian Journal of School Psychology*,*6*(1), 49–51.

Holmes, B.J. (1986, December). *Task force on school psychology report.* Paper submitted to the B. C. Psychological Association, Vancouver, B. C.

Holmes, B.J. (1980, April). *The status of school psychology training and practice in western Canada.* Paper presented at the meeting of the National Association of School Psychologists, Washington, D. C.

Hyman, I.A. (1979). Debate: Will the real school psychologist please stand up? Part 3: A struggle of jurisdictional imperialism. *School Psychology Digest*, *8*, 174–180.

McMurray, J.G. (1967). Two decades of school psychology: Past and future. *Canadian Psychologist, 8 a* , 207–217.

Perkins, M. (1990). School psychology in Ontario. *Canadian Journal of School Psychology*,*6*(1), 33–38.

Reschly, D.J. (1988). Special education reform: School psychology revolution. *School Psychology Review*, *17*, 459–475.

Saklofske, D.H., & Grainger, J. (1990). School psychology in Saskatchewan. *Canadian Journal of School Psychology*,*6*(1), 15–21.

Sarason, S.B. (1977). The unfortunate fate of Alfred Binet and school psychology. In S. Miezitis & M. Orme (Eds.), *Innovation in school psychology* (pp. 19–32). Toronto: Ontario Institute for Studies in Education.

Schmidt, W.H.O. (1976, November). The training of educational psychologists in Canada. *CSSE News*, 4–8.

School Psychology Review (1989). Mini-series on NASP at twenty, *18*, 149–224.

School Psychology Review (1989). Mini-series on the entry-level debate, *18*, 9–36.

Siegel, J.A., & Cole, E. (1990). Role expansion for school psychologists. Challenges and future directions. In E. Cole & J.A. Siegel (Eds.), *Effective consultation in school psychology* (pp. 3–17). Toronto: C.J. Hogrefe Publishers.

Stein, H.L. (1964). *The status and role of school psychologists in Canada.* Unpublished manuscript.

Sweet T. (1990). School psychology in B.C.: The state of the heart. *Canadian Journal of School Psychology*,*6*(1), 1–8.

Tindal, G., & Marston, D. (1986). Approaches to assessment. In J.K. Torgeson & B.Y.L. Wong (Eds.), *Psychological and educational perspectives on learning disabilities.* New York: Academic Press.

Trachtman, G.M. (1981). On such a full sea. *School Psychology Review*, *10*, 138–181.

Wilson, A.K., & Humphries, T. (1986). The impact of recent legislation on the role of the Canadian school psychologist. *Canadian Journal of School Psychology*, *2*(1), 1–6.

III

Regulatory Issues in Professional Psychology

7

The Nature of Regulation and Entrance Criteria[1]

Barbara Wand
Ontario Board of Examiners in Psychology, Toronto, Ontario

Where the professions are concerned, "regulation" is a term indicating regulation under a statute setting out the terms and conditions by which the members of the profession are recognized and may practise. As regulation of the professions in Canada is a responsibility of the government in each of the provinces and territories, considerable variation exists in the form it takes from province to province.

Legislation to regulate a profession follows from a decision of a government on behalf of the electorate and not from a decision of the profession in question. Although the enactment of legislation may be eased or hindered by the activities of special interest

1 Selected portions of this chapter have been adapted from "Governing the profession of psychology: Some Canadian experiences" by B. Wand, 1982, *Professional Practice of Psychology*, *3*, pp. 35–46. Copyright 1982 by the American Association of State Psychology Boards. Adapted by permission.

groups, legislation tends to be enacted to regulate a profession only when the public decides these professional services are of sufficient value or potential harm to the public to require regulation.

Similarly, revisions in a statute governing a profession, or additions to the regulations under it, are also primarily public decisions.

In enacting professional legislation, the provincial governments have done so in the belief that these statutes are in the public interest. By taking this step, each provincial government has entered into a contractual arrangement with the members of the profession on behalf of the people of that province whereby it gives legal recognition to the profession, a means of identifying the members by restrictions on the use of the professional title and, in the case of some professions, an exclusive right to practise in return for the assurance that those admitted to the profession will meet certain standards of training on entering and certain standards of conduct and competence following registration.

The Basis for Professional Regulation

It is not always clear why one provincial government introduces legislation to regulate a particular professional group when, in respect to the same group, other governments decide not to. Some insight into the process of governmental decision-making in professional regulation may be gained by studying the efforts in Ontario of the Health Professions Legislation Review (Schwartz, 1989) to apply a set of criteria in assessing the need, in the public interest, for regulation by statute.

In determining the need for regulation of the 75 professional groups under study, the Review examined each group in relation to four sets of basic criteria and concluded that of the 75, 24 professions required statutory regulation. The first set of criteria was used to determine whether or not a group should be regulated by the Ministry of Health or by some other ministry of the government. Psychology and some other professions, such as Social Work, do not fit neatly within the terms of reference of ministries of health; and unless these ministries adopt a broad conception of health in carrying out their mandate, serious flaws may be found in the legislative language used to regulate the profession of psychology. This is particularly obvious to the psychologists, for example, who use their knowledge of perception to assist in the design of traffic signs. For psychologists' clients are not always "patients" nor even "individuals", nor can their services always be considered to be "health care".

The second set of criteria were used to determine if statutory regulation was necessary at all, by examining "whether the profession's activities pose a significant risk of harm ..., whether a large proportion of the profession's members are supervised by members of another regulated profession, and whether an alternative regulatory mechanism exists for the profession" (p. 9). The third set assisted the Review in determining if regulation was "possible to implement for the group in question", by examining "whether the profession has a body of knowledge that can form the basis of its standards of practice, and whether [its] members ... are awarded a diploma or degree from a recognized Canadian post-secondary educational institution" (p. 9).

The final set of criteria were used to determine if self-regulation was a practical possibility; that is, was the leadership able "to favour the public interest over professional self-interest", would the members comply with regulation, and were the members sufficiently numerous and willing to bear the costs of self-regulation.

These criteria, "developed after research into the academic literature on professional regulation" (p. 9), set out a rational basis for making decisions about the need for statutory regulation. Nevertheless, it is obvious to participants in these processes that the determinants of the legislative outcome are not limited to factors so rational as these. The political decisions to regulate or not to regulate and the particular form that regulation will take are both affected by the pressures exerted by special interest groups. And moreover, professional legislation will be profoundly influenced by the attitudes of the public and organized consumer groups toward the professions in general.

Regulation and Consumer Attitudes

In Canada the professions have not faced the open threat of deregulation under "sunset" review of legislation as they did in the United States in the late Seventies; nor have a profession's practices been scrutinized by any agency quite like the U.S. Federal Trade Commission, a body which included in its terms of reference the study of the possible restriction in trade resulting from professional regulations. Nevertheless, the recommendations presented in the prairie provinces by the Report of the Royal Commission on Consumer Problems and Inflation (1968), in Quebec by the Quebec Commission on Health and Social Welfare (1970), in Ontario by the report of the Professional Organizations Committee under the Ministry of the Attorney General (1980) and, more recently, the Health Professions Legislation Review (Schwartz, 1989) indicate that the public scepticism which gave rise to sunset review in the United States has also existed in Canada for some time. The public is actively examining the degree to which the professions govern themselves in the public interest.

It is probably accurate to say that there is a deep and pervasive doubt in the public mind regarding the professions generally, stemming from the belief that the self-governing professions tend to act in their own economic self-interest. In fact, in a speech in 1976, the then deputy minister of the federal Department of Consumer and Corporate Affairs (Ostry, 1976), speaking in Toronto to a national conference on the professions and public policy, stated that:

> What we are seeing quite generally is a significant change in the public attitude towards self-regulation. To a greater extent than ever before, people are making invidious comparisons and questioning whether it is necessary or desirable to endow some groups with special powers. The decision in Canada's case to extend competition policy to the self-regulating professions represents, I believe, a positive and significant response to public concern on the issue. (p. 28)

The basic accusation made by these public policy makers, many of whom are economists, is that the professions do operate to restrict trade. Although there may be some substance to this accusation, it is weak if applied to the profession of psychology. For most provincial legislation regulating psychologists restricts only the use of the identifying title "psychologist", but does not restrict the provision of similar services by other practitioners, regulated or unregulated.

More telling in their application to psychologists may be the concerns of such consumer advocates as the economist, R. E. Olley (1978) who, in addition to finding that "the likelihood is high of characteristic monopoly behaviour", also finds professional groups "slow to adapt to new social conditions which require either new forms and qualities of service, or new institutional arrangements for delivering the service" (p. 82). However, Olley does not see the solution to these problems residing solely with the free operation of the market mechanism but points out that "some key conditions for efficient working of the market are not met at all in the professional service industries" (p. 88), and suggests instead that "protection of the consumer does not come from the vigourous pursuit of some simplified model's prescriptions, but from honestly and openly managed institutions which respond to changing conditions" (p. 87). The appointment of public members to professional regulatory bodies and their participation in matters of discipline is one notable instance of greater responsivenesss to public concerns to be found in professional legislation introduced in the last two decades, and an initiative which has opened the process to greater scrutiny by the public.

These examples provide some context within which the issues in the regulation of the profession of psychology may be examined. Although the small and relatively new profession of psychology has hardly been responsible for the development of public attitudes of scepticism and mistrust towards professions in general, it will have to deal with them. In the last decade the great bulk of new legislation to protect the public is evidence that consumers of professional services have a growing sense of their rights – for informed consent, respect of privacy, access to information held by the professionals they consult, and for effective recourse when the services they receive fall below the standards they consider acceptable.

Regulation of the Practice of Psychology

Over the last thirty years, for reasons that vary from province to province and are in some cases obscure, legislation has been enacted to regulate the practice of psychology in each of Canada's ten provinces and in the Northwest Territories. With the proclamation of its Psychologists Act in April, 1990, Prince Edward Island became the tenth and last province to regulate the practices of psychologists. The respective provincial governments have viewed the profession of psychology as warranting "self- governance", with the governing body composed of members of the profession, an indication that governments recognize that regulating the profession of psychology requires the special knowledge of the members. An exception is the Northwest Territories, where regulation of psychologists is carried out directly by the government.

Each professional statute identifies the organization given the mandate and responsibility to regulate the profession, specifies its composition, the manner of selection of the members of its governing council, their terms of office and so on. In legislation more recently enacted, the professional members of the governing body usually will be elected by the other members of the profession rather than appointed. This has been the case for the older professions, such as medicine or law for some time. In British Columbia, Manitoba, Quebec and Saskatchewan the regulatory body for psychology is elected by the members of the profession. In Prince Edward Island and Newfoundland, the Minister of Health appoints the members, but does it in consultation with the voluntary association of psychologists.

Typically, in newer legislation members of the public will be appointed by the government to the regulatory body. Although the purpose of professional legislation is to regulate a profession in the public interest, the participation of the "public" members is intended to ensure that this is indeed accomplished. In Alberta, British Columbia, Newfoundland, Ontario, Prince Edward Island and Quebec the members of the governing body include public representatives. Psychologists with experience in professional regulation have learned to appreciate the fresh viewpoint and the constructive suggestions brought to professional regulation by these public members.

In Canada the organizations that regulate the practice of psychology in each province differ considerably in their structure and in their relation to the voluntary associations of psychologists, as well as in the names by which they are identified. In some provinces, as in British Columbia, the "college" is both the regulatory body and the voluntary "association". Similarly, the Corporation Professionelle des Psychologues du Quebec fulfils both functions. In Newfoundland, Nova Scotia and Ontario, on the other hand, a "board of examiners" regulates the profession of psychology and a separate voluntary association acts for psychologists in organizing opportunities for continuing education, sharing knowledge through papers and meetings, and in pursuing advocacy matters. However, regardless of the model a provincial government considers appropriate for professional regulation, it is the underlying principle and the purpose of professional legislation that regulation will be conducted in the public interest.

In carrying out its mandate to govern the practice of psychology and maintain standards of competence, the regulatory body, whether "association", "board", "college" or "corporation", will review applications, specify conditions for provisional or permanent certification or licensing, set and conduct examinations, and maintain a register. In addition, and subject to the terms of the legislation, the governing body may have the additional power to require evidence of continuing education as a condition of continued registration, and may also have the power to monitor practices in order to determine continuing competence. Such additional powers over registrants beyond initial registration vary from province to province.

The governing body also has the mandate to promulgate standards of practice and conduct, and to discipline psychologists who fail to adhere to these standards. Penalties specified in legislation vary from province to province but will usually include the power to reprimand, to suspend, or to revoke a licence or certificate. The procedures for hearings into charges of professional misconduct and for appeals of the decisions of disciplinary panels are also governed by law, although they may vary across the provinces. It should be emphasized that each of the foregoing activities of the governing body has its legal implication. An applicant for registration may appeal the governing body's decision to the courts, thus placing upon the governing body the requirement of using procedures and rendering decisions to register or not to register that are fair and consistent when viewed by the courts.

As B. Quarrington (personal communication, August 15, 1990) has observed, "the members of a profession should perceive themselves as regulated and as regulators; this is the essence of self-regulation". Consequently, the distance between the members and the regulators is reduced by the participation of the members, for example, as supervisors and oral examiners, and by the efforts of the governing body to offer assistance to the members in maintaining standards, through educational efforts and through responding to requests from the members for advice on professional and ethical issues. In Ontario, the regulatory body responds annually to roughly 300 such requests from psychologists for information and advice.

Entrance to Practice

Owing to the considerable variability from province to province in the requirements for entry to the profession of psychology, this discussion considers entry criteria that could be, but which may or may not be, used by the regulatory body in a given province. The requirements for entry to the profession will include some but not necessarily all of the following: a complete resumé of the applicant's academic and occupational history, a set of references, transcripts of all university study, supervisors' reports of work experiences and satisfactory performance on written and oral examinations.

The purpose in formulating these requirements is to ensure that on entry to the profession the psychologist will be able to provide, and is likely to provide, a competent service. A competent service could be defined as an appropriate application of knowledge and skill in the service of the client. It may be assumed that competence as a psychologist in this sense will be conditional on reasonable mental health, the intent to serve the client's interest, professionalism (including an awareness and acceptance of professional obligations), willingness to be held accountable, awareness of ethical standards respecting dual relationships and other forms of conflict of interest, skill and knowledge appropriate to the chosen professional activities, and good judgment in applying this knowledge and skill. The degree to which the requirements for entry provide an adequate basis for assessment of these qualities is examined below.

Background Information

The first requirement made of an individual who is applying for entry to the profession is that he or she provide an accurate account of background and training in the discipline. To be consistent with the charter of rights and freedoms, an applicant should not be required to provide information with respect to gender, race, age, or citizenship. However, information about convictions, registration or previous rejections of applications for registration in other jurisdictions, and a complete academic and occupational history assist a regulatory body in assessing suitability for entry to the profession. Falsification of any of this information can lead to rejection of the application or, following a hearing, withdrawal of the certificate of registration or licence. Pressures that encourage truthfulness are therefore built into the application process. It is usual to require an applicant to supplement the information provided on an application form by naming psychologists who will each provide a reference.

Academic Requirements

The doctorate as the minimum academic requirement for entry to the profession of psychology is typical in North America, with legislation in 45 states in the United States and the four provinces of British Columbia, Manitoba, Ontario and Saskatchewan presently setting the doctorate as a condition for registration or licensure. In addition in Canada, Newfoundland will require a doctorate on the expiry of a "grandfather" period; and legislation to require the doctorate has been introduced in Alberta, but has not yet been proclaimed. In New Brunswick, Nova Scotia, Prince Edward Island, Québec and the Northwest Territories a masters degree is the minimum academic requirement for registration.

For many years it has been the official position of the Canadian Psychological Association that adequate preparation for the practice of psychology requires training to the level of a doctorate. A rationale for this position has been presented in a discussion by Quarrington (1989). However, the needs for psychological services differ in the provinces and territories; and it must be acknowledged that the case for requiring doctoral training for the practice of psychology is weakened in provinces or territories where doctoral programmes in applied psychology are not available in the local universities. Uniformity in educational requirements for the registration of psychologists may be delayed in Canada until educational opportunities are more uniformly distributed across the provinces.

Academic Record

The applicant is required to arrange for transcripts of all university-level studies to be forwarded directly to the regulatory body by the educational institution. Occasionally exceptions are made, for example in the case of psychologists who have left their countries under duress. In these instances signed affidavits may be accepted and the credentials verified through other means.

In evaluating the academic record, each regulatory body will conduct itself in consistency with the legislation that provides its authority. In most jurisdictions, the legislation will require that the highest degree be awarded in psychology or in a programme "primarily psychological in content" from an institution "approved" by the regulatory body. For most Canadian regulatory bodies in psychology, the acceptable Canadian educational institutions will be members of the Association of Universities and Colleges of Canada (1988) and, with some exceptions, in the United States those accredited by the regional accrediting bodies (American Council on Education, 1989). Other foreign credentials will be examined for their equivalency to programmes offered in Canadian universities.

In recent years, however, applications for registration or licensure have been made not only by graduates of programmes offered in departments of psychology in these "approved" institutions, but may be lodged by graduates of programmes located in other departments or faculties of a university, or of free-standing professional schools. In order to evaluate the extent to which these training programmes can be considered to provide training in psychology it has been necessary for each provincial regulatory body to develop its own criteria to use in evaluating a programme, regardless of its name or its administrative location. Some regulatory bodies have developed and published these criteria; others have been assisted by the concerted efforts of the Council of the National Register of Health Service Providers and the American Association of State Psychology Boards (AASPB), and more recently in Canada by a Joint Task Force of the Council of Provincial Associations of Psychologists and the Canadian Psychological Association (Dobson & Wand, 1988). These concerned groups have contributed guidelines for use in designating a graduate programme in psychology, as distinct from a programme in some other field or discipline. Although difficult, this exercise in attempting to designate a programme as a programme in psychology has been extremely important in protecting the public from practitioners whose knowledge of the fundamental concepts in psychology is inadequate.

Applicants are accepted if the academic record meets the requirement set out in the legislation. However, in most jurisdictions, the regulatory body will be concerned to see an appropriate fit between the academic programme and the work the candidate has chosen to do. When this is absent the candidate may be informed that he or she may face an extended period on the provisional register while the knowledge and skill appropriate to the area of practice is acquired. To evaluate the adequacy of this preparation, and the level of the candidate's judgment, the regulatory body may lean heavily, first on the assessment and advice of its registration committee at the time of application, then later on supervisors' assessments and on the recommendations of the oral examining committees. In the experience of the Ontario Board of Examiners in Psychology, this is a common problem and the most frequent cause of delay in obtaining registration.

Supervised Experience

In addition to obtaining the applicant's academic credentials, occupational history and personal references, the regulatory bodies in several provinces set additional requirements for registration. In six provinces the regulatory body requires that, after completion of an acceptable academic degree, the applicant work for a specified period under supervision. The Psychologists Association of Alberta, for example, specifies 900 hours of supervised work; the College of Psychologists of New Brunswick, one year for applicants who hold the doctorate, and four years when the applicant holds the master's degree; and the Nova Scotial Board of Examiners in Psychology requires two years for candidates with a doctorate and six years in the case of candidates holding the masters degree. In Ontario, the Psychologists Registration Act requires that the person "has had at least one year of experience acceptable to the Board". This is defined by the regulatory body in Ontario as a year of postdoctoral supervised experience, and in order to monitor this experience the Board admits the applicant, now termed a candidate, to a provisional register. During this year, quarterly reports on the candidate's performance are submitted by psychologists serving as the candidate's supervisor.

Although a survey of candidates recently admitted to the permanent register of psychologists in Ontario indicates that the experience is viewed positively, certain weaknesses in the present system have been noted. In particular, the supervising psychologists may evaluate the candidate only in relation to the extent to which the candidate meets the requirements of the particular job for which he or she has been hired; that is, may assess the candidate only in relation to the extent to which he or she is meeting the needs of the employing organization. The supervisor may sometimes neglect the broader question of the extent to which the candidate is ready to practise independently and the extent to which the candidate is aware of the limits of his or her competence. In such instances, the supervisor may provide inadequate feedback to the candidate or fail to provide a sufficient range of experiences on the job, with consequent delay in registration and disappointment for the candidate.

Examinations

A written examination, the Examination for Professional Practice in Psychology, is given by most psychology regulatory bodies twice a year on the same day in the United States and Canada and, by prior arrangement, in some other locations in Europe and the United Kingdom. This is a multiple choice examination consisting of 200 items, the result of the joint efforts of the regulatory bodies in the fifty states and eight Canadian provinces that are members of the AASPB. The items are developed in workshops by psychologists in various locations in the two countries, worked on by the Professional Examination Service, under contract to AASPB and approved by the AASPB Examination Committee.

A concerted effort has been made to ensure that the examination taps the knowledge and skills essential to the practice of psychology and to ensure that the items are "job related". To this end the AASPB has invested heavily in research on the examination, beginning with a job analysis of psychologists (Rosenfeld, Shimberg and Thornton, 1984) and from this identifying the knowledge and skills essential to competent performance. Given the lack of uniformity in graduate education in psychology, use of the written examination provides assurance that the candidate possesses a minimally acceptable fund of general knowledge in the discipline of psychology.

In some jurisdictions, on passing the written examination and fulfilling the requirement of supervised experience the candidate is admitted to an oral examination conducted by a panel of experienced psychologists. The thrust of this examination is not to test specific knowledge and skills, already monitored by supervisors, but to assess the candidate's readiness for practising independently. To this end emphasis is placed on assessing the candidate's judgment, awareness of personal limits of competence, and of potential ethical problems in his or her chosen area of practice. The aim is not to limit registration/licensing to supremely competent practitioners, but to ensure that those who are registered will limit their practices to areas in which they are competent, are aware of their obligations to clientsand are capable of recognizing and analyzing ethical questions as they arise.

One may ask how successful the oral examination is in determining readiness for registration and the privilege of practising independently as a psychologist. The process appears to be effective in detecting professional immaturity but less so in detecting sociopathy. Signs of emotional problems among candidates for registration are exceedingly rare and, if they are present, are usually detected at the level of supervised experience. It is therefore unusual for an oral examining committee to receive a candidate in obviously poor mental health. There is the residual problem of identifying the psychologist whose intellectual arrogance, indifference to clients, obtuseness in the face of complex ethical issues and insensitivity to the risks of bias in unfamiliar work assignments will lead to an appearance before a disciplinary panel. Neither oral examiners nor practicum supervisors appear very able to identify those who later will be found guilty of professional misconduct.

In judging suitability for registration, as in other areas of personnel selection, dependence on a single variable is suspect. Although each variable used in the screening process for admitting psychologists to the profession is vulnerable, the combination of occupational history, academic credentials, professional references, monitored supervised experience, written and oral examinations enhances the credibility of the process.

Professionalism

Unlike training programmes in law, medicine or dentistry, graduate education in psychology in Canada has been located in faculties of arts or science in the universities and not in professional schools. To a certain extent this may account for the absence, in training programmes for psychologists, of a significant emphasis on professionalism – that is, on the characteristics of the professional relationship. Early definitions of a professional (Flexner,1915; Peterson, 1976) have tended to emphasize specialized knowledge or skill, exalted aim or purity of motive. And much of psychologists' training has focused on research, the implications of research findings or the development of special techniques for helping to resolve human problems. Accordingly, too little attention may have been directed to another vital aspect of "helping", to what Tuohy and Wolfson (1978) have identified as the key element in professionalism. They state:

> Professionalism is best defined in terms of the relationship between the providers and consumers of a service. Professionalism does not refer, strictly speaking, to high levels of competence and altruism themselves. Rather it is a relationship established to ensure that specialized competence is brought to bear in the making of certain decisions and to ensure that the client's interests are fully protected in the making of these decisions. It is, in other words, an agency relationship. (pp. 112–113)

In this agency relationship, the client delegates to the professional certain decision-making authority to be exercised on the client's behalf. "The professional, in short, acts as his [or her] client's agent" (p. 113).

A survey of Canadian graduate schools of psychology conducted by Pettifor and Pitcher (1982) suggested that it is only in the clinical programmes at the graduate level, and then only in some of these, that a formal course in professional issues and ethical standards is required. Admittedly, these courses are included in an increasing number of applied programmes in psychology, but for the most part the would-be psychologist acquires a professional attitude only later, on the job. This is the case, for a significant proportion of candidates for registration, many of whom are graduates of programmes in experimental psychology and will have had no formal exposures to professional issues and standards. Although powers of analysis are considered to be among psychologists' strengths as a consequence of the research component in their training, these abilities do not seem to be directed in their training to examining their professional relations to client populations: to determining who the client is, to identifying a dual relationship, a potential conflict of interest, or potential sources of bias in their work. As a result, the year of supervised experience imposed by the regulatory body must contribute heavily to sensitizing the candidate to professional and ethical issues.

The task of ensuring entry-level competence by fostering a professional attitude could be eased if the training institutions recognized its importance for students in all programmes, including experimental psychology. As it is, they do not. In fact, significant numbers of graduate faculty in departments of psychology are ignorant of professional licensure and indifferent to the areas of practice their students may enter. It would be constructive if graduate programmes in all areas of psychology, not just in clinical psychology, placed greater emphasis on assisting students in the development of a professional attitude toward their work – toward their teaching and research as well as their direct service to clients. It is conceivable that as a consequence the regulatory bodies would see a reduction in the number of complaints against psychologists involving conflicts of interest, dual relationships with clients, violations of confidentiality, or other indications that the important "agency relationship" with the client had been inadequately understood.

In this chapter an attempt has been made to describe the authority of provincial legislatures to enact legislation to regulate the professions, and their purpose in doing so; and to identify the criteria that legislators may use in determining whether or not to regulate a professional group. Variations from province to province in the process of regulating the profession of psychology have been identified. As the legislative language used and the procedures followed in regulating the practice of psychology vary from province to province, so the requirements for entry to the profession also vary. Entry requirements that may be set in a provincial jurisdiction and the purposes they are intended to serve have been discussed, including the applicant's occupational history, references in support of the application, transcripts of academic work, supervisors' reports of work experience and performance on examinations, both written and oral. The chapter concludes with an expression of the opinion that training in the development of a professional attitude must be offered to graduate students in all areas of specialization in psychology; otherwise the graduates who have not been assisted in this way will face difficulties at a later stage in their professional work.

References

Association of Universities and Colleges of Canada. (1988). *Directory of Canadian universities, 1988–89* (27th ed.). Ottawa: Author.

Council on Postsecondary Accreditation. (1989). *Accredited institutions of postsecondary education, 1988–89*. Washington, D.C.: American Council on Education.

Dobson, K. & Wand, B. (1987). *Report of the CPA-CPAP Task Force on Designation*. Available from the Canadian Psychological Association, Chemin Vincent, Old Chelsea, Quebec J0X 2N0.

Government of Quebec. (1970). *Report of the Commission of Inquiry on Health and Social Welfare, the Professions and Society*. Vol. 7, Tome 1, Pt. 5. Quebec: Author.

Leal, H. A., Corry, J. A. & Dupré, J. S. (1980). *The Report of the Professional Organizations Committee*. Toronto: Ontario Government Bookstore.

Olley, R. E. (1978). The future of self-regulation: A consumer economist's viewpoint. In P. W. Slayton & H. J. Trebilcock (Eds.), *The professions and public policy*. Toronto: University of Toronto Press.

Ostry, S. (1978). Competition policy and the self-regulating professions. In P. W. Slayton & H. J. Trebilcock (Eds.), *The professions and public policy*. Toronto: University of Toronto Press.

Pettifor, J. L. & Pitcher, S. W. (1982). Ethics training in Canadian graduate schools of psychology. *Canadian Psychology*, *23*, 235–242.

Quarrington, B. (1990). Academic entry requirements for registration. *The Bulletin*. *16*(3), 1–3. Available from the Ontario Board of Examiners in Psychology, 101 Davenport Road, Toronto, Ontario M5R 1H5.

Rosenfeld, M., Shimberg, B., & Thornton, R. F. (1983). *Job analysis of licensed psychologists in the United States and Canada: A study of responsibilities and requirements*. Princeton, N.J.: Educational Testing Service.

Royal Commission on Consumer Problems and Inflation. (1968). *Report of the Royal Commission on Consumer Problems and Inflation*. Regina: Alberta, Manitoba and Saskatchewan's Queen's printer.

Schwartz, A. M. (1989). *Striking a new balance: A blueprint for the regulation of Ontario's health professions. The report of the Health Professions Legislation Review to the Minister of Health*. Toronto: Ontario Government Bookstore.

Tuohy, C. J. & Wolfson, A. D. (1978). Self-regulation: Who qualifies. In P. W. Slayton & M. J. Trebilcock (Eds.), *The professions and public policy*. Toronto: University of Toronto Press.

8

Codes of Ethics and Standards of Practice

Carole Sinclair
The Dellcrest Children's Centre

The Hippocratic Oath

I swear by Apollo, the Physician, by Aesculapius, by Hygeia, by Panacea, by all the gods and goddesses, that, according to the best of my ability and judgement, I will adhere to this Oath and guarantee: to hold the one who taught me this art equally precious to me as my parents; to share my assets with him and, if need be, to see to his needs; to treat his children in the same manner as my brothers and to teach them this art free of charge or stipulation, if they desire to learn it; that by maxim, lecture and every other method of teaching, I will bestow a knowledge of the art to my own sons, to the sons of my teacher and to disciples who are bound by a contract and oath, according to the law of medicine and to no one else; I will adhere to that method of treatment which, to the best of my ability and judgement, I consider beneficial for my patients and I will disavow whatever is harmful and illegal; I will administer no fatal medicine to anyone even if solicited, nor will I offer such advice; in addition, I will not provide a woman with an implement useful for abortion.

I will live my life and practice my art with purity and reverence. I will not operate on someone who is suffering from a stone but will leave this to be done by those who perform such work. Whatever house I enter, I

> will go therein for the benefit of the sick and I will stand free from any voluntary criminal action and corrupt deed and the seduction of females or males, be they slaves or free. I will not divulge anything that, in connection with my profession or otherwise, I may see or hear of the lives of men which should not be revealed, on the belief that all such things should be kept secret.
> So long as I continue to be true to this Oath, may I be granted the happiness of life, the practice of my art and the continuing respect of all men. But if I forswear and violate this Oath, may my fate be the opposite. (Perkin, 1980, p. 1584)

For professions, a sense of ethical duty and a need to articulate that duty for members has a long history. The Hippocratic Oath is one of the first known examples of a code of ethics for a profession. Written about 400 B. C., it is believed to have been a rite of induction into a specific Greek medical guild. Unlike other guild oaths, which tended to mention only a member's responsibility to the "art", one's teachers and other members (and perhaps to adhere to any standards or rules defined by the guild), the Hippocratic Oath was unusual in that it incorporated specific obligations of the physician to members of the public.

The articulation of standards of practice has an even longer history than codes of ethics. Methods for establishing diagnoses, making decisions about whether to treat and what therapy is appropriate are outlined in Egyptian papyri of the 16th century B. C., the first known documents to mention the physician's role. As long as the physician followed these standards, he/she was not held responsible if the patient died (American College of Physicians, 1984).

There has also been a long tradition of societal concern that persons practicing various occupations be controlled in some way and accountable to the society in which they function. The first evidence of this is contained in the Code of Hammarabi written by and named after the king of Babylon about 2,000 b.c. In addition to detailing laws governing adultery, alimony, witchcraft and slavery, the code specified laws and punishments (for poor technical performance) for the occupational behaviour of tavern keepers, servants and those who practise medicine. These laws stated, for example, that physicians were expected to set surgical fees according to the social status of the patient and that the punishment for killing a patient while opening an abscess was to have one's hands cut off (unless the patient was a slave, in which case replacement of the slave would be sufficient) (ACP, 1984).

The history of codes of ethics and standards of practice for professions, from these earliest recorded times to the present, has been shaped by the evolution of society and its various structures, values and expectations. To understand the current situation for Canadian psychologists, it is important to understand this history and something of the social, legal, economic and political context which has influenced the process. Therefore, before turning to specific codes of ethics and standards of practice as they relate to Canadian psychologists, the socio-political environment in which codes and standards evolved will be explored; in particular, the development of the professions that established codes of ethics and standards of practice and their motivation for doing so.

The Concept of "Profession"

The first occupations to be awarded the status of "profession" were theology, medicine and law. For centuries, these three professions were referred to as "the learned professions". Prior to 1900, architecture and engineering were added to this esteemed list. The present century has seen an explosion in the number of other occupations aspiring to and being granted the status of profession. Why? What is a profession and how is this label earned? Why are such words as "awarded", "status", "esteemed", and "earned" used when speaking of professions? One approach to answering these questions is to look at dictionary definitions of profession. A second approach is to look at studies of the sociology of professions.

Dictionary Meanings

> profession 1: the act of taking the vows that consecrate oneself to special religious service 2: an act of openly declaring or publicly claiming a belief, faith, or opinion 3: a calling requiring specialized knowledge and often long and intensive preparation including instruction in skills and methods as well as in the scientific, historical, or scholarly principles underlying

> such skills and methods, maintaining by force of organization or concerted opinion high standards of achievement and conduct, and committing its members to continued study and to a kind of work which has for its prime purpose the rendering of a public service (adapted from Webster, 1986).

The ordering of any meaning in the Webster dictionary is intentionally historical; the one known to have been used first is entered first. It is evident that the root of the concept of professions is based on religious ideas of commitment, promises, learning and service. Indeed, in ancient times, the differentiation between members of the three "learned professions" (theology, law and medicine) is somewhat difficult. The Egyptian papyri of the 16th Century b.c. referred to the physician as a priest-physician; priests and theologians were also actively involved in the first codifications of law. Such persons were accorded much status and deference in ancient societies. They were trusted, admired members of those societies, viewed as "ministering" to the needs of the people. In turn, they believed themselves to be chosen in some way by their gods and goddesses to perform public service in accordance with what they could determine were the wishes and directives of these supernatural beings.

The third Webster definition is much closer to what we currently mean when we use the word "profession". However, the word "calling" in the definition and the fact that some professions (e.g. engineering, law and medicine) still commonly practise the taking of an "oath" as an entry requirement (Kultgen, 1988) reflect the definition's religious roots. Many dimensions of this third definition can be found in the Hippocratic Oath: the long and intense preparation; maintenance of high standards of achievement and conduct; and, the rendering of service. All of these attributes would seem to be desirable. In a negative vein, however, the ancient history of the concept has brought with it attitudes that have created problems for society and for professions in this century. This is further explored below.

Sociological Meanings

Due to the burgeoning number of professions in this century, and their increased role in society (a phenomenon sometimes called "the professionalization of society"), professions have come under intense sociological study, both in terms of their characteristics and their societal influence (Kultgen, 1988). Determining the characteristics of occupations readily labelled "professions" helps to identify other occupations which could be legitimately so-labelled, as well as to provide a development plan for occupations which aspire to be professions. The following characteristics of a profession consistently appear in the literature (Gross, 1978; Jennings, Callahan, & Wolf, 1987; Newton, 1988; Rychlak, 1984; Sinclair, Poizner, Gilmour-Barrett, & Randall, 1987; Weissman, 1984):

1. Members individually and/or collectively render service to members of the public and to society.
2. Members possess a high degree of generalized and systematic knowledge and skill, requiring long and difficult education, extended practice and continuing education.
3. Members develop and promote a code of ethics, and function in accordance with this code.
4. Members function as a community that (a) controls entry requirements; (b) trains new members; (c) socializes new members into the attitudes, values and accepted practices of the community; (d) regulates and monitors the professional activities of members; and (e) develops its field of knowledge and skill.
5. Members are accountable, willing to subject their activities to scrutiny both from within their own community and from society at large.

Although all five characteristics are needed for an occupation to be considered fully professional, the latter three characteristics are of particular importance in any exploration of professional codes of ethics. They assume that an established profession will develop a code of ethics, will socialize and regulate its members in the context of a code of ethics and will be both internally and externally accountable for its ethics or lack thereof. However, within the context of the study of the sociology of professions, there is also extensive literature which questions the very existence of professions, asserts that professions have a negative impact on our society, and expresses the belief that the latter three characteristics are rarely genuine in a profession, but rather simply "window dressing" to dupe members of the public into continuing to allow a societally destructive level of power and status to a small number of persons (e.g. Gross, 1978; Illich, Zola, McKnight, Caplan, & Shaiken, 1977; Larson, 1977).

Kultgen (1988) refers to the two diverse views of professions as the functionalist and conflict perspectives. Sociologists who take the functionalist perspective "approve of what they see" (p.7), emphasizing the societally beneficial characteristics of professions. In contrast, sociologists who take the conflict perspective see professionalization as a product of class struggle which involves the domination of some groups by others and which has had many harmful features.

The conflict perspective is strengthened by the observation that medicine seems to have tried to institutionalize a sense of separateness and personal superiority through its own codes of ethics. For example, the following statements, taken from the 1847 American Medical Association Code of Ethics, appeared under the heading "Obligations of the Public to Physicians" and remained fundamentally unchanged until 1957 (cited in May, 1975):

> The members of the medical profession, upon whom is enjoined the performance of so many important and arduous duties toward the community, and who are required to make so many sacrifices of comfort, ease, and health, for the welfare of those who avail themselves of their services, certainly have a right to expect a just sense of the duties which they [members of the public] owe to their medical attendants ...
> The benefits accruing to the public, directly and indirectly, from the active and unwearied beneficence of the profession, are so numerous and important, that physicians are justly entitled to the utmost consideration and respect from the community. (p. 31–32)

Although such statements do not appear in current medical codes of ethics or the ethics codes of newly formed professions, it is the opinion of many authors that the underlying attitudes were adopted, at least in part, by these newly formed professions.

The conflict perspective has been reflected in the writing of many psychologists about their own profession. Gross (1978), in an article entitled "The Myth of Professional Licensing", postulated that all of the helping professions, including psychology, had been attempting to emulate the practices of the health and legal professions (e. g. licensing of specific acts) primarily to gain similar status in society and similar financial benefits from third-party payers. In other words, he believed the motives of such self-regulating activity to be primarily ones of self-interest. He pointed out that established professions have a history of serving the elite and of being populated by the elite, insofar as membership required prolonged university training unavailable to the "lower classes" (p. 1011).

An ad hoc committee of the Committee on Scientific and Professional Responsibility of the American Psychological Association (APA, 1964) stated that its study of professions indicated that professions tend to use controls and standards to protect members, but under the pretence of safeguarding the interests of clients. The Committee expressed concern that professional communities are in danger of "slipping over into trade unionism" (p. 170). Zemlick (1980) supported this view. In spite of the existence of a code of ethics, he expressed the belief that self-serving economic and political interests have clouded the issues of self-regulation for psychologists and have hindered psychologists from living up to the highest ethical standards. He proposed that four areas of the profession which should be guided primarily by the principle of protecting the public, showed evidence of being guided primarily by self-interest: (a) selection and training of graduate students; (b) faculty selection and retention; (c) licensing and credentialing of professionals; and (d) guidelines for protecting consumer welfare in service delivery.

Resolution of the Controversy over Professions: Contract with Society

Unlike sociologists who take the conflict perspective, psychologists and other professionals criticizing their own professions generally do not advocate the abolition of professions. Rather, they try to identify the weaknesses in order to make the profession conscious of those weaknesses and to motivate constructive action. Kultgen (1988) proposes a rapprochement between the functionalist and conflict perspectives. He postulates that the increased rate of professionalization is a natural and logical result of the progress of scientific and technological knowledge, and that a division of labour, roles and expertise is essential to today's complex society. Through the assignment of particular responsibilities to specialized experts, he believes that professionals serve the welfare of clients, employers and society as a whole. However, he and other authors (e.g. Bayles, 1989; Beauchamp & Childress, 1988; Comenisch, 1983; Flores, 1988; Frankel, 1989; May, 1975; Newton, 1988; Ravetz, 1971) agree that, in order to avoid a destructive impact on society, all professions, or occupations aspiring to be professions, must become true "moral communities", that is, groups of persons who have a genuine commitment to a clear and socially responsible ethic, show evidence of effectively socializing and regulating their members in the context of this ethic, and are actively accountable to the public for their activities.

Most of these authors conceptualize the ethical responsibilities of professions in the context of a contract with society. Unlike a basic commercial contract, the contract with society is based on principles of mutual dependence, respect, and trust (Kohlberg, 1969, 1976). As May (1975) astutely points out, professions do not provide their services as acts of philanthropy for which they are owed the never-ending gratitude and esteem of the public. Rather, the services are responsive or reciprocal acts which acknowledge the indebtedness of professionals for societal support of their training and livelihood, and for the public's active assistance in the science which nurtures each profession's field of knowledge. In return for professional autonomy, security and the ability to work in an atmosphere of public trust in the profession, the contract with society sets the expectation that each profession will pledge that it will establish those structures needed to ensure that each member will honour general ethical imperatives, be sensitive to the need for thoughtful and sound decision making in the face of ethical dilemmas, and put the welfare of members of the public (its consumers) ahead of the interests of the profession (Newton, 1988).

Codes of Ethics

In this section, the gradual evolution, particularly in North America, of international interest in psychologists' responsibilities and the embodiment of these responsibilities in codes of ethics will be traced. This will be followed by an outline of Canadian work on codes of ethics and reflections on the current uses and roles of codes. The next section will contain a discussion of standards of practice, how they relate to codes of ethics, and how they relate to professionalism.

Early Interest in Ethical Issues and Codes of Ethics

A review of articles listed in *Psychological Abstracts* from 1927 to the present provides a picture of the evolution of interest in ethical issues and codes of ethics. Table 1 presents the frequency of articles about these issues during 4 or 5 year blocks of time from 1927 to 1960, and compares them to the years 1972–1974, 1981–1982, and 1989. Rates of articles related to ethics codes and ethical responsibilities per 1,000 articles listed over each time block facilitate comparison over the total 62 years.[1]

It is evident that there were very few articles on ethical responsibilities or ethics codes prior to the end of World War II. One article (French) appeared in 1927 on "the professional secret", related to the physician's need to keep information about the patient from the patient and the patient's family. There were no further articles until one appeared in 1929 and one in 1931. Both of these were in German. One related to "the ethical borderline of the experiment" (no further information is provided in the abstract); the other discussed "the moral obligations of the psychotechnologist". In the latter abstract, eight areas of ethical concern are listed

1 Although the majority of articles listed in *Psychological Abstracts* are directly related to the field of psychology, some are related to other disciplines (e.g. medicine, social work). These latter abstracts are included in the frequency counts of Table 1 as, by virtue of their being included in *Psychological Abstracts*, they were considered to have been relevant to psychology.

Table 1. Frequencies and proportions of articles relating to ethics and professional accountability, 1927 – 1989.

	Average no. of entries per year in *Psychological Abstracts*	Average no. of articles on ethical responsibilities and codes	Average no. of articles on all forms of professional and scientific accountability*
Year(s)	n	n (n per 1,000)	n (n per 1,000)
1927–1930	4,161	2(.48)	2(.48)
1931–1935	5,705	3(.53)	3(.53)
1936–1940	6,330	1(.16)	1(.16)
1941–1945	4,461	0(.00)	0(.00)
1946–1950	5,662	15(2.65)	15(2.65)
1951–1955	8,383	28(3.34)	28(3.34)
1956–1960	8,698	13(1.50)	13(1.50)
1972–1974	24,776	126(5.09)	202(8.15)
1981–1982	27,363	272(9.94)	636(23.24)
1989	41,583	179(4.30)	349(8.39)

*Articles included in this column, in addition to articles about ethical responsibilites and codes, include entries which appear under the following headings in the *Psychological Abstracts Subject Index*: "Professional Certification", "Professional Licensing" and "Professional Standards" (all three appearing for the first time in 1972–74); "Professional Fees" (appearing for the first time in 1978–80); and, "Professional Liability" (appearing first in 1985).

(including taking the interests of the client into account as well as the interests of the employer, and not taking advantage of colleagues). The eight areas were apparently presented in the article in such a way that the abstract refers to them as a "code of ethics". Between 1932 and 1945, only three other relevant articles are included under the *Cumulated Subject Index to Psychological Abstracts 1927–1960* (1966) categories "Code of Ethics", "Ethics", "Professional (Ethics)", or "Standards".[2] One related to medical ethics, one to ethics in personnel management and one to "the morality of the scientist".

2 Although many articles appeared under the general category "Ethics", the vast majority of these relate to the relationship between psychology and moral philosophy, rather than ethical responsibilities.

Suddenly, in the five years following World War II, fifteen articles appeared. Eight articles related to the development of codes of ethics (five for psychology, three for other disciplines), five related to ethical issues faced by professionals (including text-book writing, working for an organization, and the public responsibility of social scientists), and two related to other methods of accountability for psychologists (certification and minimum standards of practice).

This sudden increase (of almost 900%) in articles related to ethical responsibility and ethics codes following World War II was probably influenced by two precipitating factors. The first was the increased application of psychology to everyday problems. Over the previous decade, North American psychologists had become increasingly involved in applications of psychology to education, clinical problems and personnel management and selection. The second, and probably more powerful, factor was the post-war discovery of atrocities that had been performed, in the name of science, on concentration camp victims during the war. In 1946, the *Nuremberg Code of Ethics in Medical Research* (1964) was developed and used in the war crimes trials in Germany to judge the practices of Nazis involved in human experimentation during the war (Mappes & Zembaty, 1981). It is the first known code of ethics to incorporate the concept of informed consent, and perhaps the first major challenge to and protection from reliance on the "beneficence" of professions.

The five articles appearing between 1946 and 1950 which related to codes of ethics for psychologists were all American in origin. Bixler and Seeman (1946) published an article advocating the development of a code of ethics for consulting psychologists, based on the values of "human rights, dignity and freedom". The Minnesota Society for Applied Psychology (1947) proposed development of a code of ethics around the principles of competence, confidentiality, professional responsibility in sharing information and avoidance of discrediting the profession. The other two articles described the beginning of efforts by the American Psychological Association to develop what was to become the first major code of ethics for psychology.

In the first of those articles, Hobbs (1948) described the 1947 appointment of the Committee on Ethical Standards for Psychologists by the president of the American Psychological Association and the criteria to be used in the development of a code of ethics.

The second article (APA, 1949) described the two-year plan for developing such a code. The first year was to be devoted to collecting and classifying descriptions of incidents requiring ethical choices; the second year was to be devoted to a critical examination of these incidents, and formulation and testing of ethical principles derived from them. In 1950, APA began publication of a series of articles (APA, 1950, 1951 a, 1951 b, 1951 c, 1951 d) which formed the basis of the provisional ethical standards adopted by its Council of Representatives on September 4, 1952 (APA, 1953).

The APA publication of these articles and its eventual adoption of a code had a profound impact on the international community of psychologists and, to a certain extent, a similar impact on the interdisciplinary community. Psychologists in both France and Germany (Bloom, 1964; Bondy, 1959; Pacaud, 1954) expressed admiration for the American process and product, and began development of their own codes of ethics; and, some work was done on an international code of ethics for psychologists (Baumgarten, 1961). Group workers and sociologists (Hall, 1952; Lee, 1953) also made specific mention of the APA process and product as a model for development of their own codes.

Twenty years later, Levy (1974) found eighty-nine human service occupational groups in the United States with a code of ethics. By May, 1990, the Office of Scientific Freedom and Responsibility of the American Association for the Advancement of Science had collected 153 codes of ethics (M.S. Frankel, personal communication, June, 1990). Of these, twelve are from countries outside the United States (including Canada) and eight are codes of international associations. The number of codes indicates both the increasing professionalization of society since World War II and the raising of consciousness about the ethical responsibilities of the professions.

Early Canadian Activity Regarding a Code of Ethics

Shortly after World War II, the Canadian Psychological Association began to discuss national standards for the certification of psychologists (Dunbar, 1990). This was occurring parallel to similar efforts in the United States (Hilgard, 1947). As part of a negotiated arrangement between the two countries, it was agreed that CPA members would be acceptable for certification by the

American Board of Examiners in Professional Psychology if the CPA by-laws contained an article regarding ethical practices and provisions for control of the ethical behaviour of its members. Although Dunbar reports that a Committee on Scientific and Professional Ethics was established by CPA and that this committee was to develop a Canadian code of ethics, he did not find any evidence of such activity in his search of archival documents. Instead, CPA adopted the 1959 revision of the APA code for a three year trial, followed by adoptions (with minor wording changes) of APA revisions in 1963 (CPA, 1963) and 1977 (CPA, 1978 a).

During the 1950s and 1960s, in keeping with the terms of the British North American Act, activity regarding certification of psychologists moved to the provinces. Many of the provinces established regulatory bodies. In addition to controlling entry into the profession, these regulatory bodies established procedures for investigating complaints about the ethical behaviour of its members. Following the CPA lead, each regulatory body reviewed and adopted various revisions of the APA code for this purpose.[3]

Such adoptions of the APA code does not mean that Canadian psychologists were completely at terms with it. The first serious sign of discontent appeared in 1973 and 1974, when CPA was considering adoption of ten principles[4] for the conduct of research with human participants. These principles had been developed by APA for addition to their 1968 code revision, and approved by APA in 1973. In a CPA document entitled *Alternative Strategies for Revising CPA's Code of Ethics*, it was stated that the ten principles were "clearly designed for the current American social and moral climate and geared to American traditions and law" (cited in Dunbar, 1990, p. 4). Although there was an expression of urgency by CPA members regarding the need to develop a Canadian code, the final decision (in 1976) was to adopt the ten APA principles. It seems that the decision was based on a number of factors, namely, the limited financial and human resources of CPA, the opinion that there were few issues in the ten principles that were

---

3 Provincial voluntary associations of psychologists consistently followed the same pattern.

4 The APA code uses the word "principles" inconsistently in its various revisions. In fact, the ten principles referred to were ten standards under the heading "Conduct of Research with Human Participants".

specific to American research alone, and the opinion that it was "cheap, easy and probably inoffensive to most members" for CPA to continue to adopt the APA code of ethics (Dunbar, 1990, p. 4).

A much greater level of discontent appeared, however, with the 1979 revision of the APA code. In response to recent court applications of the American antitrust law to professional activities (Overcast, Sales, & Pollard, 1982), APA decided to remove from its code some of its restrictions on advertising. This decision was met with much discomfort from Canadian bodies which, somewhat routinely, had considered and adopted each revision up to this time. Canadian psychologists believed that American antitrust laws tended to treat the professional relationship as a primarily commercial one, and were very concerned that too much movement in this direction would fail to protect the public from unscrupulous and self-interested professionals.[5] One after another, Canadian bodies, including CPA, decided not to adopt the 1979 APA code. It was at this point that work on a Canadian code began in earnest.

The Development of a Canadian Code

The steps taken to develop *A Canadian Code of Ethics for Psychologists*, adopted by CPA in 1986, are detailed elsewhere (Sinclair et al., 1987). In summary, the project involved a critical look at the effectiveness of the APA code in helping to meet four main purposes of ethics codes: (a) help establish a group as a profession, (b) act as a support and guide to individual professionals, (c) help meet the responsibilities of being a profession and, (d) provide a statement of moral principle that helps the individual professional to resolve ethical dilemmas. This critical look was carried out with

5 It is interesting to note that a recent decision of the Supreme Court of Canada (*Royal College of Dental Surgeons v. Rocket & Price*, 1990), although granting an appeal based on the opinion that the Royal College of Dental Surgeons' restriction on advertising was too broadly drafted and as such against the Canadian Charter of Rights and Freedoms, stated: "The importance of promoting professionalism and preventing irresponsible and misleading advertising, however, outweighs the protection of any commercial interests of professionals". (p. 5)

the hope that CPA could establish a new direction for its code, benefiting from the strength of the APA code and avoiding its weaknesses (if any). A literature review indicated that the APA code had done well in helping to meet the first purpose of establishing psychology as a profession, but that there were problems with the other three. The code seemed to be restricted in its applicability to new fields of practice (e.g. family therapy and community psychology), did not seem to meet expectations as a teaching tool for students in professional ethics insofar as its organization and explicitness were inconsistent, and was a confusing statement of moral principle. The code seemed to have been written primarily on a model of one professional and one client, was organized around "principles" which were sometimes areas of practice (e.g. Assessment Techniques) and sometimes ethical principles (e.g. Welfare of the Consumer), did not always relate standards to specific ethical principles, seemed to mix matters of etiquette with matters of ethics and offered little guidance when professional responsibilities to the client, employer, society, etc. conflicted with one another.

CPA set four objectives for its new code (Sinclair et al., 1987, p.5):

1. To develop a code that would be more conceptually cohesive and thereby a better educational tool for training in ethical practice.
2. To develop a code that would be more inclusive of recently developed areas of practice.
3. To give more explicit guidelines for action when ethical principles are in conflict.
4. To explicitly reflect the most useful decision rules (i.e. ethical principles) for ethical decision-making.

Thirty-seven hypothetical ethical dilemmas, representing the many applied, teaching and research functions of psychologists were circulated to volunteer psychologists across the country. Responses to these dilemmas were analyzed, and four major ethical principles were derived. The resulting code is organized around these four ethical principles: Respect for the Dignity of Persons; Responsible Caring; Integrity in Relationships; and, Responsibility to Society. Each ethical principle is defined through a Values Statement and is followed by a number of standards which demonstrate application of the principle and the subsumed values. The principles are ordered according to the differential weight each generally should be given when principles conflict.

The CPA code has been adopted by either the voluntary association or regulatory body, or both, in eight of the ten Canadian provinces.[6] Early opinions indicate that it is indeed a better educational tool (Eberlein, 1987, 1988); better at alerting psychologists to their social responsibilities. (Prilleltensky, 1990); more helpful in applications to community psychology (O'Neill, 1989, 1990; Pettifor, 1991) and in work with vulnerable groups (Pettifor, 1988); and, helpful in resolving ethical dilemmas of supervision (Minnes, 1987). Although some weaknesses have been identified (Sinclair, 1990; Weinberger, 1989), corrections of these are planned in future revisions,[7] thereby maintaining the responsiveness of the code to the needs of both the Canadian public and Canadian psychologists.

Content and Ethical Theory in the Canadian Code

In a recent APA publication, Bennett, Bryant, Vanderbos and Greenwood (1990) note:

> There is a tendency to write and speak about practice guidelines and ethics as if both were matters of concern only to philosophers and theorists, or as if their application were the province of saints. However, practice guidelines and ethics are developed in response to the practical concerns of people who work in a profession and people who use the services provided by the profession. (p. 17)

---

6 The Ontario Psychological Association has adopted the CPA code. However, the Ontario Board of Examiners in Psychology is still using the 1977 APA code. The Corporation Professionelle des Psychologues du Quebec cannot adopt the code as there is a common professional code (across disciplines) that is written into law. However, the CPA code is recommended to its members. The College of Psychologists of British Columbia uses the 1981 APA code, but is considering adoption of the CPA code.

7 A revised edition of the Code was approved by the CPA Board of Directors in June, 1991 (CPA, 1991; Sinclair, 1991).

In an examination of the Hippocratic Oath, it is evident that in 400 B. C. there were concerns about being grateful to one's teachers, living up to high standards of practice, doing no harm, avoiding illegal actions, staying within the limits of one's competence and maintaining confidentiality. In an analysis and critique of the ethics codes of seven professional groups (university professors, lawyers, public accountants, physicians, psychologists, engineers and journalists), Kultgen (1988, P. 241) lists fifteen modern content areas. Table 2 lists the areas in order of the frequency of their appearance in the codes of ethics of these professions and specifies related principles in the CPA code.

The list in Table 2 demonstrates that the concerns reflected in the Hippocratic Oath have been maintained for 2400 years. However, it also demonstrates that many other concerns have been added; that client autonomy and confidentiality seem to have a low priority in spite of the fact that the belief in the dignity of the individual is the basic Western ethic (Josey & Snygg, 1950); and, unless a code of ethics has a consistent and coherent logical structure, that professionals could perceive themselves to be burdened by a seemingly heavy load of conflicting responsibilities. Kultgen is somewhat brutal in his critique, pointing out that many important areas are left out of many of the ethics codes he examined, and that there is little basis provided for resolving ethical questions. In contrast, the CPA code covers all of the content areas identified by Kultgen, except for the tenth, and organizes the content areas in such a way that priorities are clearer and many common conflicts between responsibilities can be resolved. The CPA code does not deny that psychologists have responsibilities to colleagues and the profession itself; however, it places these concerns in the context of ethical theory and of each profession's overriding contract with society.

As noted by Bennett et al. (1990), most ethics codes are developed with practical concerns rather than ethical theory in mind. This presents a problem for one of the main purposes of ethics codes: to provide a statement of moral principle to guide the members of a profession. The underlying ethical theory of ethics codes is often shaky and has met with much criticism (Bayles, 1989; de Vries, 1976; Kultgen, 1988; Sinclair et al., 1987). However, due to the complex ethical questions now faced by professionals, ethicists have been co-opted into efforts to resolve ethical dilemmas,

Table 2. Common content areas in codes of ethics.

Content area (Kultgen, 1988)	Relevant ethical principles in CPA Code
1. Competence; objectivity; and honesty about qualifications.	– Principle II: Responsible Caring – Principle III: Integrity in Relationships
2. Loyalty to client, employer or institution; avoidance of conflict of interest and bribery.	– Principle I: Respect for the Dignity of Persons – Principle III: Integrity in Relationships
3. Territorial rights of colleagues; co-operation; giving proper credit; fair competition.	– Principle III: Integrity in Relationships
4. Monitoring colleagues; reporting malfeasance; preventing unauthorized practice.	– Principle II: Responsible Caring – Principle IV: Responsibility to Society
5. Protecting honour and dignity of profession; publicizing its merits.	– Principle IV: Responsibility to Society
6. Avoidance of harm to outsiders, the public, the environment.	– Principle II: Responsible Caring – Principle IV: Responsibility to Society
7. Enlargement of knowledge; research; publication.	– Principle II: Responsible Caring – Principle IV: Responsibility to Society
8. Nonexploitation of clients, students, research subjects, and animals.	– Principle II: Responsible Caring – Principle III: Integrity in Relationships
9. Truthfulness in public statements.	– Principle III: Integrity in Relationships
10. Involvement in community activities not related to the profession.	–
11. Continuing professional development.	– Principle II: Responsible Caring – Principle III: Integrity in Relationships – Principle IV: Responsibility to Society
12. Making services available to those who need them.	– Principle I: Respect for the Dignity of Persons – Principle II: Responsible Caring

Table 2 continued

13. Proper treatment of subordinates; fairness; encouraging professional development; giving credit.	– Principle I: Respect for the Dignity of Persons – Principle II: Responsible Caring – Principle III: Integrity in Relationships
14. Effort to reform institutions that bear on profession.	– Principle IV: Responsibility to Society
15. Respect for autonomy, privacy, confidentiality, and trade secrets.	– Principle I: Respect for the Dignity of Persons – Principle III: Integrity in Relationships

especially in matters of bio-ethics. This has been mutually beneficial to both ethicists and the professions.

On the one hand, ethicists have become integral members of hospital ethics committees and have had to translate “lofty moral principles” Schneiderman, 1990 (p. 23) like deontology, teleology, beneficence and autonomy into proactical decision-making guides for resolving specific delemmas.

On the other hand, codes of ethics have begun to demonstrate a more logical structure within a framework of ethical theory. The CPA code of ethics is an example of this. Each of the four principles is an ethical principle, each values statement is explained in the context of ethical theory, and many of the positions taken by the code reflect ethical theories. Rather than adopting any one particular approach, the CPA code borrows and attempts to integrate a variety of ethical theory concepts. It accepts and promotes ethics as the application of general ethical principles to specific situations, with these principles acting as guides in decision-making (normative ethics). Also, acknowledges that, for all decision-making, one is a finite human being with limited capabilities (natural law); therefore, a person could be wrong (scepticism), but must act with integrity (conscience), in keeping with his/her obligations (deontology), in the search for a satisfactory outcome (teleology).[8]

8 My apologies to all ethicists for such a simplistic explanation.

Summary

The development of a code of ethics for the profession and science of psychology in Canada has been influenced by many factors. The history of the learned professions, the recent professionalization of society, concerns about the societal role of professions, the ethical atrocities of World War II, the increased involvement of psychology in solving human problems, the work of the American Psychological Association on a code of ethics, and the growing recognition of cultural and socio-political differences between the United States and Canada all played a role. The resulting CPA code of ethics attempts to alert psychologists to the numerous ethical concerns they face, and to place these concerns in a conceptual framework which makes sense from the point of view of ethical theory and which helps psychologists to resolve dilemmas and deal with issues that are not directly dealt with by the code. To help meet Canadian psychology's contract with society, it is the task of each psychologist to learn not just the standards of the code, but also its conceptual framework, and to adopt the ethical values espoused by the code for their professional work; it is the task of the profession to help each psychologist to do so.

Standards of Practice

Unlike ethical standards, standards of practice do not articulate the underlying ethical principles or values of a profession, although they are often drawn from and should be consistent with them. Rather, they specify indicators of good quality practice.

Many of the early craft guilds had practice standards relating to quality of workmanship and such business practices as charging fees. Guild members were expected to adhere to these standards, and apprentices were trained to work according to them, unable to advance in the hierarchical structure of the guilds unless they could demonstrate both the willingness and ability to meet the expectations set by the standards. Unlike professions, guilds were established primarily to protect the craft and its members. Generally, they were not held accountable under the law for the quality of their work, but could exclude members from the guild if standards were not adhered to.

As mentioned earlier in this paper, medicine was the first known profession to articulate standards of practice and to be held accountable under the law for the delivery of its services. Medical codes of ethics, as well as most other professional codes of ethics, state that members are expected to live up to the highest standards of their profession, suggesting that there are standards other than those contained in codes of ethics. Under law, the members of all professions are seen to owe a "duty of care" to their clients. Although any member of society has this same duty (the care an ordinary, average person would exercise under the circumstances), professionals are held to a higher standard and can be sued for malpractice if they do not fulfil their duty at that higher level (Bennett et al., 1990). For the most part, courts look to the professions themselves for the standards against which professionals may be judged. Although courts will sometimes rely on the testimony of "experts" (that is professionals who will tell them what the accepted practice would be under the circumstances), written ethical and practice standards often are used as well. This fact has led to some nervousness about articulating standards in professions, for fear that some standards will be "used against us". However, such an attitude is unprofessional, by definition, insofar as it fails to live up to the contract that each profession has with society.

Another use of practice standards is in the training, screening and regulation of members of a profession. Regulatory bodies often adopt specific standards of practice as well as a specific ethics code. Training institutions are usually very careful to expose their students to such adopted standards, partly due to the fact that regulatory bodies test applicants and judge members on the basis of such standards.

The following objectives of practice standards appeared in the recent CPA document *Practice Guidelines for Providers of Psychological Services* (CPA, 1989, p. 1), and provide an excellent summary of the function and role of such standards. The word "psychologist" can be substituted by the name of any other professional.

> (1) Practice guidelines define common expectations for organizations and psychologists who provide psychological services and for the user of the

service. They provide both the provider and the user with a baseline or criteria for evaluating the quality and appropriateness of practice.

(2) Practice guidelines provide an external authority for standards of ethical and competent practice for psychologists working in situations where others may be minimally knowledgeable and minimally supportive of these standards. Situations where such guidelines may be helpful may arise in working within organizational structures, or with third-party users.

(3) Practice guidelines have significant influence on tomorrow's professionals through their incorporation into teaching models.

(4) Practice guidelines may contribute toward legislative and regulatory requirements for the practice of psychology. Guidelines may assist in providing greater legislative uniformity across Canada with regard to standards of training qualifications and competence.

(5) Practice guidelines may give specific content and structure to the profession's principles of ethical practice.

Development of Standards of Practice in North America

The development of standards of practice for North American psychologists did not begin until two decades after the development of a code of ethics. Although there is evidence that, as early as the 1930s, APA had established a committee with the primary purpose of "assessing the nature of ethics and practice guidelines within the discipline" (Bennett et al., 1990, p. 18), it took twenty years for an ethics code to appear (APA, 1953) and forty years for the first practice standards to appear (APA, 1973).

Early in 1970, the APA Board of Professional Affairs appointed a task force of psychologists who functioned in at least one of every major type of human service facility. This was a time when standards were beginning to be seen as a "vehicle of accountability" (Sinclair, 1981) and, as can be seen in Table 1, there was a burgeoning interest by North American psychologists in a broad range of issues related to professional and scientific responsibility (certification, licensing, standards, fees, liability). Courts were asking for the articulation of clear minimum standards for adequate treatment, and various groups were involved in setting standards for the accreditation of a range of different facilities (APA, 1987, Footnote 4). The first edition of *Standards for Providers of Psychological Services* was adopted four years later (APA, 1974).

A revision of these standards was approved in 1977, and a year later, CPA adopted this revision (CPA, 1978 b).

In the mid-70s, both APA and CPA had begun to consider the possibility of specialty standards, that is, standards that were specific to particular applied settings. In 1974, CPA's Applied Division established the Committee on the Practice and Delivery of Services, with six sub-committees, in order to "promote high standards of delivery in various types of settings and to encourage the development of organization patterns and administrative procedures to facilitate good practice" (cited in Dunbar, 1990, p. 5). In the meantime, following its 1977 revision of *Standards for Providers of Psychological Services*, APA began the development of *Specialty Guidelines for the Delivery of Services*[9] for clinical, counselling, industrial/organizational and school psychologists. These speciality guidelines were completed and adopted in 1981.

Although APA began its development of speciality guidelines later than CPA, it can be seen that APA was more successful. Up to the present, CPA has not developed any specialty standards. Part of the reason for this is that the CPA Committee on the Practice and Delivery of Services became aware of an intense interest in developing a Canadian code of ethics about the same time it began to look at the issue of practice standards (mid-1970s). One of its practice standards activities included a critique of the APA code of ethics as a standards document (Gilmour-Barrett, 1981) and, by the late 1970s, the efforts of the Committee on the Practice and Delivery of Service had been given over to designing a method for developing a Canadian Code of Ethics.

---

9 The reader should note that in the 1980s the word "standards" began to be substituted by the word "guidelines" in APA's revisions and additions to its practice standards documents. This was meant to reflect the fact that many of the standards/guidelines were aspirational in nature, rather than minimum behavioural expectations; that the professional practice of psychology is constantly changing; and, that no collection of standards/guidelines can direct these changes adequately (APA, 1987 a, Footnote 2). The 1989 CPA practice standards document follows this approach; however, the CPA code of ethics uses the phrase "ethical standards" rather than "ethical guidelines" in its text, reflecting the belief that a code of ethics is more permanent that a set of practice standards/guidelines, and that standards can be aspirational in nature.

This did not mean that Canadian efforts to develop practice standards discontinued. By the mid-1980s, the CPA Professional Affairs Committee had picked up the task and, in 1989, *Practice Guidelines for Providers of Psychological Service* was completed and adopted, ending the CPA practice of routinely adopting the APA document.[10] The Canadian document is directed to three levels of providers of psychological services: the larger organization or employer; the psychologist administrator/supervisor; and the individual psychologist service provider. It draws relevant standards from the CPA code of ethics and cross-references, to relevant sections of the code, those guidelines for providers that are more explicit than would be found in the CPA code of ethics.

The CPA and APA practice standards for providers of psychological services, although representing the primary efforts to develop practice standards in North America, do not represent the sole efforts. Several other practice standards of relevance to psychologists have been produced. One Canadian group has listed over forty such documents (Psychologists Association of Alberta, 1990). For example, the Canadian Psychological Association has developed guidelines for assessing sex bias in career interest inventories (CPA, 1978c); for the therapy of women (CPA, 1980); for employment of psychological assistants (CPA, 1982 a); for the use of animals in research (CPA, 1982 b); for nonsexist research (CPA, 1983; Stark-Adamec & Kimball, 1984); for the elimination of sexual harassment (CPA, 1985); for educational and psychological testing (CPA, 1987), and, for the advertisement of preschool screening tests (1990).[11] Also of interest to Canadian psychologists are the guidelines on custody/access assessments produced by a Canadian interdisciplinary committee (Kaplan, Landau, & McWhinney, 1988). American groups have produced even more guidelines, many on the same topics as those produced

---

10 As this CPA document is quite new, it has not yet been adopted uniformly across Canada, although it is anticipated that many provincial bodies will do so.

11 All of these sets of guidelines can be ordered directly from the CPA office or, with the exception of the last two documents, can be found in *Canadian Code of Ethics for Psychologists: Companion Manual* (CPA, 1988).

in Canada, but some on additional topics (e.g. see APA, 1986, 1987b, 1987c).

The number of standards documents is continually growing, making it difficult for psychologists to have detailed knowledge of them all. However, if a psychologist keeps up to date with those standards documents that relate to their own area of practice and those that are recommended or formally adopted by their provincial regulatory or voluntary bodies, much helpful direction can be found.

> As the interest in standards grows, so does the proliferation of documents. However, the common values of respect for the dignity of the individual, competence and caring in professional practice, integrity in relationships, and social responsibility (i.e. the four basic principles in the *Canadian Code of Ethics for Psychologists*) prevail. (PAA, 1990, p. 1)

Implementation of Codes of Ethics and Standards of Practice

A major controversy about codes of ethics and standards of practice has been their tendency, in addition to defining minimal behavioural expectations, to be aspirational in nature. Part of the concern, as mentioned above, is that such documents, whether aspirational or not, might be "used against us" insofar as failure to live up to standards can be the basis of complaints to voluntary associations, regulatory bodies and courts. In reaction to this fear, it is sometimes suggested that such documents should convey only clear behavioural indicators of minimally adequate performance and avoid the more ideal, aspirational standards which can often be found, especially in codes of ethics. It is the thesis of this Chapter that such a move would not be in keeping with the profession's contract with society, would be unwise, and is not necessary.

Each profession's contract with society goes beyond ensuring that members will avoid clearly unethical or prohibited behaviours in their interactions with the public; rather, it demands socialization into and acceptance of a socially responsible ethic, striving to live up to the highest standards of the profession, and the ability to make sound decisions in the face of ethical dilemmas. Guidelines or standards which expound only minimum standards contribute little to helping the profession live up to this contract.

The fact remains, however, that codes of ethics and standards of practice are used in complaints proceedings. To safeguard professionals from excessive and possibly malicious complaints based on a failure to live up to ideals, a common practice of regulatory bodies is to develop a "code of conduct" which clearly specifies practices which would be considered serious enough for formal charges of unethical conduct or what is often termed "professional misconduct". In Canada, regulatory bodies in Alberta, Newfoundland, Quebec and Ontario all use codes of conduct for their proceedings, in addition to any codes of ethics and standards of practice which they have formally adopted (also, see American Association of State Psychology Boards, 1990). The particular code of ethics used by a regulatory body acts as a constitutional document which provides the underlying ethical principles for its investigation and adjudication of complaints, and for the development of its code of conduct. Also, the code can be used as the basis of complaints which are outside of the current range of the code of conduct, but considered by the regulatory body to be of a serious nature.

Another common practice to safeguard professionals is for regulatory bodies and courts to use expert witnesses to assist in interpretation of the more aspirational standards and their application to definitions of *acceptable* (vs. *ideal*, *customary*, or *minimally adequate*) practice. In malpractice suits, courts also expect evidence of demonstrable harm or injury to the client as a direct result of the behaviour of the professional (Bennett et al, 1990).

Discussion of methods to protect psychologists from complaints of failing to live up to professional ideals may seem defensive and reactive in the light of a social contract that demands aspiration to ideals. However, it needs to be remembered that the social contract of professions does not expect the punishment of professionals for a lack of perfection. Formal complaints against professionals, whether handled judicially (e.g. in a civil court) or quasi-judicially (e.g. by a regulatory body) are serious matters and any professional against whom such action is taken deserves the same level of protection, fairness and natural justice afforded to any other citizen (Pettifor & Sinclair, 1991).

A more proactive development within professional psychology in Canada is the use of ethical and practice standards in a quality assurance framework, allowing for continuous improvement of the quality of psychological services. Many accreditation bodies (e.g. Canadian Council on Health Facility Accreditation, Ontario Association of Children's Mental Health Centres) now expect quality assurance mechanisms to be in place within facilities which they accredit. Of even more direct relevance, however, are the practice review activities in Quebec (Corriveau, 1989) and Alberta (PAA, 1989), and discussion of such in Ontario (Jackson-Whaley, Rogers, Brooker, Cebulski, & Sinclair, 1990). These activities provide a system for inspection of the professional work of individual psychologists, detection of patterns of problems which exist in the profession, and advice to the professional body for correction of such problems (e.g. through continuing education activities). Ethics codes and practice standards provide the specifics for such review activities. This more proactive approach, combined with increased training in ethical principles and decision-making in psychology graduate programmes (Eberlein, 1991), holds much promise for a "moral community" of psychologists in Canada, that is, a group of persons who have a genuine commitment to a socially responsible ethic and who are actively accountable for their activities.

References

American Association of State Psychology Boards. (1990). *Rules of conduct.* Montgomery, AL: Author

American College of Physicians, Ad Hoc Committee on Medical Ethics. (1984). Part I: History of medical ethics, the physician and the patient, the physician's relationship to other physicians, the physician and society. *Annals of Internal Medicine*, *101*, 129–137.

American Psychological Association, Committee on Ethical Standards for Psychologists. (1949). Developing a code of ethics; a first report of progress. *American Psychologist*, *4*, 17.

American Psychological Association, Committee on Ethical Standards for Psychologists. (1950). Ethical standards for the distribution of tests and diagnostic aids. *American Psychologist*, *5*, 620–626.

American Psychological Association, Committee on Ethical Standards for Psychologists. (1951a). Ethical standards in clinical and consulting relationships: Part I. *American Psychologist*, *6*, 57–64.

American Psychological Association, Committee on Ethical Standards for Psychologists. (1951 b). Ethical standards in clinical and consulting relationships: Section 3, parts II–V. *American Psychologist*, *6*, 145–166.

American Psychological Association, Committee on Ethical Standards for Psychologists. (1951 c). Ethical standards for psychologists; Section 2, ethical standards in professional relationships; Section 4, ethical standards in research; Section 5, ethical standards in writing and publishing. *American Psychologist*, *6*, 427–452.

American Psychological Association, Committee on Ethical Standards for Psychologists. (1951 d). Ethical standards for psychologists; Section 1, ethical standards and public responsibility; Section 6, ethical standards in teaching. *American Psychologist*, *6*, 626–661.

American Psychological Association. (1953). *Ethical standards of psychologists*. Washington, DC: Author.

American Psychological Association, Committee on Scientific and Professional Ethics and Conduct, Ad Hoc Committee on Ethical Practices in Industrial Psychology. (1964). Ethical practices in industrial psychology: A review of one committee's deliberations. *American Psychologist*, *19*, 174–182.

American Psychological Association. (1973). Guidelines for psychologists conducting growth groups. *American Psychologists*, *28*, 933.

American Psychological Association. (1974). *Standards for providers of psychological services*. Washington, DC: Author.

American Psychological Association. (1977). *Standards for providers of psychological services. Revised*. Washington, DC: Author.

American Psychological Association. (1981). Speciality guidelines for the delivery of services by clinical (counselling, industrial/organizational, and school) psychologists. *American Psychologist*, *36*, 639–681.

American Psychological Association. (1986). *Guidelines for computer-based tests and interpretations*. Washington, DC: Author.

American Psychological Association. (1987 a). *General guidelines for providers of psychological services*. Washington, DC: Author.

American Psychological Association. (1987 b). Guidelines for conditions of employment of psychologists. *American Psychologists*, *42*, 724–729.

American Psychological Association. (1987 c). Model act for state licensure of psychologists. *American Psychologist*, *42*, 696–703.

Bayles, M.D. (1989). *Professional ethics, Second Edition*. Belmont, CA: Wadsworth Publishing Company.

Baumgarten, F. (1961). Prinzipielle Regeln eines internationalen ethischen Kodex fur Psychologen. (The principle rules of an international code of ethics for psychologists.) *Schweizer Erziehungs-Rundschau*, (March). (From *Psychological Abstracts*, 1962, *36*, Abstract No. 1AKOOB).

Beauchamp, T.L. & Childress, J.F. (1988). Virtues and conscientious actions. In A. Flores (Ed.), *Professional ideals.* Belmont, CA: Wadsworth Publishing Company.

Bennett, B.E., Bryant, B.K., VandenBos, G.R., & Greenwood, A. (1990). *Professional liability and risk management.* Washington, DC: American Psychological Association.

Bixler, R. & Seeman, J. (1946). Suggestions for a code of ethics for consulting psychologists. *Journal of Abnormal and Social Psychology, 41,* 486–490.

Bloom, B.L. (1964). The code of ethics of the French Psychological Society. *American Psychologist, 19,* 183–185.

Bondy, C. (1959). Die ethischen Grenzen psychologischor Arbeit (Ethical limits of psychological investigations). *Psychologische Rundschau, 10,* 237–250. (From *Psychological Abstracts,* 1960, *34,* Abstract No. 5088).

Camenisch, P.F. (1983). On being a professional, morally speaking. In B. Baumin & B. Freedman (Eds.), *Moral responsibility and the professions.* New York: Haven Publications.

Canadian Psychological Association. (1963). *Ethical standards of psychologists.* Ottawa, ONT: Author.

Canadian Psychological Association. (1978 a). *Ethical standards of psychologists.* Ottawa, ONT: Author.

Canadian Psychological Association. (1978 b). *Standards for providers of psychological services.* Ottawa, ONT: Author.

Canadian Psychological Association. (1978 c). *Guidelines for assessing sex bias and sex fairness in career interest inventories.* Ottawa, ONT: Author.

Canadian Psychological Association. (1980). *Guidelines for therapy and counselling with women.* Ottawa, ONT: Author.

Canadian Psychological Association. (1982 a). *Standards for employment of paraprofessionals and psychological assistants.* Ottawa, ONT: Author.

Canadian Psychological Association. (1982 b). *Guidelines for the use of animals in research and instruction in psychology: Commentary and elaboration.* Ottawa, ONT: Author.

Canadian Psychological Association. (1983). *Short checklist for nonsexist research.* Ottawa, ONT: Author.

Canadian Psychological Association. (1985). *Guidelines for the elimination of sexual harassment.* Ottawa, ONT: Author.

Canadian Psychological Association. (1986). *Canadian code of ethics for psychologists.* Old Chelsea, PQ: Author.

Canadian Psychological Association. (1987). *Guidelines for educational and psychological testing.* Old Chelsea, PQ: Author.

Canadian Psychological Association. (1988). *Canadian code of ethics for psychologists: Companion manual.* Old Chelsea, PQ: Author.

Canadian Psychological Association. (1989). *Practice guidelines for providers of psychological services.* Old Chelsea, PQ: Author.

Canadian Psychological Association. (1990). *Guidelines for advertising preschool screening tests.* Old Chelsea, P.Q.: Author

Canadian Psychological Association. (1991). *Canadian code of ethics for psychologists. Revised.* Old Chelsea, P.Q.; Author

Corriveau, R. (1989). *How professional inspection works in Quebec.* Paper presented at the Canadian Psychological Association Convention, Halifax, Nova Scotia.

Cumulated Subject Index to Psychological Abstracts 1927–1960. (1966). Boston, MA: G.K. Hall & Company.

de Vries, P. (1976). Medical students rejecting CMA code of ethics. *Medical Post, 41* (October 12).

Dunbar, J.N. (1990). *Historical background to the Canadian Code of Ethics for Psychologists.* Paper presented at the Canadian Psychological Association Convention, Ottawa, Ontario.

Eberlein, L. (1987). Introducing ethics to beginning psychologists: A problem solving approach. *Professional Psychology: Research and Practice, 18,* 353–359.

Eberlein, L. (1988). The new CPA code of ethics for Canadian psychologists: An education and training perspective. *Canadian Psychology, 29,* 206–212.

Eberlein, L. (1991). The education of psychologists in ethical and professional conduct. In K.S. Dobson & D.J.G. Dobson (Eds.), *Professional psychology in Canada.*

Flores, A. (1988). *Professional ideals.* Belmont, CA: Wadsworth Publishing Company.

Frankel, M.S. (1989). Professional codes: Why, how, and with what impact? *Journal of Business Ethics, 8,* 109–115.

Gilmour-Barrett, K. (1981). *An analysis of the adequacy of the current interim code of ethics of the CPA as a standards document.* Paper presented at the Annual Meeting of the Ontario Psychological Association, Toronto, ONT.

Gross, S.J. (1978). The myth of professional licensing. *American Psychologist, 11,* 1009–1016.

Hall, L.K. (1952). Group workers and professional ethics. *Group, 15,* 3–8.

Hilgard, E.R. (1947). Annual report of the Policy and Planning Board of the American Psychological Association: 1947. *American Psychologist,* 2, 191–198.

Hobbs, N. (1948). The development of a code of ethical standards for psychology. *American Psychologist, 3*, 80–84.

llich, I., Zola, I.K., McKnight, J., Caplan, J., & Shaiken, H. (1977). *Disabling professions.* London: Marion Boyars.

Jackson-Whaley, I., Rogers, J., Brooker, H., Cebulski, L., & Sinclair, C. (1990). *Mandatory review of your competence. It's coming.* Symposium presented at the Annual Meeting of the Ontario Psychological Association, Toronto, ONT.

Jennings, B., Callahan, D., & Wolf, S.M. (1987). The professions: Public interest and common good. *Hastings Center Report: Special Supplement, 17* (February), 3–10.

Josey, C.C. & Snygg, D. (1950). The place of psychology in the development of values. *Personality*, Symposium No. 1, 1–6.

Kaplan, F.K., Landau, R.L., & McWhinney, R.L. (1988). *Custody/access assessment guidelines: Report of the Interdisciplinary Committee for Custody/Access Assessments.* Toronto, ONT: Ontario Psychological Foundation.

Kohlberg, L. (1969). Stage and sequence. The cognitive-developmental approach to socialization. In G.A. Goslin (Ed.), *Handbook of socializaqtion theory and research.* Chicago, IL: Rand-McNally.

Kohlberg, L. (1976). Moral stages and moralization: The cognitive-developmental approach. In T. Lickona (Ed.), *Moral development and behaviour.* New York: Holt, Rinehart, & Winston.

Kultgen, J. (1988) *Ethics and professionalism.* Philadelphia, PA: University of Pennsylvania Press.

Larson, M.S. (1977). *The rise of professionalism.* Berkeley CA: University of California Press.

Lee, A.M. (1953). Responsibilities and privileges in sociological research. *Sociology and Social Research, 37*, 367–374.

Levy, C.S. (1974). On the development of a code of ethics. *Social Work, 55*, 207–216.

Mappes, T.A. & Zembaty, J.S. (1981). *Biomedical ethics.* Toronto, ONT: McGraw-Hill.

May, W.F. (1975). Code, covenant, contract, or philanthropy. *Hastings Center Report, 5*, 29–38.

Minnes, P.M. (1987). Ethical issues in supervision. *Canadian Psychology, 28*, 285–290.

Minnesota Society for Applied Psychology. (1947). A proposal for a code of ethics for professional psychologists. *American Psychologist, 2*, 246.

Newton, L.H. (1981). Lawgiving for professional life: Reflections on the place of the professional code. In A. Flores (Ed.), *Professional ideals.* Belmont, CA: Wadsworth Publishing Company.

Nuremberg Code. (1964). Reprinted in *Science*, *143*, 553.

O'Neill, P. (1989). Responsible to whom? Responsible for what? Some ethical issues in community intervention. *American Journal of Community Psychology*, *17*, 323–341.

O'Neill, P. (1990). Ethical issues in field research: Balancing competing values. *Canadian Psychology*, *31*, 147–154.

Overcast, T.D., Sales, B.D., & Pollard, M.R. (1982). Applying antitrust laws to the professions: Implications for psychology. *American Psychologist*, *37*, 517–525.

Pacaud, S. (1954). La deontologie et l'organization de la profession. *Revue de Psychologie Appliques*, *4*, 13–19. (From *Psychological Abstracts*, 1954, *28*, Abstract No. 6872).

Perkin, R.L. (1980). The Hippocratic Oath in the 1980's. *Canadian Family Physician*, *26*, 1584–1592.

Pettifor, J. (1988). More reflections on the new Canadian Code of Ethics for Psychologists: How well does it protect and serve special populations. *Highlights*, *10*(1), 6E.

Pettifor, J. (1991). How well does the Canadian Code of Ethics serve community psychologists? *Psynopsis*, *13*(1), 11, 12.

Pettifor, J. & Sinclair, C. (1991). Enhancing fairness and justice in the ethical complaint process. *Canadian Psychology*, *32*, 63–71.

Prilleltensky, I. (1990). Enhancing the social ethics of psychology: Towards a psychology at the service of social change. *Canadian Psychology*, *31*, 310–319.

Psychologiists Association of Alberta, Practice Review Committee. (1990). *Guidelines for the practice of psychology; Annotated bibliography.* Edmonton, ALTA: Author.

Revetz, J.R. (1971). *Scientific knowledge and its social problems.* New York: Oxford University Press.

Royal College of Dental Surgeons and the Discipline Committee of the Royal College of Dental Surgeons of Ontario v. Howard Rockett, D.D.S. and Brian Price, D.D.S. and Attorney General of Quebec. Supreme Court of Canada. (June 21, 1990).

Rychlak, J.F. (1984). Newtonianism and the professional responsibility of psychologists: Who speaks for humanity? *Professional Psychology: Research and Practice*, *15*, 82–95.

Schneiderman, L.J. (1990). Still saving the life of ethics. *Hastings Center Report*, *20*(6), 22–24.

Sinclair, C. (1981). Standards as a vehicle of accountability. *Canadian Psychology*, *21*, 1–6.

Sinclair, C. (1990). Ethics code under CPA review. *Psynopsis*, *12*(4), 4.

Sinclair, C. (1991). Revised code of ethics adopted. *Psynopsis*, *13*(3), 6.

Sinclair, C., Poizner, J., Gilmour-Barrett, K., & Randall, D. (1987). The development of a code of ethics for Canadian psychologists. *Canadian Psychology*, *28*, 1–8.

Stark-Adamec, C. & Kimball, M. (1984). Science free of sexism: A psychologist's guide to the conduct of nonsexist research. *Canadian Psychology*, *25*, 23–34.

Webster's third new international dictionary of the English language: Unabridged. Toronto, ONT: Encyclopaedia Britannica, Inc.

Weinberger, A. (1989). Ethics: Code value and application. *Canadian Psychology*, *30*, 77–85.

Weissman, H.N. (1984). Professional standards from the perspective of the sociology of professions. *Professional Psychology: Research and Practice*, *15*, 471–472.

Zemlick, M.J. (1980). Ethical standards: Cosmetics for the face of the profession of psychology. *Psychotherapy: Theory, Research, and Practice*, *17*, 448–453.

9

The Education of Psychologists in Ethical and Professional Conduct

Larry Eberlein
University of Alberta, Edmonton

Psychologists often lack a sensitivity to potential ethical concerns that arise in their practices (Baldick, 1980; Welfel & Lipsitz, 1984). All manner of ethical problems arise in the field; ethical decisions will have to be made under less than optimal conditions, especially when a psychologist has never considered the issue. Awareness of this problem has led to an increased emphasis on ethics as part of professional training programmes. But too often the teaching of ethics has been tied to abstract ideals or professional codes with little relation to the daily concerns of active practice. Psychologists need better guidelines and more experience in resolving day-to-day ethical problems. Consider the following two examples:

Case 1: Dangerousness

Bob, a grade 11 student in a large urban high school, came to discuss a problem he was having with a female teacher who he felt was "putting" him down in class. Bob was very "macho" and had been studying martial arts for some time. He wished to get into the Armed Forces so he could be turned into a perfect killing machine and talked of his fascination with weapons, and the need to "blow someone away" and not be held accountable. He told of his fantasies which were both sexual and violent in nature and which at this point usually involved this teacher, but wanted this information to be held in strictest confidence. The counsellor wasn't sure whether Bob might be dangerous and considered whether this information should be kept confidential. The counsellor wondered whether the teacher might be in jeopardy and whether Bob, if unduly pressured, might harm her. What should the counsellor do to both help Bob and make sure the teacher is not harmed?

Case 2: Child Abuse

During counselling, Janet, a 24 year old mother with two young children (2 and 5) admitted that her anger, at times, overwhelms her and then she verbally abuses her younger child. She also admits to spanking the child on "odd" occasions as a form of punishment. Recently divorced, Janet is being treated for depression, low self-esteem and loss. She states that she "lives for her children". The therapist wonders about physical harm and psychological damage to the younger child's self-esteem and personal growth. The mother (client) insists she would "kill herself" if she lost her children. The number of occasions of verbal abuse or physical punishment are less than twice per week and the therapist has no objective evidence of abuse. What should the therapist do that would be best for both Janet and the children?

How to respond to these two not unusual illustrations of real professional practice problems faced by counsellors and psychologists? One might be tempted to immediately break the confidence: to report Bob to the principal, the female teacher and the police; to report Janet to the social service child abuse hotline. But the issues here, like almost every issue in professional practice, are more complex than they first appear, and any decision taken will have ethical and legal overtones, as well as a profound impact on those involved in the situation.

Often when ethical problems or dilemmas are presented, there is an immediate, impulsive response that a certain course of action is correct. This is what Kitchener (1984) calls the immediate or first level of moral thinking. While the resulting decision may be "ethical", after a risk-benefit analysis it may not be the most desirable course of action. Kitchener suggests a second, "critical-evaluative" level which requires time and reflection. Complications inherent in a situation become clear when the full implications of potential alternatives are considered. For example, what is likely to happen to the people involved if the City Police take Bob into custody or if welfare apprehends one or both of Janet's children? By contrast, what is likely to happen if the counsellor takes *no* action? Often, two or more alternatives have valid arguments which need consideration.

Ethical and legal dilemmas are seldom black and white; they involve multiple solutions. If this were not so, there would never be a need for an independent adjudication when conflicts occur. For example, Tymchuk et al. (1982) presented 12 vignettes of clinical and research situations to members of the American Psychological Association (APA) Division of Clinical Psychology, together with a proposed response. There was a strong consensus in only five situations and almost equal disagreement in four. Only on issues of sexual behaviour, client dangerousness and revealing client identity was there wide agreement. It should be noted that these latter issues were the focus of recent APA code revisions and concerns (APA Committee on Ethics, 1986). Tymchuk et al. conclude, "What may be more useful for the professional are broader and more basic decision-making standards rather than specific rules that attempt to define behaviour as 'right' or 'wrong'" (p. 420). Students have indicated that because ethical dilemmas don't generate a simple solution, one cannot overestimate the importance of reviewing underlying ethical principles, as opposed to only considering specific rules of what constitutes a right or wrong behaviour.

When clients present problems involving human relationships, these will almost always involve some conflict among the values, rights and responsibilities of the psychologist, the client, related persons, one or more agencies, other professionals and the community at large. Van Hoose and Kottler (1977) consider values to involve attitudes that influence the way people respond to ideas, events and objects. Values are part of a person's identity (whether psychologist or client); behavioural decisions "involve conflicting demands, a weighing, a balancing and finally an action that reflects a multitude of forces" (p. 173). We know that values are present in any relationship and that psychologists must confront and deal with attitudes and values within the professional relationship, as well as the respective rights and responsibilities involved. It is important to clarify values in as many foreseeable areas as possible so that future clinicians will be prepared when such situations occur. The individual psychologist may be the ultimate decision-maker; but what is the basis of that decision? What is the "moral" position of the psychologist when making this ethical decision? How do educators design a curriculum to provide students with the necessary information and experience to become professionals?

Issues and Goals of Ethics Education

During the last 40 years, most clinical programmes have introduced an education in ethics requirement at least at the doctoral level. Most reported surveys, however, do not consider the goals, issues, philosophy or approach used in teaching ethics; they only report the number of hours spent on the subject or whether a course is offered. Little guidance is offered the counsellor attempting to decide what to do about Bob and Janet. Setting legal issues aside for the moment, from an ethical perspective, several behavioural questions need consideration in setting goals or defining issues:

1. What do psychologists *do* that is ethical, and how can this be reinforced?
2. What do psychologists *do* that is unethical, and how can this be corrected?
3. What do psychologists *believe* about how they should behave, and is this a legitimate part of an ethics course?
4. *What* is the "ethical reasoning process" by which decisions are made?

To answer these and other questions, I propose that any ethics education curriculum consider the following issues and goals:

1. *Sensitivity to ethical issues.* Before being able to discuss ethical dilemmas, psychologists must be aware a problem exists. Baldick (1980) found that 17% of interns had no exposure to ethical training and 21% had less than five hours in their entire graduate programme. Interns with training were significantly better in their ability to identify ethical issues in a series of dilemmas. Even the formal training group, however, could only identify about 19 of the 44 potential ethical issues embedded in the cases presented. Welfel and Lipsitz (1984) estimate that between 5% and 10% of mental health practitioners are substantially insensitive to the ethical dimensions of their work. If nothing more, then, a course needs to sensitize students to be aware that every action they take has ethical implications and alert them to look for potential problem areas. Kitchener (1986) calls this "moral empathy". Being conversant with ethical issues in the current psychological literature will assist in this awareness.
2. *Multiple solutions.* The ethical decision-making process may occur quite rapidly in many practical situations, especially when the vast majority of psychologists consider there is only one "right" answer (as in the question of whether a psychologist should have sexual relations with a client). However, many issues are more complex because they involve competing moral values or uncertainty about possible outcomes of specific acts. This is true of issues presently being considered by the APA Ethics Committee, such as advertising, bartering services, dual relationships and the like (APA, 1986), and of new or developing techniques for which professional standards have yet to be fully explored in light of existing standards. Psychologists need to be aware that in most situations there is more than one solution that can be considered ethical. Students must learn to cope with the anxiety associated with "moral ambiguity and uncertainty" in ethical dilemmas. Sometimes in the area of professional ethics no response is very satisfying, although more than one may meet the bare requirements of ethical behaviour. By contrast, there may be no solution that is obviously good and the ethical decision-making focuses on behaviour that is

the least harmful. Thus, no matter what choice we make, we won't necessarily "feel good" about our action!

3. *Competing values and moral principles.* Tymchuk et al. (1979) found that "clarification of values plays no integral part in graduate education" (p. 1170). Yet many have stressed the importance of clarifying values and feelings as part of ethics education, one of the first being Abeles (1980). Part of this includes the realization that "how truth is spoken in therapy is as morally relevant as what truth is spoken" (Jordan & Mara, 1990, p. 111). There are many conflicts between ethical principles (such as a counsellor's focus on beneficence, often in conflict with a client's right to autonomy) with little guidance as to the correct decision. Differences exist between code provisions, between codes of different professional associations, and between codes and the legal requirements of a particular jurisdiction (Bersoff, 1975; Huey, 1986; Mappes, Robb, & Engles, 1985). Students should also be aware of the potential conflicts between their professional code provisions and the rules of the institutions or agencies where they will be working.

4. *Decision-making process.* Ethics education must help students develop a means or process to resolve these dilemmas and conflicts. This includes the goal of developing a "moral judgment" capability in students and a "moral responsibility" to act. There needs to be both presentation and use of a variety of problem solving and decision-making models to achieve this goal.

5. *Professional norms.* What are the sources of input into the decision-making process, especially from a professional standpoint? Psychologists have developed standards and written them into ethical codes, standards of conduct or other position papers and statements referring to expected professional behaviour. These are sometimes related to specific issues, such as counselling women, but may be more generic statements, such as those dealing with fellow professionals or what is appropriate advertising. Such statements do not always directly involve ethical issues but also may reflect desired professional or business relationships.

6. *Consultation.* Psychologists need to be aware that at all times, consultation is important when making decisions that can have seri-

ous legal or ethical consequences. Consultation should result in better decisions; there will be a fuller exploration using a larger number of alternatives. While psychologists are not immune from lawsuits (as it has seemed in the past), the recent trend has been toward filing of ethical complaints with a provincial regulatory body. The ability to demonstrate serious consideration of a problem and consultation with other professionals before resolving it, goes a long way toward insulating a psychologist from punitive action.

In addition to these goals, the questions arise: How can these goals be best achieved? How should a course be taught? The formal courses reviewed in the Tymchuk survey used APA standards as the basic text, with additional coverage on research standards, confidentiality, right to treatment, professional and legal issues. Wefel and Lipsitz's review indicates that in addition to simply reviewing a code, many writers feel that "ethics education must broaden its base and include instruction in moral philosophy" (1983 b, p. 322). Consideration of personal values and the ability to reason on moral issues are considered essential. Fine and Ulrich (1988) recommended a meld of psychology and philosophy, while Kitchener (1986) suggested integrating current research on the psychological processes underlying moral behaviour and applied ethics with the ethical decision-making process. Jordan and Meara (1990) argue for the inclusion in ethical training of "virtue ethics" a focus on "who shall I be?" as a psychologist. This chapter proposes a blend of philosophical underpinnings and the presentation of case studies using a problem-solving decision-making process, part of which utilizes the new Canadian Psychological Association Code of Ethics for Psychologists (CPA, 1988; Eberlein, 1987, 1988 a, 1990 a). Before considering a proposed curriculum for ethics education, however, a brief historical review might help place ethics education into perspective.

An Historical Perspective

The first formal programme of ethics education for North American psychologists began in Canada. In 1947 the University of Ottawa included a regular ethical component in its counselling course, according to a 1956 survey by de Palma and Drake. This survey found professional training in ethics to be a recent phenomenon, which coincided with the emergence of clinical psychology as a separate emphasis in psychology. The most common opinion in 1956 was that ethics "can be handled best as part of a more inclusive course dealing with professional problems" (p. 555). The APA code of ethics and journals were the preferred sources of reference.

Canadian graduate programmes in psychology were surveyed by Pettifor and Pitcher (1982). They found 55% offered formal courses in ethics (more often than not a component of another course), while 30% offered ethics training only by informal methods. The remaining 15% did not believe ethics education was necessary. When material in ethics was required, it was usually mandatory only for clinical students.

Some psychologists have argued that no formal training in ethics is necessary, especially at a master's level, because an ethical problem will be handled in context and in conjunction with the student's supervisor. This assumes that students (or their supervisor) will recognize the existence of an ethical problem a factor often not true for the novice therapist. (The weakness in this position has been further discussed by Handelsman, 1986.) What if Bob and Janet's counsellors had never encountered the dilemma posited in these cases during their training experience?

Students and master's level graduates often are not bound by ethical guidelines because they belong to no professional association. There are often no licensure laws and such graduates may or may not work under the supervision of a psychologist who belongs to the CPA or is covered by a provincial regulating body. Psychology, however, must emphasize that any graduate student who intends to practise or aspires to be part of a profession should have more than a passing contact with professional issues.

While there is evidence of an increasing emphasis on education in ethics, there is little information in the literature about the content of such courses. Welfel and Lipsitz (1983 b) suggest more information and research are necessary. They ask, for example, what activities occur in these courses, do they have an impact on behaviour, do they sensitize practitioners, and which approaches are most effective? "How do practitioners, when recognizing an ethical dilemma, sort through the complex considerations involved in making ethical decisions?" (p. 321).

In designing an ethics course suitable for the training of professional psychologists at both the master's and doctoral level, two main themes have been identified through an examination of what has historically been considered important in such a course component. These themes are explored below, firstly under the heading of Role of Professional Codes, and secondly under the heading of Teaching Models. The interested reader may want to consider each model's strengths, weaknesses, commonalities and differences, and then evaluate what has been lacking in past programmes.

Role of Professional Codes in Ethics Education

Groups of practitioners striving to gain recognition and identification as professionals often initially adopt a "code of professional conduct". This is a poor substitute for a true code of ethics. The latter, which attempts to identify and make explicit a maturing profession's underlying values, provides behavioural expectations which follow from these values.

In 1953 the APA adopted its first ethical code which largely reflected desirable behaviour a teleological approach (Nagy, 1989). This code (later adopted with modifications by the CPA and most provincial bodies) has been revised and updated every few years as new issues were considered by the profession. A code of ethics "serves as a vehicle for professional identity and a mark of the maturity of the profession" (Mabe & Rollin, 1986, p. 294). The movement to certification and licensing required such a code be available and current, but in psychology the code was still largely a set of professional expectations or rules.

It does not necessarily follow that such a code will be useful for helping a psychologist develop an awareness of the moral and evaluative nature of moral reasoning in ethical decision making.

On the contrary, as one student has suggested, it might lessen awareness, especially when this is one of the ways the psychologist gains "recognition and identification" as a professional. The very existence of the code may confine the level of ethical awareness to an institutional or societal orientation and thus limit the awareness of ethical reasoning to the one stated within the code or demonstrated within a model.

The CPA reliance on the American model was changed in 1986 using a totally different approach to reflect an emphasis on moral or ethical principles (see Sinclair et al., 1987, and Chapter 8, this volume). About the time the new CPA code was adopted, the APA set up a revision task force, the goal of which was to create a new ethical code "which is more useful in decision-making, educational, and relevant to the work and lives of psychologists in every subspecialty area" (Nagy, 1989, p. 1). The APA (1990) organized its proposed code of 165 paragraphs under six principles, in part reflecting the Canadian model.

By contrast, the Canadian Committee desired a document that would be comprehensive, systematic and useful for educational purposes. It had to be integrated and more than a new or codified list of existing rules. The Committee adopted a structure based on four principles (reflecting the moral principles of autonomy, beneficence, nonmaleficence, justice and fidelity):

- Principle I: Respect for the Dignity of Persons (36 standards)
- Principle II: Responsible Caring (43 standards)
- Principle III: Integrity in Relationships (36 standards)
- Principle IV: Responsibility to Society (23 standards)

When compared with other professional codes, I consider the new Code of Ethics for Canadian Psychologists to be better organized, more coherent and more directly related to the underlying principles which psychologists need to consider. As a result it is more useful for a practising psychologist and offers a better educational tool than is true with most other existing codes.

The ordering of the four ethical principles and 138 standards provides both professional expectations and a focus for ethics education. There is an awareness of the moral and value issues involved when trying to reach a personal, ethically-oriented decision. In addition, the problem-solving or process approach involving the critical-evaluative level of moral reasoning is used by the CPA Ethics Committee. This is readily adaptable for use in a coherent, and extended course in ethics; for use during in-service training sessions; and for workshops emphasizing ethics and other professional issues.

The new CPA code also provides an opportunity to look at hypothetical situations and anticipate potential problems; it encourages discussion of the meaning and application of the four principles to these situations. This is what Tymchuk (1986) calls *ethics futurology*, the "anticipation of what would be appropriate in a given circumstance in the absence of other guides". (p. 39). New and emerging issues can be considered by evaluating possible alternatives in light of the four principles: Does the proposed action respect the dignity of the client and other persons involved? Is it responsible caring for these persons? Is the psychologist being accurate and honest? Does the proposed action promote the welfare of others and meet the psychologist's responsibility to society?

If all the answers are "yes", the alternative is probably ethical, even if may not be the most useful solution. If some of the answers are "no" or "uncertain", a further review of the conflicting values and code standards is required. The final resolution of such a dilemma may be based on personal conscience but there will have been an explicit review of the four principles.

Because these codes and decision-making processes stress the importance of ethics and moral reasoning, it is important for both the professional and student to maintain an open mind to question even these codes and models, not to select one pathway by overlooking or excluding other pathways.

Teaching Models Using Ethical or Moral Development

Abeles (1980) presented one model for a teaching seminar in ethics for clinical psychology doctoral students. This was a ten week seminar (three hours per week) with a regular course outline and assigned readings. With the use of critical incidents and readings covering a variety of relevant topics, students were challenged to look at their own values in responding to the material. Topics covered included assessment, therapist and client values, normality-abnormality, research, models and theories of counselling and psychothcrapy from a values perspective, and professional and training issues. The approach appears to be inter-personal and intellectually challenging rather than purely didactic, and does not appear to rely heavily on a specific Code of Ethics.

A somewhat different approach involves moral and value education and a philosophical focus on the decision-making process. Rest (1984), for example, proposes that there are four major interactive components which comprise the moral (ethical) decision-making process. Component I involves an awareness that a moral problem exists, imagining what courses of action are possible, and the consequences of each course of action and its effect on the welfare of each party involved. Component II invokes the decision-making process to identify the morally right or ideal response. Component III relates to personal values and involves choosing among courses of actions, each of which involves different values and motivations. Rest asks, "Would a person ever choose the moral alternative, especially if it involves sacrificing some personal interest or enduring some hardship?" (p. 25). Will a person choosing a highly moral action be able to put it into practice? Component IV of the process, the plan of action, will indicate to what extent the ethical ideal can or will be actually implemented. In effect, the action in component IV will indicate the ability or willingness of a person to put his or her words into practice.

Other educators have used the work of Kohlberg (1969) in the area of moral development to generate models for ethical growth and development (similar to child development) but there have been criticisms of this approach because of its emphasis on cognition (Gillon, 1979). Nonetheless, a developmental approach (with a cognitive emphasis) offers a useful basis for research (Welfel & Lipsitz, 1983a; 1983b). Proponents see ethical reasoning as a form of moral reasoning. Goldman and Arbuthnot (1979) describe a similar course designed for undergraduates entering medical school, the content of which includes ethical and professional problems that medical doctors actually experience.

Van Hoose and Paradise (1979) offer a developmental model which describes five levels of ethical thought (based upon Kohlberg): a punishment orientation, an institutional orientation, a societal orientation, an individual client orientation, and what the authors consider the highest moral or ethical orientation, one based upon principle or conscience. These are described as "qualitatively discrete stages" reflecting "an underlying continuum of ethical reasoning" (p. 37). To complement this model Van Hoose and Paradise (1979, pp. 113–160) have developed the Ethical Judgment Scale (EJS) which purports to measure a person's position on this continuum. While the EJS has limited value as a research tool (Doromal & Creamer, 1988), it has definite educational value in focusing discussion on 25 ethical dilemmas for psychologists (Eberlein, 1988 b).

Finally, Jordan and Meara (1990) have argued for the inclusion of "virtue ethics" in the ethics module. While ethical principles facilitate selection of appropriate answers to the question of "What do I do?" "virtue ethics" focuses on the question of "What shall I be?" This, they claim, helps explain why different, competent psychologists, using the same decision-making paradigm will choose different alternatives for action.

Ethics Education in the 1990s – A Personal Perspective

To achieve the education goals mentioned above, we need to look at both curricular content and the teaching process. Ten topic areas, including most professional issues of concern to current practising psychologists, are presented in Table 1. The subdivisions were designed to be included in ten 3-hour sessions of a regular semester course. The topics also can be used as a base for half-day, in-service programmes or longer workshops. A particular topic area can be emphasized and enlarged to meet the needs of a particular audience.

Source material for these topics can be found in books on ethics for psychologists, preferably those with a philosophical component (e. g. Carroll, Schneider & Wesley, 1985), a general legal compendium such as that provided for the National Register of Health Service Providers in Psychology (Stromberg, et al., 1988), special topic areas (e. g. *Marriage*, Huber & Baruth, 1987; *Behavior Modification*, Stolz, 1978; *Psychotherapy*, Thompson, 1990; *Business Practices*, Wood, 1988) and material provided by national and provincial psychological associations (e. g. CPA, 1988).

Some of the best content resources are students and workshop participants who can provide personal experiences and professional dilemmas for group resolution. A good example are the two dilemmas presented at the beginning of the chapter, both provided by students. There is also a substantial body of recent journal articles relevant to the above topics, in the current psychological literature. I prefer that students find and critically evaluate these articles. It helps them become familiar with the literature and encourages them to integrate the material with their own values and also share what is valuable with their peers.

An *ethical diary* can help in this respect, reflecting both readings and case material. As students work with clients they could keep a diary of their cases, recording ethical issues as they arise and how the student perceives and handles these issues. Such a diary with an ethical focus would help students clarify their own biases

The use of such a diary should sensitize students to ethical issues and may also help strengthen the problem-solving, decision-making process. The diary may lead students to be more aware of the values and biases which inhibit optimum care for certain clients, as well as their feelings about these clients, and help them put these into context when working out ethical decisions.

The ten topics and their presentation through lectures, readings, critiques, select cases and guest speakers requires a lot of time and represents a tremendous amount of information to be absorbed in a relatively short time. However, it is much easier to learn and retain information when that information has a high probability of affecting the student in the future as a practising professional. Students have commented that it is personally important for them to know both that they differ from others on a particular issue, but also, and perhaps more significantly, "*why*" do they differ? Small groups and class discussions can facilitate this knowledge. This is why, in teaching ethics, process is as important as content.

The Case Approach to Ethics and Professional Issues

The process component asks the question, how is content presented and how is it utilized in class sessions? The same issue is important for in-service sessions and professional workshops. The use of actual professional problems encourages a realistic appraisal of a specific professional issue in the context of the work environment. As one student suggested: "I consider the case approach to ethics training to be the most valuable component. It enables students to develop their 'sensitivity' to ethical problems, and also encourages the application of the decision-making tools in a nonthreatening context". Another student suggested it might be useful at the beginning of the course to present a case, have the students indicate their initial course of action and then document their "educated" course of action (perhaps over time) after discussion of the principles involved.

One of the more comprehensive sources for cases is *Ethics in Psychology: Professional Standards and Cases* (Keith-Spiegel & Koocher, 1985). The authors' experience on the APA ethics committee helped provide a comprehensive review of all areas of psychological practice; 385 actual cases illustrate the APA 1981 principles involved. In most of the cases, reasonable psychologists came to reasonable conclusions about the ethical judgments or behaviour involved. Although the book is an excellent guide to the thinking of professional ethics committees, it is not always helpful in resolving a particularly difficult issue, on which reasonable psychologists differ.

Many professions have adopted a mentor model or a case study approach for the education of those newly entering the field. Law and medicine, for example, used an apprenticeship model during their early years as a profession. More recently, law schools adopted and still use a case-law approach to teach basic legal principles and legal reasoning. Many business schools have also adopted a case study approach for use in their MBA programmes. Psychology training programmes and some texts (see e.g. Corey, 1991) combine some use of a "mentor" model in training clinical students with actual case material, both in the teaching of new trainees and in applying psychological theory to real problems.

The use of real cases is useful for the study of professional issues in psychology particularly if the cases involve one or more professional issues with one or more ethical dilemmas. Ethical cases abound in casebooks put out by professional associations (APA, 1987; Callis, 1976; CPA, 1988; Huber & Baruth, 1987) and in the professional literature. Many of these cases, however, do not offer real dilemmas dilemmas where different psychologists, each using the same ethical code and standards of behaviour, reach quite different conclusions about the appropriate course of action to take.

Psychology has not yet reached the point where we can always say, "there is only one course of action the psychologist can take". Psychology is still an art, as much as a science, where choices must be made by the individual psychologist. These choices are based on training and experience, and also on the moral beliefs and ethical values intrinsic to the individual psychologist. As a result, individuals will differ on their respective choices of action.

Neither is the profession static in its view of appropriate professional behaviour. Standards which were once ambiguous have been clarified and sharpened over time. As one example, in the United States, the Federal Trade Commission legally forced the APA to remove ethical restrictions on professional advertising. As another, through legislation, lawsuits and code revisions, it seems clear that sexual involvement with a client is now considered unacceptable professional behaviour and is often illegal conduct. Likewise, since the 1976 California legal decision in *Tarasoff*, psychologists are aware of a legal duty to identify reasonably foreseeable dangers and protect those endangered by acts of a psychologist's client. Psychologists are also mandated reporters of child abuse situations. While these standards may seem clear, specific cases can be found where the answer is not at once obvious. (This assumes that persons reading the case are willing to think about the case rather than choosing an action based upon a "knee-jerk" reaction or a literal, rigid decision process.) The cases of Bob and Janet should be considered in this light. These were provided by psychologists in training (modified to preserve privacy) and were seen by the trainees to represent real ethical dilemmas.

Groups of 3 or 4 participants can be asked to analyse these (or similar) cases based on a problem-solving model (see below) or an ethical principle approach. Both are valuable and necessary to broaden the base of ethical decision making. An alternative is to work through a series of graded cases that present more and more difficult dilemmas which tax and refine the student's decision-making ability.

An ethical or moral principle model seeks an analysis based on the principles of autonomy, beneficence, nonmaleficence, justice and fidelity. For example, can we preserve Bob and Janet's autonomy and right to privacy, while being sure no harm comes to the other teacher or Janet's children? What really is in the best short and long term interest of Janet's daughters? This model directs attention away from reliance for answers on specific ethical code standards to an understanding of the underlying ethical principles. Discussions focus on individual values relating to each principle, encouraging psychologists to consider their belief structures and personal value systems.

The goal of this approach is to move the study of ethics away from a purely abstract, cognitive perspective. Nevertheless, resolving real cases through group consensus or individual reflection still can remain abstract and cognitive to an inexperienced student, or even a professional not personally confronted by a particular ethical issue. In addition, the affective component merits consideration. Psychologists will have "feelings" about an issue when it directly affects them. How, then, can educators include *affect* as part of the decision-making process? Kilpatrick observes that even a balanced, "dispassionate discussion of values ... may habituate students to the notion that moral questions are merely intellectual problems rather than human problems that naturally call up strong emotion" (1986, p. 189).

Consider, for example, a discussion of the pitfalls when becoming personally involved with a client. Over time strong emotions often develop in what some call transference–countertransference issues between therapist and client. Can a student who hasn't had this experience make an adequate decision in an *affective* vacuum? If, as a group explores alternative actions that a therapist could have taken, will an experienced therapist readily and publicly discuss these experiences and the associated feelings? The challenge is one of achieving individual personal involvement in the discussion of real cases.

Problem-Solving Models

Several authors have developed problem-solving models, and these tend to involve a similar process, but with different emphases. Van Hoose and Paradise (1979), for example, suggest five steps, one of which looks to an external locus of control and asks: "Do any rules or guiding principles exist to help resolve the dilemma?" (p. 57). Keith-Spiegel and Koocher (1985) offer a useful eight-step model adapted from Tymchuk (1981). Included is step 7: "Present any evidence that the various consequences or benefits resulting from each decision will actually occur" (p. 20). Tymchuk (1986) provides an illustration of the ethical decision making process involving seven steps: who should participate, choice of alternatives, who should decide, which alternative to implement (including risk-benefit analysis), review, implementation and evaluation. Of particular importance is a review of the short-term, ongoing and long term consequences; and the psychological, social and economic costs. The CPA Ethics Committee proposed a seven-step process (Table 2), using ideas from both Tymchuk and Van Hoose, and included it in the preamble to the new code. The important final step is often left out of other models and requires a psychologist to assume responsibility for the consequences of the action taken.

Rather than relying solely on any of the above models, I have found it more useful to go back to the original questions used in developing the CPA Code (Sinclair, et al., 1987). These questions were asked of a number of psychologists responding to a series of dilemmas in an effort to discover the basis on which a course of action was recommended. I have modified these questions so as to partially replicate the process by which the CPA code was developed. These are the questions, then, for use when considering a dilemma:

1. Indicate the individuals and/or groups that need to be considered in arriving at a solution to the dilemma posed by the situation.
2. Take each of the individuals or groups that you feel should be considered and explain in detail what consideration each is owed and why, particularly in terms of the rights and responsibilities involved.
3. List 3, 4 or 5 reasonable, alternative courses of action.
4. Provide a risk-benefit analysis of each alternative considering: (a) the short-term, on-going and long-term consequences; and (b) the psychological, social and economic costs and benefits.
5. Defend your choice of one alternative (or sequence of steps).

Conclusion

Ethical dilemmas abound in the daily practice of our profession we either lack sensitivity to some of them or choose to avoid them. For example, most psychologists are generally aware of the legal and ethical concepts of confidentiality and informed consent (Everstine, et al., 1980). However, they may not be aware that 96% of clients want to be apprised of information pertaining to confidentiality, 46% before the first session (Miller & Thelan, 1986). Psychologists may also not sense the ethical dilemma present in the content and timing of discussions about confidentiality. They may assume that because a client enters into a relationship, the client has consented to whatever happens in the session and the way in which the psychologist uses the material later.

Ethical dilemmas exist. The dilemmas involve multiple solutions and involve conflicting values. Previous educational programmes often have been inadequate in providing students with a model to use for resolution of these dilemmas. The problem solving approach suggested here has been shown to be an effective educational tool. A recent study at the University of Victoria found that students exposed to a three-hour ethical decision-making workshop scored significantly higher on the quality of their ethical decisions than those without the practical experience (Gawthrop & Uhlemann, 1991). Even where a full course requirement is not practical, this suggests that psychologists will benefit from a shorter-term experience.

Currently all provincial associations provide workshop experiences for their members, and there is a trend toward attendance at such workshops to maintain certification as professional psychologists. The material discussed in this chapter should be of interest to those responsible for these continuing education programmes. Psychology educators have an obligation to students to make them aware of potential ethical pitfalls in the profession.

Two cases were presented at the beginning of this chapter, both of which involve the issue of confidentiality and whether the counsellor or therapist should break the promise of privacy made to the client at the beginning of counselling. In the one case courts (and some jurisdictions by statute) have proclaimed a duty to protect potential victims from harm. In the second case, all jurisdictions (with the exception of the Yukon Territory) mandate reporting of suspected child abuse. Is either of these a case in which confidentiality *must* be broken? What are the criteria that apply and who decides? An ethics education programme cannot determine the outcome in these cases, but students should be aware that a problem exists and the educational programme must provide ways to consider the dilemma and possible alternatives before action is taken. In the two situations presented, confidentiality should probably be compromised at least to the extent that the counsellor or therapist consult and work through the problem with another professional who is also bound by the promise of confidentiality. Legal and ethical principles must be applied to the cases, but the final decision will be based on the experience and judgment of the psychologist as a professional, including a personal value component.

A better educational programme, such as the one proposed, would address the issues of sensitivity to ethical issues, multiple solutions to a dilemma, the competing values involved in the problem, alternative decision-making processes, norms and expectations of the profession and appropriate consultation. Furthermore, both the content and process components of a programme would be specially tailored to meet the needs of students in training.

Acknowledgements

The author would like to thank the following for reading and commenting on an earlier draft of this chapter: Carole Sinclair, Chair of the CPA Ethics Committee, and the students Lynda Grant, John Hogg, Sandra Inamasu, Beverly Krest, Margaret Marean, Marie Mitchell and Sara Yarwood. Student comments or quotations in the chapter are attributable to these students.

References

Abeles, N. (1980). Teaching ethical principles by means of value confrontations. *Psychotherapy: Theory, Research and Practice, 17*, 384–391.

American Psychological Association, Report of the Ethics Committee. (1986). *American Psychologist, 41*, 694–697.

American Psychological Association. (1987). *Casebook on ethical principles of psychologists* (Rev. ed.). Washington, DC: Author.

American Psychological Association. (1990, June). Ethical principles revised. *Monitor, 21*(6), 28–32.

Baldick, T. L. (1980). Ethical discrimination ability of intern psychologists: A function of training in ethics. *Professional Psychology, 11*, 276–282.

Bersoff, D. N. (1975). Professional ethics and legal responsibilities: On the horns of a dilemma. *The Journal of School Psychology, 13*, 359–376.

Canadian Psychological Association. (1988). *Canadian Code of Ethics for Psychologists: Companion manual.* Old Chelsea, Quebec: Author.

Callis, R. (1976). *Ethical standards casebook* (2nd ed.). Washington, DC: American Personnel & Guidance Association.

Carroll, M. A., Schneider, H. G., & Wesley, G. R. (1985). *Ethics in the practice of psychology.* Englewood Cliffs: Prentice Hall.

Corey, G. (1991). *Case approach to counseling and psychotherapy.* Pacific Grove, CA: Brooks/Cole.

de Palma, N., & Drake, R. M. (1956). Professional ethics for graduate students in psychology. *American Psychologist, 11*, 554–557.

Doromal, Q. S., Jr., & Creamer, D. G. (1988). An evaluation of the Ethical Judgment Scale. *Journal of College Student Development, 29*, 151–157.

Eberlein, L. (1987). Introducing ethics to beginning psychologists: A problem-solving approach. *Professional Psychology: Research and Practice, 18*, 353–359.

Eberlein, L. (1988 a). The new CPA Code of Ethics for Canadian psychologists: An education and training perspective. *Canadian Psychology, 29*, 205–212.

Eberlein, L. (1988 b). The use of the Ethical Judgment Scale for ethics education. *Canadian Journal of Counselling, 22*, 242–245.

Eberlein, L. (1990 a). Client records: Ethical and legal considerations. *Canadian Psychology, 31*, 155–166.

Eberlein, L. (1990 b). *Course outline for Educational Psychology 597.* Edmonton: University of Alberta.

Everstine, L., Everstine, D. L., Heymann, G. M., True, R. H., Frey, D. H., Johnson, H. G., & Seiden, R. H. (1980). Privacy and confidentiality in psychotherapy. *American Psychologist, 35*, 828–840.

Fine, M. A., & Ulrich, L. P. (1988). Integrating psychology and philosophy in teaching a graduate course in ethics. *Professional Psychology: Research and Practice, 19*, 542–546.

Gawthrop, J. C., & Uhlemann, M. R. (1991). *Effects of the problem-solving approach in ethics teaching.* Unpublished manuscript, University of Victoria, Faculty of Education, Victoria, B.C.

Gillon, R. (1979). Commentary. *Journal of Medical Ethics, 5,* 180–181.

Goldman, S. A., & Arbuthnot, J. (1979). Teaching medical ethics: The cognitivedevelopmental approach. *Journal of Medical Ethics, 5,* 170–181.

Handelsman, M. M. (1986). Problems with ethics training by "osmosis". *Professional Psychology: Research and Practice, 17,* 371–372.

Huber, C. H., & Baruth, L. (1987). *Ethical, legal and professional issues in the practice of marriage and family therapy.* Columbus: Merrill.

Huey, W. C. (1986). Ethical concerns in school counseling. *Journal of Counseling and Development, 64,* 321–322.

Jordan, A. E., & Meara, N. M. (1990). Ethics and the professional practice of psychologists: The role of virtues and principles. *Professional Psychology: Reasearch and Practice, 21,* 107–114.

Keith-Spiegel, P., & Koocher, G. P. (1985). *Ethics in psychology: Professional standards and cases.* Hillsdale, NJ: Erlbaum.

Kilpatrick, W. K. (1986). Moral character, story-telling and virtue. In R. Knowles & G. McLean (Eds.), *Psychological foundations of moral education and character development* (pp. 183–199). New York: University Press of America.

Kitchener, K. S. (1984). Intuition, critical evaluation and ethical principles: The foundation for ethical decision in counseling psychology. *The Counseling Psychologist, 12*(3), 43–55.

Kitchener, K. S. (1986). Teaching applied ethics in counselor education: An integration of psychological processes and philosophical analysis. *Journal of Counseling and Development, 64*, 306–310.

Kohlberg, L. (1969). Stage and sequence: The cognitivedevelopmental approach to socialization. In D. Goslin (Ed.), *Handbook of socialization theory and research.* Chicago: RandMcNally.

Mabe, A. R., & Rollin, S. A. (1986). The role of a code of ethical standards in counseling. *Journal of Counseling and Development, 64*, 294–297.

Miller, D. J., & Thelen, M. H. (1986). Knowledge and beliefs about confidentiality in psychotherapy. *Professional Psychology: Research and Practice, 17*, 15–19.

Mappes, D. C., Robb, G. P., & Engels, D. W. (1985). Conflicts between ethics and law in counseling and psychotherapy. *Journal of Counseling and Development, 64*, 246–252.

Nagy, T. F. (1989). Revision of *The ethical principles of psychologists:* APA task force's progress report Three years later and ready for review. Paper presented at the Annual Convention of the American Psychological Association, August 11–15, 1989, New Orleans.

Pettifor, J. L., & Pitcher, S. W. (1982). Ethics training in Canadian graduate schools of psychology. *Canadian Psycholopy, 23,* 235–242.

Rest, J. R. (1984). Research on moral development: Implications for training counseling psychologists. *The Counseling Psychologist, 12*(3), 19–29.

Sinclair, C., Poizner, S., GilmourBarrett, K., & Randall, D. (1987). The development of a code of ethics for Canadian psychologists. *Canadian Psychology, 28,* 1–8.

Stolz, S. B. (1978). *Ethical issues in behavior modification.* San Francisco: Jossey-Bass.

Stromberg, C. D., et al. (1988). *The psychologist's legal handbook.* Washington, DC: The Council for the National Register of Health Service Providers in Psychology.

Tarasoff v. Regents of the University of California, 131 Cal. Rptr. 14, 551 P.2d 334 (1976).

Thompson, A. (1990). *Guide to ethical practice in psychotherapy.* New York: Wiley.

Tymchuk, A. J. (1981). Ethical decision making and psychological treatment. *Journal of Psychiatric Treatment and Evaluation, 3,* 507–513.

Tymchuk, A. J. (1986). Guidelines for ethical decision making. *Canadian Psychology, 27,* 36–43.

Tymchuk, A. J., Drapkin, R. S., Ackerman, A. B., Major, S. M., Coffman, E. W., & Baum, M. S. (1979). Survey of training in ethics in APAapproved clinical psychology programs. *American Psychologist, 34,* 1168–1170.

Tymchuk, A. J., Drapkin, R., MajorKingsley, S., Ackerman, A. B., Coffman, E. W., & Baum, M. S. (1982). Ethical decision making and psychologists' attitudes toward training in ethics. *Professional Psychology, 23,* 412–421.

Van Hoose, W. H., & Kottler, J. A. (1977). *Ethical and legal issues in counseling and psychotherapy.* San Francisco: JosseyBass.

Van Hoose, W. H., & Paradise, L. V. (1979). *Ethics in counseling and psychotherapy: Perspectives in issues and decision making.* Cranston, RI: Carroll Press.

Welfel, E. R., & Lipsitz, N. E. (1983a). Ethical orientation of counselors: Its relationship to moral reasoning and level of training. *Counselor Education and Supervision, 23,* 35–45.

Welfel, E. R., & Lipsitz, N. E. (1983 b). Wanted: A comprehensive approach to ethics research and education. *Counselor Education and Supervision, 22,* 320–332.

Welfel, E. R., & Lipsitz, N. E. (1984). The ethical behavior of professional psychologists: A critical analysis of the research. *The Counseling Psychologist, 12*(3), 31–41.

Wood, R. H. (1988). *Protecting your mental health practice: How to minimize legal and financial risk.* San Francisco: Jossey-Bass.

10

The Union of Regulatory and Fraternal Roles: The Professional Corporation Model of Regulation

Luc Granger
Université de Montrèal

The influence of regulation upon the practice and development of a profession depends largely upon the judicial tradition from which the regulatory process emanates. The fact that Canada, for instance, was originally founded by two groups of people belonging to two different political and judicial systems, greatly coloured the way in which professional psychology is regulated.

In 1774, eleven years after the signing of the "traite de Paris" (which gave England the control of what was formally called "La nouvelle France") the "Quebec Act" was passed by the British parliament. This event was in good part due to Sir Guy Carleton, who was later to become Lord Dorchester. The "Quebec Act" confirmed, among other things, the fact that the French Civil Code would still be applied in the new British colony and that much of the French civil tradition would be maintained. Despite the fact that this piece of Canadian history may appear rather irrelevant with regard to understanding the regulation of psychology in Canada, it is in fact highly pertinent. Contrary to what was to happen in the rest of the country, the Province of Quebec would thus still retain a civil code of law based to a large extent upon the French legal tradition instead of the British tradition of Common Law. When the new profession of "psychologist" was eventually to be regulated in Quebec two centuries later (1962) it would be done according to that French legal tradition. This tradition has created a system of professional regulation which in many ways parallels the systems in the other provinces, and yet is also very different.

Until 1972, all professions regulated in Quebec were done so by a private bill or act, as is still done in most of the other Canadian provinces. These bills in Quebec derive from the French model of the professional corporation, or guild, which follows a tradition dating back to the Middle Ages. In 1020, the dyers of the town of Tiel in the Netherlands founded one of the first guilds, and asked the King for a special charter. The dyers made this request for three main reasons: to increase their wealth, to obtain a royal privilege permitting them to avoid legal suits by taking an oath of honour, and to organize an annual meeting (Poirier, 1990). In exchange for a royal privilege which would grant them a monopoly on certain trades and professions, these professional corporations were responsible for the training of apprentices and for the quality control of the products and services they were providing.

In 1962 the Quebec Professional Corporation of Psychologists (the CPPQ) was established by a private bill in the Quebec legislature. It was established upon the same tradition as had been all previous professional corporations: in exchange for certain commercial or social privileges a professional group is responsible for controlling the admission into the profession, as well as the quality of the services provided by its membership.

Due to increasing complaints from the public that the professional corporations were promoting their own interests and protecting their own members, the State intervened. In 1973, following the recommendations of an inquiry commission, the government decided to put all the professional corporations under one "umbrella" law which would define their professional and social rights and responsibilities. This law is called the Professional Code (Government of Quebec, 1989). The Professional Code continues to maintain the principle of selfgovernment and selfcontrol by the profession itself, which was the main characteristic of the professional system. However, it also firmly established the protection of the public as the first and foremost mandate of the professional corporations. The principle function of the professional corporations therefore became the protection of the public, and not promoting the interests of the profession or of its practitioners, as had been traditional since the Middle Ages.

The Professional Code states that "The principal function of each corporation shall be to ensure the protection of the public. For this purpose it must in particular supervise the practice of the profession by its members" (Section 23). It also states (Section 28) that each corporation shall "consist of the professionals who are members of it, and shall be a corporation within the *meaning of the Civil Code*". As is evident from the wording of the law, this mandate does not preclude other kinds of activities that a particular corporation may choose to exercise. However, all other activities must remain subordinate to the main mandate, which is the protection of the public.

In Quebec the corporations were, therefore, officially given the role of regulatory boards without losing their right to remain, at the same time, fraternal organizations as long as this second role did not interfere with the first. This is not to say that in Quebec certain professions do not have separate fraternal organizations. However, these separate fraternal organizations function more as labour unions, usually bargaining with the government for higher fees and better working conditions. What this means for the profession of psychology in Quebec is that the CPPQ serves simultaneously as the regulatory board and as the fraternal organization. Two of the main functions of a fraternal organization in psychology are usually "public representations" and "lobbying efforts". The CPPQ, being both a regulatory body and a fraternal organization, has the right, therefore, to perform these dual activities.

The remainder of this chapter will demonstrate how a single organization can effectively assume the role of regulatory body and fraternal organization, and will show the consequences of such a situation on the development of professional psychology. The situation is not that different from that in several other provinces. British Columbia and New Brunswick, among others, have only one psychological organization which assumes both the regulatory and fraternal roles (American Association of State Psychology Boards, 1990). The uniqueness of the CPPQ stems from the fact that in 1972, when the Professional Code was adopted, the new corporation had to be built on the basis of the first one. This first corporation, which in 1962 was conceived along the model of the traditional professional corporation, was as preoccupied with the interest of its own members as with the protection of the public. The new CPPQ then had to start promoting the protection of the public as preponderant over the promotion of the profession.

The CPPQ as a Regulatory Body

The Professional Code gives the CPPQ three main regulatory powers in order to ensure that the public is well protected:

1. The CPPQ has a say in establishing the admission criteria to the profession.
2. It has the right to inspect psychologists to ensure maintenance of adequate standards of practice.
3. It can effect disciplinary actions when there is a breach of the Code of Ethics.

Each of these powers must be exercised according to the Professional Code, with the responsibility being assumed by the president and the CPPQ Board.

The president is elected by the members for a 2-year term, renewable without limit if he or she decides to run and is reelected. The Board comprises 20 members of the profession elected according to regional criteria (also for a 2-year term) and four lay persons appointed by the government (usually for a 3-year term).

Admission Criteria to the Profession

Section 184 of the Professional Code states that "the government1, after consulting with the Office, the Conseil des universités, the teaching establishments and the corporation concerned may, by regulation (a) determine which diplomas issued by the teaching establishments he indicates give access to a permit or a specialist's certificate."

With regards to psychology, the system works as follows: first the CPPQ establishes the minimum curricula requirements – in terms of academic credits in psychology and number of hours of practicum and internship – that should characterize an academic programme for it to be considered as giving access to the CPPQ and to the title of psychologist. These minimum requisites are then presented and discussed with the universities, which must decide at what graduate level (doctorate or master's) their programmes meet those criteria. They then inform the CPPQ of the exact denomination of each of their programmes which meet the criteria. A regulation proposal which nominally designates, for each university, the diplomas which give access to the CPPQ and the title of "psychologist" is subsequently presented for adoption by the CPPQ to the "Office des professions", the governmental agency responsible for supervising all professional corporations. As such, the criteria for diploma approval are based more upon the content of each diploma rather than upon the academic level of that diploma (i.e. master's vs. doctorate).

Two aspects of the curriculum-based admission process are worth mentioning. The first is that, contrary to popular belief, Quebec law does not state that a master's degree is *the* universal degree which permits access to the CPPQ and to the title of psychologist. The kind of diploma necessary for CPPQ membership will vary depending upon the specific curriculum of the university from which a student graduates. For example, if someone is graduating from the Department of Psychology at McGill University in Montreal, a PhD in clinical psychology is the necessary diploma for membership to the CPPQ The Department at McGill does not offer a terminal master's degree in Clinical psychology containing the minimum curriculum requirements deemed necessary by the CPPQ and has chosen to include these minimum requirements in the clinical PhD programme. If, on the other hand, a student graduates from the Department of Psychology at the Université de Montreal, the degree necessary for CPPQ admission and registration as a psychologist is an MPs (master of psychology)[1] degree or a PhD (researchintervention), depending upon the subspecialty that the student has chosen.

In reality, the admission requirements to the Quebec profession of psychology are multilevel criteria similar in structure to the requirements for the medical profession. An individual can be admitted into the Quebec "Corporation professionnelle des médecins" after having either 4 years of medical study and 2 years of family medicine, which will qualify him or her as a general practitioner, or 4 years of medical study and 4 years of specialization (e.g. psychiatry, cardiology or paediatrics), which will then give him or her a specialist's certificate. Similarly, an individual can be admitted to the CPPQ after fulfilling the necessary academic requirements, either through a specific master's-level programme (usually 2 years of study after a baccalaureate in psychology) or through a specific doctoral programme (usually 4 years of study after a baccalaureate in psychology). A graduate diploma (master's or doctorate) obtained from outside the province will be evaluated for the academic and professional suitability before being recognized by the CPPQ.

The second aspect to the admission process is that the principle mandate of the CPPQ is to establish the *minimum standards* necessary for public protection. In other words, those standards must guarantee that a newly admitted psychologist possesses the minimal skills necessary to provide a reasonably adequate service to the public. The curriculum requirements of the CPPQ are, there-

---

1 It is well worth mentioning that, due to the general structure of study in Quebec, particularly considering the existence of CEGEP, a student completing an applied master's programme has often accumulated almost as many credits from courses and internships in psychology as a student enrolled in a PhD programme in another province. The main difference is in the research thesis requirement, which is nonexistent or minimal for most applied psychology programmes.

fore, not established to ensure production of "ultimate" or "super" psychologists. This is not to say, however, that the curriculum requirements are substandard. The salient point is that the curriculum should reflect the demands which are minimally required in order to protect the public, a principle used in all jurisdictions across Canada. The differences between the different provincial regulations reflect the way in which each jurisdiction applies that general principle in different social and political contexts. It is important to note that the aforementioned principle does not preclude universities from offering optimal or maximal curricula. In fact, all the PhD-level diplomas which are listed in the admission regulation of the CPPQ usually contain more than is deemed necessary to meet the CPPQ's minimum requirements.

Inspection of the Members

Once the CPPQ has allowed an individual the right to the title "psychologist", it is obliged to oversee the member's professional competence. This obligation is accomplished by means of a professional inspection committee. Section 109 of the Professional Code states that "a professional inspection committee is established within each corporation". Section 112 states that "The committee shall supervise the practice of the profession by the members of the corporation and it shall in particular inspect their records, books, registers, medications, poisons, products, substances, apparatus, and equipment relating to such practice."

Because the Professional Code is a general law which covers over 40 professional corporations, some of the items mentioned in section 112 clearly do not apply to psychology. Nevertheless, the Code provides a clear mandate for the CPPQ and emphasizes its legal obligation to exert control over the practice of its members. This mandatory quality control is implemented by means of a controlled random process. A certain number of psychologists' names are chosen randomly each year according to certain criteria such as private practice vs. public service, urban vs. rural, etc. These criteria are established by the professional inspection committee with the approval of the Board. The selected psychologists must submit to a process of professional inspection. If any aspect of their practice is deemed unsatisfactory, the Board has the right to impose additional supervised training and to restrict certain areas of their practice for a designated time period.

Discipline

The CPPQ is also mandated to see that its members behave professionally and act in accordance with the Code of Ethics. This is ensured by the adoption of a mandatory Code of Ethics, according to Section 87 of the Professional Code, which states that:

> The Bureau [board of directors] must make, by regulations, a code of ethics governing the general and special duties of the professional toward the public, his clients and his profession, particularly the duty to discharge his professional obligations with integrity. Such code must contain, *inter alia:*
> (1) provisions determining which acts are derogatory to the dignity of the profession; (2) provisions defining , if applicable, the professions, trades, industries, businesses, offices or duty incompatible with the dignity or practice of the profession; (3) provisions to preserve the secrecy of confidential information that becomes known to the members of the corporation in the practice of their profession; (4) provisions respecting the right of any person having recourse to the services of a professional to take cognizance of the documents regarding him in any record made by the professional about him and to obtain copies of those documents.

If a person feels that a psychologist has acted in an unprofessional manner, a complaint must be filed with the secretary of the committee on discipline. This complaint will then be investigated by a special officer, called the "syndic". The syndic is appointed by the Board and is a member of the corporation. The syndic investigates the matter, and enforces the provision of any information or document relating to such enquiry (Sections 121–122). The syndic is granted immunity by the law (Section 193), and cannot be prosecuted for acts done in good faith during the performance of his or her duty. Based upon the results of the inquiry, the syndic decides whether a complaint is to be lodged before the discipline committee. The discipline committee is composed of two psychologists appointed by the Board and a lawyer appointed by the government who acts as chairperson. The discipline committee hearings are public except in situations where the committee decides that, in the interest of morality or public order, professional secrecy must be maintained and/or a person's privacy or reputation be protected. In such cases, the hearings are either held *in camera*, or the publication or release of information or related documents is banned (Section 142). It is interesting to note that the discipline committee has the same power as the Superior Court to subpoena witnesses to appear and answer, and to take punitive measures in case of refusal (Section 147). If the syndic decides against lodging a complaint, any individual can choose to bring the complaint before the discipline committee (Section 128).

The number of complaints for which an inquiry has been deemed necessary has remained relatively stable over the last 4 years (varying between 35 and 50 per year, with a mean of 39.5). The four main motives of complaint in the last 4 years have been:

1. Child custody evaluation (59)
2. Not following the standards of practice (13)
3. Breach of confidentiality (10)
4. Sexual abuse by the therapist (10)

(Corporation professionnelle des psychologues, 1987–88, 1988–89, 1989–90, 1990–91).

The CPPQ as a Fraternal Organization

As previously stated, the law does not preclude the CPPQ from exercising mandates which, in other jurisdictions, would usually fall within the domain of the fraternal organization. However, these mandates must always be exercised with the primary objective of protecting the public and supervising the practice of profession, although of course such activities may, in fact, help to promote the profession itself.

Over the last few years the successive presidents and Board members of the CPPQ have decided that the Corporation should broaden its concept of public protection. In view of the possible conflict of interest inherent between protection of the public and promotion of the profession, this issue was discussed at length. Some argued that any kind of promotional activities would violate the mandate of protection of the public. The issue was finally resolved in the following manner: in view of the fact that mental adjustment (in a broad sense) is considered by many to pose one of the greatest health concerns (Epp, 1988), professional psychology surely has a fundamental role in the management of such problems. It could then be argued that protecting the public not only means protecting the public from incompetent psychologists but also from charlatans. It was therefore argued that promotional activities would not be seen as conflicting with the mandate of protecting the public, as long as these activities always had the goal of providing the public with adequate information to help it make an informed choice.

It was then decided that, in addition to its usual regulatory role, the CPPQ should: (1) make sure that the highest quality of service is provided by its members; (2) make certain that the public is aware of those services; and (3) make sure that those service are readily available to the public.

The Quality of the Services

In addition to professional inspection and discipline, an effective measure to help psychologists maintain their competence is to provide them with good continuing education programmes. In order to do so, a knowledge of what psychologists do and what they need as part of their working environment is essential.

Over the last 10 years the number of psychologists in Quebec has doubled, with increasing diversification in the nature of their work. The recognition of specialties has therefore become a much discussed issue in Quebec, as in the rest of Canada (Canadian Psychological Association, 1988). After a lengthy analysis of the subject of specialization, the CPPQ Board concluded that, although likely desirable in the long run, it would be premature to establish legally codified specialties. To do so the CPPQ would have to ask the Government for permission to grant specialist's certificates. This would imply the adoption of very specific academic requirements for obtaining those certificates by a psychologist. In addition, this would produce a very restrictive definition of specialties, and also preclude any uncertified psychologist from presenting him- or herself as specializing in the field covered by a certificate.

The Corporation nevertheless did recognize the need for a supple structuring of the profession, so as to inform the public and organize continuing education activities, as well as to promote the development of the profession itself and, in the long run, the emergence of legally codified specialties. A policy concerning the regrouping of psychologist by fields of practice was subsequently adopted. According to that policy, to be officially defined as a field of practice by the board of CPPQ a field must: (1) have a sufficiently well specified clientele; (2) have a significant number of psychologists working in that area; and (3) be seen as necessitating a certain amount of specialized knowledge for a psychologist to work in the field.

With these criteria in mind, professional psychology as it is practised in Quebec was to be subdivided into different professional fields of practice.

To date, nine fields have been officially defined and recognized: Educational psychology, Clinical psychology, Industrial/organizational psychology, Mediation, Forensic psychology, Community psychology, Neuropsychology, Psychogerontology, and Teaching and Research. The delineation of new domains is ongoing, as advocated by continual professional development. Psychologists affiliated with these different fields are encouraged to structure themselves into special interest groups and to apply for financial and administrative support from the CPPQ to do so. In addition, they also receive support to organize continuing education workshops, to make public statements and to present briefs to the government requesting increased availability of psychological services in their respective fields.

This structuring of the profession is crucial as regards governmental lobbying and providing the CPPQ with the necessary expertise in informing the public. This structuring process in terms of professional domains or field also plays a fundamental role in overseeing the organization of continuing education programmes. The CPPQ offers support to more than 60 annual continuing education workshops, not counting the increasing number of continuing education workshops or seminars offered by hospitals, universities and private corporations. The CPPQ also negotiates with university departments of psychology for the organization of long-term continuing education programmes.

Public Representation

To permit the public to make informed choices with respect to professional services, the CPPQ must alert the public to the kind and quality of professional services that psychologists can provide. This information has been provided in a number of ways over the last few years. Leaflets have been disseminated to the general public informing them of the many aspects of a psychologist's role, helping them make appropriate choices for services and informing them of their rights if an inadequate choice has been made. Support and resources have been given to news media wanting to interview or present psychologist's work. The CPPQ, along with a number of other professional groups in the health domain, has even participated in the financing of a television series called "Comment ca va?", which explores the different facets of common health or behavioural concerns.

The CPPQ is also involved in widely publicized statements concerning events confronting the public (e.g. the testimony of small children against their parents in the criminal court, the sexual abuse of patients by health professionals and the psychological consequences of long term unemployment). The corporation also awards an annual prize to any group or person (from the political arena, the media or the general public) who makes a significant contribution to helping people take better care of their psychological health. This event is highly publicized, attracts much public attention and reinforces the importance of individual responsibility for psychological health.

The CPPQ has also joined forces with other interested groups to publicly address important social questions such as the overconsumption of medication by the elderly, violence in children's television broadcasting, a sexual abuse prevention programme for schoolage children and the psychosocial effects of unemployment. It is important to note that with these issues the CPPQ always delineated its primary involvement and expertise in terms of the psychological aspects of these concerns only.

How can the results of those actions be evaluated? In order to explore the public's perception of psychologists, in 1985 the CPPQ had a professional survey group ask a representative sample of the Quebec population the following question:

> If you were having personal problems that you were not able to solve by yourself, such as marital problems, depression, or sexual problems, which one of the five following specialists would you spontaneously consult?

The five professional groups mentioned were medical doctors, social workers, psychiatrists, psychologists and priests. This same question was asked again to a comparable sample 5 years later (Cote, 1991). Figure 1 shows the comparative results for the different professions during the 5-year interval. As we can see, in 1985 medical general practitioners were far ahead of the others in terms of public preference, with psychologists lagging quite far behind in second place (with a 10% difference). By 1990, the percentage of the sample choosing general practitioners and psychologists was virtually the same (37.1% vs. 36.9%). All groups *except* psychologists have decreased in public stature.

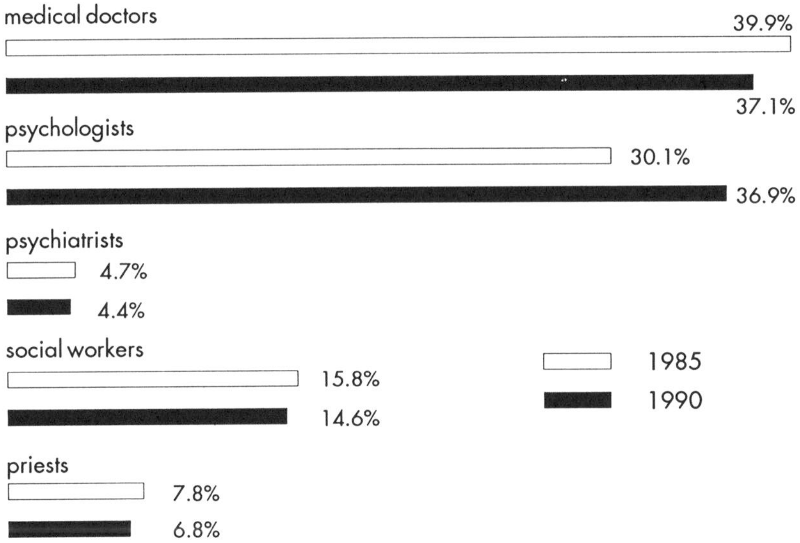

Figure 1. Evolution of public preference for five helping professions over a 5-year interval.

In addition, the 1990 survey asked individuals who had consulted a psychologist to specify the role each of the following played in their decision to consult: the confidentiality of the service provided, the quality of the human contact with a psychologist,

Figure 2. Percentage of people in the sample citing each of the five reasons as motivating their decision to consult a psychologist.

the reliability of the diagnosis, the absence of medication and the professional quality of the service provided.

Figure 2 shows the comparative results for these five reasons. It is worth noting that the professional aspects of the service provided (namely the confidentiality of the service, the reliability of the diagnosis and the general professionalism of the service) were the main determinants of the decision to consult.

The results of the 1990 survey also show that 31.3% (almost one third) of the Quebec population knew of someone who had consulted a psychologist, and that half of that percentage (15.4%) had themselves consulted one. The data indicate that psychologists currently enjoy a good deal of credibility, and that their competence and integrity make them soughtout professionals (Poirier, 1991).

Availability of Service

If people are convinced that psychological health is as important as physical health, an adequate service should be available to every citizen of our country. The CPPQ has invested much human and financial effort in the pursuit of this goal. The Corporation has ardently lobbied several bodies – the provincial government, the federal government (the GST collective effort), insurance companies and employers – in an effort to bring about increased availability of services to the public.

For some years now, the CPPQ has been continually present at different governmental levels, lobbying and submitting briefs to various parliamentary commissions on health, welfare, the school system, etc. In keeping with its general public position, the CPPQ always clearly circumscribes its expertise (and the expertise of its members) to the psychological domain of these varying issues. As such, the Corporation constantly limits its interventions and suggestions to the psychological aspects. It has been frequently pointed out by politicians that this type of welldefined involvement gives great credibility to an organization's public position. Consequently, this kind of input is considered to be much more professional than that of lobbying groups which take a public position on each and every aspect of a question without having the expertise to do so. It has also been pointed out that this role of "expert" should always characterize the lobbying of a professional corporation whose legal mandate is protection of the public.

In the course of recent years, briefs have been presented and lobbying efforts have been made regarding a range of issues: the reform of the health system, the reform of the welfare system, the reform of the law vis-à-vis "la protection de la jeunesse", the implementation of the law regarding international adoption, the question of the exceptions made by the minister for age of admission to school, the availability of a joint psychologist–lawyer mediational service instead of a court appearance in the case of a divorce, the crime prevention policies, the importance of film and video classification by age of viewers to name just a few.

The CPPQ and many individual psychologists have also taken upon themselves the responsibility of providing services which are not readily available. For example, in the case of the Polytechnique massacre in December 1989, the CPPQ mobilized a number of psychologists who offered free phone consultation to anyone in need. The same kind of effort was made during the Oka crisis in June, July and August 1990. Free consultation is also offered on Valentine's day each year, so that people can talk to a psychologist about any kind of problem they are experiencing. The CPPQ also organizes and supervises free services, offered by volunteer psychologists for different community groups.

The results of these efforts are beginning to materialize. Just a few years ago the CPPQ was mostly reactive and virtually ignored by the policy makers. Now, it is rapidly becoming an organization which is often consulted proactively by the government. For example, psychologists were recently included in Law 170, bearing on international adoption, as the only professionals, other than social workers (already included in the law), deemed qualified to produce the psychosocial evaluations required by that law (Corporation Professionnelle des psychologues, 1990–91).

The CPPQ as a Regulatory Body and Fraternal Organization: Consequences for the Profession

There are many effects accruing from the fact that the CPPQ is at the same time the regulatory and fraternal organization. Most of these ramifications, however, stem from the one principal consequence, which is that *all the registered psychologists in Quebec are also members of the same fraternal organization.*[2] This fact, combined with a particular regulatory aspect concerning the admission criteria to the profession in Quebec, makes the CPPQ the largest fraternal organization of registered psychologists in Canada, and one of the biggest in North America.

As already discussed, in Quebec the profession of psychology is a multilevel entry profession. The consequence of this situation is that the sociological profile of the profession is different in Quebec than in most of the other provinces and territories in the country. Because of the multilevel entry, many professionals who would not be registered as a psychologist in another province can be a member of the CPPQ and thus be considered as psychologists in Quebec. If we compare Quebec with Ontario, where there is a

2 There are some other fraternal organizations of psychologists in Quebec. One in particular is called the "Association des psychologues et chercheurs en psychologie", but their goals, means and social impact remain much more limited than those of the CPPQ.

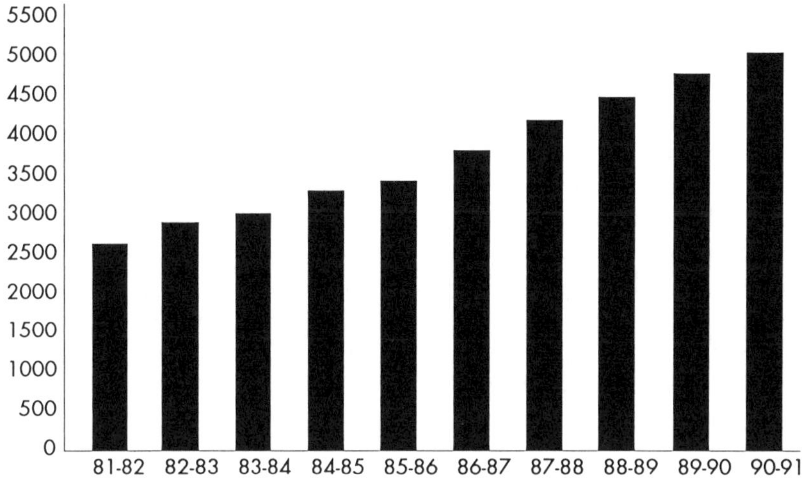

Figure 3. Number of registered psychologists in Quebec from 1981 to 1991.

strict PhD requirement for registration, there are about the same number of *doctoral-level psychologists* per capita in each province. The difference is that, in Quebec, the term "psychologist" encompasses a broader variety of professionals with a wide range of domains, but who will all have at least a master's degree in psychology and some supervised practical training. This situation has created a dramatic increase in the number of registered psychologists in the last ten years, as can be seen from Figure 3. One corollary of the increased membership is financial. With almost 5000 members and annual dues of $290, the CPPQ has an annual budget of almost $2,000,000 ($1,765,783 for 1990–91; Corporation Professionnelle des Psychologues, 1990–91). This budget gives the Corporation incredible financial means and manpower with which to pursue its various goals. There is money to maintain a full-time president and a central office with more than 14 full-time paid employees. A quick analysis of the annual reports of the last few years (Corporation Professionnelle des psychologues, 1988–89, 1989–90, 1990–91) shows that approximately one third of the budget is spent on regulatory business. This leaves two thirds for fraternal endeavours. These financial resources allow the organization to keep abreast of events in health, social and educational fields, at both provincial and federal levels.

A second consequence is that psychology, due to the huge number of psychologists in the market, is increasingly represented in a variety of surroundings. This increased exposure consequently helps to convince the public of the value of the services being provided by the psychological profession.

A third effect is that this huge number of psychologists has created a powerful political presence that can no longer be ignored by the provincial government. The CPPQ can, for example, easily organize a lobbying effort where, in a few days, almost all of Quebec MPs will have been met by one or more psychologists from each riding and informed of certain public consequences of intended governmental reforms.

Conclusion

The fact that the CPPQ is at the same time a regulatory and a fraternal organization has had a significant impact on the development of the profession in Quebec. It is clearly increasing the availability of high quality psychological services to the public of this province, and this reflected by the high public regard for the profession. Even if, at first glance, it may seem that the coexistence of the regulatory and fraternal side in the same professional organization may bring about serious ethical problems, the vitality and the popularity of professional psychology in Quebec proves that this is not necessarily the case. The important point to emphasize is that, if the union is to be successful, the fraternal activities must always remain subordinate to the goal of providing better public professional services.

References

American Association of State Psychology Board (1990). *Handbook of Licencing and Certification Requirements for Psychologists in North America.* Montgomery: AASPB.

Cote, D. (1991). Les révélations d'un sondage. *Psychologie Quebec*, *8*, 1.

Corporation Professionnelle des psychologues. (1987–88). *Rapport Annuel 1987–88*. Outremont: CPPQ.

Corporation Professionnelle des psychologues. (1988–89). *Rapport Annuel 1988–89*. Outremont: CPPQ.

Corporation Professionnelle des psychologues. (1989–90). *Rapport Annuel 1989–90*. Outremont: CPPQ.

Corporation Professionnelle des psychologues. (1990–91). *Rapport Annuel 1990–91*. Outremont: CPPQ.

Epp J. (1988). *La santé mentale des canadiens: Vers un juste équilibre*. Ottawa: Ministre de la santé nationale et du bien être social.

Government of Quebec (1988) *Professional Code, R.S.Q. Chapter C26*. Quebec: Editeur officiel du Quebec.

Poirier, M. (1990). Qui dort dine. *Psychologie Quebec*, *7*, 2.

Poirier, M. (1991). L'image publique du psychologue. *Psychologie Quebec*, *8*, 2.

Ritchie, P. L., Hogan ,T.P., & Hogan, T.V. (Eds.). (1988) *Psychology in Canada: The state of the discipline, 1984*. Ottawa: Canadian Psychological Association.

IV

Applications of Professional Psychology to Canadian Society

11

Applications of Psychology to Health Care

Margaret T. Hearn
University Hospital, London, Ontario

David R. Evans
University of Western Ontario

The Nature and Scope of Applications

A major conceptual shift in the definition of health occurred at the International Health Conference held in New York on 22 July 1946, when the representatives of 61 nations signed the Constitution of the World Health Organization (World Health Organization, 1970). In the Constitution nine principles were included as basic to "... the happiness, harmonious relations and security of all peoples" (World Health Organization, 1970, p. 1). Among these principles were the following:

- "Health is a state of complete physical, mental and social well-being and not merely the absence of disease or infirmity."
  and

– "The extension to all peoples of the benefits of medical, psychological and related knowledge is essential to the fullest attainment of health."

With the acceptance of these principles, the 61 nations established the World Health Organization under the terms of Article 57 of the Charter of the United Nations. Thus, the importance of applications of psychology to health care was recognized.

However, it took almost another quarter century for psychologists to act upon this conceptual shift in any significant way. In a review of the development of health psychology around the world, Stone (1990) indicated that "Suddenly, in the last years of the 1960s, a number of psychologists noticed that there were vast territories in the health system that were psychologically underdeveloped" (p. 14). In Canada during this period similar arguments were being made at provincial and national meetings of psychologists (R. G. Berry, personal communication, December 20, 1990).

Health psychology is considered by most to describe the application of psychology to health care, and hence the two phrases can be used interchangeably (Matarazzo, 1987; Webster, 1967). The definition most widely cited and ascribed to is that of the American Psychological Association, Division of Health Psychology. This definition is as follows:

> Health psychology is the aggregate of the specific educational, scientific, and professional contributions of the discipline of psychology to the promotion and maintenance of health, the prevention and treatment of illness, the identification of etiologic and diagnostic correlates of health, illness and related dysfunction, and the analysis and improvement of the health care system and health policy formation. (Stone, 1990, p. 5).

One further definition is that included in early versions of the Canadian Register of Health Service Providers in Psychology (1988):

> A 'Health Service Provider in Psychology' ... is a psychologist ... whose professional practice includes the delivery of health promotion, or preventive services, or direct assessment and therapeutic interventions services to individuals, couples, families, or groups whose growth, adjustment, or functioning is actually impaired or is demonstrably at risk for impairment. (p. 11).

There are a number of ways in which the application of psychology to health care can be conceptualized within the above definitions. First, there is the model outlined by Dunn (1986), who visualizes psychologists providing clinical services, consulting, teaching, and doing research focused on the health care system, other health care providers, and patients. In his article he presents these functions and foci in matrix form with examples (Dunn, 1986, p. 47). Second, Peters (1988) envisages three approaches to health care, treatment/rehabilitation, prevention, and promotion directed toward three domains of health: physical, mental, and social. He views health psychology as confined to the physical domain of health. Third, there is the position of Kaplan (1990), who after reviewing several models in health psychology, including the biomedical and biopsychosocial models, advocated the behavioural model. He argues that "Health outcomes are behavioral, and one way to modify them is to modify behavior" (p. 1218). He goes on to argue that "Medicines, surgeries, and behavioral interventions are complementary methods of enhancing behavioral health outcomes. Often one alternative is superior in terms of efficacy and efficiency.... Ultimately, treatments should be favored if they produce the most benefit at the lowest cost" (p. 1218).

No doubt the application of psychology to health care lies in a synthesis of these three positions in which psychologists concentrate on clinical service, consulting, teaching and research at all levels of the health care system directed toward intervention, prevention and health promotion with the goal of enhancing physical, psychological and social well-being.

There have been few surveys of the activities of psychologists in Canada. As a result it is hard to determine the number of psychologists, who are involved either full time or part time in health care. Martin, Ritchie and Sabourin (1988) in preparation for Opinicon II, 'The State of the Discipline Review for Psychology' held in 1984, surveyed some 7,000 practising psychologists in Canada. A total of 1,085 (15.5%) responded to the survey. Of those who responded it was estimated that 138 (13.4%) were employed in health care settings, and another 184 (17.9%) were employed in mental health care facilities. Hunsley and Lefebvre (1990) sent a 13-page questionnaire to a random sample of 300 listees in the 1988 Canadian Register of Health Service Providers. A total of 88 (29.3%) of the sample responded. In this survey

12.5% of the respondents indicated that their primary institutional affiliation was to a general hospital, and 6.8% indicated their secondary institutional affiliation was to a general hospital. It is difficult to place much confidence in either study because of the low response rate.

To gain a more precise estimate of the number of psychologists in the country engaged in health care facilities the registers of each province were reviewed. The total number of psychologists resident in each province was determined, along with the number of psychologists indicating their institutional affiliation as a health care facility. A health care facility was any general hospital, or any nonhospital setting modified by the term health. These data are shown in Table 1. The data for Quebec and Ontario were extrapolated from recent surveys carried out by OBEP and CPPQ. In order to gain more accurate national data it would be helpful if all regulatory bodies did an annual survey of the psychologists in their jurisdiction. Using these data, the average number of psychologists in health care settings across the country is 17%, with above average levels in Ontario, Quebec, and Newfoundland, and below average levels in the remaining provinces and territories.

Table 1. Canadian psychologists in health care.

Province	No. of resident registered psychologists	No. of psychologists in health care[1]
British Columbia	788	63 (9%)
Alberta	1487	No data
Saskatchewan	80	5 (8%)
Manitoba	128	12 (9%)
Ontario	1610	336 (21%)
Quebec	4133	767 (19%)
New Brunswick	140	11 (8%)
Nova Scotia	226	31 (14%)
P.E.I.	13	0.5
Newfoundland	69	17 (25%)
Territories[2]	8	0.5 (6%)
Total	7174	1243 (17%)

[1]These data do not include persons providing mental health services, nor do they include any estimate of the number of private practitioners providing exclusively health care.
[2]Data were available for the Northwest Territories only.

History and Development

Although a history of academic psychology in Canada has emerged (Wright & Myers, 1982), there is little documentation about the history of applied psychology and even less about the history of health care psychology. In the United States, an extensive body of knowledge about health care psychology and psychologists has resulted from information collected by the American Psychological Association (APA) and the divisions of health psychology and rehabilitation psychology. In Canada, the Canadian Psychological Association (CPA) has neither been funded nor had the internal resources to collect such information from health care psychologists.

The proliferation of psychologists in health care settings over recent years may leave the impression that psychology is a new profession to the health care system. To believe this is to deny the contributions of psychology to medical education and practice during this century (Matheson, 1983). As occurred in the United States, the initial entry of psychology into the field of health care practice was through medicine, specifically through medical schools. The difficulty that psychology had in defining its role within medical schools is outlined by Bott (1928), professor of psychology and director of the psychological laboratory at University of Toronto. In his paper he noted the lack of responses from Canadian schools to a survey on the status of psychology in medical schools in 1911. Although the emphasis in medical schools in Canada was increasingly on scientific, clinical, and research aspects of disease, there were attempts by psychologists to emphasize the importance of human factors. Bott (1928) described the important role of the Psychology Department at the University of Toronto in developing a medical school programme which stressed the importance of psychological factors in life adjustments. Associated with this training were a number of settings where students were placed and among which was the Department of Health.

Not only did psychology have difficulty in defining its role within medical schools, difficulty was encountered also in defining its place within health care. According to Matheson (1983), the difficulty that psychology had in developing as a profession in the health care field was twofold. One reason was the emphasis placed by the medical profession on "germ theory", which led to the exclusion of psychological and social factors from the field of health. The other reason was the more academic experimental orientation of psychology, which was perceived as having limited relevance to health care. These two factors inhibited the development of professional psychology in Canada for some years.

Because of the central role that hospitals play in health care, no discussion of health psychology can occur without reference to the development of departments of psychology within the general hospital system. A review of the available literature yielded little information on the history of departments of psychology within general hospitals, or on the recent status of such departments. Accordingly, a sample of hospitals across the country (see Appendix A) was contacted in an effort to obtain this information. The hospitals surveyed were not randomly chosen or inclusive of all hospital departments. Rather, an attempt was made to include general hospitals in each province with identified psychology service units that reflected the type and variety of psychological services available. Directors of psychology departments in the general hospitals surveyed were asked to outline the number and service assignments of their staff, and the status of quality assurance and internship activities. They were asked also to comment on the research activities of their staff and the nature of future plans for their departments. Only the history component of the survey will be addressed here. The information pertinent to other issues will be included as it is discussed.

Psychology departments in Canadian public hospitals came into being in a variety of ways. By far, the largest number of departments have their origins in departments or divisions of psychiatry. A few departments have their origins in rehabilitation programmes developed for war veterans. Others began as laboratories for university programmes, or were associated with child guidance clinics/paediatric facilities. More recently, psychology departments have been set up as independent units of new hospitals, or as the result of an amalgamation of separate divisions or units of psychology within or between hospitals.

Of the hospitals contacted, the earliest health service by psychologists to patients was reported for Toronto General Hospital, now part of The Toronto Hospitals (Goldsmith, personal communication, November 1990; Myers, 1974). Subsequent to World War I, E. A. Bott was invited by the then superintendent of the Toronto General Hospital to set up a rehabilitation programme for disabled veterans. The programme, initially set up in the psychology laboratory at the University of Toronto, and later transferred to Hart House at the University of Toronto and the Christie Street Hospital, included psychological testing and training in the use of prosthetics and the retraining of transplanted muscles.

By 1948, a consultation service, including a number of fulltime psychology staff and headed by Dr. Morgan Wright, was established within the Department of Medicine at Toronto General Hospital. Activities of this service were broadbased and included not only assessment and treatment but also the identification of factors associated with healing. In pursuit of the latter, studies were undertaken to evaluate the effect of the hospital environment on patient care. The studies revealed environmental factors associated with healing, and the information arising from the study was used by other hospitals.

While the application of psychology to the rehabilitation of World War I veterans appears limited to the Toronto General Hospital, the post-Second World War involvement of psychologists was more extensive. There were psychologists associated with such hospitals as Camp Hill in Halifax, Sunybrook in Toronto, Westminster in London, and Colonel Belcher in Calgary. These psychologists were originally located in psychiatry departments until the federal government divested itself of these facilities in the 1970s. Over time these departments have been integrated into larger independent departments of psychology within amalgamated health centres.

The first volume of the *Canadian Psychologist* appeared in 1951, and a perusal of its contents throughout the 1950s gives evidence of the link between psychology and health care. Positions for psychologists in general hospitals are advertised in various provinces, and reports of presentations on health care topics are found in the programmes of the CPA annual meeting. The 1951 programme contained a paper reporting a survey of chronic disease (Canadian Psychological Association, 1951). The 1952 annual proceedings included papers on psychology in a general hospital and pain (Canadian Psychological Association, 1952). The 1955 conference listed papers on arthritis, pain, multiple sclerosis and skin diseases (Canadian Psychological Association, 1955).

Psychology was represented also in the public and political arena with respect to health issues. In 1951, the *Canadian Psychologist* reported the appointment of a Nova Scotia psychologist to the Prince Edward Island Department of Health. The participation of a psychologist on a panel to discuss constructive employee health programmes was reported in the Bulletin of the Maritime Psychological Association (Maritime Psychological Association, 1956). The topic of the panel was "Building a Healthy Working Team". In 1961, the CPA was requested to submit a brief to a Royal Commission on Health Services, appointed to inquire into existing health facilities and their future needs (Douglas, 1960).

During the 1950s, psychology developed closer links with health. A name that is featured consistently with this growth is that of Morgan Wright. Associated with the early development of the Psychology Department within Medicine at Toronto General Hospital, Dr. Wright then became a consultant to a Medical Arts Clinic in Regina, where he worked with forty five physicians who wished the expert advice of a psychological consultant "to round out their diagnostic needs" (Wright, 1955). Among the requirements listed for the position were history taking, knowledge of the community, counselling and psychotherapy skills, and an internship in a general hospital, which was considered a much preferred and relevant placement to a psychiatric setting. In 1957, Dr. Wright moved to the Psychology Department at the University of Manitoba, with a joint appointment in psychiatry. From this position he established the Psychology Department that is today part of the Health Sciences Centre in Winnipeg.

During the 1950s and 1960s, psychology departments began to increase in numbers in general hospitals. As occurred in the Health Sciences Centre in Winnipeg, many psychology departments originated within divisions of psychiatry. The Jewish General Hospital in Montreal listed five staff positions in *The Canadian Psychologist* in 1963. In some instances, departments that were functioning at a more autonomous level found themselves absorbed into departments of psychiatry for periods of time. This occurred at both Toronto General Hospital and the University Hospital, Saskatoon. In other provinces however, notably Nova Scotia (Canadian

Psychological Association, 1958), psychology departments were established as separate departments and administered as such as early as 1947.

Two factors appeared to influence the development of psychology departments as autonomous entities. One factor was the number of psychology staff. As the number of psychologists employed by a hospital grew, it became difficult to accommodate them within departments of psychiatry. In some instances this led to the demise of psychology. In other instances psychology was given autonomy within psychiatry or advocated successfully to report directly to hospital administration. The other influential factor was the move toward the establishment of independence of departments of psychology when new hospitals were established. This began in the 1960s, and since then the practice of setting up independent departments of psychology reporting directly to hospital administrations has spread.

During the 1970s, the inherent limitations of the bioscientific approach to medicine which had dominated the field since 1911 began to be recognized (Matheson, 1983). A key issue in this recognition was the awareness of the very limited increase in life expectancy that had occurred since 1950 in spite of large expenditures of capital on the bioscientific approach (Lalonde, 1974; Hetzel, 1980; Barsky, 1988). Public acknowledgement that substantial increases in health care costs had little impact on life expectancy led to a reorientation within medicine, from a focus on reduction of morbidity to that of improving quality of life. This move from an emphasis on adding years of life to adding life to years facilitated the emergence of clinical health psychology. Liaisons between psychology and medicine have become commonplace, and increasing numbers of psychologists work with physicians and their traditional patient populations (Burstein & Loucks, 1982). The advent of health care psychologists with expertise in particular medical areas, for example, neurology, geriatrics and pain, is reflected in the development of CPA sections. Section 8, health psychology, was formed in 1980; section 17, gerontology, was formed in 1985; and section 23, neuropsychology, was formed in 1987.

In addition to those health care psychologists who work in health facilities, there are a large group of psychologists who carry out health-related service activities in private practice. One of the earliest recorded examples of such work is described by Wright (1960), who outlined the activities of a group of psychologists in Hamilton. They accepted referrals from medical practitioners and occupational/vocational settings. Among the referrals listed were head injury assessments, treatment of a psychosomatic ulcer and liaison with a rehabilitation programme.

The Nature of Practice

A number of developments in the last decade have affected the practice of health psychologists. Among these are the following:

- *The inclusion of psychology in national and provincial legislation empowering psychologists and increasing their scope of practice.* One example of this is the exemption from the Goods and Services Tax of psychological services delivered by psychologists listed in the Canadian Register of Health Service Providers in Psychology (CRHSPP). Other examples are the inclusion of psychologists among those responsible for monitoring a client's ability to drive under the Motor Vehicle Act in British Columbia, and the recognition in Ontario of the prime therapeutic role played by psychologists in the rehabilitation of those affected by motor vehicle accidents under the Insurance Act.
- *The development of standards for reviewing psychology departments as part of the process by which the Canadian Council on Health Facilities Accreditation (CCHFA) accredits hospitals.* Developed for the Canadian Psychological Association in 1981 by an Ontario Psychological Association subcommittee, the CCHFA standards for psychology were utilized first in 1984, establishing minimal quality assurance standards under which a hospital psychology department could operate. Recent revisions to these standards (1989) require psychology services to be organized under a qualified psychologist who reports directly to senior management, specify that qualifications of the director of the service and staff psychologists include listing in CRHSPP, and provide for heightened standards of operation

and more involvement for psychologists in the decision-making process.

- *The development of standards by the Canadian Psychological Association (1984) for accrediting internship programmes in hospitals*, thus establishing a national level of internship training.
- *The development of workload measurement systems enabling the cost efficiency of psychology services to be examined and improved.* Although individual hospital psychology departments have utilized various workload measurement models for some years, including the Measurement Information Systems (MIS) resulting from a cost-shared venture of the federal and provincial governments and the provincial hospital associations, there has been no universally accepted model, and hence no comparable data. One exception to this was a comparison of psychologists in Canadian pain centres (von Bayer & Genest, 1985). In 1988, under the auspices of Health and Welfare Canada and with the cooperation of the Canadian Psychological Association, the National Hospital Productivity Improvement Program (NHPIP) formed a national group of psychologists representing general, children's, rehabilitation, psychiatric and chronic care hospitals. The task of the group was to develop a workload measurement system for psychology that could be used in a variety of facilities. This project is now at the field testing stage and has become the mandate of the newly formed Management Information Systems (MIS) group formed as a result of a merger of the NHPIP group with the MIS group.
- *Organization of health care psychologists into interest groups for the purpose of improving clinical, research, and organizational functions.* These include the various health sections of CPA and organizations of chief psychologists such as the Ontario Chief Psychologists Association (OCPA). The latter was formed in 1983 and incorporated in 1987 for the purpose of supporting chief psychologists in developing and improving the practice of applied psychology in hospitals governed by the Public Hospitals Act.

Two surveys of psychologists involved in the practice of health care have been undertaken in recent years. A survey of psychologists in Canadian medical schools (Arnett & Martin, 1981) examining the professional activity of this group reported that psychodiagnosis and therapy accounted for 22% of the staff psychologist's time, in comparison with 16% for formal and informal teaching activities and 27% for research. Further information about the nature of these activities was beyond the scope of the survey. The most detailed information on hospital psychology resulted from a comprehensive examination in 1982 of hospital psychology in Canada (Arnett, Martin, Streiner, & Goodman, 1987). Of the 493 Canadian hospitals surveyed, 340 (69%) responded, and 184 (54%) reported psychologists on staff. Information reported included type of hospital, numbers of staff, administrative and organizational models and issues, reimbursement, professional and academic status of staff, and clinical, research, and teaching activities. The hospitals responding included general (61%), psychiatric (14%), children's (4%), rehabilitation (4%), chronic care (2%), and geriatric (1%). Involvement of psychologists in clinical service and research was reported for a wide range of health care areas that were once regarded as the exclusive domain of medicine (Arnett et al., 1987).

In order to provide more recent information on current activities of psychologists in general hospitals, including teaching and children's hospitals, the facilities listed in Appendix A were surveyed as indicated earlier. In the survey 29 hospitals were contacted and agreed to participate. The sample of 29 hospitals employed 408 psychology personnel, for an average of 1 full-time equivalent staff member for every 47 beds. There was great variability in hospitals with respect to staffing levels. Active outpatient clinics and involvement of staff in community programmes was more predictive of department size than was number of hospital beds. No attempt was made to categorize numbers of staff by academic degree. However, many respondents made reference to the high proportion of doctoral-level psychologists employed.

In the hospitals surveyed it was very common for psychologists to be assigned to specific areas of service. In some teaching hospitals these areas of service were referred to as "Institutes" or "Centres of Excellence". As well, many psychology departments had developed some specific programmes of their own, for example, pain, biobehavioural or industry-oriented programmes to which patients were referred from both within and without the hospital. In some instances these programmes are revenue gener-

Table 2. Clinical areas serviced by general hospital psychologists.

Adolescent medicine	Enuresis	Occupational health
Affective disorders	Epilepsy	Oncology
Anaesthesiology	Exercise/nutrition	Orthopaedics
Behaviour therapy	Facial maxillary	Pain
Biobehavioural	Family court clinic	Perinatal
Biochemical disease	Forensic	Psychoeducational
Brain tumour	Gastroenterology	Psychosomatic medicine
Burns	Geriatric	Psychiatry
Cardiovascular disorders	Haematology	Rehabilitation
Child abuse	Headache	Renal dialysis
Child and family	Hearing impaired	Respiratory
Child development	HIV (AIDS)	Rheumatic diseases
Parenting education	Home care development	Sexual abuse
Cranial-facial	Infant/parent	Sexual disorders
Cystic fibrosis	ICU	Sleep disorders
Developmentally handicapped	Internal medicine	Smoking
Diabetes	Liaison	Social skills
Eating disorders	Memory dysfunction	Stress disorders
Emergency	Myelomeningocele	Visually impaired
Employee assistance	Multiple sclerosis	Weight control
Encopresis	Neonatology	Workers' compensation
Endocrine	Neurology/neurosurgery	

ating for the department, and are perceived as the direction in which psychology must proceed if it is to establish a secure future role in health care. In general hospitals which were exclusively devoted to children, clinical practice tended to be divided evenly between models where the practice was to allocate psychologists to services and models where the practice was to centralize referrals and then develop specific psychological programmes to meet the overall needs of the various patient populations.

Overall, survey data indicated that 37% of psychology staff provide services that are mental health or psychiatrically oriented, 41% provide service to defined medical areas, and 22% provide services described as primarily neuropsychological in focus. As well, a number of general hospital psychology departments have staff affiliated with external programmes such as court clinics, employee assistance programmes, and workers compensation clinics. An overview of clinics/services/units in which psychologists function is found in Table 2. The large number of these services is a clear indication of the degree to which hospital psychologists have become involved in the health care field.

Table 3. Characteristics of general hospital departments surveyed.

Independent department of psychology	24 (83%)
Section of psychiatry	5 (17%)
Active quality assurance programmes	23 (83%)
One-year internship (majority paid)	22 (76%)
APA/CPA approved internship	4 (14%)
CPA only approved internship	4 (14%)
Pre-site visit by APA/CPA	2 (7%)
Active research programmes	22 (76%)

Only two administrative/organizational models within which psychologists work were identified in the current survey (see Table 3). Independent departments of psychology with direct accountability to an administrative officer of the hospital were reported by 83% of the hospitals, while departments of psychology that are organized as divisions or sections of psychiatry were reported by the remaining 17%. Of the five hospitals reporting the latter model, one indicated that the setting up of an autonomous department was underway. A number of departments surveyed commented on the growth of psychology as a department since gaining autonomy or as a result of the integration of scattered psychological services in their facilities into a viable department better able to plan and offer service to the hospital. In both of these instances, the establishment of a psychology department reporting directly to administration appears to have stemmed from an acknowledgement of the role to be played by psychologists in the broader medical areas of the hospital, and/or the emphasis placed by the CCHFA on the necessity of health professionals implementing the type of quality assurance standards that are only possible if a profession is appropriately organized within a facility.

A wide range of quality assurance activities were reported by departments. Apart from performance appraisals, which are mandatory in most hospitals, the most commonly used quality assurance measure reported was the retrospective chart audit, which occurs when individual patient charts are examined for fit with existing standards and when the appropriateness of an assessment or treatment programme is reviewed. Peer reviews, data base audits, evaluations of existing psychological programmes, quantity of work completed and satisfaction surveys of patients and referral sources were among other activities reported by respondents.

The growth of psychology as a health care profession and the seeking of CPA/APA accreditation by university departments has led hospital psychology departments to focus increasingly on the development of 1-year internship positions in order to accommodate university graduate students seeking such placements as part of their graduate programmes. Of the hospitals surveyed, 22 (76%) reported the availability of 50 internship positions. Some hospital departments have obtained CPA approval (14%); some have obtained both APA and CPA approval (14%); some are in the process of being accredited (7%). In the Quebec sample, the hospitals surveyed were associated with the McGill programme and internships were unpaid. Wherever internships were established, departments viewed the arrangement as one of mutual benefit for both intern and department – the intern received the benefit of the department's experience and knowledge, while the department benefitted from the stimulation of the intern's new knowledge and enthusiasm.

Contributions to Research

One form of application that psychologists make to health care is research. Since many psychologists in Canada hold a PhD, an orientation toward research as an integral part of day to day activity might be assumed. Essentially there are three groups of psychologists that make contributions to research in the health care field. The first group is psychologists doing research in core areas of psychology that may impact on health care. A second group is psychologists, based in universities and research centres, doing health related research. The third group is psychologists doing research in health care settings. Most basic research, whether general or health related, is done in Canada by academics or psychologists in full-time research establishments. The contributions of this latter group are important, and their work tends to be well known and easily accessible. Of equal importance, but perhaps less well known and less accessible, are the contributions of psychologists in health care settings. Of the hospitals surveyed 76% of respondents reported active research programmes in a variety of areas.

An obvious way to assess the research activities of psychologists in health care settings is to carry out a survey. This is impossible, because there is no accurate registry of psychologists in health care settings available at this time. Another possibility is to survey those psychologists who are listed in the Canadian Register of Health Service Providers in Psychology and who render health care services. The most recent listing for 1990 preempted the Goods and Services Tax legislation incorporating the Canadian Register, and the new Health Facilities Accreditation Standards requiring listing by health facility psychologists. Hence, as Hunsley and Lefebvre (1990) have pointed out, only a minority of registered psychologists is as yet listed in the Canadian Register. Another difficulty with survey research is the low response rate by Canadian psychologists, 15.5% in the 1984 Canadian Psychological Association Survey (Martin, Ritchie, & Sabourin, 1988) and 29.3% in the Hunsley and Lefebvre (1990) survey. The ideal, if a listing of all psychologists in health care facilities were available, would be to search for the publications of each in *Psychological Abstracts, Index Medicus*, and the *Science* and *Social Science Citation Indexes*. An alternative method, and the most tangible approach at this time, was to assay the abstracts of the Canadian Psychological Association annual meetings for the past 5 years.

The data base employed to identify the research activities of psychologists in health care facilities was the abstracts for the annual meetings of the Canadian Psychological Association from 1986 to 1990 (Canadian Psychological Association, 1986, 1987, 1988, 1989, 1990). These meetings were held in Toronto, Vancouver, Montreal, Halifax and Ottawa, respectively. To accommodate the possibility that persons from more proximate areas to the annual meeting would be overrepresented in the presentations for a given year compared to those from more distant locations, the data employed were totals across the 5-year period. Given thaat the locations were representative geographically, it was felt that totals would give a fair representation of activity across Canada at this time. Work in progress often appears initially in the form of papers or posters at annual meetings; hence, the results of the current analysis are perhaps more indicative of activity than a review of published research. A limitation to this approach is that not all psychologists in health care settings present at Canadian Psychological Association annual meetings.

Each published abstract from the annual meetings of the Canadian Psychological Association for 1986 to 1990 was reviewed, and when at least one author had an affiliation with a health care facility, that abstract was included in the current investigation. Then, these abstracts were coded as to the location of their author(s), the sample used, the topic and the area of psychology into which the study fell. The latter data were tabulated according to the location of the author, area of medicine, area of health psychology and area of contribution. Percentages were calculated and graphical representations of each set of data were made.

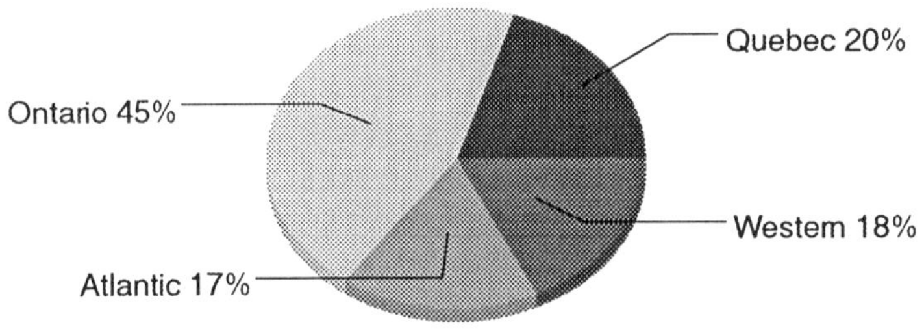

Figure 1. Papers by health facility psychologists at CPA annual meetings 1986–1990: Regional distribution.

The regional distribution of papers presented by health facility psychologists at the Canadian Psychological Association annual meetings between 1986 and 1990 is shown in Figure 1. For summary purposes the four Atlantic, and the four Western provinces were grouped together for comparative purposes along with Ontario and Quebec. If the percentages of presentations are corrected for the percentage of health care psychologists in each region then Ontario and the Western provinces contribute at roughly the same rate, 2.16:1 and 2.18:1 respectively. In contrast, Quebec and the Atlantic provinces contribute at a much lower rate, 1.08:1 and 1.25:1 respectively. It is noteworthy that when the annual conference was held in Montreal the rate of presentations by health care psychologists in Quebec was much higher, 1.94:1, and was similar to the rates for Ontario and the Western provinces. The regional differences are perhaps less a reflection of the amount of research being done in various locations, than of the involvement of psychologists in the annual meetings of the Canadian Psychological Association. Despite this fact it was concluded that the studies surveyed did give a reasonable representation of the activities of health care psychologists in Canada.

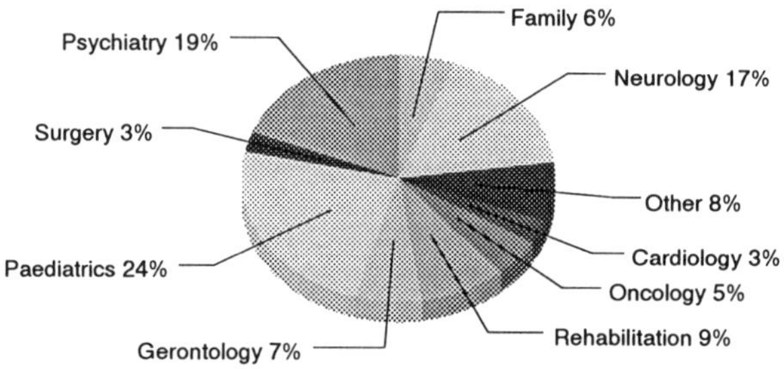

Figure 2. Papers by health facility psychologists at CPA annual meetings 1986–1990: Distribution by medical specialty.

Perhaps one point of interest is the degree to which health care psychologists are doing research in the various specialties of medicine. Based upon sample characteristics and topic, each study was assigned to an area of medicine. The results of this tabulation are shown in Figure 2. The three classic areas of medicine to which health care psychologists have historically provided services – psychiatry, neurology and paediatrics – account for 60% of research activity. It is clear that health care psychologists are extending their research into many other areas of medicine, including rehabilitation medicine, gerontology, family medicine, surgery and oncology. It is probable that as health care psychology matures this trend to move into other areas of medicine will continue.

As each abstract was reviewed it was assigned to an area of health psychology. The proportion of research in each speciality of psychology over the 5 years of abstracts is shown in Figure 3. It should be noted that the distinction between children and adults was not maintained for this aspect of the survey. Given that only 16% of studies had to do with psychopathology, it is obvious that health care psychologists have become emancipated from psychi-

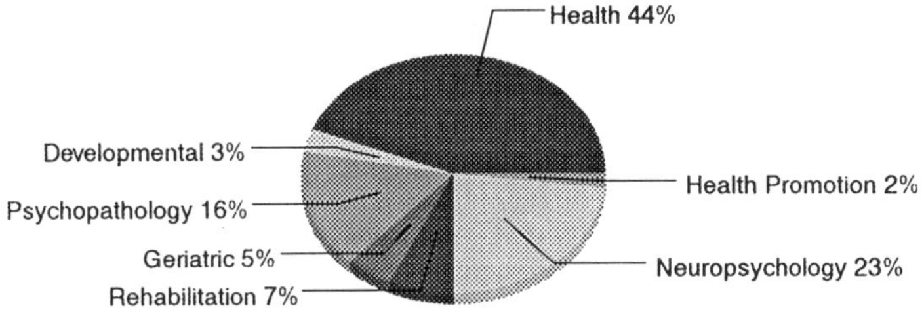

Figure 3. Papers by health facility psychologists at CPA annual meetings 1986–1990: Distribution by psychological specialty.

atric units. As might be expected, research in the areas of health psychology and neuropsychology was well represented, 44% and 23% respectively. Health promotion, rehabilitation and geriatric psychology appeared as other areas in which research was being accomplished. With the shift in emphasis from acute care to health promotion and the aging of the Canadian population it is anticipated that research in these areas will increase. The research in developmental psychology was focused on neonatal development of babies and infants in hospital and their future development, representing a point of contact between health care facilities and normal behaviour.

A final concern of the survey was the type of research being carried out by psychologists in the major domains of psychopathology, neuropsychology and health psychology. To answer this question developmental studies were excluded, cognitive rehabilitation and neuropsychology studies were combined, and geriatric psychology and health promotion studies were included with health psychology. The focus of these abstracts was classified as theory, treatment, programme evaluation, psychometrics or assessment.

The orientation of the research by the major groupings within health care facilities are presented in Figure 4. Studies in the psychopathology area are much more focused on theory than treatment and measurement issues, perhaps because these areas are well developed in the mental health domain. Papers in health psychology were focused on theory and treatment questions, and far less on measurement problems. In contrast to health psychology and psychopathology, most studies in neuropsychology were concerned with psychometric and assessment issues. No doubt, once

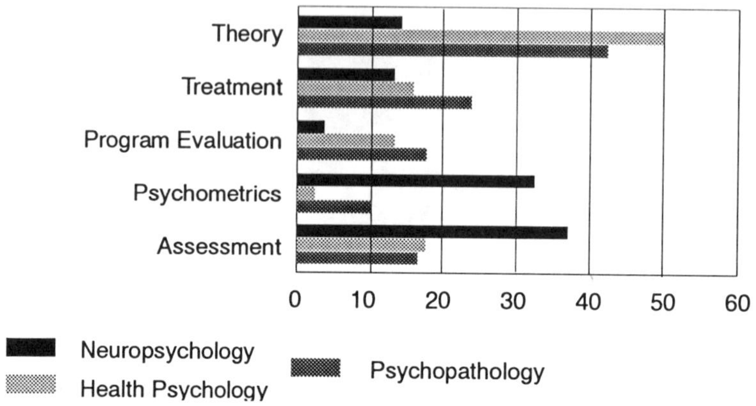

Figure 4. Papers (%) by health facility psychologists at CPA annual meetings 1986–1990: Focus of paper.

Canadian neuropsychologists complete the development and standardization of their measures, they will turn their attention to intervention issues with the clientele they serve.

The foregoing provides an overview of research in quantitative terms, but it is equally important to look at the content of research by health care psychologists. A general search, and a search by health care practitioner, were made of the literature to identify publications on the application of psychology to health care. Recognizing the limitations noted above, health care practitioners were identified by scanning the pages of the Canadian Register of Health Service Providers in Psychology. The publications for each listee were identified by searching the *Psychological Abstracts*. The *Canadian Journal of Behavioural Science*, and *Canadian Psychology* were also reviewed for relevant articles. The identified research is presented according to contributions to psychopathology, health psychology, pain, neuropsychology and rehabilitation, and to the newer areas of interest, geriatric psychology and prevention/health promotion.

Before considering these areas in turn it should be noted that in the past decade a number of special issues relevant to the application of psychology to health care have been published by the Canadian Psychological Association. The first, which appeared in 1983, was on clinical health psychology (Neufeld, 1983). The next, edited by Clemens (1985), contained articles on the interface between psychology and various aspects of medicine. The more recent special issues were focused on more specific topics, child and adolescent health (McGrath, 1988) and the psychology of aging and gerontology (Fry, 1989). These volumes have included reports of ongoing research and theoretical reviews by psychologists in universities and health care facilities across Canada.

A major contribution of Canadian psychologists to the type of psychopathology that is most frequently encountered in health as opposed to mental health care facilities has been in the area of depression and suicide. A special issue of the *Canadian Journal of Behavioural Science* was devoted to clinical depression (McLean, 1989). This issue included articles by many of the leading theorists and researchers in the area on the aetiology, assessment, treatment and prevention of depression (Costello, & Devins, 1989, Gotlib, & Wiffen, 1989; McLean, & Carr, 1989, Zemore, & Rinholm, 1989). Shaw, Dobson and Vallis, and their coworkers have done considerable research on the development of the cognitive behavioural assessment and treatment of depression and the training of therapists (Dobson, & Shaw, 1986; Shaw, & Dobson, 1988; Olinger, Kuiper, & Shaw, 1987; Vallis, Shaw, & Dobson, 1986). Contributions in the area of suicide among general hospital patients have been made by Barnes (1985, 1986), and Eaton and Reynolds (Reynolds, & Eaton, 1986; Eaton, & Reynolds, 1985). McNeil and Harsany (1989) have provided an interesting discussion concerning differential etiological factors among young and old depressed individuals and the implications of these factors for health psychologists.

Studies and reviews in the health psychology domain range across numerous topics, including sexuality, paediatric psychology, eating disorders, and treatment methods to name just a few. A number of psychologists at Jewish General Hospital are involved with the assessment and treatment of sexual dysfunctions and related disorders, including erectile dysfunction, secondary orgasmic dysfunction and the effects of transurethral prostatectomy (Fichten, Libman, & Brender, 1986; Fichten, Libman, Takefman, & Brender, 1988; Libman, 1989; Libman, Creti, & Fichten, 1987). Arnett and his coworkers at the University of Manitoba have also been active in this area (Arnett, Prosen, & Toews, 1986). The range of activity in paediatric psychology is demonstrated by the work of Ramsay and Zelazo (1988) at Montreal Children's Hospital on the treatment of failure-to-thrive infants, that of Manley and his colleagues at British Columbia Children's Hospital on various facets in the treatment of eating disorders and smoking (Manley, Tonkin, & Hammond, 1988; Manley, & Boland, 1983), and that of Whitsett and his coworkers at Alberta Children's Hospital on measurement issues in psychophysiology (Whitsett, Robinson, & Kaplan, 1987). Other researchers have been interested in various forms of treatment in the management of such conditions as irritable bowel syndrome (Lynch & Zamble, 1987), juvenile diabetes mellitus (Rose, Firestone, Heick, & Faught, 1983) and cardiac function (Bouchard, & Labelle, 1982). Another focus in health psychology has been on the evaluation of a range of medical interventions, such as transplant procedures and in vitro fertilization (Evans, Hearn, Levy, & Shatford, 1989; Hearn, Yuzpe, Brown, & Casper, 1987; Newton, Hearn, & Yuzpe, 1990). As psychologists extend their service into all aspects of health care it is anticipated that research contributions will be made in many other areas of paediatric and adult assessment and treatment.

Psychologists in universities and health facilities have made extensive contributions in the investigation and treatment of the psychological aspects of pain, many of which are internationally recognized. At McGill, Ronald Melzack (1989, 1987, 1984) has made an outstanding contribution to the area of pain research, a contribution that was recognized by the Canadian Psychological Association Award for Distinguished Contributions to Psychology as a Science in 1986. His subsequent D.O. Hebb Memorial Lecture in 1987 was entitled *Phantom Limbs, the Self and the Brain* (Melzack, 1989). Craig and his colleagues at the University of British Columbia (Branson, & Craig, 1988; Craig, 1987, Reesor, & Craig, 1988) have contributed to the literature on the psychological factors associated with pain in both children and adults. Two psychologists at the University of Saskatchewan, Genest (Genest, 1983; Genest, & Genest, 1987) and von Baeyer (von Baeyer, Bergstrom, Brodwin, & Brodwin, 1983; von Baeyer, & Genest, 1985; von Baeyer, Johnson, & McMillan, 1984), have completed research on the application of psychology to specific patient groups, such as those suffering back pain and rheumatoid arthritis. Vallis (1984), who is now at Camp Hill Hospital in Halifax, evaluated the relative importance of the various components used in the treatment of pain by stress inoculation. Contributions in the paediatric area have been made by Kuttner and Lepage (1989) at the British Columbia Children's Hospital, P.A. McGrath, de Veber, and Hearn (1985) at the Children's Hospital of Western Ontario, and Guibert, Firestone, and P.J. McGrath et al. (1990) at the Children's Hospital of Eastern Ontario.

In the area of neuropsychology and rehabilitation there are a number of Canadian psychologists who are active researchers. There are several psychologists in universities who have contributed to research in neuropsychology, Knights at Carleton, Rourke at Windsor, Milner at McGill, Gates at Victoria, and Kimura at Western, and many have been recognized by awards for their contributions. However, as more and more neuropsychologists establish their practices in health facilities, more of the research is being done in these settings. Byrne and his colleagues at the Izaak Walton Killam Hospital for Children in Halifax have contributed research into the neuropsychological assessment of children and the developmental impact of children's neurological disorders (Byrne, Backman, & Smith, 1986; Byrne, & Gates, 1987; Byrne, & Miller, 1988). Stuss, who has recently moved to the Baycrest Centre in Toronto, and his coworkers have made a consistent contribution in the study of psychological impairments associated with several neurological conditions (Stuss, & Benson, 1984; Stuss, Guberman, Nelson, & Larochelle, 1988; Stuss, & Guzman, 1988). Not all studies have dealt with patient populations: Jason, Pajurkova and Lee (1989) at the University of Calgary Medical Clinic investigated the impact of mountaineering on cortical functioning in members of an Everest expedition. Finlayson, Alfano and Sullivan (Alfano, & Finlayson, 1987; Finlayson, Alfano, & Sullivan, 1987; Finlayson, Sullivan, & Alfano, 1986) at the Chedoke-McMaster Hospitals perhaps epitomize the new wave of neuropsychologists in Canada with their interest in assessment and theoretical issues on the one hand, and their work on rehabilitation on the other. A number of other psychologists in Canada are also involved in issues related to rehabilitation (Carlson, 1985; Young, Collins, & Hren, 1983), and Fichten and her colleagues in Montreal have published a number of papers on the reactions of the nondisabled to college students with physical disability in an effort to identify required components in the rehabilitation process (Amsel, R., & Fichten, C. S., 1988; Fichten, Amsel, Bourden, & Creti, 1988; Fichten, & Bourden, 1986).

In addition to those areas of health care noted above psychologists are beginning to be more involved in two emerging areas, geriatric psychology and prevention/health promotion concerns. Gottlieb (1987, 1989) at the University of Guelph has provided theoretical reviews of the role of the family and other social support groups in the care of medical patients and the elderly. Other psychologists have been concerned to investigate the assessment of the elderly, and the impact of various treatment strategies with this population (Bonardi, Pencer, & Tourigny-Rivard, 1989; Rosberger, & MacLean, 1983). Prevention activities have involved such topics as substance abusers (Davis, & Glaros, 1986; Evans, Nesbitt, Pilgrim, & Potts, 1985) and potential scalding of children (Webne, Kaplan, & Shaw, 1989). Much of the work to date on health promotion has focused on the management of stress by a variety of strategies (Sinyor, Golden, Steinert, & Seraganian, 1986; Weinstein, & Conry, 1983). With the current programmes sponsored by the Federal and Provincial governments aimed at these areas, it is anticipated that there will be increased research in these domains in the future.

Future Directions

The foregoing sections of this chapter indicate the current scope and nature of the applications of psychology to practice and research in health care in Canada. Ahead lie a number of clear directions and some dilemmas. As psychology in general gains in independence and stature, similar advances will accrue for practitioners in the health care domain. This leads to the dilemma of moving toward independence on the one hand, and yet fostering cooperation among the growing number of professionals who contribute to the biopsychosocial model of health. Given the high cost of health care, new methods of service delivery are imperative. For psychologists in health care the dilemma rests between the need to consolidate their current excellent and necessary services while developing new models and directions of service delivery. There are also directions that must be followed in research, training and advocacy, irrespective of how these dilemmas are resolved. Before concluding this chapter it is important to overview each of these issues in terms of the future of health psychology.

In the survey of adult and children's general hospital departments of psychology a common theme in terms of future activities was the goal of making the role of psychologists in health care more visible and more formalized. This goal extended from the need to foster the continued existence of psychology in some hospitals to the development of psychology-led programmes in others. Another emerging theme was the need for psychology to obtain defined hospital privileges and the right to participate on an equal footing with other senior health professions in the governance of hospitals. In essence the goal expressed is that identified by Matheson (1983) almost a decade ago when he exhorted health psychologists to become "independently responsible professionals" (p. 8).

As the focus of health care becomes more behavioural the argument for the independence of psychological practice is strengthened. Evidence exists that between 30% and 70% of individuals consult primary care physicians for behavioural rather than physical problems (Diekstra, 1990; Jansen, Methorst & Kerkhof, 1990). Further, there is increasing awareness that much illness stems from behavioural pathogens, such as smoking, overeating, and lack of exercise, rather than biological pathogens (Holtzman, Evans, Kennedy & Iscoe, 1987; Lacroix, 1987). These observations suggest an important role for psychologists in health care if they are willing to take up the challenge levelled by Matheson (1983).

A number of statutory hurdles remain to be crossed in the attainment of independence as health care professionals. Recent changes in the accreditation standards for health care facilities will assist the move to independence. However, as Lacroix (1987) points out, much of the current enabling legislation pertaining to health care across Canada can be interpreted as limiting severely the potential of psychologists in health care research and practice. Psychological associations at all levels are following the call by Lacroix (1987) to get organized and change the law to reflect both reality and the public need. This form of change is demanding of resources, is time consuming, and at times is daunting, but without it, true independence as a profession will not be obtained. A major thrust of the Practice Directorate of the American Psychological Association has been to obtain full privileges in hospitals for psychologists (Enright, Resnick, DeLeon, Sciara & Tanney, 1990). By the end of 1990, hospital practice legislation, allowing psychologists full privileges, was in place in California, Georgia, the District of Columbia, and North Carolina, and some 20 other state associations, plus at least one provincial one, were working to obtain statutory authority for hospital privileges for psychologists (Enright et al., 1990). In 1990 the Public Hospitals Act in Ontario was under review, and the Ontario Psychological Association was actively involved in the review process. It remains to be seen what the outcome of these activities will be. A frequent argument against extending privileges to psychologists is the need for privileged health care professionals to have fully developed quality assurance programmes. Most hospital psychology departments are developing quality assurance programmes, such as the programme outlined by Goodman, Goodman, McGrath & Goldsmith (1987), but a national standard for quality assurance awaits development.

While it is important that psychologists obtain independence for the full impact of psychology's contribution to health care to be realized, the multifaceted nature of both health and illness demands that an atmosphere of cooperation among health care practitioners be fostered. Jansen et al. (1990) point out cogently that factors leading to health and illness are psychological, social and physical, thus, there is a need for professionals in each of these areas to contribute to research, practice and public policy with relative equality and respect. Diekstra (1990) makes a more encompassing plea for cooperation:

> People including health personnel and their elected representatives should work together to promote health, prevent disease, alleviate unavoidable disease and disability, improve the process of being born and growing up, insure that all are healthy enough to work productively and to participate in the social life of the community, and finally, facilitate growing old gracefully and dying in dignity. (p. 53)

In sum, it is important that if psychologists are to make their maximal contribution to the health care system they will have to pursue the seemingly disparate goals of independence and cooperation simultaneously.

Respondents to the survey indicated several future directions for service delivery. These included the extension and enhancement of current services in health and neuropsychology, the consolidation of mental health programmes, and the extension of services into the community under a variety of delivery models to a range of client groups. Two areas of future development identified both in the literature and by those surveyed are services for the older adult (Martin et al., 1988; Taylor, 1990), and a move toward health promotion and prevention (Diekstra, 1990; Holtzman et al., 1987; Martin et al., 1988). Both Diekstra (1990) and Holtzman et al. (1987) suggested that future applications of psychology to health care involve the development of new and innovative service delivery systems aimed at methods of promoting health, changing life styles and reducing behavioural pathogens.

These emerging directions are well supported in principle by all levels of government, from the World Health Organization (1981) to the federal and provincial ministries responsible for health (Berry, 1988), and most are extending resources tentatively into these areas. As several of the respondents surveyed suggested, there is a need to review and perhaps revise current methods of service delivery to accommodate accumulated experience in applying psychology to health care, the emerging trend toward a proactive rather than a reactive health care system, and the increasing emphasis on cost effectiveness.

Hunsley and Lefebvre (1990) in their survey of health service providers in psychology found that only 31% were involved in research, spending on average 4.4% of their time or approximately 1.5 hours per week in such activities. Of the departments surveyed most had several active research projects, but many argued for more time and resources for research. If psychology is to recognize its potential application to health care there is an urgent need to secure personnel and resources aimed at applied research in health care facilities. As Taylor (1990) noted, research will continue to be directed toward the specification of " ... models and pathways whereby psychological and social factors can be integrated into the biology of health and illness in multifactorial causal chains" (p. 46). This direction is also envisaged by Jansen et al. (1990). Taylor (1990) suggested that perhaps psychology has come of age in that psychologists are increasingly the principal investigators in research projects with a team of health professionals, instead of acting as advisors or consultants on the research of other health professionals. It is evident that much of the fine research already being carried out by health care psychologists in Canada should be encouraged and extended.

Several authors have identified life style factors as an important and urgent focus of future research (Diekstra, 1990; Holtzman et al., 1987; Jansen et al., 1990). Some of the more important questions are as follows:

1. What life style factors are health enhancing? (Diekstra, 1990)
2. How can healthy life styles be engendered across the board? (Health Education Unit, WHO regional office for Europe, 1986)
3. How can unhealthy life styles be changed? (Diekstra, 1990; Jansen et al., 1990)
4. How can healthy life styles be maintained? (Jansen et al., 1990)

As these questions are answered, a collateral question relates to the identification of the most appropriate delivery system. Should health be facilitated on an individual basis, through educational groups, or by community empowerment (Diekstra, 1990; Holtzman et al., 1987); in the workplace, through educational settings, in health care malls, or in other community based facilities (Holtzman et al., 1987; Oberman, 1984)?

With increased numbers of psychologists entering the health care field the training of health psychologists in Canada must be considered. The *Directory of Training Opportunities in Behavioral Medicine* (Society of Behavioral Medicine, 1988) lists few training programmes in Canada, and those listed appear to add health psychology or behavioural medicine courses, practica and research to a clinical, experimental or general PhD programme. A number of other options worthy of consideration include, a health psychology PhD programme, a clinical PhD programme with a major concentration in health psychology, or a postdoctoral training programme in health psychology following a clinical PhD programme. Resolution of this issue rests with groups such as the Health Psychology section of the Canadian Psychological Association, organizations of Chief Psychologists in Hospitals, or the Canadian Register of Health Service Providers in Psychology. Aside from the issue of how the programme of training is to be structured, there is the added concern of what the curriculum should include: for example, Bresler (1988) has outlined a doctoral programme that focuses on "Health Promotion in the Community" (p. 87). If in fact mental health has given way to health as the major focus of clinical psychologists, then all that may be needed is to reorient current clinical programmes away from a psychopathological orientation toward a proactive health orientation.

Enright et al. (1990) have argued that "The goal of psychology's expanded role in [health care] is to ensure that consumers have full benefit of and access to the most up-to-date behavioral science knowledge" (p. 1064). Knowledge is not static, and will develop only to the degree that applied research in health care is facilitated by both public and government agencies. Only then can it be given appropriate priority by health psychologists. There is also the concern of universal access to health psychologists (Holtzman et al., 1987), either through public funding, or through the methods outlined by Ritchie et al. (1988). If the healthy life style model is in fact extended such that individuals consult a psychologist once a year for a life style check up, some mode of facilitating this activity will be required. It is interesting that vast sums of public and private monies are extended to support the illness industry, while little is expended on health. Health psychologists in Canada must begin to promote and market their activities if their importance is to be recognized and fostered (Jansen et al., 1990). The multiple goal of increasing applied research, enhancing accessibility to psychological services, and marketing is essential if health psychologists are to meet the challenge provided by the World Health Organization in 1946 of extending to all peoples the benefits of psychological and related knowledge, which was deemed essential to the fullest attainment of health (World Health Organization, 1970).

Appendix A: Hospitals Surveyed

Vancouver General Hospital, Vancouver, British Columbia
UBC Health Sciences Centre Hospital, Vancouver, British Columbia
B.C. Children's Hospital, Vancouver, British Columbia
Shaughnessy Hospital, Vancouver, British Columbia

Calgary General Hospital, Calgary, Alberta
Foothills Hospital, Calgary, Alberta
Tom Baker Cancer Centre, Calgary, Alberta
Alberta Children's Provincial General Hospital, Calgary, Alberta
Holy Cross Hospital, Calgary, Alberta

University Hospital, Saskatoon, Saskatchewan

Winnipeg Health Sciences Centre, Winnipeg, Manitoba

Victoria Hospital, London, Ontario
Children's Hospital of Western Ontario, London, Ontario
University Hospital, London, Ontario
Peterborough Civic Hospital, Peterborough, Ontario
Chedoke-McMaster Hospital, Hamilton, Ontario
Ottawa Civic Hospital, Ottawa, Ontario
Children's Hospital of Eastern Ontario, Ottawa, Ontario
Windsor Western Hospital, Windsor, Ontario
Toronto General Hospital, Toronto, Ontario
Sunnybrook Medical Centre, Toronto, Ontario
Kingston General Hospital, Kingston, Ontario

Jewish General Hospital, Montreal, Quebec
Montreal General Hospital, Montreal, Quebec
Montreal Children's Hospital, Montreal, Quebec
Royal Victoria Hospital, Montreal, Quebec

Hopital Docteur Georges L. Dumont, Moncton, New Brunswick

Victoria General Hospital, Halifax, Nova Scotia
Camp Hill Hospital, Halifax, Nova Scotia
Izaak Walton Killam Hospital for Children, Halifax, Nova Scotia

The General Hospital, St. John's, Newfoundland

References

Alfano, D. P., & Finlayson, M. A. (1987). Comparison of standard and abbreviated MMPIs in patients with head injury. *Rehabilitation Psychology*, *32*, 67–76.

Amsel, R., & Fichten, C. S. (1988). Effects of contact on thoughts about interaction with students who have a phsical disability. *Journal of Rehabilitation*, *54*, 61–65.

Arnett, J. L., & Martin, R. M. (1981). Psychologists in Canadian medical schools. *Professional Psychology*, *12*, 237–245.

Arnett, J. L., Martin R. M., Streiner, D. L., & Goodman, J. T. (1987). Hospital psychology in Canada. *Canadian Psychology*, *28*, 161–171.

Arnett, J. L., Prosen, H., & Toews, J. A. (1986). Loss of libido due to stress. *Medical Aspects of Human Sexuality*, *20*, 140–148.

Barnes, R. A. (1985). Women and self injury. *International Journal of Women's Studies*, *8*, 465–474.

Barnes, R. A. (1986). The recurrent self-harm patient. *Suicide and Life Threatening Behaviour*, *16*, 399–408.

Barsky, A. J. (1988). *Worried sick: Our troubled quest for wellness.* Toronto: Little Brown & Company.

Berry, R. G. (1988). "A debtor to his profession." *Canadian Psychology*, *29*, 174–186.

Bonardi, E., Pencer, I., & Tourigny-Rivard, M. F. (1989). Observed changes in the functioning of nursing home residents after relocation. *International Journal of Aging and Human Development*, *28*, 295–304.

Bott, E. A. (1928). Teaching of Psychology in a Medical Course. *Bulletin of the Association of American Medical Colleges*, *3*, 289–304.

Bouchard, M. A., & Labelle, J. (1982). Voluntary heart rate deceleration: A critical evaluation. *Biofeedback and Self Regulation*, *7*, 121–137.

Branson, S. M., & Craig, K. D. (1988). Children's spontaneous strategies for coping with pain: A review of the literature. *Canadian Journal of Behavioural Science*, *20*, 402–412.

Bresler, C. (1988). Health promotion in the community: Development of a curriculum for predoctoral clinical psychologists. *Professional Psychology: Research and Practice*, *19*, 87–92.

Burstein, A., & Loucks, S. (1982). The psychologist as health care clinician. In T. Millon, C. Green, & R. Meagher (Eds.), *Handbook of clinical health psychology*. New York: Plenum Press.

Byrne, J. M., Backman, J. E., & Smith, I. M. (1986). Developmental assessment: The clinical use and validity of parental report. *Journal of Pediatric Psychology*, *11*, 549–559.

Byrne, J. M., & Gates, R. D. (1987). Single-case study of left cerebral hemispherectomy: Development in the first five years of life. *Journal of Clinical and Experimental Neuropsychology*, *9*, 423–434.

Byrne, J. M., & Miller, C. L. (1988). Developmental course of early cardiac-somatic integration. *Infant Behaviour and Development*, *11*, 43–53.

Canadian Psychological Association. (November, 1951). *The Canadian Psychologist*, *1*, 3.

Canadian Psychological Association. (December, 1952). *The Canadian Psychologist*, *2*, 4.

Canadian Psychological Association. (April, 1955). *The Canadian Psychologist*, *4*, 27–47.

Canadian Psychological Association (1986). Abstracts annual meeting of the Canadian Psychological Association, Toronto. *Canadian Psychology*, *27*, No. 2 a.

Canadian Psychological Association (1987). Abstracts annual meeting of the Canadian Psychological Association, Vancouver. *Canadian Psychology*, *28*, No. 2 a.

Canadian Psychological Association (1988). Abstracts annual meeting of the Canadian Psychological Association, Montreal. *Canadian Psychology*, *29*, No. 2 a.

Canadian Psychological Association (1989). Abstracts annual meeting of the Canadian Psychological Association, Halifax. *Canadian Psychology*, *30*, No. 2 a.

Canadian Psychological Association (1990). Abstracts annual meeting of the Canadian Psychological Association, Ottawa. *Canadian Psychology*, *31*, No. 2 a.

Canadian Register of Health Service Providers in Psychology (1988). *Canadian Register of Health Service Providers in Psychology 1988*. Ottawa: Author.

Carlson, P. M. (1985). Psychology in rehabilitation: Principles and practices. *Ontario Psychologist*, *17*, 4–9.

Clemens, W. J. (Ed.). (1985). Special issue: The interface between psychology and medicine. *Canadian Psychology*, *26*, 81–173.

Costello, C. G., & Devins, G. M. (1989). Screening for depression among women attending their family physicians. *Canadian Journal of Behavioural Science, 21*, 434–451.

Craig, K. D. (1987). Consequences of caring: Pain in the human context. *Canadian Psychology, 28*, 311–321.

Davis, J. R., & Glaros, A. G. (1986). Relapse prevention and smoking cessation. *Addictive Behaviors, 11*, 105–114.

Diekstra, R. F. W. (1990). Psychology, health and health care. *Psychology and Health, 4*, 51–63.

Dobson, K. S., & Shaw, B. F. (1986). Cognitive assessment with major depressive disorders. *Cognitive Therapy and Research, 10*, 13–29.

Dunn, R. J. (1986). General hospital psychology. *Canadian Psychology, 27*, 44–50.

Eaton, P., & Reynolds, P. (1985). Suicide attempters presenting at an emergency department. *Canadian Journal of Psychiatry, 30*, 582–585.

Enright, M. F., Resnick, R., Deleon, P. H., Sciara, A. D., & Tanney, F. (1990). The practice of psychology in hospital settings. *American Psychologist, 45*, 1059–1065.

Evans, D. R., Hearn, M. T., Levy, L. M. L., & Shatford, L. (1989). Modern health technologies and quality of life measures. In R. C. King & J. K. Collins (Eds.), *Social applications and issues in psychology* (pp. 243–250). Amsterdam: Elsevier.

Evans, D. R., Nesbitt, L. M. L., Pilgrim, A. E., & Potts, S. M. (1985). The Community Alcohol Use Scale: A scale for use in prevention programs. *American Journal of Community Psychology, 13*, 715–731.

Fichten, C. S., Amsel, R., Bourdon, C. V., & Creti, L. (1988). Interactions between college students with physical disabilities and their professors. *Journal of Applied Rehabilitation Counseling, 19*, 13–20.

Fichten, C. S., & Bourdon, C. V. (1986). Social skill deficit or response inhibition: Interaction between disabled and nondisabled college students. *Journal of College Student Personnel, 27*, 326–333.

Fichten, C. S., Libman, E., & Brender, W. (1986). Measurement of therapy outcome and maintenance of gains in behavioral treatment of secondary orgasmic dysfunction. *Journal of Sex and Marital Therapy, 12*, 22–34.

Fichten, C. S., Libman, E., Takefman, J., & Brender, W. (1988). Self-monitoring and self-focus in erectile dysfunction. *Journal of Sex and Marital Therapy, 14*, 120–128.

Finlayson, M. A., Alfano, D. P., & Sullivan, J. F. (1987). A neuropsychological approach to cognitive remediation: Microcomputer applications. *Canadian Psychology, 28*, 180–190.

Finlayson, M. A., Sullivan, J. F., & Alfano, D. P. (1986). Halstead's Category Test: Withstanding the test of time. *Journal of Clinical and Experimental Neuropsychology*, *8*, 706–709.

Fry, P. S. (Ed.), (1989). Special Issue: Psychology and Aging and Gerontology. *Canadian Psychology*, *30*, 505–615.

Genest, M. (1983). Coping with rheumatoid arthritis. *Canadian Journal of Behavioural Science*, *15*, 392–408.

Genest, M., & Genest, S. (1987). *Psychology and health*. Champaign, IL: Research Press.

Goodman, J. T., Goodman, M. I., McGrath, P. J., & Goldsmith, L. J. (1987). Quality assurance in psychological services. *Canadian Psychology*, *28*, 172–179.

Gotlib, I. H., & Wiffen, V. E. (1989). Stress, coping and marital satisfaction in couples with a depressed wife. *Canadian Journal of Behavioural Science*, *21*, 401–418.

Gottlieb, B. H. (1987). Marshalling social support for medical patients and their families. *Canadian Psychology*, *28*, 201–217.

Gottlieb, B. H. (1989). A contextual perspective on stress in family care of the elderly. *Canadian Psychology*, *30*, 596–607.

Guibert, M. B., Firestone, P., McGrath, P. J., Goodman, J. T., & Cunningham, J. S. (1990). Compliance factors in the behavioural treatment of headache in children and adolescents. *Canadian Journal of Behavioural Science*, 22, 37–44.

Health Education Unit, World Health Organization Regional Office for Europe (1986). Life-styles and health. *Social Science and Medicine*, *22*, 117–124.

Hearn, M. T., Yuzpe, A. A., Brown, S. E., & Casper, R. F. (1987). Psychological characteristics of in vitro fertilization participants. *American Journal of Obstetrics and Gynecology*, *156*, 269–271.

Hetzel, B. S. (1980). *Health and Australian Society*. Ringwood Australia: Penguin.

Holtzman, W. H., Evans, R. I., Kennedy, S., & Iscoe, I. (1987). Psychology and health: Contributions of psychology to the improvement of health and health care. *International Journal of Psychology*, 22, 221–267.

Hunsley, J., & Lefebvre, M. (1990). A survey of the practices and activities of Canadian clinical psychologists. *Canadian Psychology. 31*, 350–358.

Jansen, M. A., Methorst, G. J., & Kerkhof, A. J. (1990). Health psychology in international perspective: A summary and some thoughts for the future. *Psychology and Health*, *4*, 83–89.

Jason, G. W., Pajurkova, E. M., & Lee, R. G. (1989). High-altitude mountaineering and brain function: Neuropsychological testing of members of a Mount Everest expedition. *Aviation, Space, and Environmental Medicine, 60*, 170–173.

Kaplan, R. M. (1990). Behavior as the central outcome in health care. *American Psychologist, 45*, 1211–1220.

Kuttner, L., & LePage, T. (1989). Face scales for the assessment of pediatric pain: A critical review. *Candian Journal of Behavioural Science, 21*, 198–209.

Lacroix,, R. (1987). Stumbling blocks to the practice of health psychology: A Canadian perspective. *Canadian Psychology, 28*, 280–284.

Lalonde, M. A. (1974). *A New Perspective on the Health of Canadians.* Ottawa: Government of Canada.

Libman, E. (1989). Sociocultural and cognitive factors in aging and sexual expression: Conceptual and research issues. *Canadian Psychology, 30*, 560–567.

Libman, E., Creti, L., & Fichten, C. S. (1987) Determining what patients should know about transurethral prostatectomy. *Patient Education and Counseling*, 9, 145–153.

Lynch, P. M., & Zamble, E. (1987). Stress management training for irritable bowel syndrome: A preliminary investigation. *Clinical Biofeedback and Health An International Journal, 10*, 123–134.

Manley, R. S., Tonkin, R., & Hammond, C. (1988). A method for the assessment of body image disturbance in patients with eating disorders. *Journal of Adolescent Health Care*, 9, 384–388.

Manley, R. S., & Boland, F. J. (1983). Side-effects and weight gain following a smoking cessation program. *Addictive Behaviors, 8*, 375–380.

Martime Psychological Association (1956). Notes and News. *Bulletin of the Martime Psychological Association, 5*, 21–23.

Martin, R. M., Ritchie, P. L.-J., & Sabourin, M. E. (1988). The state of psychological practice in Canada: Current status and directions for the future. In P. L.-J. Ritchie, T. P. Hogan, & T. V. Hogan (Eds.), *Psychology in Canada: The state of the discipline, 1984.* (p. 73–119). Old Chelsea, Quebec: Canadaian Psychological Association.

Matarazzo, J. D. (1987). Relationships of health psychology to other segments of psychology. In G. C. Stone et al. (Eds.), *Health psychology: A discipline and a profession.* (pp. 41–59). Chicago: University of Chicago Press.

Matheson, G. (1983). Health psychology: An opportunity, a responsibility. *The Ontario Psychologist, 15*, 4–10.

McGrath, P. A., de Veber, L. L., & Hearn, M. T. (1985). Multidimensional pain assessment in children. In H. L. Fields, R. Dubner & F. Cervero (Eds.), *Advances in pain research and therapy*, 9. New York: Raven Press.

McGrath, P. J. (Ed.), (1988). Special Issue: Child and Adolescent Health. *Canadian Journal of Behavioural Science, 20*, iii–vi, 359–470.

McLean, P. D. (Ed.). (1989). Special Issue: Clinical Depression. *Canadian Journal of Behavioural Science, 21*, iii–viii, 353–493.

McLean, P. D., & Carr, S. (1989). The psychological treatment of unipolar depression: Progress and limitations. *Canadian Journal of Behavioural Science, 21*, 452–469.

McNeal, J. K., & Harsany, M. (1989). An age difference view of depression. *Canadian Psychology, 30*, 608–615.

Melzack, R. (1989 a). Measurement of nausea. *Journal of Pain and Symptom Management, 4*, 157–160.

Melzack, R. (1989 b). Phantom limbs, the self and the brain (the D. O. Hebb Memorial Lecture). *Canadian Psychology, 30*, 1–16.

Melzack, R. (1987). The short-form McGill Pain Questionnaire. *Pain, 30*, 191–197.

Melzack, R. (1984). The myth of painless childbirth (the John J. Bonica lecture). *Pain, 19*, 321–337.

Myers, C. R. (1974). Edward Alexander Bott (1887–1974). *Canadian Psychologist, 15*, 292–296.

Neufeld, R. W. J. (Ed.). (1983). Special Issue: Clinical Health Psychology. *Canadian Journal of Behavioural Science, 15*, 301–438.

Newton, C. R., Hearn, M. T., & Yuzpe, A. A. (1990). Psychological assessment and follow-up after in vitro fertilization: Assessing the impact of failure. *Fertility and Sterility, 54*, 651–659.

Oberman, A. (May, 1984). Components of health promotion. *Family and Community Health, 7*, 1–11.

Olinger, L. J., Kuiper, N., & Shaw, B. F. (1987). Dysfunctional attitudes and stressful life events: An interactive model of depression. *Cognitive Therapy and Research, 11*, 25–40.

Peters, R. D. (1988). Mental health promotion in children and adolescents: An emerging role for psychology. *Canadian Journal of Behavioural Science, 20*, 389–401.

Ramsay, M., & Zelazo, P. R. (1988). Food refusal in failure-to-thrive infants: Nasogastric feeding combined with interactive-behavioral treatment. *Journal of Pediatric Psychology, 13*, 329–347.

Reesor, K. A., & Craig, K. D. (1988). Medically incongruent chronic back pain: Physical limitations, suffering, and ineffective coping. *Pain, 32*, 35–45.

Reynolds, P., & Eaton, P. (1986). Multiple attempters of suicide presenting at an emergency department. *Canadian Journal of Psychiatry, 31*, 328–330.

Ritchie, P. L.-J., Wilson, R. F., Berry, R., Boulay, M., King, M., & Sabourin, M. E. (1988). The funding of psychological health care services. *Canadian Psychology*, *29*, 187–205.

Rosberger, Z., & MacLean, J. (1983). Behavioral assessment and treatment of "organic" behaviors in an institutionalized geriatric patient. *International Journal of Behavioral Geriatrics*, *1*, 33–46.

Rose, M. I., Firestone, P., Heick, H. M., Faught, A. K. (1983). The effects of anxiety and management training on the control of juvenile diabetes mellitus. *Journal of Behavioral Medicine*, *6*, 381–395.

Shaw, B. F., & Dobson, K. S. (1988). Competency judgements in the training and evaluation of psychotherapists. *Journal of Consulting and Clinical Psychology*, *56*, 666–672.

Sinyor, D., Golden, M., Steinert, Y., & Seraganian, P. (1986). Experimental manipulation of aerobic fitness and the response to psychosocial stress: Heart rate and self report measures. *Psychosomatic Medicine*, *48*, 334–337.

Society of Behavioral Medicine (1988). *Directory of training opportunities in behavioral medicine*. Knoxville, TN: Author.

Stone, G. C. (1990). An international review of the emergence and development of health psychology. *Psychology and Health*, *4*, 3–17.

Stuss, D. T., & Benson, D. F. (1984). Neuropsychological studies of the frontal lobes. *Psychological Bulletin*, *95*, 3–28.

Stuss, D. T., Guberman, A., Nelson, R., & Larochelle, S. (1988). The neuropsychology of paramedian thalamic infarction. *Brain and Cognition*, *8*, 348–378.

Stuss, D. T., & Guzman, D. A. (1988). Severe remote memory loss with minimal anterograde amnesia: A clinical note. *Brain and Cognition*, *8*, 21–30.

Taylor, S. E. (1990). Health psychology the science and the field. *American Psychologist*, *45*, 40–50.

Vallis, T. M., Shaw, B. F., & Dobson, K. S. (1986). The cognitive therapy scale: Psychometric properties. *Journal of Consulting and Clinical Psychology*, *54*, 381–385.

von Baeyer, C. L., Bergstrom, K. J., Brodwin, M. G., & Brodwin, S. K. (1983). Invalid use of pain drawings in psychological screening of back pain patients. *Pain*, *16*, 103–107.

von Baeyer, C. L., & Genest, M. (1985). Role of psychologists in Canadian pain centres. *Canadian Psychology*, *26*, 140–147.

von Baeyer, C. L., Johnson, M. E., & McMillan, M. J. (1984). Consequences of nonverbal expression of pain: Patient distress and observer concern. *Social Science and Medicine*, *19*, 1319–1324.

Webne, S., Kaplan, B. J., & Shaw, M. (1989). Pediatric burn prevention: An evaluation of the efficacy of a strategy to reduce tap water temperature in a population at risk for scalds. *Developmental and Behavioral Pediatrics, 10*, 187–191.

Webster, E. C., (Ed.), (1967). *The Couchaching conference on professional psychology.* Montreal: McGill University.

Weinstein, M. S., & Conry, R. (1983). A survey of stress management practices and attitudes in community health settings in B.C. *Canadian Journal of Community Mental Health*, 2, 71–78.

Whitsett, S. F., Robinson, J. W., & Kaplan, B. J. (1987). A comparison of three approaches for the determination of baseline levels of physiological activity. *International Journal of Psychophysiology*, 5, 53–61.

World Health Organization. (1970). *Constitution of the World Health Organization in basic documents* (21st ed.). Geneva: World Health Organization.

World Health Organization (1981). *Global strategy for health for all by the year 2000.* Geneva: [Author].

Wright, M. (1955). On private group practice for the clinical psychologist. *The Canadian Psychologist*, 4, 9.

Wright, M. (1960). Professional psychologist at work. *The Canadian Psychologist, 19*, 24–27.

Wright, M. J. & Myers, C. R. (1982). *History of academic psychology in Canada.* Toronto: C.J. Hogrefe Inc.

Young, G. C., Collins, D., & Hren, M. (1983). Effect of pairing scanning training with block design training in thhe remediation of perceptual problems in left hemiplegics. *Journal of Clinical Neuropsychology*, 5, 201–212.

Zemore, R., & Rinholm, J. (1989). Vulnerability to depression as a function of parental rejection and control. *Canadian Journal of Behavioural Science, 21*, 364–376.

12

Counselling Psychology: Development, Identity and Issues

Bryan Hiebert
University of Calgary

Max R. Uhlemann
University of Victoria

Introduction

It is somewhat presumptuous for us to write a chapter on the "state of the art" of counselling psychology in Canada. Counselling psychologists are an extremely diverse group, practising in a wide variety of settings and operating from many different, often diametrically opposing, theoretical and procedural perspectives. Who can presume to speak on their behalf? Who could do justice to the diversity and leave all sectors feeling like they have been given decent representation? We will try.

Depicting the nature of counselling psychology in Canada is a difficult, albeit important task. A check of the usual data bases (ERIC, Psychological Abstracts, Med Lars) revealed that virtually nothing definitive has been written about counselling psychology in Canada. Even attempts to address issues in this field from a Canadian perspective are rare, and those that exist are overlaid with an American perspective (cf. Friesen, 1983; Lecomte, Dumont & Zingle, 1981). For the most part it would seem that counselling psychologists in Canada have been willing to accept American perspectives and positions as being appropriate for Canadians. Yet some differences do exist in the way the profession has developed in Canada. Also, societal differences between Canada and the United States may mean that American statements regarding professional practice are not directly transferable. Furthermore, American attempts to define counselling psychology have produced no consistent description of its professional identity (cf. Whiteley, 1984; Zytowski & Rosen, 1982). Therefore, it is important to try to delineate the Canadian perspective.

We begin this chapter by describing how counselling psychology became a professional entity in Canada and how that developmental process was similar to and different from what happened in the United States. Then, we describe the current Canadian scene, basing our description on a survey asking counselling psychologists to describe their profession. Finally, we provide some thoughts on future directions of counselling psychology in Canada by outlining the issues and problems that remain to be addressed if counselling psychology is to continue to develop as a viable specialization within the broad field of psychology. Thus, we see this chapter as an initial step in helping define more clearly the nature of counselling psychology in Canada. We trust that it will not be the final word on our Canadian professional identity.

Developmental Roots

The title "counselling psychologist" suggests affiliation with two professions: counselling and psychology. Therefore, in compiling a definition both affiliations must be taken into account. The definition problem is exacerbated because the title suggests both a domain and a process: While counselling psychology is a domain of practice, counselling is also a process that is a part of other psychological disciplines (Whiteley, 1984).

In both Canada and the United States, counselling psychology has its two main professional ties, respectively. The counselling professional affiliations are with the Canadian Guidance and Counselling Association (CGCA) and the American Association for Counseling and Development (AACD); the psychological professional affiliations are with the Canadian Psychological Association (CPA) and the American Psychological Association (APA). Counselling psychology as a specialization within the broad field of psychology is represented in the Counselling Psychology Section (current membership 180) of the Canadian Psychological Association. The section was formed in 1986 and has since moved to establish its own newsletter, *Matrix*, and implement accreditation procedures for training programmes and internships in counselling psychology. The structure and composition of CPA, and the similarities and differences with APA, are outlined elsewhere in this book and will not be repeated here. The counselling component of counselling psychology, however, remains to be described.

Important differences exist between the structure of the CGCA and the AACD which give counselling a different professional character in the two countries. The AACD is a national umbrella organization with divisions focusing on various areas of counselling application: This provides a national voice for school counsellors, college and university counsellors, career counsellors, counsellor educators, etc., and each contributes to a united voice for counsellors as a whole. In Canada, the CGCA (current membership 1300) was formed on a geographical basis with each province represented on the board of directors (the provinces of Ontario, Quebec and New Brunswick have both an anglophone and a francophone director). In response to the professional affiliation needs of various counselling specializations, a myriad of independent professional organizations were created, some at a national level and others at a provincial level. This has resulted in a wide array of professional organizations that have stakeholder interest in the field of counselling. For example, in a recent project involving the first author (Hiebert, in press), there are eight national organizations, each independent from the other and each having a stakeholder interest in career counselling for youth. Undoubtedly, national projects directed at other counselling specialties would require similar diverse representation.

The matter is further complicated because some counselling specializations have no national representation. For example, because education (schooling) is a provincial matter in Canada, school counselling is organized on a provincial basis, and no national voice exists for school counsellors. Conger (1989) has pointed out the substantial contribution to career counselling by the research and programme development commissioned by Employment and Immigration Canada. At the time of writing, however, no national organization exists for career counselling specialists. This situation undoubtedly reduces the impact that counselling can have on national policy makers.

Summary

The developmental roots of counselling psychology in Canada are relatively brief and complicated by a title suggesting affiliation with both counselling and psychology. This complication is exhibited in the profusion resulting of professional associations. Professionals who view themselves more as counsellors may be more likely to affiliate themselves with one or more of the regional or national counselling organizations, such as the CGCA, while professionals who view themselves more as psychologists may affiliate themselves with their provincial psychological associations or the Counselling Psychology Section of CPA. Counselling is not well represented at the national level in Canada; unlike in the United States, there is no organization and there are no counselling-oriented professionals to provide a unified voice for specialist or generalist counsellors. It seems to us that the identity of counselling psychology in Canada and the primary professional affiliation for Canadian counselling psychologists is yet to be identified.

Counselling Psychology: The Search for Professional Identity

We encountered a dilemma in attempting to define counselling psychology because virtually all such attempts have been American in context. Our choice was whether to rely on past American definitions to describe counselling psychology in Canada or to construct a particularly Canadian definition. We chose the second alternative and approached it empirically.

Survey of Counselling Psychologists

Method and Sample

In order to get a representative picture of the nature of counselling psychology in Canada, a six-page open-ended questionnaire was sent to all registered members of the counselling psychology division of the CPA and the counsellor educator's chapter of the CGCA. The questionnaire asked the recipients to define counselling psychology and indicate how it was different from counselling and from other branches of psychology. It also asked respondents to indicate the nature of their clients' concerns and the nature of their interventions. Finally, it asked respondents to identify what they saw as the future developmental path for their profession.

A total of 300 questionnaires were distributed, of which 32 were returned as having incorrect addresses and 23 were returned in usable form. This represents a return rate of about 9%. One surprising observation was that only 21 names appeared on both CPA and CGCA lists. It seems that most people declare their professional affiliation with either counselling *or* psychology, but not with both. About 70% of the respondents listed counselling psychology as their primary or secondary professional affiliation. Of these, three-quarters had doctoral-level training, most having graduated from counselling psychology programmes. Thus, the picture presented in the remainder of this section represents the perspective regarding counselling psychology of 16 of our peers.

The combination of such a wide distribution and the lengthy open-ended questionnaire format perhaps virtually assured a low return rate, though it is not dramatically different from that obtained in other similar investigations (e.g. Sinclair, Poizner, Gilmor-Barrett & Randall, 1987; Spokane & Hawks, 1990), nor is the final number that different from many ethnographic studies. Undoubtedly, we could have increased the return rate by shortening the questionnaire or making the response format more structured (cf. Hunsley & Lefebvre, 1990; Sinclair, et al., 1987), or by selecting a smaller subset of potential respondents (cf. Spokane & Hawks, 1990). However, we reasoned that it was important to gain input from as wide a base as possible and to use a format that would not restrict responses. In the end, we decided that the collective opinions of those responding would paint a more representative picture of Canadian counselling psychology than merely relying on our own views. Therefore, we have used their responses as a guide in preparing the following descriptions. Nevertheless, we do acknowledge that the small sample size should caution readers against overdrawing on the survey results for conclusions about our field.[1]

Data Aggregation

A content analysis was conducted on the answers to each question to develop a categorization system that emerged naturally from the raw data (cf. Glaser & Strauss, 1967; Smith,1987). Where possible, accepted terms from extant literature were used for category labels, e.g. terms in the APA Division 17 definition or Morrill, Oetting and Hurst's (1974) classification of client problems. In all cases, care was taken to provide an accurate aggregation of respondent descriptions rather than to fit those descriptions into categories where they did not belong. The entire data set was coded independently by two raters, and where coding discrepancies existed, the category descriptors were redefined until consensus was achieved on all responses, thus satisfying the criterion of intersubjectivity (cf. Stone, 1985).

---

1 Readers wishing a copy of the questionnaire, or a copy of the raw data (i.e. the participants' responses), may contact the first author.

Defining Counselling Psychology

From the responses to our questionnaire, a composite definition of counselling psychology emerged in terms of professional identity and areas of practice.

Professional Identity

Respondents overwhelmingly identified counselling psychology as a specialization within the broad field of psychology. The focus in counselling psychology was thought to be working with "normal" (vs. pathological) clients, living in community (rather than institutional) settings, who were experiencing any number of developmental life issues or personal life crises. The realm of practice was identified as primarily remedial or rehabilitative, in the attempt to resolve a discrepancy between the demands or problems people face and their skills for dealing with those problems. Counselling psychology was seen as differing from counselling in that counselling psychologists had more extensive psychological backgrounds and operated from a more scientific and research-oriented base. Furthermore, counselling psychologists were trained at a more advanced level (doctoral rather than master's), practised in more varied types of work settings and worked with a broader spectrum of clients, both in terms of variety and severity of client problems. Counselling psychology was thought to be different from other psychological specialties in that it was more interactive, and in that the focus of the interaction was more educational in nature, focusing on the client's life situation and perceptions. There was agreement that while assessment and diagnosis were often a part of counselling psychology, the focus was more on interactive techniques that support client growth and change, rather than on labeling and diagnosis.

Areas of Practice

Three-quarters of the respondents who identified themselves as counselling psychologists indicated they saw clients as a regular part of their work; the remainder worked in academic settings where they did not see clients. Half of the respondents who saw clients did so in private-practice settings, with the rest working in school or university counselling environments. Descriptions of the types of clients seen were consistent with the definition of counselling psychology provided by respondents. Most clients were normally functioning adults or children from a broad cross-section of society.

The types of client problems fell nicely into Morrill et al.'s (1974) framework. The largest category of concerns was remedial, addressing people currently experiencing difficulties or with a diagnosed problem. The problem areas included unemployment, marital tension, bereavement, abuse (sexual, emotional, physical or substance), stress and anxiety, interpersonal conflicts (marital tension, relationship problems) and chronic illness. The second largest category of concerns was preventive, focusing on people who were at risk of developing particular types of problems but who had not yet done so. These included adolescents with career concerns, special needs clients and students with low self-esteem. The primary intervention in this category was some form of skill training aimed at giving clients greater resources for dealing with likely problems. Only two respondents reported working with clients within a developmental framework, where the focus was on working preventatively with all clients, not just those who were identified as being "at risk". The focus in these cases was on promoting self-esteem or working in career-related areas.

Future Directions

In order to get some sense of where the profession was heading, we asked respondents to comment on the future direction of research, theory development, professional issues, professional organizations and areas of practice. We suggested that if they saw a difference between where they thought the profession was heading and where they would like the profession to be heading, they should separate those two ideas.

Research

Our respondents clearly felt that the trends in Canadian counselling psychology research would continue to reflect prevalent thrusts in the North American literature, and that this was a positive direction. Specifically, the prediction was for a continued emphasis on applied research, focusing on specific client groups and/or specific interventions addressing the basic question "Which kinds of interventions work best with which types of clients?" It was predicted that future studies would pay more attention to counsellor/client process variables instrumental in promoting success in counselling, thus continuing another recent trend in counselling research. This was seen as an attempt to improve the success rate of various interventions and to provide a data base to aid in the selection of "best" treatment combinations. It was predicted that career development issues, women's issues and special client populations would continue to be strong research areas, and that there would be a continuing thrust towards qualitative methodology. In every case these were thought to be positive developments.

Theory Development

There was a strong belief that the future direction of theory development in counselling psychology would focus on how various theoretical perspectives can be brought to bear on understanding people as whole entities operating in their natural environments. Cognitive theories were thought to be of particular importance, especially with regards to understanding and facilitating client change processes. This emphasis on developing more integrated and holistic theories was seen as positive, although some resignation was also expressed to the effect that whatever happened in Canada would probably follow the developments occurring in the United States.

Professional Issues

Accreditation, certification and licensure were mentioned as central future professional concerns by two-thirds of our respondents. Accreditation was thought to be important because it would promote a more uniform calibre of training. Certification and licensure were thought to be important in promoting the credibility of psychologists, a particularly important theme in times of dwindling financial resources. Third-party reimbursement was thought to be a major professional issue needing to be addressed, especially by those in private practice. Ethical and legal issues were identified as requiring attention because such problems were seen as increasing, and because respondents regarded the preparation in these areas provided by their training programmes as being inadequate.

Two strong positions emerged regarding the nature of professional organizations pertaining to counselling psychology: One group expressed the need for related professional organizations to work more closely together and to strive to remove territorial barriers between professional groups; the other group expressed a need for developing a stronger unique professional identity for counselling psychology to make it more distinct from clinical psychology and from counselling. The authors view this as an important professional issue and discuss it in more detail below.

Service Delivery

According to our respondents, remedial or rehabilitative concerns will continue to dominate the practice of counselling psychologists. The prevailing view was that the current array of client problems would probably persist in the foreseeable future, although they might increase in intensity. Regarding intervention methods, there was some feeling that self-help groups would become a more important intervention mode, and that computer applications are particularly promising methods for intervention delivery. There was agreement that intervening with a third party on behalf of the client (advocacy) would become more necessary, and that generally more emphasis would need to be placed on interventions taking place outside the psychologist's office and in community-based facilities. There also was the strong opinion that interventions aimed at an educative and developmental level would become increasingly important. These would be primarily preventative programmes aimed at the general population, rather than only at persons identified as being "at risk". Health and lifestyle development was identified as being a particularly important area.

Summary

Questionnaire results indicate that counselling is perceived as a specialty within psychology, the practitioners of which provide primarily remedial or rehabilitative and preventative assistance to "normal" clients experiencing developmental life problems or personal life crises. Those counselling psychologists seeing clients as a regular part of their work do so in private practice, public schools or university settings. Counselling psychologists were thought to be different from counsellors by typically having had more education and relying more on research for intervention planning. Our sample predicted a continuing increased emphasis on applied research examining various interventions for specific client groups and counsellor-client process variables that enhance counselling outcomes. They believed that future theory development would move toward producing more integrated and holistic theories of people in their natural environments. Service delivery was seen to be primarily remedial or rehabilitative in nature, with "at-risk" populations, although educative and developmental interventions would likely increase with public interest in health and lifestyle issues. Professional issues identified as requiring future attention included accreditation, certification, licensure and ethical-legal education. Participants were notably divided on whether to direct energy to remove territorial barriers among professional groups or to develop a stronger identity for counselling psychology. Generally speaking, Canadian counselling psychologists were optimistic in their view of the future of counselling psychology in Canada and indicated considerable similarity between their wishes for the future development of the profession and what they expected actually would take place.

Professional Issues

We stated at the beginning of this chapter that we saw two alternative ways to approach the task of defining counselling psychology in Canada: to use existing literature to compare and contrast counselling psychology with similar disciplines like clinical psychology and counselling; or to focus on the Canadian context, comparing it, where appropriate, to the American scene. We chose to focus on a Canadian perspective, rather than rely on the American literature, to determine our professional identity; for even though Canadian literature is sparse, we felt that it was important to begin examining our professional identity as Canadians, rather than simply assuming roles defined by our American colleagues. Thus, we first present some professional issues that have been addressed, or are in the process of being addressed, by Canadians, and then we turn to other professional issues that we believe to be important, but that have not yet – to the best of our knowledge – been addressed in the Canadian context. Our purpose here is not to attempt to resolve outstanding issues (we believe that to be the responsibility of professional groups with a stakeholder interest in counselling psychology), but to present various facets of the issues under discussion. It is our hope that outlining these issues will facilitate future debate and/or research to determine a Canadian position on these professional matters.

Professional Standards

Any discussion of professional standards usually includes accreditation, licensure and certification. *Accreditation* signifies that a particular training programme has satisfied criteria that a.professional association deems necessary to prepare competent practitioners. Programmes that wish to be accredited by a professional association apply primarily to that association and follow the evaluation procedure that the association has established. *Licensure*, on the other hand, refers to the legal right to practise in a particular field or to give oneself a particular professional designation. Provincial legislation is necessary in order to establish a licensing mechanism, and once in place, use of the particular professional title is restricted to those who have complied with the licensing procedure. *Certification* is less restrictive than licensure, for it does not require provincial legislation: It pertains only to standards established by a professional group which signify adequate preparation to practise. Certification typically carries little recognition outside of the professional group issuing the certificate, though it does provide some assurance to the public that professionals have received adequate training – at least in the eyes of the professional organization issuing the certificate. The current state of affairs regarding each of these areas is elaborated below.

Accreditation

There are no studies pertaining to the accreditation of Canadian programmes in counselling psychology. Yet the need for programme accreditation is apparent in data stemming from the United States, where APA-accredited programmes consistently have attracted more than twice as many applicants as nonaccredited programmes (Cameron, Galassi, Birk & Waggener, 1989; Galassi & Moss, 1986; Tipton, 1984). Nevertheless, the AACD also has an accreditation programme. The question then becomes "With whom should our programme affiliate, the AACD or the APA?" Some programmes in the United States have opted for accreditation with both professional bodies, although that option seems to be becoming increasingly unviable (See Wittmer, 1988).

As Martin (1988) has pointed out, it looks like Canada is heading down the same contentious path. As of this writing, the CGCA has prepared accreditation guidelines for master's programmes in counselling which have been approved by the Board of Directors and are ready for pilot testing. The Counselling Psychology Section of the CPA has prepared doctoral accreditation guidelines for both training programmes and internship programmes in counselling psychology, both of which have been approved by the Board of Directors. Canada may avoid some of the difficulties existing in the United States if the CGCA confines itself to addressing the needs of master's level training and the CPA focuses on doctoral level training. But should CPA doctoral programme accreditation standards affect the content of master's degrees or the CGCA move to include doctoral-level training in its accreditation programme, the Canadian scene also will be fraught with difficulty. It is our view that unless discussions take place between the CPA and the CGCA, and unless they choose to work together to avoid duplication, counselling psychology programmes in Canada will not have profited from the experiences of their American counterparts: They will face the same dilemma of choosing between well-intentioned, but competing professional standards.

Professional Standards and Our Primary Affiliation

Although counselling psychology has two professional roots, it is our view that a primary affiliation with psychology, rather than with counselling, is probably best for the profession. Ritchie (1990) points out that one of the criteria that a profession typically must fulfil is legal recognition (p. 224). Every Canadian province has legislation restricting the use of the term "psychologist" to those who have met provincial education standards, passed both written and oral examinations and complied with certain supervised practice guidelines. In every case, the knowledge criterion is satisfied by successful completion of the *Examination in the Professional Practice of Psychology*. In six provinces (British Columbia, Manitoba, Newfoundland, Prince Edward Island, Saskatchewan and Ontario), a doctoral degree is the minimum level of training, whereas two provinces (Alberta and Quebec) require a master's degree and two provinces (New Brunswick and Nova Scotia) prefer a doctoral degree, but will accept a master's degree if the applicant has additional supervised professional experience.

In Canada, the use of the term "counsellor", on the other hand, is not controlled in this manner. In the United States, at the time of writing, legislation licensing counsellors exists in 36 states (Clawson, personal communication), 33 of which require the successful completion of an examination as part of the licensing process. (See Brooks & Gerstein (1990) for a summary of credentialling issues in the United States.) In 29 states, the examination of the National Board for Certified Counsellors is used, while three states have developed their own examination. The CGCA recently voted against the principle of using an examination as the basis for certification and instead elected to use graduate-level training as the sole certification criteria. Thus, since some sort of external examination is an inextricable part of the licensing process in both Canada and the United States, licensing of counsellors in Canada does not appear likely in the near future, and counselling will continue to lack this indicator of a profession.

Another indication of the importance of external standards governing professional practice – and a testimony to the importance of a unified voice for a professional group – is a recent ruling that psychologists who are listed with the Canadian Register of Health Service Providers in Psychology will be exempt from the

Goods and Services Tax. King (1990) acknowledges that it was because psychologists had "acted and spoken as one in pursuit of a worthy goal" (p. 1) that this exemption was granted. Because of the diversity of counselling organizations, and in spite of the CGCA's attempts at reproachment with other counselling organizations, a unified voice for counsellors does not appear imminent. Finally, a further factor suggesting a closer affiliation with psychology than counselling is that the CPA seems to be moving more quickly to implement its accreditation programme, and to do so on more fronts (both training and internship) than the CGCA.

To our knowledge, Canadian studies addressing differences in the practice of counsellors and counselling psychologists have yet to be conducted. However, data from the United States (e.g. Watkins, Campbell & McGregor, 1989) indicate that counsellors usually hold a master's degree and spend more of their working time in personal and vocational counselling than in teaching and research. Given that attempts to define counselling psychology consistently include research activity, or at least practice-based on research, an observation confirmed by our data, it would appear that a closer professional affiliation with psychology would be natural. However, we hasten to add that a matter as important as this should be debated at the national forums of both professional associations.

Whither Our Home?

Most counselling psychology programmes in Canada and the United States are housed in faculties of education rather than departments of psychology. Although the appropriateness of this affiliation has seen little examination in Canada, it has been the subject of much debate in American journals (cf. Lent, Lopez & Forrest, 1988; Sprinthall, 1990; Westfield, Meadows & Talbert, 1987), and we think it is an important area to address. Therefore, we will depart momentarily from our focus on Canadian perspectives to summarize the American debate.

Some have argued this position on the basis that counselling is essentially an educational endeavour (Hiebert, 1989; Martin & Hiebert, 1985; Sprinthall, 1990). Sprinthall (1990) reminds us that the roots of counselling psychology lie in education, prevention and development – not in diagnosis and treatment, an observation also apparent in Whiteley's (1984) documentation of the history of counselling psychology. Sprinthall (1990) continues by pointing out that the theoretical basis for understanding normal life-span development has increased over the past two decades to the point that "we now have a cleaner successive approximation as to how humans grow and develop than that provided by any competing paradigm" (p. 459). Thus, the theoretical foundation for educational and developmental orientations seems to be more solid than in the past and located primarily in faculties of education.

Still, there is a move in many circles towards blurring the boundary between counselling and clinical psychology. This is reflected in the increasing number of counselling psychology graduates working in private-practice settings, the large numbers of clients being "treated" from a remedial perspective and the quest for third-party reimbursement. However, such a merger is not without danger. Horan (1989) pointed out that a large proportion of research in counselling psychology is directed at areas like career education, vocational counselling and preventative and developmental interventions, often undertaken in school contexts; and that these areas of interest typically do not receive strong support in psychology departments. Sprinthall (1990) makes a related point in arguing that abandoning the life-span developmental framework of counselling psychology for the diagnosis/treatment focus of clinical psychology will result in also abandoning the scientist-practitioner model in favour of a practitioner model that will invariably end up focusing on remediation and leaving "those who have the greatest need for assistance out of the service loop" (p. 460).

From the responses of Canadian counselling psychologists it would appear that we are already proceeding down the road to reproachment. A large proportion of our respondents were involved, either full or part time, in private practice; the largest portion of their client case loads was remedial in nature; and around half of them were in favour of striving to remove territorial barriers between different client service professionals. However, an equal number of respondents favoured channeling more energy into developing a stronger professional identity for counselling psychology and identifying more clearly how it is similar to and different from other professional groups. Considerable inconsistency and confusion, in terms of philosophy, intervention, client population, work setting and professional title, currently exists between training programmes for both counsellors and counselling psychologists and the locations of those programmes. We suggest that it is in the best interest of each professional identity to sort out this confusion. Neither a department of psychology nor a faculty of education will long support a programme that is inconsistent with the department or faculty missions. Consistency between the programme thrust and the department or faculty mission is necessary for counselling psychology regardless of where its home ultimately is located.

Scientist-Practitioner

Canadian counselling psychologists reported that one factor separating counselling psychologists from counsellors is that the former are more likely to operate from a research base. Whiteley (1984) also points out that attempts to define counselling psychology have persistently contained a statement that one of the functions of counselling psychologists is to conduct research with the potential to produce more effective practitioners. This would suggest that a scientist-practitioner approach, in which research plays an integral role in practice (cf. Howard, 1985), would have particular relevance for counselling psychologists.

In light of this, it is somewhat surprising to find reports that the research productivity of American counselling psychologists is balefully low. Carkhuff (1968) estimated that for more than 90% of counselling psychologists the last piece of research conducted was their doctoral dissertation. Gelso (1979) confirmed this perspective 11 years later, indicating that the modal counselling psychologist published no research following the doctoral degree. Walton (1982) found that 60% of his sample, most of whom were academics, published less than one article per year (see Hiebert, 1988, for a summary). Similar observations were reported in Fitzgerald and Osipow's (1986) occupational analysis of counselling psychology, which found that 75% of counselling psychologists spent 14% or less of their time in research activities (reviewing literature, preparing manuscripts or conducting field studies). Most recently, Zimpfer and DeTrude's (1990) survey of doctoral graduates further revealed that only 25% had published one or more articles in the year preceding their survey.

If research is one of the cornerstones of our profession, then we would expect far more emphasis on applied research in training programmes and a greater, or at least more obvious, display of research endeavours by those involved in the practice and training of counselling psychologists. Some might argue that the importance of research for practising counselling psychologists might be addressed by teaching practitioners to be good consumers of research even if they are not actively involved in research themselves. We would counter that people not involved in research are unlikely to maintain a research-driven orientation to their practice. For example, Fitzgerald and Osipow (1986) discovered that very few counselling psychologists review literature. Howarth (1989) reviewed 10 recent books dealing with client interventions and found that only one of them addressed the necessity of evaluating client outcome in an empirically defensible manner. As Coons (1990) points out, in our consumer-driven society, it will become increasingly necessary to demonstrate tangibly that counselling has made a difference in the lives of clients. This will be difficult to do if practitioners spend little time reviewing literature, if sources describing client interventions do not elaborate explicit procedures for obtaining such tangible demonstrations and if counselling psychologists do not have a procedural orientation that fosters placing client intervention within a research-driven framework.

Ivey (1980) contends that there is a growing consensus that counselling psychologists in the future "will be searching for a logical consistency in their procedures ... [and that] ... as this consistency evolves, [idiosyncratic] eclecticism ... will lose favor to systematic metatheoretical approaches that provide a rationale for what one is doing" (p. 119). It is interesting to note that many authors advocate moving away from single-theory approaches and sloppy-minded, idiosyncratic eclecticism. In some cases, a new model deriving from theoretical commonalities is recommended (cf. theoretical integration, Beitman, 1989), while in other cases the new model is guided by the impact of client qualities and specific procedures and techniques (cf. prescriptive [technical] eclecticism, Lazarus, 1989). (See Corey, 1991; Norcross & Greneavage,

1989; Smith, 1982 for a more complete discussion of the movement towards theoretical and procedural integrationism.) We believe that such systematic metatheoretical approaches will not develop in an empirical vacuum, and that the logical consistency in procedures is unlikely to be discovered without a strong research-practitioner focus amongst counselling psychologists. Sprinthall (1990) agrees, suggesting that it is time to re-root counselling psychology in the scientist-practitioner model, to underscore our unique distinctiveness from clinical psychology and to re-establish our mission as emphasizing educational and preventive measures focused on promoting growth.

The main point in the preceding discussion is that if research is to be a central part in the definition of counselling psychology, then it will needs to be a central part in the practice of counselling psychologists. The data from the United States portray a separation between what people say and what they do with regards to this area. There is a need, in our view, for Canadian studies addressing the match between professional definition (which includes an emphasis on research) and actual practice of counselling psychologists; for as Lichtenberg (1986) pointed out, the lack of research productivity suggests a seemingly growing separation between research and practice which could well result in counselling psychology separating itself from its very identity.

Training Issues

Although the Canadian literature is noticeably quiet on this topic, several issues pertinent to the preparation of counselling psychologists have been raised in the American literature. Some of these, like programme accreditation, licensure and certification, were dealt above. Other issues, like whether master's- or doctoral-level training is appropriate preparation (see Watkins et al., 1989), are largely non sequiturs for the research productivity rates of master's-level psychology programmes is similar to the overall productivity rates in psychology (Gordon, 1990). Furthermore, the use of the term "psychologist" is a matter of provincial legislation in Canada. Therefore, we will address only briefly the content of training programmes in counselling psychology.

Surveys of counselling psychology training programmes in the United States (Cameron et al., 1989; Galassi & Moss, 1986; Tipton, 1984) have consistently indicated that substantial proportions of graduates in counselling psychology are finding employment in private-practice settings. This is the second largest and the fastest growing category of employment. Cameron et al. (1989) also pointed out that graduates generally do not find employment in the places where they intern. Moreover, although many graduate programmes have formal internship or practicum placement arrangements with college and university counselling centres, these also do not provide experience in the types of settings in which the graduates will subsequently be working. The question then arises, "Are our programmes preparing students for the settings in which they are finding work?" Galassi and Moss (1986) suggest they are not. It seems to us that this pattern is not different from the situation in Canada.

However, the natural response to re-tool the content of our training programmes to match more closely the work environments of our graduates contains an inherent difficulty: It leads in precisely the direction that, as Sprinthall (1990) cautions, takes us away from our professional roots. Fitzgerald and Osipow (1986) point out that an examination of the way counselling psychologists spend their time and their job-related behaviours suggests that "we appear to have come a long way from the scientist-practitioner model" (p. 543). Moreover, the trend away from a research base and a developmental or educational practice focus is more apparent for younger counselling psychologists. Fitzgerald and Osipow (1986) conclude that the single most identifiable characteristic of counselling psychology, namely, career/vocational development and counselling, "appears to be eroding as the foundation of the discipline" (p. 543). They point out that this shift is ironic because it is occurring "at a time when clinical psychologists are discovering vocational psychology and career development" (p. 543).

Perhaps it would be better to spend more energy developing a stronger sense of professional identity – a more salient idea of what counselling psychologists do – instead of altering the content of training programmes to prepare graduates for more clinical-oriented settings. Our data support this contention, in that while self-help groups and advocacy roles with an educational or developmental focus were seen to be more important in the future, current practice did not closely match those future roles. Perhaps a stronger sense of the appropriate roles and spheres of practice for counselling psychologists would have resulted had there been a closer match between the current intervention thrusts of our sample and their vision of future developments. Our central point is that when a discrepancy exists between the content of training programmes and the current practices of graduates of those programmes, at least two viable corrective procedures exist: One is to *alter the content of the training* to give people the skills they need to service the client group with which they are working; the other is to take steps to *change the sphere of practice* so that it more closely matches the areas in which the person was trained. In the American literature cited earlier, the thrust seems to be on the first of these alternatives. Nevertheless, we view both as viable alternatives and foresee a stronger sense of professional identity as the means to achieving the second alternative. Perhaps counselling psychology should curb its haste to abandon its professional roots and identify more closely with its clinical cousin. Moving in this direction would mean concentrating more completely and explicitly on developing the skills, and sense of mission, that would enable graduates to address more adequately the needs of clients that lie within the traditional spheres of practice for counselling psychologists.

When considering the match between professional identity, the content of training programmes and the skills required for future employment, it is important to have a clear idea of which is the tail and which is the dog. In our view, a strong sense of professional identity is central and should predominate all facets of graduate training. The content of training programmes, and the resulting skill repertoires of graduates, should result logically from the view of the professional identity of counselling psychology upon which the programme is based – not vice versa. In other words, training programmes should be built on a mission statement that outlines the conceptualization of counselling psychology as a profession, and that conceptualization should guide the content of the training programme and not derive by default from the collection of courses embedded in the programme. We are not suggesting that professionals should abandon attempts at reproachment between counselling and clinical psychology; we are only saying that it is important to consider the long-term impact before programmes are refocused to meet a "need" that may not be in the best interest of the profession.

Summary

In this section we have presented a number of professional issues requiring attention by counselling psychologists. Accreditation of programmes and internships may become a confusing matter similar to that found in the United States unless representatives of the CGCA and the CPA quickly begin working to sort out their territorial areas of interest. Several factors, including provincial control of professional title through external standards, speed of implementation of programme accreditation standards and emphasis on research in practice, may indicate that counselling psychology is better served by a primary identification with psychology. Whether the best home for counselling psychology is in a faculty of education or a department of psychology is at present unclear when views on both sides of the matter are examined. What is clear is that there is a need for counselling psychology to develop consistency within relevant factors affecting the profession so that a secure home is ultimately assured. We suggest that the scientist-practitioner model will continue to serve counselling psychology well in the future, because of our continued emphasis on a research orientation to training and practice and because of the growing consumer orientation towards accountability in service delivery. When considering training issues, it is important to scrutinize programme change in relation to a clear professional identity and concern for the long-term effects on the profession. The answers to these professional issues will influence the identity of the profession and as a result they deserve serious and systematic attention by the professional organizations interested in representing counselling psychology. If we do not undertake to resolve these issues ourselves, others may do it for us and we may not like the result.

Conclusion

Counselling psychology in Canada appears to be a viable profession with a relatively brief developmental history, except in relation to its American counterpart. Two important considerations arise from this statement, the first pertaining to our status as a profession, the second dealing with the sparsity of literature investigating a Canadian perspective.

When we say "counselling psychology is a viable profession" we mean that it satisfies the criteria usually espoused as being necessary for recognition as a profession (cf. Friesen, 1983; McCully & Miller, 1962; Ritchie, 1990). The most troublesome of these criteria – and the one that will therefore require considerable future attention – is the one dealing with the possession of a body of knowledge unique to the profession, not generally known by the public and based on scientific research (cf. Ritchie, 1990). The uniqueness of the knowledge base in counselling psychology is somewhat problematic because counselling is a process shared by numerous other groups, both professional and nonprofessional. A further problem also arises from the requirement that the knowledge base be developed from scientific research. Emener and Cottone (1989) point out that the lack of a research-driven theoretical base for counselling techniques has been a constant source of criticism. Although we would hasten to add that, based on Coons' (1990) treatise, perhaps counselling psychology is no more culpable in this regard than other branches of psychology. Yet in our view this underscores the importance of maintaining a scientist-practitioner approach and an emphasis on research in counselling psychology training programmes.

The second consideration pertains to the absence of professional documentation of a Canadian perspective on counselling psychology. The few reports that do exist (e.g. Friesen, 1983; Lecomte et al., 1981) seem to represent a "Canadian perspective" largely because the writers are Canadians, not because they focus on the state of affairs in Canada or review Canadian research. Such Canadian-focused research does exist in other spheres, for example, Gfellner and Hundleby's (1990) review of Canadian research on adolescence, Hiebert's (1985) review of Canadian research on teacher stress and Jevne's (1981) study investigating counsellor competencies. To our knowledge, the data given earlier in this chapter represent the first attempt to identify how Canadian counselling psychologists perceive their profession. It is vital to the development of counselling psychology in Canada that further research be conducted focusing on the central issues in our profession, many of which we have raised in this chapter. The issues we raised earlier (e.g. the content of training programmes, the research endeavours of counselling psychologists, the match between the espoused cornerstones of professional identity and one's practice of the profession, etc.) all lend themselves to empirical scrutiny. It is time for Canadian counselling psychologists to take up the challenge and use their espoused research focus to address these professional issues.

Finally, there is a definite need for counselling psychologists to select and promote a national organization to serve as a forum and coordinating entity for the profession. The basic question "Are we counsellors or psychologists?" likely will continue to plague people in the field. Will the question continue to be phrased in dichotomously or is there some room for reproachment? Do those seeking an answer need to affiliate with an existing professional organization, develop a new one to represent their interests or divide their loyalties amongst several professional organizations? At present the answers are uncertain.

Perhaps the answer to the counsellor-psychologist question is not as important as the process of debating the issue. The question will continue to remain central to the professional identity of counselling psychologists and is therefore worthy of attention by the existing national stakeholder associations, those involved in training counsellors and counselling psychologists and individuals working in the field. The answer obtained will affect the choice of professional affiliation, which in turn will affect the development of the respective professional identity. Perhaps the criteria for selection should be the organization with the most resources and infrastructure to develop our professional identity (whatever that might evolve to be) and with the strongest ability to speak with a knowledgeable national voice for the profession. Without all, or at least most, of the personal and organizational resources located within one organization, it is likely that the professional evolution of counselling psychology in Canada will lack direction. We would hope for increased personal and organizational resolve to address this professional issue in order to advance our developing profession in Canada. It is our hope that an orderly and collaborative decision can be made concerning these professional issues.

We stated at the outset of this chapter that we intended to provide a nonpartisan "state-of-the-art" description of counselling psychology in Canada. Perhaps our discussion has raised as many questions as it has addressed, but we believe the issues are ones that require debate. Certainly, this is not the final word on the professional identity of counselling psychology in Canada; but we hope it is an important word – one that will encourage others to address a Canadian perspective on the issues central to the professional identity of counselling psychology in Canada.

Acknowledgement

The authors wish to thank Nancy Arthur, Rey Carr, Corinne Koehn, Lee Handy and David de Rosenroll for their helpful comments on the draft version of this chapter, and Gwen Hartrick for her assistance with data analysis.

References

Beitman, B.D. (1989). Why I am an integrationist (not an eclectic). *British Journal of Guidance and Counselling*, *17*, 259–273.

Brooks, D.K., & Gerstein, L.H. (1990). Counselor credentialing and interprofessional collaboration. *Journal of Counseling & Development*, *68*, 477–490.

Cameron, A.S., Galassi, J.P., Birk, J.M., & Waggener, N.M. (1989). Trends in counseling psychology training programs: The council of counseling psychology training programs survey, 1975–1987. *Counseling Psychologist*, *17*, 301–313.

Carkhuff, R.R. (1968). A "non-traditional" assessment of graduate education in the helping professions. *Counselor Education and Supervision*, *8*, 252–261.

Clawson, T. (1990). Personal communication regarding administration and use of the National Board for Certified Counselors Examination.

Conger, D.S. (1989). *Some contributions to vocational psychology in Canada*. Ottawa: Canada Employment and Immigration Commission.

Coons, W.H. (1990). The crooked path. *Canadian Psychology/Psychologie Canadienne*, *31*, 138–146.

Corey, G. (1991). *Theory and practice of counseling and psychotherapy* (4th ed.). Pacific Grove, CA: Brooks/Cole.

Emener, W.G., & Cottone, R.R. (1989). Professionalization, deprofessionalization, and reprofessionalization of rehabilitation counseling according to criteria of professions. *Journal of Counseling and Development*, *67*, 576–581.

Fitzgerald, L.F., & Osipow, S.H. (1986). An occupational analysis of counseling psychology. *American Psychologist*, *41*, 535–544.

Friesen, J.D. (1983). Counselling psychology: A discipline. *Canadian Counsellor*, *17*, 147–154.

Galassi, J.P., & Moss, N.L. (1986). Training in counseling psychology: 1985 data and trends. *Counseling Psychologist*, *14*, 471–477.

Gelso, C.J. (1979). Research in counseling: Methodological and professional issues. *Counseling Psychologist*, *8*(3), 7–35.

Gfellner, B.M., & Hundleby, J.D. (1990). The status of Canadian research on adolescence: 1980–1987. *Canadian Psychology/Psychologie Canadienne*, *31*, 132–137.

Glaser, B.G., & Strauss, A.L. (1967). *The discovery of grounded theory: Strategies for qualitative research*. Chicago: Aldine.

Gordon, R.A. (1990). Research productivity in master's-level psychology programs. *Professional Psychology*, *21*, 33–36.

Hiebert, B. (1988). Modeling: An important aspect of counsellor education. *Guidance & Counselling*, *3*(5), 28–37.

Hiebert, B. (1989). Meeting the accountability challenge. *NATCON-15*. Toronto: Ontario College Counsellor's Association.

Hiebert, B. (in press). Creation and mobilization of counselling resources for youth. *Canadian Vocational Association Journal*.

Hiebert, B. (1985). *Stress and teachers: The Canadian scene*. Toronto: Canadian Education Association.

Horan, J. (1989, March). Counseling psychology training in Colleges of Education: Issues of integration and focus. Symposium presented to the Annual Conference of the American Educational Research Association, San Francisco, CA.

Howard, G.S. (1985). Can research in the human sciences becomes more relevant to practice? *Journal of Counselling and Development*, *63*, 539–544.

Howarth, I. (1989). Psychotherapy: Who benefits? *Psychologist*, *2*, 150–152.

Hunsley, J., & Lefebvre, M. (1990). A survey of the practices and activities of Canadian clinical psychologists. *Canadian Psychology/Psychologie canadienne, 31*, 350–358.

Ivey, A. (1980). Counseling 2000: Time to take charge! In J. M. Whiteley & B. Freiz (Eds.), *The present and future of counseling psychology* (pp. 113–123). Monterey, CA: Brooks/Cole.

Jevne, R. (1981). Counselor competencies and selected Canadian counsellor educators. *Canadian Counsellor, 15*, 57–63.

King, M.C. (1990). From the president. *Bulletin of the Canadian Register of Health Service Providers in Psychology*, *4*(1), 1–2.

Lazarus, A.A. (1989). Why I am an eclectic (not an integrationist). *British Journal of Guidance and Counselling, 17*, 248–258.

Lecomte, C., Dumont, F, & Zingle, H.W. (1981). Research in counselling psychology: Changing emphasis in a Canadian perspective. *Canadian Counsellor, 16*, 9–20.

Lent, R.W., Lopez, F.G., & Forrest, L. (1988). Counseling psychology in colleges of education: A time to leave home? *Counselling Psychologist, 16*, 488–491.

Lichtenberg, J.W. (1986). Counseling research: Irrelevant or ignored? *Journal of Counseling and Development, 64*, 365–366.

Martin, J. (1988). Professional identities: Reflections of a Canadian in America's heartland. *Counselor Education and Supervision, 27*, 298–300.

Martin, J., & Hiebert, B. (1985). *Instructional counseling: A method for counselors.* Pittsburgh, PA: University of Pittsburgh Press.

McCully, C.H., & Miller, L.L. (1962). *Challenge for change in counselor education.* Minneapolis, MN: Burgess.

Morrill, W.H., Oetting, E.R., & Hurst, J.C. (1974). Dimensions of counselor functioning. *Personnel and Guidance Journal, 52*, 354–359.

Norcross, J.C., & Greneavage, L.M. (1989) Eclecticism and integration in counseling and psychotherapy: Major themes and obstacles. *British Journal of Guidance and Counselling, 17*, 227–247.

Ritchie, M.H. (1990). Counseling is not a profession – yet. *Counselor Education and Supervision, 29*, 220–227.

Sinclair, C., Poizner, S., Gilmor-Barrett, K., & Randall, D. (1987). The development of a code of ethics for Canadian psychologists. *Canadian Psychology/Psychologie canadienne, 28*, 1–8.

Smith, D. (1982) Trends in counseling and psychotherapy. *American Psychologist, 37*, 802–809.

Smith, M.L. (1987). Publishing qualitative research. *American Educational Research Journal, 24*, 173–183.

Spokane, A.R., & Hawkes, B.K. (1990) Annual review: Practice and research in career counseling and development, 1989. *Career Development Quarterly*, *39*, 98–128.

Sprinthall, N.A. (1990). Counseling psychology from Greyston to Atlanta: On the road to Armageddon? *Counseling Psychologist*, *18*, 455–463.

Stone, C.R. (1985). Qualitative research: A viable psychological alternative. *Psychological Record*, *35*, 63–75.

Tipton, R.M. (1984). Trends and issues in the training and development of counseling psychologists. *Counseling Psychologist*, *12*, 111–112.

Walton, J.M. (1982). Research activity and scholarly productivity among counselor educators. *Counselor Education and Supervision*, *21*, 305–311.

Watkins, C.E., Campbell, V.L., & McGregor, P. (1989). APA-affiliated master's-level counselors. *Counseling Psychologist*, *17*, 289–300.

Westfield, J.S., Meadows, M.E., & Talbert, F.S. (1987). Issues faced by counseling psychology programs located in colleges of education. *Counseling Psychologist*, *15*, 624–625.

Whiteley, J. M. (1984). A historical perspective on the development of counseling psychology as a profession. In S.D. Brown & R.W. Lent (Eds.), *Handbook of counseling psychology* (pp. 3–55). New York: John Wiley & Sons.

Wittmer, J. (1988). CACREP or APA: A counselor educator's personal view. *Counselor Education and Supervision*, *27*, 291–294.

Zimpfer, D.G., & DeTrude, J.C. (1990). Follow-up of doctoral graduates in counseling. *Journal of Counseling and Development*, *69*, 51–56.

Zytowski, D.G., & Rosen, D.A. (1982). The grand tour: 30 years of counseling psychology in the *Annual Review of Psychology*. *Counseling Psychologist*, *10*(1), 69–81.

13

Contemporary Issues in School Psychology

D. H. Saklofske
University of Saskatchewan

H. L. Janzen
University of Alberta

School psychology is a dynamic area of both professional and academic psychology. While school psychology may be considered to be as old as clinical psychology, its growth, identity and organization have not been as great or dramatic as that of clinical psychology, especially in Canada. School psychology in Canada has become much more obvious in only the past ten years. There are well-established university training programmes and a great amount of activity both provincially and nationally to develop professional school psychology associations. There is a growing body of Canadian research focusing on school and educational psychology that is being published in Canadian journals. All provinces employ professionals to deliver psychological services to schools, although the roles and task performed are quite variable because of Canada's great physical and cultural diversity.

In this chapter we describe contemporary issues in Canadian school psychology. I doinf so we pay particular, attention to the roles and functions of school psychologists, as well as the recent efforts to establish a professional identity, and provide an overview of the research that is both produced and consulted by them. Illustrations of school psychology applications, including the clientele and work settings, reflect both the traditional and changing roles of Canadian school psychologists.

Roles and Functions of School Psychologists

In the USA, descriptions of what school psychologists do can be found in various journal articles and books; at the same time, organizations such as the National Association of School Psychologists have recommended particular competencies for school psychologists in relation to both indirect and direct pupil service dimensions. There is no general statement that articulates the roles and functions ascribed to Canadian school psychologists. Each province, and even individual school boards, may have their own job or task descriptions. For example, while some job descriptions list several general functions such as assessment and reporting to and consulting with teachers and parents, others such as Quebec have listed 41 different psychological services that are provided by either school psychologists, or by other specially trained educational personnel.

The Canadian "mosaic" makes it very difficult to offer broad, sweeping statements about what it is that school psychologists actually do. However, there are some commonalities that stem from the view of the school psychologist as a professional, trained in both psychology and education, whose purpose is to support individual student growth and improve the quality and effectiveness of the educational process through the use of psychological skills and knowledge (Livingston, 1973; Haverstock & Millman, 1991).

Given the history of clinical and school psychology, which was entrenched in the "testing movement", it might be expected that the testing function would still be an important one today. Statements such as "school psychology was born in the prison of a test, and although the cell has been enlarged somewhat, it is still a prison" (Sarason, 1977, p. 27), and descriptions of the school psychologist's role as the "gatekeeper of special education" (Ysseldyke, Reynolds & Weinberg, 1984), certainly reflect the importance and dominance of the assessment function. Just as the medical doctor must diagnose a person's condition and needs before prescribing a particular treatment, school psychologists will always be requested to engage in diagnostic assessment based on data obtained from formal (e. g. intelligence, personality, achievement) and informal tests, observations, interviews, case histories and so forth.

However, the assessment needs of today have gone far beyond the routine and limited administration of "mental ability tests", and testing is now viewed in the appropriate context of assessment as an ongoing activity and one that is crucial to the decision-making process (e. g. placement in special programmes, determination of most effective teaching strategies or programmes, further referral for treatment of depression or attentional problems). Thus, school psychologists are leaving the "prison", and while comprehensive assessment rather than "testing" is still an important function, it is placed more appropriately in the context of direct and indirect services to individual students, teachers, parents and schools.

A recent survey conducted by Dumont (1989) and a 1991 issue of the *Canadian Journal of School Psychology* provide provincial overviews of school psychology, including information on service delivery roles and functions. There seems to be considerable commonality in the practices of school psychologists, reflecting both traditional (assessment) and newer roles (consultation, programme development). The factors that more or less determine what psychologists do are related to local and provincial educational mandates, the characteristics and needs of the school population, the number of school psychologists employed together with the size of their caseloads and the psychologist to student ratio, their training and professional orientation, rural vs. urban work locations and the general strength and "recognition" of the profession in each of the provinces. For example, a rural school division, with schools scattered over great distances, which is primarily interested in hiring a person to administer tests to teacher-referred children for designation purposes is most likely to select a "different" school psychologist than the large urban office that is looking for an individual who is specially trained to perform neuropsychological assessments or who can function as a member of a multidisciplinary team offering programme consultation to teachers of developmentally delayed children.

Keeping in mind that services provided by school psychologists vary across Canada as a function of many factors, it may still be helpful to employ examples of both the expected and actual roles and tasks performed by school psychologists. First is a summary of the specific goals of school psychology services for the Province of Quebec, as summarized in a paper by Gagné and Boivin (1991):

1. To detect, identify and diagnose in close collaboration with teachers, problems encountered by students with regard to their progress in school and their intellectual, social, and emotional development.
2. To intervene directly with students and groups of students who encounter problems with their progress in school and with their intellectual, social and emotional development.
3. To assist students in understanding their experiences, and in acquiring attitudes and behaviours that are conducive to their personality development and to satisfactory human relations, and scholastic success.
4. To make an active contribution, by offering support to educators, to the solution of problems encountered by students in their intellectual, social and emotional development.
5. To encourage in educators skills and attitudes conducive to the students' intellectual, social and emotional development.
6. To promote forms of physical and social organization that will foster the students' development.

While the above statement lists the basic goals of school psychology (at least for Quebec), and thus gives some indication of the roles proposed for school psychologists, we can turn to a recent survey of actual functions performed by school psychologists in Saskatchewan (Neudorf, 1990). A two-part questionnaire requesting information on professional training and experience and the various tasks performed by educational psychologists was sent to 50 psychologists employed by the Boards of Education in Saskatchewan. Based on the 37 (74%) returned questionnaires, Neudorf (1990, p. 37) reported that the most frequently performed tasks included:

> 1) Administering individual tests to children to identify specific learning disabilities, 2) Reporting findings of individual assessments to parents, 3) Planning individual programmes with teachers for children with learning disabilities, 4) Discussing with parents and teachers realistic expectations of specific students with learning disabilities, 5) Conducting assessments to determine strengths and weaknesses of students in relation to learning styles.

Neudorf also found a similarity of tasks performed by urban and rural psychologists with approximately the same amount of time being given to diagnosis, assessment, consultation and programme planning. Given some of the similarities between Saskatchewan and Manitoba, it is interesting to note that an almost equal amount of effort is given by school psychologists employed by the Child Guidance Clinic in Winnipeg to assessment, direct intervention and collaboration/consultation (Bartell, 1991).

Perkins (1991) discussed the roles of Ontario school psychologists under several headings. Prevention activities intended to identify and plan for special needs children include early screening, consultation, inservice and curriculum and programme development. Assessment includes the administration of tests but also observation, programme evaluation and consultation. Perkins reports that about 1/3 of the students attending metropolitan Toronto schools were born into non-English-speaking families. This situation necessitates culture fair assessment and bilingual testing as well as dynamic assessment and continuous performance appraisal of students. Intervention activities may include counselling, remedial instruction and educational programming. The identified client(s) may be the individual or group (student, teacher, parent) as well as the school system.

Gagné and Boivin (1991) have traced the responsibilities of Quebec school psychologists from predominantly a testing role to today's focus on "prevention and personal growth, whose objectives are the optimum development of the students' abilities and of their intellectual, emotional and social potential". Descriptions of the roles of school psychologists in other provinces such as

Prince Edward Island (Lechowick, 1991) and Nova Scotia (Haverstock & Millman, 1991) also stress such activities as assessment, intervention and prevention as well as the increasing role of consultation.

Finally, there seems to be some blurring of professional lines between various practitioners in school settings. Some teachers have been trained (rightly or wrongly) to administer intelligence tests, both school counsellors and psychologists may be trained and involved in the individual treatment of children with social or emotional problems, and special education teachers may develop and implement teaching strategies grounded in contemporary cognitive psychology and information processing theory. No matter what the actual specific functions performed by school psychologists, Frost (1983) argued that:

> Unless the school psychologist can successfully differentiate him/herself from these other professionals, then he/she will be absorbed by them ... the only way a school psychologist can demonstrate individuality, and worth to the employing system, is to be a psychologist and convey to the clients information and services based on psychology in its various forms – social, cognitive, clinical, etc. (p. 9)

School Psychology Applications: Some Examples

Here, we describe some contemporary issues that school psychologists face on a regular basis. By presenting these issues, we are indirectly commenting on the areas of training that a school psychologist would be wise to choose with respect to being prepared for these varied and complex problems of our modern society and schools.

Programme Placement and Diagnostic Classification

> *Referral 1:* I am referring this child for psychological and educational testing. His strengths are in math, but he cannot cope with the Grade 3 reading material. His spelling is very poor, his grammar weak and he cannot sit still long enough to gain much from a lesson. What can I do to help him?

Since school psychologists primarily work in the schools, most of the referrals come largely from teachers and/or school principals who are faced with developing individual programmes for special needs children or placing them in special classes designed to ameliorate their learning difficulties. While mainstreaming (i.e. educating exceptional children in regular classrooms) is emphasized for all students, today's schools offer a wide range of programme alternatives. Special classes exist for the learning disabled, the gifted and talented, the mentally handicapped and those for whom English is a second language. Other programmes exist for those who in the past were deemed to be slower learning students. These are now called by various names such as learning assistance programmes, opportunity programmes, resource centres or learning centres.

A teacher may make a referral indicating that the student is having difficulty in learning to read or write. The question may relate to knowing if the student is "ready" and has the "ability" to benefit from the regular classroom curriculum and instruction. Not infrequently, the issue is whether or not this child is truly learning disabled and hence requires special programme placement or special programming within the regular classroom. At other times, a quite pleasant diversion for the school psychologist, is the identification of gifted and talented individuals. Other referrals may be expected for those students who may have language difficulties sensory (visual, auditory) and motor impairment or for those who are mentally handicapped. The school psychologist's job is to determine the kind and extent of special school programmes when the regular classroom programme no longer can meet the child's learning needs.

For example, the teacher might state that a child is reversing numbers and letters, cannot read at his/her expected age or grade placement level, will not sit still and listen, often gets into trouble with other students, has difficulty concentrating, has messy handwriting and other similar behaviours. A first step for the school psychologist might be to engage the student in psychological and educational testing to determine the child's strengths and weaknesses and level of performance on achievement tests. Following the diagnosis, the school psychologist would write a psychological report making recommendations for intervention strategies in the school and possibly also at home. A brief example of such an assessment following referral is included in Appendix A.

Retention or Promotion

> *Referral 2:* I am having trouble deciding what to do with this student. I think he should repeat the grade, but I am not sure. His grades are all in the bottom of the class. He is big for his age. Should I repeat or refer him to the next grade, but with resource room help? I need to know before the end of May.

Another common concern that school psychologists face, usually at the end of a school year, is whether or not a child should be passed or failed. While this question was previously often handled by the regular classroom teacher, less often the case today. Teachers request supporting information that might help them determine whether it would be appropriate to have a child retained in the same grade or whether the child should be promoted but with special education intervention. Teachers recognize that there are social as well as educational factors that determine whether or not the student would be better off in the same classroom or promoted to the next grade. This is a difficult question especially when the parents want the child to be promoted while the teachers may argue the benefits of retention or vice versa. The research on retention and promotion is equivocal at best; one can find research papers that both support or do not support it. The school psychologist, therefore, may be called in to assist the decision-making process. Analysis of previous educational and personal factors and psychological testing would be the first stage of work for the school psychologist in assisting the teacher, followed by further individual assessment as required.

Behaviourial and Emotional Problems

> *Referral 3:* B has become increasingly more withdrawn in the classroom. He seldom interacts with others and spends much of his time alone. At other times, he is very sullen, irritable and even aggressive and has recently been in several verbal and physical fights at school. His school work has slipped and everything seems like an effort for him. I would like him to see the psychologist for some individual help.

Approximately 10%–15% of all referrals to school psychologists relate to behavioural, emotional and social difficulties. A parent might call the school and report that her child is being "beat up" on the way home from school. This parent would like the school to do something about it. A teacher might notice that a child is afraid and lonely and has no friends in school. She or he would like the school psychologist involved in determining whether counselling or any classroom interventions might be helpful in improving this child's psychological well being. A parent contacts the school psychologist and reports that their child has great difficulty sleeping at night. The child often wakes up with nightmares and night terrors. She would like some advice as to how to handle the situation and some information as to what might be causing this problem. These are only a few of the many referral reasons of this kind. Parents worry about the child's self-esteem and social development. They wish their child to be happy and motivated to go to school. Sometimes the behavioural problems are so great that the child refuses to go to school. School phobia, a not uncommon psychological condition well known to school psychologists, may not be so much a problem of being afraid of the school as it is a concern over leaving the home. Adolescent and childhood depression is another issue that school psychologists must understand and deal with (Saklofske & Janzen, 1987; Saklofske, Janzen & Paananen, 1987).

In order to adequately assist parents and teachers with behavioural, emotional and social problems, school psychologists require training in child psychology, learning theories, instructional strategies, individual and group counselling skills and social psychology. They may refer the child to the school counsellor or provide the therapy themselves, if they have time. In other cases, depending on the problem and the available resources, they are likely to refer parents to community agencies, medical doctors and clinics for assistance. However, the school psychologist is a key resource person, and consultant for the teacher and parent, providing suggestions helpful for the school setting.

A few words are in order here regarding the similarities and differences between clinical and school psychologists. School psychologists practise mainly in school contexts and apply their knowledge to school-age clients whereas clinical psychologists frequently work in mental health settings. While training programmes may be quite similar, a major difference is in the work setting and the issues that arise. Psychological problems presented to the school and clinical psychologists are essentially the same but how they are addressed is as much a function of where the problem is referred as by who it is referred to. However, school psychologists are also specifically trained to focus on the promotion of effective learning, educational measurement, educational programming, consultation/collaboration with other educational professionals and other concerns specifically related to the mandate of the schools.

Problems Arising out of Dysfunctional and Conflictive Families

> *Referral 4:* Would you please talk to this child. Her father and mother have divorced recently and she is tearful and angry. I cannot seem to get her to do any work. She just sits there and stares out the window. She will not play with other children. The mother has given permission for you to counsel this child.

The divorce rate in Canada has doubled in the last 30 years. While cohabitation has increased by 400% in the province of Alberta in the last decade, the province of Alberta has one of the highest divorce rates, now standing at 42%. Thus, the issues for the school psychologist arising out of these circumstances are multiple and varied. Children come to school feeling afraid, depressed and angry. They may sit in the classroom, yet worry about whether they will ever see their Dad or Mum again who has just left home. They try to concentrate on their school work but their feelings of anxiety, fear, confusion and possible depression or even anger are likely to interfere with learning and achievement. The parents come to the school and wish an interview with the school psychologist to determine how to best handle the situation now that the family is separated.

In other cases, the problem may be one of step-parenting. For example, the father has just remarried and the daughter has great difficulties accepting her new stepfather. She lashes out with verbal abuse against both parents and they want to know how to most effectively manage and resolve this situation. The school psychologist is familiar with these scenarios. They realize that children do not leave their worries and fears at home when they come to school. Parents today realize that the school psychologist may be one specialist who could help them and assist them with these very difficult problems that impact on children.

Parenting and Child Management Issues

> *Referral 5:* I would like Student B to be seen by the school psychologist. Lately, she has been a very difficult child to manage at home. She has become bossy and often teases her younger brother. She lies about her school work and we feel she is being negatively influenced by several of her friends.

An increasing concern of parents today is the issue of how to raise their children and how to manage their child's behaviours. By far the most common referrals from parents to the school psychologist are issues dealing with sibling rivalry, temper tantrums, refusing to do their school work, staying out late and other similar concerns arising out of the home. Of lesser concern, but still an issue for some parents today are the requests to determine the cause of enuresis and encopresis. School psychologists require a knowledge of the principles and practices of child management in the home and school. While many of these problems are typical ones in any home, some families may not have the necessary parenting skills to know what to do. The school psychologist is, therefore, asked to become involved in order to give them some assistance. A number of such home problem areas and suggested management strategies may be found in two recent books by Janzen, Paterson & Blashko (1989 a, 1989 b).

Referrals from and to Other Health Professionals

> *Referral 6:* I have been student C's family doctor for the past 10 years. We are attempting to better control his overactive and excitable behaviour with a different medication and would be grateful for your assessment of C's academic and social behaviour in school. It would be helpful to discuss this new course of treatment and our expectations for C.

While previously described issues rose out of the context of the school and the home, there are many other specialists in the community that look to the school psychologist for assistance. The local health unit which has a team of nurses, social workers and speech therapists, will frequently call to gain some assistance with a child. The school psychologist thus works in collaboration with the health unit staff to develop a programme for treatment in the schools, home and in the health units. Family doctors may call on the school to assist them in the assessment of hyperactivity, attention-deficit disorder, epilepsy and many other medical conditions, and especially to consider the psychological and educational implications of these conditions. The school psychologist, therefore, needs to be knowledgeable and aware of the various physical and mental health problems that impact on school learning. Sometimes the school psychologist will refer a child to the family doctor for diagnosis and possible medical treatment and arrange to coordinate the exchange of information between the doctor, parents and teachers. The local Social Services units have social workers who are directly involved with families in which there is alcohol abuse, physical and sexual abuse, single parent concerns and many other family and social problems such as custody or temporary guardianship. The school psychologist's role in these cases is to provide psychological diagnostic information as well as develop a plan that may assist that child to function in the school and home.

Summary

The above paragraphs have sampled only a few of the contemporary issues that a school psychologist is faced with on a day-to-day basis. Many school psychologists will have over 200 referrals for problems such as these each year. One can see that while the school psychologist has been largely identified as an expert in psychological and educational diagnosis, they must also have an understanding about a wide range of human problems, knowing how to intervene and to explain to parents, teachers and the student, the issue at hand. Indeed, school psychologists must be responsive to all of society's problems and not just to those that arise from within the school context. Parents as well as other mental health professionals directly access the school psychologist's expertise in order to ensure a more complete service to school children and adolescents.

Work Settings of School Psychologists

The School Setting

Today's school psychologists are hired by a school district to provide service to the teachers, administrators and parents within those schools. While most of their work is focused on psychological diagnosis, report writing, planning individualized educational programmes, offering guidelines for various psychological intervention, in-service education and consultation, many school psychologists wish to become more involved in individual and group counselling activities. Schools often do have counsellors, especially at the high school level, who are involved in individual and group treatment of students. Nevertheless, most school psychologists have been trained in intervention strategies (e. g. individual and group counselling, cognitive-behaviour modification) and are becoming increasingly involved in both a greater counselling and consultation role.

The Community Setting

It is estimated that roughly 30% of all referrals now come from outside the school itself. Social workers, mental health consultants, drug and alcohol-abuse counsellors, speech and language therapists, medical doctors and community health nurses all make referrals to the school psychologist when the problems faced by children in the community directly impacts on the nature of their educational programme. It is not unusual, therefore, for the school psychologist to spend as much time consulting with these mental health specialists as they do with teachers and parents. A child's educational life cannot be separated from the larger social context of family and community. Intervention programmes can be coordinated that will involve community mental health workers, and others working closely with the school psychologist, to effect more positive and long-lasting change at home, at school and in the community.

Industry

While referrals from industry are still quite uncommon, they're likely to increase in the future. Both small and large companies that have formed the work-base in the community are beginning to realize that school psychologists have a role to play with respect to consultation in the business world. Some school psychologists have offered their services to industry in relation to personnel selection, programme development and continuing education, group processes to increase work productivity and stress reduction. Some school psychologists have been hired directly by businesses to develop employee assistance programmes that assist employees with problems of stress, substance abuse, retraining, etc.

Hospitals

School psychologists have accepted positions in the hospitals. Most larger hospitals today have a psychology unit and the psychologist usually works closely with psychiatrists, pediatricians and other medical specialists with respect to patient treatment and assessment. School psychologists who have been trained in psychological diagnosis as well as intervention techniques are in an excellent position to be hired by the psychology department in the hospitals. Many of the PhD graduates in school psychology from the University of Alberta, for example, are now working in hospital psychology departments; in fact, there are a number of directors of psychology units in the hospitals that were initially trained as school psychologists.[1] Their skills in diagnosis, treatment, consultation and programme development and evaluation are welcomed by hospital boards as providing a needed service in this setting.

Maximum and Minimum Security Environments

School psychologists who have a special interest in working with young offenders and convicted criminals, may work in forensic units in the hospitals, youth centres for young offenders and prisons. The solicitor-general's department of each province is one of the largest employers of psychologists, some being school psychologists. Again, the emphasis here would be on assessment and recommendation for treatment. School psychologists are in an excellent position to provide service to this environment with respect to assistance with psychiatric referrals for diagnosis. The solicitor general's departments across this country are concerned with initial in-depth psychological evaluation of convicted criminals with respect to subsequent programmes at these institutions. Thus, school psychologists have been placed in these environments to provide psychological evaluation, assist in determination of learning disorders, offer educational programmes for inmates, develop individual and group treatments and provide consultation on social, emotional and personality problems associated with incarceration.

Private Practice

While the issue of private practice was relatively unheard of several decades ago, it is now quite common for school psychologists, upon completion of their graduate degree, to engage in private

---

1 *Editors' note:* The editors question to what extent the University of Alberta experience generalizes to other parts of the country where doctoral programmes in clinical psychology have developed.

practice. Approximately 10% of PhD graduates in school psychology are now setting up their own professional business much the way lawyers, doctors and other specialties have done over time (Fagan, 1989; Janzen, 1987). With the regulation of professional practice well in place in Canadian provinces, school psychologists are finding that their training has given them an advantage in being able to become established in a private practice setting. Each provincial association sets guidelines and rules for this practice, and school psychologists are able to manage the rigours of the daily work because of their training and experience with the many issues that were referred to them within the school setting. Some of the private practice is in individual therapy, evaluation for child custody, issues surrounding support for psychiatrists in the treatment of patients on an out-patient basis and many other concerns. School psychologists are valued in a consulting role by the courts, medical clinics, legal firms and social service agencies. This has clearly been a major role change for school psychologists in recent years. The fact that they've been able to quite adequately maintain a successful private practice suggests that their skills and knowledge are well suited to this new endeavour.

Media Psychology

Media psychology is discussed last because it is the newest of all settings in which school psychologists are involved. In fact, the City of Edmonton has been one of the first that sought the use of psychologists and psychiatrists for "on-air" service to the public. In 1982, Dr. Robbie Campbell, a psychiatrist, began a radio programme called "That's Living". Within a year two trainers of school psychologists, Dr. John Paterson and Dr. Henry Janzen, became involved as media psychologists on this programme, which was broadcast from Mondays to Fridays for one and a half hours a day. While eight minutes of the programme was spent on developing a particular theme or topic for the day, its basic function prrmme was to help callers with their personal problems. Thousands of listeners are helped daily with respect to common human problems. School psychologists clearly have a role to play in this area. In 1985, "That's Living" won a major award from the Canadian Broadcasting Association for service to the public.

The provincial as well as the Canadian Psychological Associations in Canada have been made well aware of this new role of the media for school psychologists and other psychological specialists (Janzen, 1987; Janzen, Paterson & Blashko, 1989a, 1989b). Their training in mental health, psychological diagnosis, educational strategies, personality theory, learning and instructional approaches, to name a few, has prepared them for work in the media. By far the most pleasant outcome of the work on radio has been that the public has come in direct contact with psychologists. Many people today feel more comfortable in calling upon a psychologist for advice than they have in the past.

Media psychology in Canada is in its infancy and this particular programme in Edmonton is the only one of its kind here in Canada. In contrast, the United States has been involved in media psychology for several decades. Psychologists of every specialty are beginning to realize the power of the media in not only publicizing the nature and work of psychologists in general but in education and prevention as well.

Rural vs. Urban Settings

Canada is a large country with vast areas that are sparsely populated. While the urban school psychologist often works as a part of a team and addresses the problems and issues that arise out of referrals that come to a central location, the rural school psychologist is sometimes seen to be everything to everyone. Indeed, the rural school psychologist is much like the chameleon who has to change his colours depending on the situation. Rural school psychologists often are the only professional resource with a specialty training that the community and schools can draw upon. That doesn't mean that the urban school psychologist does not have to meet the demands of many presenting problems. They do. However, the urban school psychologist is in a better position to draw upon other specialists such as speech therapists, social workers, psychiatrists, medical doctors and many other mental health professionals.

A problem faced by rural school districts is finding and retaining qualified school psychologists. For example, the turnover of school psychologists in Northern Saskatchewan led to the first author being requested to assemble a team of psychologists and special education personnel from the University of Saskatchewan to provide the required services. The team travels to various schools once a month, sometimes flying into remote areas that are otherwise, inaccessible. The range of services provided include assessment and referral to other agencies but the greatest emphasis is placed on consultation leading to development and implementation of programmes that can be carried out by teachers and possibly also at home.

Professional Identity and Organization

Opinions vary on the current status of school psychology within both the professional (other specialty areas of psychology and education) and public arenas. While Dawson (1982) optimistically stated that Canadian school psychology was moving into "adolescence", others contend that it is a very young and not well-defined branch of psychology, at least in Canada. Janzen (1987) wrote that the profession in Canada is now experiencing the very growing pains that American school psychology has already passed through. Many of these issues of professional identity are tied to efforts to develop school psychology associations. Questions that are currently being addressed by Canadian school psychologists include: what is a school psychologist and how is this distinct from other psychology specializations, what training is required and what are the entry level requirements for the profession (masters degree vs. PhD, certification standards) and are the concerns of school psychologists best addressed by associations separate from other branches of psychology.

These issues are reflected in the recent creation of provincial and national school psychology associations as well as the relatively new Canadian Psychological Association interest section on school and educational psychology. The formation of the Canadian Association of School Psychologists (CASP) was, in the main, due to the efforts and vision of Dr. Barry Frost. In 1984, Dr. Frost called a meeting in Calgary which included Dr. Carl Anserello (British Columbia). Dr. Don Saklofske (Saskatchewan) and Retha Finch-Carriere (Manitoba). This steering committee was later expanded to include Drs. Buff Oldridge (British Columbia), Ruth Frost (Alberta) and Marjorie Perkins (Ontario). The first CASP annual conference was held in Winnipeg in 1987, followed by Toronto, Edmonton and Saskatoon venues; the 1991 conference will again be held in Toronto. In its brief existence, CASP can boast members from across Canada. The *Canadian Journal of School Psychology*, publication of which started in 1991, complements the existing newsletter (*Cognitions*). Standards for Professional Practice have been developed, and CASP has further adopted the CPA ethics code.

At a provincial level, the greatest activity occurred in western Canada during the 1980s; strong provincial associations have formed in British Columbia (B. C.), Alberta, Saskatchewan and Manitoba. However, there has been some considerable controversy associated with some of these developments, especially in relation to the use of the title "psychologist". In 1986, the B. C. Psychologists Association was granted an injunction by the Supreme Court of B. C. against the newly formed B. C. Association of School Psychologists over the use of the title "psychologist". Although the injunction was lifted a year later, considerable confusion and even animosity between the two groups was observed during this period. The British Columbia Association of School Psychologists (BCASP) is now in the process of developing and instituting formal certification procedures that will hopefully lead to a clear identity and regulation of the profession. It is estimated that there are about 200–250 school psychologists working under a variety of occupational designations employed across the 75 school districts in B. C.

Alberta has a long tradition of school psychology (Janzen & Massey, 1991). Certainly, university training programmes were well established in the 1960s and the Psychology Department at the Calgary Board of Education under the direction of Dr. Carl Safran during this time served as a model of such a service. The Alberta Association of School Psychologists (AASP) was only formed in 1981 but rather than break completely from the Psychologists Association of Alberta (PAA), it requires members to be both registered as chartered psychologists in PAA and employed or trained as school psychologists. Further AASP members are bound by the CPA Code of Ethics adopted by PAA and also the Standards of Practice developed by the National Association of School Psychologists in the USA. It will be interesting to observe the impact of possible changing certification requirements to the PhD level in the near future since most school psychologists are still trained to the masters degree level.

The Saskatchewan Educational Psychology Association (SEPA) has about 90 members although not all are employed by school boards. Again, problems centre around the identity and designation of school psychologists since most are not eligible for certification in the Saskatchewan Psychologists Association because of the PhD entry requirement. An important development in deploying and maximizing the use of school psychologists in this largely rural province is the Shared Services programme whereby several boards may jointly employ and share a school psychologist. A major problem for Saskatchewan school boards is to find and retain qualified psychologists, especially in northern areas (Eidness, 1988; Saklofske & Grainger, 1991)

Bartell (1991) reported that there are 105 practising school psychologists in Manitoba employed mainly by the Child Guidance Clinic of Greater Winnipeg and the Government of Manitoba Child Care and Development Branch. They comprise one of six specialty designations of school clinicians who are certified by the Board of Teacher Education and Certification. Guidelines have been in place since 1974 prior to the emergence of the Manitoba Association of School Psychologists earlier last decade. Again, only a small number of these psychologists are also registered by the Psychologists Association of Manitoba (PAM) which requires the PhD degree for entry. Current discussions between the two associations are centred around the development of a specialty of school psychology within PAM that could grant Associate status to those with masters degrees.

Mental health services for schools were begun in Ontario in 1919, and today there are more than 1000 individuals employed to provide psychological services to schools (Perkins, 1991). The title of "school psychologist" is not formally used since there is no provision for specialty certification and only PhD holders are eligible for a certificate of registration from the Ontario Board of Examiners in Psychology. Instead the more common reference is to psychoeducational consultant, psychometrist or teacher diagnostician. Within the Ontario Psychological Association (OPA) is the Section of Psychologists in Education, and the OPA has recently developed a policy statement on psychological services in schools. School psychology at the nondoctoral level is also represented within the Ontario Association of Consultants, Counsellors, Psychometrists, and Psychotherapists. As well, the Association of Chief and Senior Psychologists of School Boards in Ontario provides a forum for the discussion of issues of relevance to the delivery of psychological services in schools.

In Quebec, the title of psychologist is regulated by the Professional Code and practitioners must also be a member of the Corporation professionnelle des psychologues du Québec. Again, since many school psychologists are not eligible for provincial registration, Gagné and Boivin (1991) report that the title "counsellor in reeducation" is used by school boards for their approximately 600 psychologists and counsellors. Within the Corporation professionnelle des psychologues du Québec is a newly formed interest section of elementary school psychologists, the Groupe d'intérêt en psychologie scolaire.

The Atlantic provinces and northern Canada vary in the organization and regulation of school psychology practitioners. For example, the Psychological Association of Prince Edward Island is a voluntary organization, and until recently there was no certification act that would impact on the four currently practising school psychologists (Lechowick, 1991). However, Prince Edward Island had its first Act proclaimed this year. Nova Scotia has more than 40 individuals offering psychological services in schools (Haverstock & Millman, 1991). Psychologists registered under the Psychologists Act of Nova Scotia require a master's degree; others are referred to by other titles such as "psychometrist". School psychologists have formed an interest group with the Association of Psychologists of Nova Scotia but have not been successful in also doing so within the Nova Scotia Teachers' Union. New Brunswick's psychologists are regulated by the College of Psychologists Act which requires at least a master's degree. There is both a Francophone and an Anglophone division with in the Department of Education that employs psychologists. For example, 34 psychologists are hired by the Francophone division. Finally, Webster (1991) states that the first Yukon school psychologist was hired in 1973 and is responsible to the Yukon Department of Education in Whitehorse. The school psychologist is referred to as the Coordinator of Assessment and Counselling Services and performs both a consultation and resource role to schools and school based teams.

School Psychology Research in Canada

School psychologists are contributors to and consumers of psychological research literature spanning a wide range of topics, including development, learning, personality, intelligence and cognition and assessment. They also consult the publications from other related fields ranging from special education and counselling to psychiatry. Much like psychologists employed in hospitals or mental health clinics, the school psychologists' clientele can include very young children in kindergarten, high school adolescents, adults enrolled in educational upgrading programmes, developmentally delayed, gifted, emotionally disturbed and learning disabled students. Further, school psychologists provide direct as well as indirect and consultation services to teachers and other educational personnel (e.g. counsellor, principal, speech and language personnel, special education consultants) the parents and various community agencies (e.g. the courts, hospitals, social services) and allied professionals within the human services delivery systems (e.g. psychiatrists, social workers). The kinds of services provided by school psychologists range from psychological and educational assessments, direct intervention, prevention, consultation, programme development, inservice training to advocacy. Thus it would be common to find Canadian school psychologists reading the *Alberta Journal of Educational Research* (March, 1990) issue focusing on classroom and curriculum-based assessment, the *McGill Journal of Education* special issue entitled "International Perspectives on School-Based Assessment" (Winter 1990, vol. 24, no. 3) or specific articles in this same journal such as "Non-discriminatory assessment of culturally different students" (Lewis & Samuda, 1989).

University faculty, trainers and school psychologists engage in a considerable amount of applied research activity that has direct application for practice. Dumont (1989) described several factors that influence the kind and amount of school psychology research carried out in Canada. Since education is under provincial control, "educational values and research priorities expressed as political pressures and funding incentives that are directed to institutions that do research in educational and school psychology differ considerably from province to province" (p. 209). Both the multicultural composition and rural character of Canada are also important factors in determining research priorities. Dumont's review examines some of the recent Canadian research contributions in the areas of pupil assessment, intervention, exceptionality (e.g. gifted learners) and second language learning.

The results of Canadian school psychology research may be found in various well-established journals published in the United States such as the *Journal of School Psychology*, *Psychology in the Schools* and the *School Psychology Review*, the latter published by the National Association of School Psychologists, as well as related journals such as the American Psychological Association's *Journal of Educational Psychology* and *Psychological Assessment*, or the *American Educational Research Journal* and the *Review of Educational Research*, both published by the American Educational Research Association.

There are fewer publication outlets in Canada for school psychology research. Until recently, school psychology and related research published in Canada was most likely to be found in such journals as the *Alberta Journal of Educational Research* (e.g. "Predictive validity of the Canadian Readiness Test and selected measures of cognitive development for grade one reading and mathematics achievement"; Collis, Ollila & Yore, 1986), the *Canadian Journal of Behavioural Science* (e.g. "Canadian content in the WISC-R: Bias or jingoism"; Beal, 1988), the *Canadian Journal of Special Education* (e.g. "Predictors of childhood depression: Literature review and empirical findings by Saklofske, Janzen & Paananen, 1987; Logo and Special Education by Michayluk & Saklofske, 1988) and the *McGill Journal of Education* (e.g. "School psychology in Canada; An evolving profession" by Dumont, 1988; "School-based assessment research in Canada" by Saklofske & Janzen, 1990).

While other Canadian publications sometimes contain work by or of interest to school psychologists (such as Common and Frost's article on the use of standardized intelligence tests with native students published in the *Canadian Journal of Native Education*, 1988, or Michayluk and Saklofske's paper on the effects of LOGO with emotionally disturbed children published in 1988 in the *Canadian Journal of Educational Communication*), it is the newsletters and smaller journals from the various Canadian provincial school psychology organizations that focus most directly on the applications of psychology in the schools. Of course, books and book chapters written by Canadian psychologists with titles such as "A cognitive approach to intelligence: Attention, coding and planning (Kirby & Das, 1990), "Assessment and placement of minority students" (Samuda, Kong, Cummins, Lewis & Pascual-Leone, 1989), "Testing for diagnostic purposes", (Saklofske & Janzen, 1991) and "Individual differences in children and adolescents: International perspectives" (Saklofske & Eysenck, 1988) published here or abroad have much to offer school psychologists.

Another indication of the research activity and interests of Canadian school psychologists can be seen in presentations made at conferences such as those sponsored by the provincial school psychology associations, the Canadian Association of School Psychologists (CASP) and the school and educational psychology section of the Canadian Psychological Association. For example, the 1990 CASP conference, jointly hosted by the Saskatchewan Educational Psychology Association, spanned three days and included topics ranging from intelligence, behavioural assessment, social skills, cognitive approaches to assessment and intervention and the effects of psychoactive drugs to workshops on attention deficit disorder and symposia on the treatment and intervention roles of school psychologists.

One further example of the research efforts of school psychologists is the development and publication of tests and assessment programmes. Some examples of assessment instruments recently developed in Canada include:

- The Canada French Immersion Achievement Test, which measures spelling, arithmetic, word identification and passage comprehension of children in grade 1–7;
- The Canadian Comprehensive Assessment Program (Danley, Wick & Smith, 1982, 1983 a, b), measuring cognitive abilities, achievement and school attitudes;

- The British Columbia Quick Individual Educational Test (Wormeli, 1983);
- The Students Perception of Ability Scale (Boersma & Chapman, 1985); and
- The Frost Self Description Questionnaire (Frost, 1979).

The *Canadian Journal of School Psychology* (*CJSP*) was first published in 1985, and it is now established as the major vehicle for school psychology research and clinical applications. An examination of the contents of this journal provides a good sample of the kind of applied research that Canadian school psychologists are both producing and reading. In general, these studies can be loosely categorized according to several related themes.

The use of tests in assessment and diagnosis continues to occupy many pages in *CJSP*. For example, DiPasquale (1986) describes the "temporal plot" for interpreting WISC-R results; Holmes (1977) suggests some "edu-clinical" interpretations of WISC-R data; while Mueller, Dennis and Short (1986) argue that the use of WISC-R profile analysis is not effective in distinguishing between various groups of exceptional children. Other investigations have reported on the use of tests in determining school readiness (Simner, 1987) and diagnosing learning disabilities (Andrews & Janzen, 1988; Hackhoffer, 1988; Saklofske & Yackulic, 1987; Wiss & Burnet, 1988), as well as on specific instruments such as the DIAL-R (Derevensky & Mardell-Czudnowski, 1986) or WISC-R (Koe & Oldridge, 1987) in identifying special needs children. Other papers examine the accuracy and use of behavioural observation in the classroom as a source of assessment data (Merrell, 1989). Since many of the frequently used test instruments are developed and normed outside of Canada, it is important to determine the appropriateness of these tests in the Canadian setting. Thus even brief nonverbal tests such as the Matrix Analogies Test (Naglieri, 1985) require some systematic study before employing them as routine assessment instruments (Saklofske, Yackulic, Murray & Naglieri, 1991).

The multicultural composition of Canada and our commitment to the protection and promotion of minority rights are also reflected in contemporary school psychology research and writings. Some of this research compares the performance of culturally different groups such as Gardner's (1986, 1988) analysis of the K-

ABC and WISC-R performance of Cantonese-, Punjabi- and English-speaking children. Other investigations focus on the use of particular tests such as the WISC-R with native children (Scaldwell, Frame & Cookson, 1985), which has led to a clearer articulation of the problems concerning the assessment of native students (Goldstein 1988). Williams (1988) examined the reading and information processing skills of native and non-native children, and concluded that "environmental factors outweigh ethnicity ... experiential background in a cultural context must be seen as a major determinant of information processing ability" (p.45). Several other papers published in *CJSP* offer insight into the cross-cultural adjustment difficulties felt by foreign students and young immigrants (Ishiyama, 1989) as well as useful suggestions for cross-cultural assessment (Massey, 1988).

Intervention, prevention and programme strategies are another major theme found in the Canadian school psychology research literature. For example, the *CJSP* includes regular "case study reviews" and "clinical hints". Cole (1986) has developed a model of "parent-teacher mediated intervention" in the identification and treatment of childhood depression. Beal (1986) reports on the effectiveness of a group intervention programme for developing more adaptive and acceptable behaviours in children at school. Koe and Meiners (1989) have provided and extensive description for identifying and treating depressive episodes in children.

Lastly, a number of other important topics and issues have been addressed in the Canadian school psychology literature. Such papers include the impact of recent legislation as well as litigation on the practice of school psychology (e.g. Kimmins, Hunter & McKay, 1985; Wilson & Humphries, 1986), the use of computers in the practice of school psychology (Hunter, 1989), the effect of summer vacation on the written language of learning disabled students (Morton & Siegel, 1988) and an examination of birth date on various developmental indices in the first several years of schooling (Finch & Braid, 1988), and the range of topics extends to studies of school dropout (Pawlovich, 1986) and descriptions of fetal alcohol syndrome (Williams, 1986).

Current Status and Future of School Psychology in Canada

While much has been spoken and written about the past, present and future of American school psychology in books (e.g. Gutkin & Reynolds, 1990), journals (e.g. Fagan, 1986, 1989) and at conferences (Spring Hill and Olympia conferences), it is more difficult to find similar descriptions of the Canadian scene. Obviously, this is because school psychology in Canada is still a relatively young specialty area. Also, most provincial organizations and CASP were only formed very recently, in contrast to the strong American organizations at the state and national levels (APA Division 16, NASP), including the recent National School Psychology Certification Program. Dumont (1989) reminds us that a national assessment of the "condition" of Canadian school psychology is complicated by the lack of definition of the profession, the changing nature of schools, the blurred lines between disciplinary specialties, provincial control of education and the vast geographic landmass containing a relatively small but culturally diverse population.

Both writers are familiar with the training programmes for and practice of school psychology in Canada through our research and professional practice activities. During a sabbatical leave from the University of Alberta several years ago, the second author had the opportunity to visit school psychology training programmes and school boards employing school psychologists across Canada. Again, while the identity of the specialty of school psychology in relation to other specialty domains (clinical, industrial/organizational and counselling) in the USA seems to have become much clearer in recent years, the situation is less so in Canada. School psychologists have a "chameleon-like" image. University training programmes need to prepare school psychologist to undergo "binary fission" as they enter the work place since it is impossible to teach the school psychologist all the necessary skills that are required in day-to-day practice. School psychologists are expected to work as psychologists, specialist teachers, programmers, evaluators, counsellors, administrators etc., and to be both "artist and scientist". The shift in roles and identity over recent years has been from that of diagnostician (or even the more limited "testing" function) to consultant. However, while school psychology has drawn heavily from other branches of psychology, especially clinical psychology, it has not developed so much on the basis of its own body of knowledge. While the school psychology literature is replete with discussions of the applicability of various techniques and strategies to school psychological practice, there remains a lack of unifying structure for organizing these roles and functions into explicit conceptualizations of practice. Without a clear, unified conceptualization of practice which is based on a recognized body of knowledge, school psychology will continue to be highly malleable to "bandwagon" trends and remain vulnerable to criticism of its effectiveness as a profession.

School psychologists will continue to provide both direct and indirect services. However, these will be cast within contemporary frameworks reflecting competency-based, criterion- and curriculum-based measurement practices, intervention techniques drawn from other areas of applied psychology, vocational guidance and career education, system analysis and systems organization, decision-making models, crisis intervention, affective education, substance abuse prevention and intervention, contemporary lifestyle factors, sociopolitical issues, consultation approaches, and a wide range of knowledge related to neuropsychology, behavioural medicine and cognitive and instructional psychology. School psychologists will increasingly function as facilitators, change agents and as child advocates in such areas as mainstreaming, school-wide testing practices, curriculum development and implementation and school-family-community service coordination.

We would conclude with the view that school psychology may be the most interesting of the four broad specialty areas of psychology since it is certainly one of the most variable and diverse; i.e. dynamic. The changing roles of schools in contemporary society and the opportunity to facilitate learning and psychological well-being in children, adolescents and adults in various learning environments places school psychology in the forefront of both academic and professional psychology.

Appendix A: Confidential Psychological Report

Name:	Student A	Date of Birth:	August 21, 1982
Age:	8–3	Assessment Date:	December 2, 1990
Sex:	Male	School:	
Grade:	3		

Reason for Referral

Student A, an 8 year 3 month old boy, was referred by his teacher and mother for testing. While A's first language is not English, there is a suggestion that Student A has attentional problems, based on his tendency to not pay attention, nor to complete schoolwork. He is also very impulsive, restless and easily distracted. They want to confirm this so that he can receive appropriate help within his school. Student A does not complete his work in class and so until recently his mother spent two to three hours a night working with him on it. She stated that she hopes to learn from this psychological and educational assessment what the extent of his difficulties are and whether there are learning difficulties and/or attentional ones.

Tests Administered

- Stanford-Binet IV (SBIV)
- Peabody Individual Achievement Test (PIAT)
- Developmental Test of Visual-Motor Integration (BEERY)
- The Murphy-Meisgeier Type Indicator for Children (MMTIC)
- The Perception of Ability Scale for Students (PASS)

Summary

The most important information from this testing session may not be intelligence scores or achievement test results. Although these are informative, they may be of limited value or even misinterpreted if considered apart from the behavioural observations. Student A has considerable difficulties sitting still and quiet, even in a highly structured situation and when presented with a task. He tends to respond impulsively and does not appear to attend to details. It is likely that these behaviours are even more problematic in environments with more distractions and less individual attention and structure. These behaviour patterns are consistent with attention deficit disorder.

In a one-on-one situation, Student A is able to function at an average level on intellectual and school related tasks. He shows some weaknesses in reading comprehension and spelling, but not to the extent that they should be labelled a "learning disability". He also demonstrates possible weakness in visual-fine motor coordination. Since Student A's problem behaviours are likely to be similar or even greater in most other environments, his typical performance is likely to be below the levels seen here.

His perception of his own ability indicates that he may not see his behaviour or level of performance as presenting any problem, at least he wishes to convey this impression. He does not appear particularly motivated to change.

Recommendations

1. Further inquiry should be made into possible need for medication (e.g. Ritalin) and cognitive-behaviour therapy for hyperactivity and attentional difficulties.
2. Student A is likely to work better in a one-on-one, highly structured environment.
3. Student A needs to develop strategies to control his impulsive tendencies. He should be given tasks which require him to work carefully and learn to remind himself to stop and check whether he has considered everything before acting or answering. Learning to give himself instructions to go slowly, check that he has done everything and correct any mistakes can help in a variety of situations.
4. In working on reading and spelling, determine whether Student A's knowledge of two languages is confusing him. Help him to

conceptually separate these languages as much as possible and to learn where their rules differ.

5. Encourage Student A to read recreationally; whatever he enjoys will help him develop reading skills.
6. Assure Student A that everyone makes mistakes, including him, and encourage him to learn from his mistakes rather than denying them or blaming them on some outside factors. Stress that he is responsible for his performance but is not expected to be perfect.

Thank you for referring Student A to me. If you have questions regarding this report, please contact me.

School Psychologist.

Test Results December 2/90 (Client's Name)

Stanford-Binet IV

Verbal Reasoning	*SAS*
Vocabulary	60
Comprehension	52
Absurdities	44
Area SAS	105
Abstract/Visual Reasoning	
Pattern Analysis	49
Matrices	48 (estimate)
Area SAS	97 (estimate)
Quantitative Reasoning	
Quantitative	50
Number Series	45 (estimate)
Area SAS	94 (estimate)
Short-Term Memory	
Bead Memory	47
Memory for Sentences	49
Memory for Digits	51
Memory for Objects	47
Area SAS	96
Composite SAS:	98 ± 5*

*At the 95% confidence level.

PIAT

Test	Raw Score	Age Equiv.	%ile Rank	Standard Score
Mathematics	34	8–5	53	101
Reading Recog.	29	8–2	43	97
Reading Compre.	25	7–9	31	93
Spelling	25	7–6	24	89

BEERY

VMI Raw Score:	11	Percentile:	8
VMI Age Equiv.:	5–10	Standard Score:	5

PASS

Scale	Raw Scores	Classification
Full Scale	51 ±7*	Average
1. General Ability	10 ± 3*	Average
2. Arithmetic	11 ± 2*	Average
3. School Satisfaction	4 ± 3*	Below average
4. Reading/spelling	7 ± 2*	Average
5. Penmanship/neatness	10 ± 2*	Average
6. Confidence	6 ± 2*	Above Average
Misrepresentation Index	6	Above Average

*at the 95% confidence level

MMTIC (Murphy-Meisgeier Type Indicator for Children)

Preference Scores:	*Type*:
EI = 50	U
SN = 63	S
TF = 70	F
JP = 66	U

References

Alpert, J.I. (1985). Change within a profession: Change, future, prevention, and school psychology. *American Psychologist*, *40*, 1112–1121.

Andrews, J., & Janzen, H. (1988). Objectifying the kinetic school drawing (KSD): A comparison of LD vs. non LD Grade 5 students. *Canadian Journal of School Psychology*, *3*, 27–52.

Bartell, R. (1991). School psychology in Canada: The state of the art in Manitoba. *Canadian Journal of Psychology*, in press.

Bateson, D. (1989). A psychometric refresher. *Canadian Journal of School Psychology*, *5*, 23–30.

Beale, A.L. (1988). Canadian content in the WISC-R: Bias or jingoism. *Canadian Journal of Behavioural Science*, *20*, 154–166.

Beale, A.L. (1987). An activity group intervention for school children with behavioural problems. *Canadian Journal of School Psychology*, *3*, 47–56.

Boersma, F.J., & Chapman, J.W. (1985). *Manual for the Students' Perception of Ability Scale.* University of Alberta, Edmonton, Alberta.

Brown, O.T., & Minke, K.M. (1986). School psychology graduate training: A comprehensive analysis. *American Psychologist*, *41*, 1328–1338.

Cole, Ester, (1987). Parent-teacher mediated intervention: A growth promoting process. *Canadian Journal of School Psychology*, *3*, 33–46.

Collis, B., Ollila, L.O., & Yore, L.D. (1986). Predictive validity of the Canadian Readiness Test and selected measures of cognitive development for grade one reading and mathematics achievement. *The Alberta Journal of Educational Research*, *32*, 2–11.

Common, R.W., & Frost, L.G. (1988). The implications of the mismeasurement of Native students' intelligence through the use of standardized intelligence tests. *Canadian Journal of Native Education*, *15*, 9–30.

Danley, R.R., Wick, J.W., & Smith, J.K. (1982). *School attitude measure teacher's manual.* Toronto: Gage

Danley, R.R., Wick, J.W., & Smith, J.K. (1983 a). *Developing cognitive abilities test: Teacher's manual.* Toronto: Gage.

Danley, R.R., Wick, J.W., & Smith, J.K. (1983 b). *Canadian comprehensive assessment program: Achievement series teacher's manual.* Toronto: Gage.

Dawson, D. (1982). The future of school psychology in Canada. *The NASP Canada/Mexico Newsletter*, January, 4–8.

Derevensky, J.L., & Mardell Czudnowski, C. (1986). The use of the DIAL-R for the early identification of children with special needs in a Canadian population. *Canadian Journal of School Psychology*, 2, 27–34.

DiPasquale, G. (1986). The temporal plot: another tool for WISC-R profile interpretation. *Canadian Journal of School Psychology, 2*, 55–60.

Dumont, Florent, & Karen-Fine, Esther (1989). School psychology in Canada: A selective review of recent research trends. *Professional School Psychology*, 4, 209–217.

Dumont, F. (1987). School psychology in Canada: An evolving profession. *The McGill Journal of Education*, 22, 101–116.

Dumont, F. (1989). School psychology in Canada: Views on its status. In P. Saigh & T. Oakland (Eds.), *International perspectives on psychology in the schools* (pp. 211–222). Hillsdale, NJ: Erlbaum.

Eidness, B.W. (1988). A study of the effectiveness of Shared Services Program in Saskatchewan. *News and Views*, 6, 10–18.

Fagan, T.K. (1986). The historical origins and growth of programs to prepare school psychologists in the United States. *Journal of School Psychology, 24*, 9–22.

Fagan, T.K. (1989). School psychology: Where next? *Canadian Journal of School Psychology*, 5, 1–7.

Finch R., & Braid, V. (1988). The effect of birthdate on a child's overall development: concept development, self-concept, fine and gross motor skills. *Canadian Journal of School Psychology*, 3, 53–60.

Frost, B.P. (1979). *The Frost Self Description Questionnaire: Extended Scales*. Department of Educational Psychology, University of Calgary, Calgary, Alberta.

Fulgenzi, J., Holland, C.J., & Daly, R.M. (1986). Transfer effects of a home-based remediation program to the school setting: a study in directive parental counselling. *Canadian Journal of School Psychology*, 2, 19–26.

Gagné, N., & Boivin, G. (1991). The situation of Québec school psychology services. *Canadian Journal of School Psychology*, in press.

Gardner, J. (1986). A comparison of the K-ABC and WISC-R for Cantonese, English, and Punjabi speaking Canadians. *Canadian Journal of School Psychology*, 2, 45–54.

Gardner, J. (1988). Factor structure of the K-ABC for Cantonese, English, and Punjabi speaking Canadians. *Canadian Journal of School Psychology*, 4, 49–60.

Goldstein, C. (1988). Cautions concerning assessment of native Indian students. *Canadian Journal of School Psychology*, 4, 17–20.

Gutkin, T.B., & Reynolds, C.R. (1990). *The handbook of school psychology* (2nd ed.) New York: Wiley.

Hackhofer, W. (1988). Brain insult as a predictor of specific learning disabilities in school-aged children: Reproductive causality revisited. *Canadian Journal of School Psychology*, 3, 1–7.

Haverstock, C., & Millman, E. (1991). School psychology in Nova Scotia – 1990. *Canadian Journal of School Psychology*, in press.

Holmes, B. (1987). WISC-R interpretation: An edu-clinical orientation. *Canadian Journal of School Psychology*, *3*, 1–4.

Hunter, W.J. (1989). School psychological applications of computer technology. *Canadian Journal of School Psychology*, *5*, 31–40.

Ishiyama, F.I. (1989). Understanding foreign adolescents' difficulties in cross-cultural adjustment: A self-validating model. *Canadian Journal of School Psychology*, 5, 41–56.

Janzen, H.L. (1984). Changes in education and the school psychologist: Erosion or explosion of excellence? *Alberta psychology*, 13, 8–11.

Janzen, H.L. (1987). American influences on school psychology and a new role for a trainer of school psychologists. *The School Psychologist*, *41*, 4–6.

Janzen, H.L., & Massey, D. (1991). State of the art of school psychology in Alberta. *Canadian Journal of School Psychology*, in press.

Janzen, H.L., Paterson, J.G., & Blashko, C. (1989 a). *That's Living*. Edmonton: Three Pears Publishing.

Janzen, H.L., Paterson, J.G., & Blashko, C. (1989 b). *That's Living, Too*. Edmonton: Three Pears Publishing.

Janzen, H.L., & Saklofske, D.H. (1991). Testing for diagnostic purposes. In L. Stewin, R. Short & S. McCann (Eds.), *Educational psychology: Canadian perspective*. Toronto: Copp Clark Pitman.

Kimmins, R., Hunter, W., & McKay, A.W. (1985). Educational legislation and litigation pertaining to the practice of school psychology in Canada. *Canadian Journal of School Psychology*, *1*, 1–10.

Kirby, J.R., & Das, J.P. (1990). A cognitive approach to intelligence: Attention coding and planning. *Canadian Psychology*, *31*, 320–333.

Koe, G., & Meiners, D. (1989). Some suggestions for treating major depressive episodes in children. *Canadian Journal of School Psychology*, *5*, 9–22.

Koe, G., & Oldridge, O. (1987). Interpretation of the WISC-R. *Canadian Journal of School Psychology*, *3*, 5–10.

Lechowick, F. (1991). School psychology in Prince Edward Island. *Canadian Journal of School Psychology*, in press.

Lewis, J., & Samuda, R.J. (1989). Non-discriminatory assessment of culturally different students. *The McGill Journal of Education*, *24*, 253–266.

Livingston, R.M. (1973). *The role of the educational psychologist employed by the Saskatchewan Department of Public Health*. Unpublished master's thesis, University of Regina.

Massey, D.L. (1988). Cross-cultural psychological assessment: A clinical model of service delivery. *Canadian Journal of School Psychology*, *4*, 21–38.

Merrell, K. (1989). Validity issues in direct behavioral observation: Applications for behavioral assessment in the classroom. *Canadian Journal of School Psychology*, *5*, 57–62.

Meyers, J., Wurtz, R., & Flanagan, D. (1981). A national survey investigating consultation training occurring in school psychology programs. *Psychology in the Schools*, *18*, 297–302.

Michayluk, J.O., & Saklofske, D.H. (1985). Some effects of LOGO with emotionally disturbed children. *Canadian Journal of Educational Communication*, *14*, 4–7.

Michayluk, J.O., & Saklofske, D.H. (1988). Logo and special education. *Canadian Journal of Special Education*, *4*, 43–48.

Morton, L., & Siegel, L. (1988). Summer vacation effects on aspects of written language in the learning disabled. *Canadian Journal of School Psychology*, *3*, 9–18.

Mueller, H.H., Dennis, S.S., & Short, R.H. (1986). A meta-exploration of WISC-R factor score profiles as a function of diagnosis and intellectual level. *Canadian Journal of School Psychology*, 2, 21–44.

Naglieri, J.A. (1985). *Matrix Analogies Test: Examiners Manual.* Toronto: Charles E. Merrill Publishing Company.

Neudorf, J. (1989). *The role and tasks of educational psychologists in Saskatchewan*. Unpublished master's thesis. University of Regina.

Paananen, N., & Janzen, H.L. (1980). Survey of Canadian school psychology programs. *Canadian Psychology*, *21*, 14–16.

Paananen, N., & Janzen, H.L. (1986). Incidence and characteristics of depression in elementary school children. *Canadian Journal of School Psychology*, 2, 7–19.

Paterson, J.G., & Janzen, H.L. (1980). Psychologists in the media: An analysis and history of CJCA's "That's Living" program. *Alberta Psychology*, *16*, 11–13.

Pawlovich, W. (1986). Early school leaving as perceived by leavers, parents, teachers/principals and stay-ins. *Canadian Journal of School Psychology*, 2, 1–18.

Perkins, M. (1991). School psychology in Ontario. *Canadian Journal of School Psychology*, in press.

Reynolds, M., & Janzen, H.L. (1987). Personal constructs in school psychology. *School Psychology International*, *8*, 11–20.

Saklofske, D.H., & Eysenck, S.B.G. (1988). *Individual differences in children and adolescents: International perspectives*. London: Hodder and Stoughton.

Saklofske, D.H., & Grainger, J. (1991). School psychology in Saskatchewan. *Canadian Journal of School Psychology*, in press.

Saklofske, D.H., & Janzen, H.L. (1987). Children's Depression. In A. Thomas & J. Grimes (Eds.), *Childrens' needs: Psychological perspectives.* Washington, DC: NASP.

Saklofske, D.H., & Janzen, H.L. (1990). School-based assessment research in Canada. *The McGill Journal of Education, 25*, 5–23.

Saklofske, D., Janzen, H.L., & Pannanen, N. (1987). Predictors of childhood depression: Literature review and empirical findings. *Canadian Journal of Special Education, 3*, 1–14.

Saklofske, D.H., & Yackulic, R.A. (1987). Identifying learning disabled children: An analysis of some measurement problems. *Canadian Journal of School Psychology, 3*, 11–20.

Saklofske, D.H., Yackulic, R.A., Murray, W.M., & Naglieri, J.A. (1991). Canadian children's performance on the Matrix Analogies Test: Short Form. *Canadian Journal of School Psychology*, in press.

Samuda, R.J., Kong, S.L., Cummins, J., Pascual-Leone, J., & Lewis, J. (1989). *Assessment and placement of minority students.* Toronto: Hogrefe.

Sarason, S.B. (1977). The unfortunate fate of Alfred Binet and school psychology. In S. Miezitis & M. Orme (Eds.), *Innovation in school psychology* (pp. 19–32).

Scaldwell, W., Frame, J., & Cookson, D. (1985). Individual intellectual assessment of Chipewa, Muncey and Oneida children using the WISC-R. *Canadian Journal of School Psychology, 1*, 15–21.

Simner, M. (1987). Predictive validity of the teacher's school readiness inventory. *Canadian Journal of School Psychology, 3*, 21–32.

Webster, J. (1991). School psychology services in The Yukon. *Canadian Journal of School Psychology*, in press.

Williams, D. (1988). Developmental trends in information processing and reading: a cross-cultural comparison. *Canadian Journal of School Psychology, 4*, 39–48.

Williams, D.G. (1986). Fetal alcohol syndrome: historical review and present concerns. *Canadian Journal of School Psychology, 2*, 35–46.

Wilson, A.K., & Humphries, T. (1986). The impact of recent legislation on the role of the Canadian School psychologist. *Canadian Journal of School Psychology, 2*, 1–6.

Wiss, C., & Burnett, W. (1988). The application of the Boder Test of reading-spelling patterns to the assessment of learning disabilities in French immersion poor readers. *Canadian Journal of School Psychology, 4*, 61–70.

Wormeli, C.T. Jr. (1983). *Manual for the BC QUIET*. University of British Columbia Education Clinic. Vancouver, B. C.

Ysseldyke, J.E., Reynolds, M.C., & Weinberg, R.A. (1984). *School psychology: A blueprint for training and practice*. Minneapolis, MN: National School Psychology Inservice Training Network.

14

Modern Developments in the Profession of Industrial/Organizational Psychology

Steven F. Cronshaw
University of Guelph

This chapter describes the professional practice of industrial/organizational (I/O) psychology in Canada. It is divided into five sections. In the first, a detailed description is given of the scientist-practitioner model presently driving the practice of I/O psychology. As well, a discussion is presented outlining the various mechanisms and structures that have been put in place to support both the science and practice of I/O psychology. In the second section, we examine in some depth what I/O psychologists do when they practise their profession. Among other things, we review survey data reporting the extent to which Canadian I/O psychologists are currently involved in a number of competency areas. In the third section, the graduate training requirements set by the field are outlined. In the fourth section, ethical codes espoused by psychologists are discussed and the relevance of these codes to I/O psychology is explored. In the fifth and last section, one possible future for I/O psychology in Canada is presented. We see how the professional activities of I/O psychologists must adapt to changing organizational requirements as the Canadian economy realigns in response to external events, especially the globalized world economy.

In keeping with the spirit of this book, this chapter deals primarily with the *professional* aspects of I/O psychology in Canada. There is little mention of such matters as how *theory* is developed in I/O psychology, or of the *methods* that I/O psychologists use when, for example, they conduct a job analysis or validate an employment test. These issues of theory and method are of course important, but are dealt with at length elsewhere (e.g. in a book by Cronshaw, 1991).

The Scientist-Practitioner Model as a Basis for the Profession of I/O Psychology

Before embarking on the discussion in this section, it is useful to clarify terms. Given that this book examines the practice of professional psychology in Canada, it is useful at the outset to develop a common understanding of what is meant by the word "profession", at least for the purposes of this chapter. Accordingly, a profession is defined here as *a service-related work role requiring a specialized knowledge base and a lengthy, intensive academic preparation.* This definition accords reasonably well with Webster's dictionary and should resonate with professional psychologists reading this chapter. One happy consequence of coming up with this definition is that it saves a lot of guesswork about what content to put into this chapter. That is, much of the space here is devoted to examining both what I/O psychologists have to know (i. e. their "specialized knowledge base") as well as how they are trained (i. e. their "lengthy, intensive academic preparation").

Some readers may note, perhaps with some concern, that formal registration with a provincial board has not been included as a part of the definition of what comprises a "profession". This omission is bound to raise the ire of some who view registration as a *sine qua non* for admission into the ranks of professional psychology but, at least for the moment, this chapter will stay with the more general and inclusive definition of a "profession", and come back to the contentious issue of licensure at a later point.

Having defined the term "profession", the scientist-practitioner model will now be explained in more detail (fully recognizing that many readers will be very familiar with this term and may offer their own definitions in preference to this one). According to the scientist-practitioner model, the I/O psychologist fulfils two roles. The first role is that of a scientist who discovers new knowledge through basic and applied research. The second role is that of a practitioner who applies the principles developed by the scientist. Each I/O psychologist is expected to serve in both roles, although individual psychologists may emphasize one role over the other at a particular point in time. For example, some I/O psychologists have moved from business settings to university positions (or vice versa) at some time in their careers. Those I/O psychologists in academe often hone their applied skills by taking on consulting contracts; many I/O psychologists working in industrial, government, consulting or military settings publish their research in the major journals read most often by academic I/O psychologists (e.g. *Journal of Applied Psychology*, *Personnel Psychology*). Despite the fact that I/O psychologists (in their role as pundits) sometimes lament the existence of the "scientist-practitioner gap", I/O psychologists in academic and field settings often speak the same language and share many of the same concerns. In other words, the dual roles of science and practice function in a *complementary* fashion, at least as they apply to I/O psychology. They support and mutually reinforce each other.

How does the "scientist-practitioner model" mesh with the definition of the "profession" of I/O psychology given earlier? Here a distinction between means and ends might help. The knowledge base generated by the scientist and the practical skills possessed by the practitioner might best be viewed as the *means* to achieve the *ends* that I/O psychologists seek, where the primary ends sought by the I/O psychologist are the competent performance of a role in assisting organizations to solve "people" problems, primarily those large organizations in the industrial, business, government and military sectors. In other words, the knowledge base and skills acquired by the I/O psychologist under the guidance of the scientist/practitioner model (i. e. the means) provide the wherewithal to accomplish the competent performance of the professional role required of an I/O psychologist (i. e. the ends). Naturally, the role of the I/O psychologist does not remain static; rather, the duties required in that professional role change over time, to stay in line with the demands of the client population. These changes reverberate back to the scientist, requiring him or her to undertake the necessary research in new areas as they open up to the practitioner, and to the practitioner, requiring him or her to update skills through workshops, reading of scientific journals and other professional development activities.

What Keeps the Professional in I/O Psychology "Professional"?: An Examination of Licensing Bodies and Professional Associations

The maintenance of a service-related work role as specialized and demanding as that of the professional psychologist requires support mechanisms. In the first instance, a mechanism is needed to provide the lengthy training required by entrants to the profession. The resulting knowledge and skill base must be sufficient to ensure that all those entering the field are competent to practise I/O psychology. (This training component will be dealt with in a subsequent section of this chapter.) Beyond the initial training required of I/O psychologists, additional mechanisms exist to maintain and reinforce professional identity. Foremost among these is *registration*. Given the importance of the registration process, it will be discussed first, with particular reference to effects on I/O psychologists. Then, in the following section, we will discuss another type of support mechanism for I/O psychology – membership in provincial and national psychological associations.

The Primary Support Mechanism for the Profession of I/O Psychology: Provincial Registration Acts and Boards

All provinces in Canada have passed legislation requiring anyone representing himself or herself to the public as a psychologist to hold a certificate of registration (with some exceptions for individuals at universities and in government service). These registration acts require those registered as psychologists to have a basic minimum education in psychology, usually a PhD. In addition, registrants may be required to pass a registration exam and undergo a period of supervised practice. Registration acts are enforced by provincial boards which are set up to monitor complaints against registered psychologists. These boards may investigate complaints, convene hearings and levy penalties against those psychologists proven to be guilty of professional malpractice. In the most serious cases, psychologists may be dropped from the permanent registers in the respective provinces, so revoking those individuals' rights to practise as psychologists. For an in-depth treatment of the registration process, readers are referred to the chapter by B. Wand in this volume.

Provincial registration acts regulate professional practice by I/O psychologists, even though these acts were originally written with Health Service Providers (HSPs), such as clinical and counselling psychologists, in mind. For example, in Ontario, The Psychologists Registration Act defines "professional misconduct" to mean, among other things, "... failure to maintain a record for each client that does not contain ... (i) the client's name, address, telephone number, if any, and date of birth". Let us consider the situation where a large corporation has asked a registered I/O psychologist to conduct a job analysis. On whom does the psychologist keep such a client record? On the senior human resources manager who serves as company liaison on the project? On the workers and supervisors who actually provide the job analysis information? Is a request to these people for their date of birth even legitimate, given the nature of the work by conducted by the I/O psychologist? Or do we list the corporation as the "client" and record "date of birth" as the time when the Articles of Incorporation were signed in the lawyer's office? In short, there is a justifiable concern among some I/O psychologists about the "goodness of fit" provided by provincial registration acts to at least some of the services provided by I/O psychologists and to the unique needs of clients who require management consulting, rather than health-related, services.

Of equal concern is the ability of provincial boards, comprised mainly of HSPs, to dictate the standards of practice for a specialized non-HSP subfield such as I/O psychology. As well, concerns have been raised about the fact that individuals possessing a master's degree in I/O psychology are not eligible for registration in most provinces. Unable to label themselves as "psychologists", many of these people lose their primary identification with psychology after a period of time, often assuming labels such as "human resources manager" and the like. These individuals tend to join personnel and human resource management associations, foregoing professional activities with psychologists, and are permanently lost to the psychology profession.

The preceding discussion shows that some I/O psychologists have concerns about how well the requirements of provincial registration acts match the realities of practice in the field of I/O psychology. One manifestation of this concern is the issue of *specialty designation*, which has received much discussion among Canadian psychologists over the past several years. The Canadian Psychological Association (CPA) and the Council of Provincial Associations of Psychology (CPAP) have jointly established a Task Force to assess the viability of setting up a structure for specialty designation in selected subfields of psychology (including I/O). Importantly, representatives from the provincial registration boards sit on CPAP, so the initiative toward specialty designation has some support from the regulatory boards which might eventually enforce it.

What is involved in specialty designation? As Catano (1987) points out, specialty designation would go beyond the generic registration presently in place in the provinces across Canada in that such a mechanism would "certify" that a psychologist has expertise in a particular subfield of psychology, such as I/O. At present, every candidate meeting the provincial boards' standards is placed on the Register, so granting him or her access to the specialized work role we call the "profession" of psychology. This registration process does not "certify" that an individual psychologist possesses expertise in any specialty area, such as I/O or educational psychology. Psychologists are largely left to police themselves under a code of ethics which limits psychological practice to one's self-judged area of expertise (although, in egregious cases, psychologists providing incompetent services outside their area of expertise may be disciplined by the provincial regulatory board).

In contrast, specialty designation would require psychologists to demonstrate at least minimal training and competence in their chosen specialty area before being listed on a specialty "register". A number of mechanisms are potentially available to enforce a system of specialty designation, including a provincial system whereby each province would develop its own designating mechanisms, a system operated by CPA, or a joint CPA-CPAP mechanism of designation. After one of these mechanisms is set up, I/O psychologists might be listed in a specialty register similar to the National Registry of Health Care Providers in Psychology presently in place for clinical psychologists.

Where do Canadian I/O psychologists stand on the issue of specialty designation? A survey conducted in 1987 by the Section on I/O Psychology of CPA suggests that most Section members support the idea of specialty designation for I/O psychologists in Canada if this specialty designation process involves an assessment and certification of at least minimal competence to practise in the field (Section on Industrial/Organizational Psychology, 1987). In contrast, the Section members completing the specialty designation survey disagreed on what structure should be set up for achieving specialty designation. (Some of the structures potentially available include those listed at the end of the previous paragraph.) However, even if professional psychologists across Canada can reach general agreement on a structure for implementation, specialty designation may be some time in coming due to the logistical difficulties of setting up regulatory boards, establishing minimal educational requirements, and the like (in regard to educational requirements, the I/O psychology profession in Canada has already developed graduate training guidelines, as explained in the third section of this chapter). Regardless of the delay in achieving specialty designation, if it comes at all, I/O psychologists will closely monitor this issue because it strikes to the heart of how I/O psychology will be defined and who will define it.

Whatever the difficulties experienced by I/O psychologists in the present system of "generic" provincial registration, the importance and centrality of the present registration mechanism is not in dispute.[1] Those I/O psychologists wishing to practise their profession outside of universities and the government service must conform their activities to stipulations set down by provincial registration boards, whatever the difficulties and inconsistencies are experienced by individual I/O psychologists in conforming to this process.

Other Support Mechanisms for the Profession of I/O Psychology: Provincial, National and Foreign Psychology Associations

As discussed in the previous section, registration is mandatory for all I/O psychologists who wish to practise, although some provinces exempt psychologists in universities and government from the requirement to hold a registration certificate. The stance of the individual psychologist vis-à-vis the provincial registration boards is one of a regulated professional reporting to an enforcement body to which he or she is accountable for his or her standards of professional practice. The enforcement body has the legal right to deny the individual the right to practise psychology under its jurisdiction if he or she does not meet the stipulated standards of training and practice. In contrast, the stance of the psychologist vis-à-vis provincial, national and foreign psychology associations is very different from that of a provincial regulatory board. The psychologist's membership in these associations is *voluntary* – the psychologist is not required under any statute to join any of these associations and may discontinue membership at any time without jeopardizing his or her legal right to a professional practice. Although these associations may, and sometimes do, discontinue members due to infractions of ethical codes, the associations have no power to require these individuals to discontinue the pro-

1 This statement must be qualified in light of recent attempts in the Province of Ontario to exempt psychologists outside the health care field from the requirement to become registered. If the coverage of provincial registration acts is restricted to health care providers, I/O psychologists will no longer be accountable to provincial registration boards. Such legislation would have a major influence on how I/O psychology is practised in the various jurisdictions across Canada.

fessional practice of psychology. These powers only reside in the provincial regulatory boards.

A major difference between provincial regulatory boards and the various psychological associations is therefore the fundamental distinction between *enforced regulation* and *voluntary membership*. However, despite the voluntary nature of membership in psychological associations, these associations play a vital part in supporting the profession of I/O psychology. Consequently, we will consider the associations commonly joined by Canadian I/O psychologists and the part that they have to play in supporting the activities of I/O psychologists in the professional sphere. We will start with the provincial psychological associations, move to the level of the national association (i.e. the CPA) and then lastly examine foreign associations often joined by Canadian I/O psychologists.

Involvement of I/O Psychologists in Provincial Associations of Psychology

A number of I/O psychologists across Canada have joined the associations in their provinces of residence. Some of these provincial associations have interest groups of I/O psychology affiliated with them. For example, the Ontario Psychological Association has an interest group called the Section on Industrial and Organizational Psychology (SIOP). This group has an elected executive and conducts regular meetings in which members exchange information about their activities and interests in the area of I/O psychology. I/O interest groups at the provincial level can be contacted, in the provinces where such groups have been formed, through the executive offices of the respective psychological associations.

Involvement of I/O Psychologists in the Canadian Psychological Association

The CPA serves as the national voice for psychology in this country. The CPA has affiliated with it a number of sections which represent the interests of various specialty areas in psychology (e.g. social, programme evaluation). The I/O Section is one of the most active in CPA. Founded in 1975, it has an elected executive and operates under a set of by-laws. The section has become involved in a number of key issues important to I/O psychologists in Canada, including specialty designation (discussed earlier), accreditation of graduate programmes in I/O psychology (see the section on training later in this chapter), planning for I/O activities at the annual CPA conferences and representation of I/O concerns to external agencies and print media. The I/O Section has a regular newsletter which is sent to all of its members (about 170 in total). A contact person for the Section can be reached through the Executive Office of the CPA in Old Chelsea, Quebec.

The CPA is the parent body of the Section on Industrial and Organizational Psychology. CPA publishes three journals, two of which are potential outlets for research and writing by I/O psychologists. The *Canadian Journal of Behavioural Science* publishes a wide range of empirical studies, including work by I/O psychologists in areas such as organizational commitment and group processes. *Canadian Psychology (CP)* publishes articles in areas of theory, research and practice that are of interest to a broad cross-section of psychologists, including of course ones that are of considerable interest to I/O psychologists. Most notably, an issue of *CP* published in 1988 (Vol. 29, No. 1), and edited by Victor Catano and John Tivendell, is entirely devoted to the science and practice of I/O psychology in Canada. Readers wishing to gain a theoretical and technical overview of I/O psychology in Canada are referred to this first-rate source.

Involvement of I/O Psychologists in Other National and Foreign Associations

The subfield of I/O psychology overlaps a great deal (in content, if not in method) with personnel and human resources management as taught in business schools. In fact, some of the leading academic I/O psychologists in Canada have been located in business schools, even though they keep a close connection with psychology through the I/O Section of CPA and other mechanisms. Some I/O psychologists who work in academic institutions, whether psychology departments or business schools, choose to join the *Administrative Sciences Association of Canada (ASAC)*. ASAC publishes a regular, high-quality journal called the *Canadian Journal of Administrative Sciences*. This journal occasionally publishes empirical research by Canadian I/O psychologists and so should not be overlooked as either a publishing outlet or as a source of research information in such areas as work attitudes and employment testing.

A number of Canadian I/O psychologists have joined the Society for Industrial and Organizational Psychology, Inc. (SIOP), which is based in the United States. SIOP is affiliated with both the American Psychological Association (APA) and the American Psychological Society. It is home for the largest concentration of I/O psychologists in the world, and many of the top experts in the area are active members of SIOP. The society publishes a regular, high-quality newsletter called *The Industrial Psychologist* or *TIP* (actually, the newsletter is more akin to a glossy journal). The APA publishes the *Journal of Applied Psychology (JAP)*, which many consider to be the premier journal for I/O psychology. As well, SIOP has close ties to *Personnel Psychology (PP)*, which is published by private concerns out of Houston, Texas. Canadian I/O psychologists are prominently seen at the annual conferences of SIOP and Canadian I/O psychologists consider *JAP* and *PP* to be important outlets for their work.

Many members of SIOP are also members of the Academy of Management, once again based in the United States (the Academy of Management is the US counterpart of ASAC). The Academy publishes three important journals (the *Academy of Management Journal*, the *Academy of Management Review* and the *Academy of Management Executive*), to which I/O psychologists frequently contribute. Some Canadian I/O psychologists have chosen to join the Academy of Management and regularly attend their annual conferences.

What Do I/O Psychologists Do?

Now that we have examined with whom I/O psychologists associate and what they read, we will consider the more difficult question: What do I/O psychologists practising as professionals in Canada actually *do*? Unfortunately, the answer to this question must remain somewhat speculative because no survey on this issue has yet been conducted (other than periodic surveys conducted by the I/O Section of CPA, and possibly sections of provincial psychological associations, to assess their members' interests). Even if a complete survey of professional activities was available, one would have to qualify its results because the implicit understanding on the part of the survey researcher as to "what I/O psychologists do" will influence who will be included as respondents in the survey (e.g. Are people conducting human factors research or designing job evaluation systems to be included in a survey of I/O psychologists?). In a sense, then, such surveys are self-fulfilling prophecies, with the survey outcome largely predetermined by the nature of the sample preselected for inclusion in the study. Of course, a second way (and, some would say, a preferable way) of identifying what I/O psychologists do is conduct a detailed job analysis. However, to my knowledge, no one in Canada has tried this approach yet. Of course, the results of the job analysis, as with the surveys, are influenced by the type of people interviewed by the job analyst in the first place. If human factors people are not asked to participate in job analysis interviews, the job that the I/O psychologist does will be noticeably devoid of human factors applications.

In the absence of surveys and job analyses on the job of the I/O psychologist in Canada, I will attempt initially to outline what I/O psychologists do in Canada by drawing on his observations. These observations will be augmented with another source, albeit of a less direct nature than a survey of job activities or a job analysis; specifically, I will summarize and discuss the results of a survey of member interests conducted by the Section on Industrial and Organizational Psychology of the CPA.

This discussion about what Canadian I/O psychologists do will begin with some personal observations of the I/O scene in this country. There appear to be two distinctly different models of I/O psychology operating in Canada. The first model will be referred to here as the "home-grown clinically based model" of I/O psychology. The second will be called the "Midwest American systems-based model" of I/O psychology. There is a wide philosophical gulf between these two groups, and a tendency for these two groups to operate in isolation from each other. As no one (to my knowledge) has yet documented this phenomenon, some observations will be made on where each model is practised and how the models differ.

The "Home-Grown Clinically Based Model" of I/O Psychology

This model of I/O psychology appears to be most prevalent among psychologists working out of consulting firms in large Canadian cities. These consulting firms undertake a range of activities for their clients in business, industry and government, but are often involved in the selection, development and promotion of middle- and upper-level managers. Many of the psychologists who carry out such activities are not trained in I/O psychology *per se*, but have received PhDs in other specialty areas of psychology, most notably, clinical, social and experimental. On a philosophical level, many of these individuals appear to be operating with a primary focus on the "treatment" of individual managers or executives who are the source of performance problems in client organizations. Often, this treatment, which may be personnel selection or outplacement, requires assessment through the use of standard psychological instruments or clinical interviews, feedback and interpretation of the results to the individual manager/executive and (where appropriate) some sort of work counselling. Of course, the selection of managers and executives involves a variation on this theme: the assessment and feedback/interpretation component is kept, but there is no longer-term commitment to the individual by the psychologist if that individual is screened out through the selection process.

In sum, then, the home-grown clinicallybased model of I/O psychology focuses on the assessment and treatment of individuals, usually managers and executives, often with the help of standardized psychological instruments and clinical interviews.

Earlier in the chapter, the *registration* process extant in provincial jurisdictions across Canada was discussed. The provincial registration boards seem to have in mind the home-grown clinically based model when they think of I/O psychology. However, as we shall see below in the discussion of the Midwest American systems-based model, there are a significant number of professional psychologists in Canada who hold very different assumptions from clinical school about how I/O psychology should be practised.

The "Midwest American Systems-Based Model" of I/O Psychology

This model of I/O psychology is most prevalent among those working out of in-house positions in government (including large government-regulated industries), the military and academia. Many of these individuals received their PhDs from I/O psychology programmes in Canada and the United States. The following quote from an American I/O psychologist summarizes very well how these individuals practise (and teach) I/O psychology:

> The core activities of practising I/O psychologists are clear: the design and validation of selection systems, job analysis, the design and evaluation of performance systems, the design, delivery and evaluation of training programmes, attitude survey research and organizational interventions based on survey results, and the design and evaluation of compensation systems. The redundancy in the last sentence is intentional: the repeated use of "design and evaluation of systems" highlights the fact that most of the work of I/O psychologists does not involve one-on-one work intended to benefit a *single* [emphasis added] individual, as may be the case with much clinical, counselling and school psychology work. (Sackett, 1986, p. 21)

Cronshaw (1991) has characterized this view of I/O psychology as "objectivist". Objectivists rely heavily on research design and statistical analysis in their work and have a mistrust of clinical judgment in most, if not all, matters in which I/O psychologists become involved. To put it compactly, if a bit simplistically, the systems person "reads the numbers", whereas the clinical person "reads the person". However, the differences don't end here. At least some of the clinical types and the systems types have decided that they don't like the way that the other group does business. The clinical people see the systems types as too numbers-oriented and impractical; the systems types complain that the clinical people are subjective and unscientific. In this game, the systems types have an advantage – they control, by and large, the research journals frequented by I/O psychologists (e.g. *Journal of Applied Psychology*, *Personnel Psychology*). The research in these journals is overwhelmingly systems-oriented and objectivist. However, the clinical person typically doesn't read them. In short, we have two solitudes in professional I/O psychology.

Two I/O Solitudes?: Divergences Between the Clinical and Systems Models

In the previous discussion, it was observed that the adherents of the clinical and systems models occupy two solitudes[2]. This split manifests itself in various ways. As one example, I/O psychologists of the "clinical" persuasion often elect to affiliate with provincial psychological associations, if in fact they decide to join psychological associations at all. These people are not often seen, for example, at the national and international conferences frequented by I/O psychologists of the "systems" persuasion (e.g. the annual conference of the CPA, the conference of the Society for Industrial and Organizational Psychology in the United States). On the other hand, the systems people may avoid the provincial associations and often forego registration.

The philosophical stances of the clinical and systems camps come into direct conflict in the literature of I/O psychology. To illustrate this point, we will begin by assuming that the prototypical journals of I/O psychology are represented by the *Journal of Applied Psychology* and *Personnel Psychology*, previously described in this chapter. These journals are in the words of Cronshaw (1991) "objectivist". The typical research in these journals employs rigorous research designs and statistical analysis. The judgmental model implicit in this work can be best characterized as statistical as opposed to clinical. In fact, sometimes these journals report results which directly challenge the accuracy and usefulness of clinical judgment for making people decisions in organizations. For example, Ryan and Sackett (1987, 1989) have recently published two empirical papers which call into question the usefulness of individual assessments, as traditionally undertaken by the clinical camp, for making various decisions in organizations (e.g. who to select or promote into a managerial position). Such incidents suggest that, due to basic philosophical differences, a full

---

2 Some I/O psychologists, most notably from the "clinical" camp, have recognized this problem and are making efforts to bridge the gap with the other group. However, it remains to be seen whether sufficient understanding can be developed between the two groups to allow them to work together on a regular basis.

reconciliation between the clinical and systems camps will be difficult to achieve in the foreseeable future.

Interest Areas of I/O Psychologists: The Results of a Survey

The personal observations on the "clinical" and "systems" variants of professional I/O psychology presented earlier in this chapter, which are conjectural at best, still do not provide enough detailed information to fully inform the reader about what I/O psychologists do. Fortunately, a source does exist to provide this more complete picture. The Section on Industrial and Organizational Psychology of CPA has conducted surveys to assess membership interests across and within in the various subareas of I/O psychology. The results of the most recent such survey (conducted by the Section on Industrial and Organizational Psychology, 1988) are presented over the next few pages. In the original survey, I/O Section members reported their interests in 32 subareas (e.g. employee selection, organization development). For the purposes of this chapter, these 32 subareas are classified into three broader areas: industrial/personnel, organizational and other.

The pie chart in Figure 1 reports the total number and percentage of survey respondents who had interests in each of the three broader areas (note that respondents could indicate interests in more than one subarea, so at least some of the responses reported in Figure 1 are repeats from the same people). As Figure 1 shows, about half of the responses from the total survey sample fell into the broad area of industrial or personnel psychology, with the remainder of the responses divided among organizational psychol-

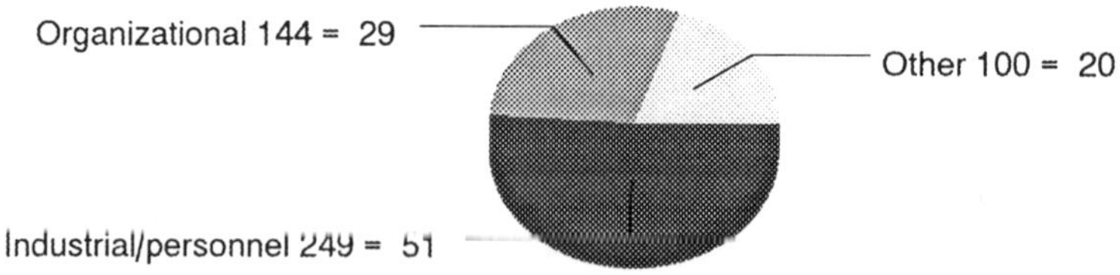

Figure 1. Number of responses (= %) from Canadian I/O psychologists indicating interests in three major areas of I/O psychology.

ogy and other topics. (The other category is comprised of subareas which could not be classified into either industrial/personnel or organizational psychology.) The strong expressed interest of the survey respondents in traditional industrial/personnel topics (e. g. employee selection, performance appraisal, training and development) is noteworthy and probably reflects the close historical ties of industrial psychology with large bureaucratic organizations in industry, business, government and the military.

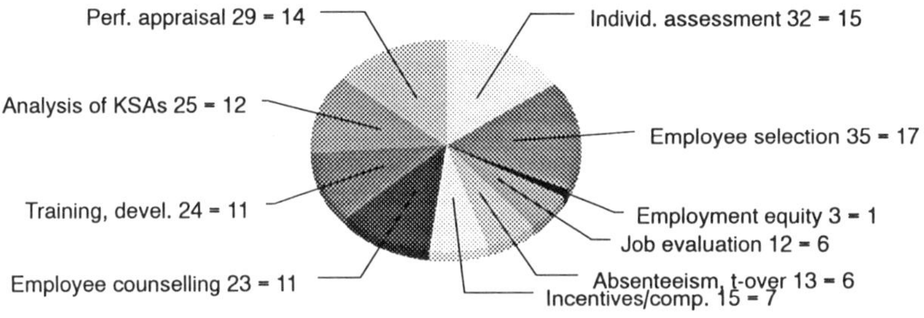

Figure 2. Number of responses (= %) from Canadian I/O psychologists indicating interests in 10 subareas of industrial/personnel psychology.

The last three figures in this chapter show a breakdown of each of the three broader areas into their constituent subareas. In Figure 2, ten subareas of industrial/personnel psychology are presented, along with the number and percentages of responses in each subarea. Interestingly, over half of the responses fell into the following four subareas, all of which are highly prototypic of the systems approach to industrial or personnel psychology: employee selection; performance appraisal; analysis of *k*nowledges, *s*kills and *a*bilities (KSAs); and training and development. However, the clinical approach to I/O psychology is also represented by a relatively strong interest in individual assessment and employee counselling. The number of I/O psychologists expressing an interest in employee counselling in Figure 2 is particularly significant, especially given that the training and education of I/O psychologists discussed in the next section does not prepare individuals to assume a counselling role. Many of these respondents represented in Figure 2 may in fact be trained in clinical PhD programmes (having adopted the label of "I/O psychologist" later). Whatever the explanation, however, these survey results suggest greater clinical involvement in the practice of I/O psychology than would be revealed by looking only at training/education guidelines for I/O psychologists and scientific journals such as the *Journal of Applied Psychology*.

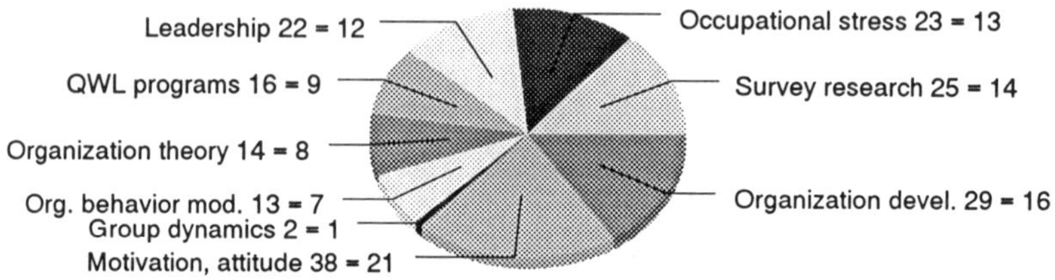

Figure 3. Number of responses (= %) from Canadian I/O psychologists indicating interests in nine subareas of organizational psychology.

Figure 3 presents a breakdown of the responses in the organizational area. About two thirds of the responses are concentrated in four interest areas: organization development, survey research, occupational stress and leadership. Of these four subareas, only occupational stress is left unaddressed by the training and education guidelines for I/O psychology given in the following section of this chapter. At least some I/O psychologists undertaking drganization development interventions and occupational stress management may be working from the clinical approach; otherwise, the systems approach comes out quite prominently in Figure 3.

The last figure (Figure 4) presents the number and percentage of respondents indicating an interest in what have been classified as other topics in I/O psychology. Most surprisingly, programme evaluation emerges as the other subarea of greatest interest to the membership of the Section on Industrial and Organizational Psychology (many psychologists view programme evaluation as a part of applied social psychology). Less surprisingly, research methods emerges prominently as an interest area of I/O psychologists. In addition, there is some interest in the subareas of technological impact, marketing research and industrial/labour rela-

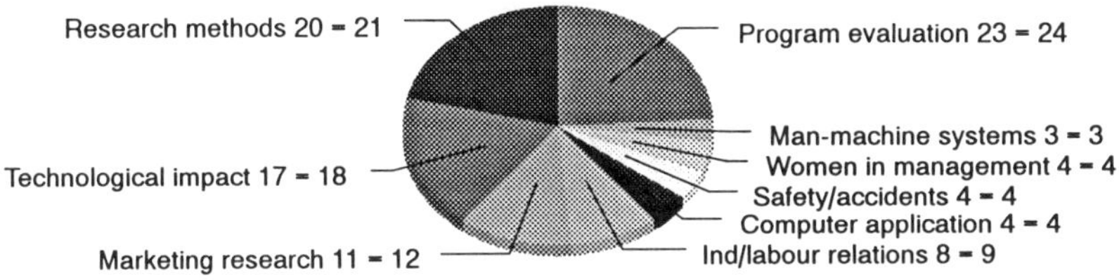

Figure 4. Number of responses (= %) from Canadian I/O psychologists indicating interests in nine supplementary subareas associated with I/O psychology.

tions. Perhaps the most notable feature of Figure 4 is the wide range of other interests held by I/O psychologists in Canada which cannot be classified into either of the traditional areas of industrial and organizational psychology.

Before leaving the discussion of the interest survey done by the Section on Industrial and Organizational Psychology, two limitations of the survey should be noted. First, not every Canadian who calls himself or herself an I/O psychologist is a member of the Section on Industrial and Organizational Psychology of CPA, and not all members of the Section responded to the survey. As a result, the survey results reported here may not be fully representative of Canadian I/O psychologists as a group. Second, expressions of interests by I/O psychologists do not guarantee that these people actually do these things in field. Again, the survey is an assessment of Section member interests, rather than a direct measure of the *activities* that they undertake on a daily basis. Nevertheless, one should reasonably expect to find a correlation between expressed interests and professional activities, although it is impossible to say how strong that correlation would be.

In conclusion, then, the survey of member interests yields some insight into what professional I/O psychologists do in Canadian organizations. Even if this document might be criticized as presenting an incomplete or unrepresentative view of what I/O psychologists do, it can be countered that this source presents the *best* picture that we have at present time. Further work, hopefully of the job analysis variety, would be beneficial in providing a more definitive picture of what I/O psychologist in Canada do.

Training Requirements for I/O Psychologists

Another way of establishing what I/O psychologists do is to examine the training requirements for the profession. These training requirements have been set down by the Section on Industrial and Organizational Psychology of the CPA (see the first section of this chapter for a discussion of the role of the I/O Section within CPA). It should be noted at the outset that these training requirements are consistent for the most part with the Midwest American systems-based model, which is not surprising, given that the training document developed by the Section on Industrial and Organizational Psychology (i. e. *Guidelines for graduate training and education in industrial and organizational psychology in Canada*, 1989) was based on a set of training guidelines published by the Society for Industrial and Organizational Psychology, Inc. (1982) in the United States. The membership of the Society is overwhelmingly systems-oriented, so it follows that the *Guidelines* have a distinctly objectivist and systems-based orientation.

Given the fundamental importance of graduate training and education to I/O psychology, it is useful to review the training model presented in the *Guidelines for graduate training and education in industrial and organizational psychology* (1989). Table 1 presents the content areas which should be included in the training and education of I/O psychologists, according to the *Guidelines*. Importantly, a survey was conducted in which members of the Section on Industrial and Organizational Psychology of CPA were asked to rate the extent that each of these areas in Table 1 was necessary for the training and education of I/O psychologists. On the basis of these results, the content areas were grouped into three categories of core, complementary and secondary (as reported in Table 1). The areas classified as *core* are considered necessary to the practice of I/O psychology and should be thoroughly covered in I/O graduate programmes. The areas classified as *complementary* should be the subject of some training in all graduate programmes. More established graduate programmes should ensure competence in these complementary areas. The *secondary* content areas should receive at least basic coverage at either the graduate or advanced undergraduate level. The writers of the *Guidelines* clearly intended to indicate the priorities that university adminis-

Table 1. Education and Training Strategies by Content Area from the *Guidelines for Graduate Training and Education in Industrial and Organizational Psychology in Canada*

Content area	Education strategy					
	Graduate course work	Advanced undergrad. courses	Independent study/ research	Supervised experience	On-the-job training	Professional workshop
Core Areas						
1. Ethical, legal and professional context of I/O psychology	HR	A	A		A	A
2. Organization theory	HR	A	A	A	A	
3. Work motivation theory	HR	A	R	A		
4. Statistical methods/ data methods	HR	R	A	A	A	A
5. Research methods	HR	R	A	A	A	
6. Personnel selection, placement and classification	HR	A	A	HR	A	
7. Performance appraisal/feedback	HR	A	A	HR	A	
8. Measurement of individual differences	HR	R	A	A	A	
Education strategy						
9. Organizational development theory	HR	A	A	A	A	A
10. Job and task analysis	HR	A	A	HR	R	A
11. Criterion development and theory	HR	A	A	A	A	A

Table 1 continued

Content area	Education strategy: Graduate course work	Advanced undergrad. courses	Independent study/ research	Supervised experience	On-the-job training	Professional workshop
Complementary Areas						
12. Individual assessment	HR	R	A	R	R	A
13. Training: Theory, programme design and evaluation	HR	A	A	R	R	A
14. Attitude theory	HR	R	A			
15. Career development theory	HR	A	R	A	A	A
16. Human performance/ human factors/ergonomics	HR	A	A	A	A	
Education strategy						
Secondary Areas						
17. Small group theory and process	HR	R	A	A	A	
18. Decision theory	HR	A	A			
19. Programme evaluation	HR	A	A	A	A	A
20. Consumer behaviour	R	A	A			
21. Fields of psychology	A	HR	A			
22. History and systems in psychology	R	HR	A			

Note. The above table is reproduced from Section on Industrial and Organizational Psychology (1989). The entries in the table are interpreted as follows: HR = a "highly recommended" training strategy for the content area; R = a "recommended" training strategy; A = an "acceptable" strategy.

trators should consider when investing resources in graduate training and education in I/O psychology (i.e. the greatest emphasis should be placed on the core areas, followed by complementary and, finally, secondary content areas).

In addition to indicating how priorities should be set in graduate training and education in I/O psychology, the *Guidelines* offer recommendations for how training and education can be provided for achieving competence in each of 22 content areas. These training and education strategies are listed along the top of Table 1 from left to right as follows: graduate course work; advanced undergraduate courses; independent study/research; supervised experience; on-the-job training; and professional workshops. As indicated in the legend at the bottom of Table 1, the importance of each training/education strategy is given for all 22 content areas (e.g. graduate coursework in the ethical, legal and professional context of I/O psychology is "highly recommended" in any graduate programme offering a PhD in I/O psychology). Obviously, the information contained in this table provides an excellent basis for the design of curricula in graduate programmes of I/O psychology.

Appendix A at the end of this chapter presents a summary description for each of the content areas listed in Table 1. A close reading of the descriptions there provides a good overview of the competency areas identified by the membership of the Section on Industrial and Organizational Psychology as "core", "complementary" and "secondary" to their discipline. These descriptions, particularly of the "core" areas, also match closely the topic coverage in major journals in I/O psychology, such as the *Journal of Applied Psychology* and *Personnel Psychology*. As well, the content areas listed in Table 1 and Appendix A overlap to a considerable extent with the survey of I/O Section member interests reported in the previous section of this chapter.

Implicit in the training guidelines summarized in Table 1 is the centrality of statistics and research methods to the science and practice of I/O psychology. As in psychology more generally, the profession of I/O psychology trains all of its mew members in empirical methods. Through the use of empirical measurement and field research designs, I/O psychologists seek objective indicators of the efficacy of their behavioural science interventions (e.g. personnel selection, organization development). In doing so, they are able to provide critical input to clients who try to justify their behavioural science interventions through self-fulfilling hypotheses. In short, I/O psychologists bring an empirically based scepticism to information that is not found in most other professions in the business world.

Ethics and the I/O Psychologist

Early on in this chapter, a profession was defined as a service-related work role requiring a specialized knowledge base and lengthy, intensive academic preparation. In keeping with this definition, much of the foregoing material in this chapter was devoted to describing the types of activities that I/O psychologists engage in, the specialized knowledge base they possess, and the content and approach of the intensive academic preparation required. Yet there is an additional dimension of the I/O psychology profession – that of *ethics* – which is even more complex than, and at least as important as, the material already discussed. Ethics, the principles of conduct governing the I/O profession, sets the boundaries around what the I/O psychologist may do in pursuing his or her service-related work role. Ethics does this by explicitly articulating and advocating the rights of the people and groups who are impacted by what I/O psychologists do. As such, ethical principles are critically important statements of who I/O psychologists are, how they define themselves and how they relate to other individuals and groups in society.

Ethical issues in I/O psychology are extremely complex and can not be fully dealt with in the limited space available here. Rather than attempt the unrealistic goal of resolving the many complex substantive issues in this area, I will attempt to achieve the following two limited objectives: (1) To show the reader where the primary documents on ethics for I/O psychologists can be found; (2) To outline in brief the major concerns experienced by the I/O profession in applying the ethical principles discussed in the first part. This approach, although modest in scope, should give the reader sufficient background to access other sources on the subject of ethics in I/O psychology, if he or she desires to pursue this topic in more depth.

Ethical Documents for I/O Psychologists

Earlier in this chapter, we examined the licensing bodies and professional associations most relevant to I/O psychologists. This prior work now simplifies our discussion of ethics somewhat because most of these licensing and professional bodies have published one or more codes of ethics. In fact, a review of the ethical codes developed by these bodies will provide a complete list of the materials most relevant to the ethics discussion contained in this section of the chapter. The reader should note however that these ethical codes differ in content and scope; for example, the *Code of Ethics* developed by the CPA was intended to apply to all psychologists in CPA, not just to I/O psychologists, so the content is necessarily broad and the *Code* makes few, if any, specific references to I/O psychology *per se* (Canadian Psychological Association, 1986 a, 1988). This should not be taken to imply an inherent inferiority of ethical documents such as the *Code* for I/O psychology but, rather, that some work will be required on the part of I/O psychologists to carefully interpret and apply these general ethical principles within the contexts that are most familiar to them.

Provincial Registration Acts and Boards

A previous discussion dealt with provincial registration acts and boards where it was noted that individual psychologists are governed by a mechanism of enforced regulation. The boards set up under provincial registration acts are free to adopt ethical principles that apply to all psychologists under those jurisdictions. For example, the Ontario Board of Examiners in Psychology (OBEP) has developed and adopted the *Standards for Professional Conduct* espousing eight ethical principles to be followed by psychologists registered in Ontario (Ontario Board of Examiners in Psychology, 1986). As previously discussed, OBEP has quasi-legal powers under provincial legislation to enforce the *Standards for*

Professional Conduct and to sanction psychologists found in violation of those ethical standards.

Canadian Psychological Association

CPA members are governed by the *Code of Ethics* (Canadian Psychological Association, 1986a). Unlike the *Standards for Professional Conduct*, the *Code* must rely more on moral persuasion than force of law to gain compliance among CPA members. Although a hearings board could be convened for violations of the *Code* by CPA members, the Association does not have the authority to restrict the practice of anyone found guilty of unethical practice (at worst, the offending member would be dropped from CPA membership). The CPA *Code* is a document which was carefully prepared with broad input from the CPA membership. As such, it has gained considerable support from the psychological community in Canada, including many I/O psychologists.

Foreign Psychology Associations

On the international scene, the American Psychological Association (APA) has published several documents on professional ethics for its membership, including *Ethical principles for psychologists* (1990), *Standards for the providers of psychological services* (1977) and *Ethical principles in the conduct of research with human participants* (1982). APA has published specialty guidelines directed to I/O psychologists (American Psychological Association, 1981) and Division 14 of APA has produced an ethics casebook for I/O psychologists (Lowman, 1985). Some other foreign associations, in which Canadian I/O psychologists sometimes hold membership, also have their own ethical standards (e.g. Academy of Management in the United States).

Issues in the Application of Ethical Principles to I/O Psychology

The above descriptions of ethical codes relevant to the practice of I/O psychology in Canada raises two obvious questions requiring further comment. These two issues are briefly discussed under the following two headings.

How Does the Practising I/O Psychologist Decide Which Codes Apply to Him or Her?

The previous discussion shows that a number of ethical codes potentially apply to each practising I/O psychologist. How does he or she know which codes apply? That question is answered quite simply by referring to that individual's provincial registration or membership in psychological associations. The psychologist will be ethically accountable to all those bodies in which he or she holds registration or membership. It is conceivable, and in fact sometimes happens, that the psychologist holds registration or membership in several bodies simultaneously. This situation must be somewhat disconcerting for the individuals involved given that the application of just one code to one's professional practice is a complex endeavour, quite apart from the balancing of requirements under several codes. And what happens if the ethical principles of one body contradict the principles espoused by another? Even though the different ethical codes appear (at least on the face of it) to be reasonably consistent in their treatment of ethical dilemmas, there exists no systematic investigation into whether application of the different codes would lead to the same, different or even contradictory actions in those situations typical of practice in I/O psychology. Research of this type would provide a very useful service in clarifying the ethical requirements for I/O psychologists across several codes.

How Can Ethical Codes Be Applied Where They Do Not Specifically Refer to Concerns of I/O Psychologists?

As previously shown, ethical codes differ in the extent to which they address the immediate concerns of I/O psychologists. Some codes, such as the specialty guidelines for I/O psychologists (American Psychological Association, 1981) and the Division 14 Casebook (Society for Industrial and Organizational Psychology, 1985), more directly address the concerns of I/O psychologists than do more general documents such as the CPA *Code of Ethics*.

For example, the Division 14 Casebook analyses in the ethical implications of numerous written cases submitted by I/O psychologists; whereas, the CPA *Code of Ethics* is an umbrella document for all Canadian psychologists which serves as a guide to the development of more specific standards for particular areas such as I/O psychology (Canadian Psychological Association, 1986 a).

The answer to the above question is therefore as follows: Where ethical codes do not yet address the concerns of Canadian I/O psychologists with enough specificity, the I/O profession bears the responsibility to establish where the relevant linkages are. Harvey (in press) has begun this task for Canadian I/O psychologists by developing a proactive ethical model for organization research drawing on the CPA *Code of Ethics*. Interested readers are referred to this important work as an example of how the I/O psychology profession in Canada can better grapple with the complex ethical issues facing the field. Nevertheless, much work remains to be done before the I/O psychology profession in Canada can claim to have fully articulated the ethical implications of its practice across the various competency areas listed in Appendix A.

The Future of I/O Psychology in Canada

Having considered the state of I/O psychology in Canada, we will now look to how the field might evolve in future. However, in order to fully appreciate where I/O psychology in Canada may be going, a glance to its historical roots is needed. Therefore, the first part of this final section of the chapter is devoted to a brief historical summary of the origins of I/O psychology in Canada. I will then speculate as to where the field may be going and present some observations as to how professional I/O psychology will need to change to be effective in the globalized world of the 21st century.

Cronshaw (1991) traces the roots of industrial psychology back to the mid-1800s, at which time the large-scale industrialization of the Canadian economy began. In particular, the period from 1870 to 1920 saw extensive changes, including: a rapid increase in the number of factories in the country, growth in the size of manufacturing facilities, a shift of people from the agricultural sector to the manufacturing sector, the decline of craft work and an increase in the number of office workers (Krahn and Lowe, 1988). In other words, this period saw the rise of large bureaucratic organizations through which production work was organized.

At the end of this period, industrial psychologists started to appear on the Canadian scene to build practices in and around these bureaucratic organizations. Webster (1988), in his historical review of industrial psychology in Canada, identifies the first practising industrial psychologist in Canada as Gerald P. Cosgrave, who in 1928 became the Personnel Supervisor in the Employment Department of Sun Life Assurance Company in Montreal – a date which seems to accord well with the previously described rate of industrialization and bureaucratization in Canada. There were relatively few industrial psychologists practising in Canada before World War II, but the post-war period saw a steady expansion of their number (Webster, 1988). That expansion continues to this day and will likely accelerate well into the next century.

The review of historical trends in Canada done by Cronshaw (1991), combined with an extensive reading of the Canadian literature in industrial psychology, shows that the rise of industrial psychology in Canada is inextricably linked to large-scale industrialization of this country and that industrial psychologists have historically served the needs of large bureaucratic organizations in business, industry, government and the military. Although Cronshaw (1991) did not study the organizational side of Canadian I/O psychology in this way (and so must qualify his remarks on organizational psychology accordingly), the thesis is offered that organizational psychology emerged at least partially as a reaction to the perceived shortcomings of Taylorism and scientific management, with which traditional industrial psychology is closely allied.

The rise of the human relations school of management, to which organizational psychology is allied, is traced by many back to the Hawthorne studies conducted in the USA during the 1930s (e.g. Morgan, 1986). Although the interpretations of the Hawthorne studies vary, this work is often cited as support for efforts to humanize the work environment and reduce the adverse effects of bureaucracy on people and productivity (e.g. through studying leadership and group dynamics). Many organizational psychologists, although not by any means all of them, will find a close affinity with the "humanizing" tendencies of both the Hawthorne studies and its intellectual heirs (e.g. participative management). When examined historically, it is clear that organizational psychology made widespread gains in Canada during the post-World War II period, at the same time that industrial psychology achieved its considerable growth.

So how does all of this play out against the future growth and progress of I/O psychology in Canada? To use a popular metaphor: If industrial psychology in bureaucratic organizations is the original *thesis* that professional I/O psychologists started with early in this century, then the "humanized" version of organizational psychology which has arisen in the post-World War II period is its *antithesis*. Further, if commentators on the Canadian business scene are correct, the antithesis is coming into the ascendance, not only among the ranks of I/O psychologists, but among business and industrial leaders more generally. This is evidenced by the increasing interest in participative management by Canadian business and industries, at least partially in response to the need to become more competitive in the face of a globalized world economy. It appears that professional I/O psychologists in Canada will have to increasingly offer their services in non-bureaucratic, participative organizations as opposed to their traditional bureaucratic venue.

So what is the problem? The problem is that many of the concepts and techniques developed by I/O psychologists, particularly on the "industrial" side of things, are predicated on a bureaucratic context. Cronshaw (1991) demonstrates that the traditional competency areas of industrial psychology (e.g. job analysis, selection, performance appraisal) are geared toward the hiring and assessment of highly controlled individual workers in bureaucratic settings and, with a few exceptions, are suited only to that purpose. Participative management, on the other hand, requires a shift of focus to self-regulating *work groups* where the workers have considerable discretion. Many of the concepts required for practising I/O psychology in participative settings (currently latent in the literature of organizational psychology) must be developed, then a firm research base (which is meagre at present), must be developed to support the application of these concepts in Canadian organizations.

We can now come to closure on the discussion about the future of I/O psychology in Canada, at least as it might unfold into the next century. I/O psychologists in this country will have to invest much effort in developing alternative models of science and practice which are better suited to the realities of organizations in the 21st century (i. e. nonbureaucratic, participative forms of organization).[3] As a good beginning, more effort must be devoted to integrating the subareas of "I" and "O" psychology, which at present remain only tenuously linked. To be sure, the challenges and risks inherent in developing these new models are very great, because we will have to substantially redefine the field of I/O psychology from the "old" to the "new". However, Canadian I/O psychologists must invest the effort and resources in such change if the profession of I/O psychology is to continue to grow and contribute to Canadian society to its full potential.

Epilogue

Now is the opportunity to try to achieve synthesis and closure on all that has preceded in this chapter. It seems that I/O psychology has much going for it as subfield of professional psychology. As this chapter shows, the profession of I/O psychology has the following positive features in its favour:

1. An extensive support base provided by the registration process and various psychological associations;
2. A well-established scientific literature;

3 Not all Canadian organizations will change to nonbureaucratic, participative forms. It is unlikely that the military or government will abandon bureaucratic management in the foreseeable future. For these organizations, traditional "industrial" psychology is well suited. However, for other organizations, mostly in the private sector, which are moving to highly participative forms of management, I/O psychologists must develop alternative models of science and practice. These models will complement, rather than entirely replace, much of what is found in the literature in present-day I/O psychology.

3. A clear mandate for educational institutions offering graduate training in I/O psychology; and
4. A strong demand for I/O services in the marketplace.

Despite these strengths, the profession of I/O psychology faces the following challenges:
- the split between clinical and systems camps in I/O psychology;
- a shortage of Canadian graduate programmes to offer the necessary training in I/O psychology;
- the full integration of ethical codes into the practice of I/O psychology; and
- the need to adapt concepts and methods in I/O psychology to the rapidly changing global marketplace.

Overall, however, the prognosis is very good for the continued viability of the science and practice of I/O psychology in that the field has much to offer to Canadian society in an era when so much work is accomplished through collective effort of people channelled through formal organizations. However, this promise will only be fully realized if all constituencies with an interest in promoting I/O psychology (including university psychology departments, the CPA and provincial associations of I/O psychologists) resolve to work together in a coordinated way to advance I/O psychology as a subfield within psychology.

When asked to write this chapter (and in readily agreeing to do so), I did not fully realize the breadth of the issues that would have to be dealt with, from the registration process to matters of graduate training to ethics to an historical overview of the field itself. In thinking and writing on these matters, however, I have come to a better appreciation of where the profession of I/O psychology has come from and where it might be headed. In this, the writing of the present chapter has been a beneficial exercise and has brought some new insights. I hope that the reader can also take something away from this chapter for his or her quiet reflection or for discussion with colleagues.

Finally, in closing the chapter, the following thoughts occurred to me while writing, but did not fit neatly into the topics presented earlier. These thoughts take the form of exhortations to the I/O community in Canada.

The first exhortation is that we must not forget our roots in the broader discipline of psychology. I/O psychology draws its strength from the larger discipline and needs to maintain its bonds with the larger psychological community to ensure its long-term viability.

The second exhortation is that we should give more consideration to alternative conceptions of science in addition to the traditional objectivist model. Science takes many forms – there is great strength in diversity of opinions and approaches. There are many available niches for I/O psychologists and the primary limit on where we can go as a field is where we believe we can go.

The third exhortation is that we must continue to fully embrace our role as scientist-practitioners. There is much to be achieved by bringing science and practice together to address the people problems in work organizations within our urbanized society. The profession of I/O psychology is uniquely positioned to solve many of these problems and our continued efforts can produce lasting benefits for future generations of Canadians.

Acknowledgements

I would like to thank Tom Foard of RHR Canada Ltd. for his insightful comments on an earlier draft of this chapter and Steve Harvey for materials and discussion on ethical issues. All opinions expressed in this chapter are solely those of the author.

Appendix A: Brief Descriptions of Content Areas Listed in the Guidelines for Graduate Training and Education in Industrial and Organizational Psychology in Canada

Core Areas

1. *Ethical, legal and professional context of I/O psychology* – Knowledge of: relevant ethical guidelines (e.g. *Canadian Code of Ethics for Psychologists*, Canadian Psychological Association, 1988); relevant federal, provincial and local laws, statutes, regulations and legal precedents (e.g. *Bona fide occupational requirement policy*, Canadian Human Rights Commission, 1988); labour/management dynamics and how collective agreements work; professional norms, standards and guidelines (e.g. *Guidelines for educational and psychological testing*, Canadian Psychological Association, 1986 b).
2. *Organization theory* – How structure, functions, processes and other organization-level constructs impact on the behaviour of individuals in complex organizations (e..g, classical and contemporary theories of organizations, organizational structure, organizational design, technology, processes of organizational policy formulation and implementation).
3. *Work motivation theory* – How conditions within the individual and his/her environment influence the direction, strength and persistency of effort in work settings. Includes knowledge of theory, research and motivational practices in organizations.
4. *Statistical methods/data analysis* – The application of various statistical techniques used in the analysis of data from empirical research, including descriptive and inferential statistics as well as parametric and nonparametric methods.
5. *Research methods* – The methods, procedures and techniques used in the conduct of empirical research in I/O psychology (including, but not limited to, development of study designs,

reliability and validity of measures, sampling procedures and research ethics).

6. *Personnel selection, placement and classification* – The theory and techniques involved in the effective matching of individual needs, preferences, skills and abilities with the personnel requirements of organizations. In particular, the individual must keep current with human rights legislation and tribunal/court decisions related to selection, placement and classification.
7. *Performance appraisal/feedback* – The measurement and evaluation of individual work performance and use of this information for administrative and developmental purposes. Must have a thorough understanding of rating scale construction and use, as well as skill in designing a complete performance appraisal and feedback system.
8. *Measurement of individual differences* – The assessment of unobservable psychological traits (e.g. general cognitive ability, spatial ability). Must have a sound background in both classical and modern measurement theories and their respective areas of application.
9. *Organization Development theory* – The theory and research relevant to changing individuals, groups and organizations to improve effectiveness (including, but not limited to, attitude change, career planning, team building and group training, survey feedback, conflict management, job redesign, management by objectives, human resource accounting, flexible working hours and quality circles).
10. *Job and task analysis* – Knowledge of the theory and techniques used to generate information about jobs, the physical and social context of this work and the attributes needed by individuals performing the job. Individuals should have skills in applying job analysis techniques to real world situations.

Complementary Areas

11. *Criterion development and theory* – The measurement of individual, group and organizational effectiveness against criteria or standards (includes, but is not limited to, single vs.

multiple criteria, criterion dynamics, characteristics of acceptable criteria).

12. *Individual assessment* – The application of psychological tests, interviews and appraisals to individuals for a variety of work related purposes (e.g. career, educational, rehabilitation and employee counselling). Individuals should have skills in the following: assessing the relevant psychological attributes; identifying, developing, selecting and/or using the appropriate means for these assessments; and communicating the results and interpretation of the assessment in verbal or written form.
13. *Training: Theory, programme design and evaluation* – The theory and techniques used to design, set up and evaluate large-scale instructional programmes in industry, business and government (including, but not limited to, needs assessment, writing of instructional objectives, application of learning principles, choice of training media and evaluation of training programmes).
14. *Attitude theory* – Knowledge of literature on attitude theory, attitude measurement and attitude change, with an emphasis on how attitudes are formed and changed, and how they are related to behaviours (e.g. how individual intentions to quit the organization affect actual turnover behaviour).
15. *Career development theory* – Knowledge of theories and research which describe the nature of positions held and resultant experiences during an individual's lifespan of experiences with work organizations (including, but not limited to, individual aptitudes and interests, specific skill training and development, early work history, occupational choice and preretirement planning).
16. *Human performance/human factors/ergonomics* – Emphasizes the interaction of human behaviour and task environments (including, but not limited to work station design, workload measurement, control systems, information display systems and person-computer interactions).

Secondary Areas

17. *Small group theory and process* – Requires an understanding of the research and theory related to interpersonal behaviour

of people in small groups (including leadership, interpersonal influence, group effectiveness, conformity, conflict, role behaviour, group decision making).

18. *Decision theory* – Knowledge of how decision makers use inferential procedures to make decisions in uncertain situations (including the Brunswikian lens model, Bayesian inference and cognitive information processing). Can be used to integrate existing research in I/O areas such as vigilance behaviour, employee selection, choice behaviour and human performance in complex environments.
19. *Programme evaluation* – Knowledge and skill in evaluating the impact and effectiveness of programmes, functions and policies aimed at improving organizational effectiveness, quality of work and work life, safety in the work place, etc., with particular attention to human resource management interventions (including knowledge of formative and summative evaluation, experimental and quasi-experimental design, evaluability assessment, cost-benefit analysis and utility analysis).
20. *Consumer behaviour* – The systematic study of the relationship between producers (or distributors) and consumers of goods and services (e.g. consumer preferences for product features, consumer attitudes and motivation), including skill required to appropriately apply social science methodologies to consumer research.
21. *Fields of psychology* – Knowledge of basic research in the following areas: Biological bases of behaviour; Cognitive-affective bases of behaviour; Social bases of behaviour; and Individual differences.
22. *History and systems in psychology* – Knowledge of the intellectual heritage of psychology which will allow integration of I/O psychology into the broader discipline.

Note. To improve readability, the entries in this Appendix are given in the same order as the content areas in Table 1. They are paraphrased summaries of information given in the Society for industrial and Organizational Psychology's (1982) *Guidelines for education and training at the doctoral level in Industrial/Organizational psychology* and the Section on Industrial and Organizational Psychology's (1989) *Guidelines for graduate training and education in Industrial and Organizational Psychology in Canada.* References to US equal employment opportunity laws/policy and psychological standards (as given in the Society document) are revised to reflect the corresponding Canadian sources.

References

American Psychological Association (1977). *Standards for the providers of psychological services.* Washington, DC: Author.

American Psychological Association (1981). Specialty guidelines for the delivery of services by industrial/organizational psychologists. *American Psychologist, 36,* 664–669.

American Psychological Association (1982). *Ethical principles in the conduct of research with human participants.* Washington, DC: Author.

American Psychological Association (1990). Ethical principles of psychologists. *American Psychologist, 45,* 390–395.

Canadian Human Rights Commission (1988). *Bona fide occupational requirement policy.* Author: Ottawa.

Canadian Psychological Association (1986 a). *A Canadian code of ethics for psychologists.* Old Chelsea, Quebec: Canadian Psychological Association.

Canadian Psychological Association (1986 b). *Guidelines for educational and psychological testing.* Author: Ottawa.

Canadian Psychological Association (1988). *Canadian Code of Ethics for psychologists: Companion manual.* Author: Canadian Psychological Association.

Catano, V.M. (1987). A primer on specialty designation. *Bulletin of the Section on I/O Psychology (Canadian Psychological Association, 3(4),* 22–25.

Cronshaw, S.F. (1991). *Industrial psychology in Canada.* Waterloo, ON: North Waterloo Academic Press.

Harvey, S. (in press). An application of the CPA Code of Ethics in planning field research: An organizational case. *Canadian Psychology.*

Krahn, H.J., & Lowe, G.S. (1988). *Work, industry & Canadian society.* Toronto: Nelson Canada.

Lowman, R.L. (Ed.). (1985). *Casebook on ethics and standards for the practice of psychology in organizations.* College Park, MD: Society for Industrial and Organizational Psychology, Inc., Division 14 of the American Psychological Association.

Morgan, G. (1986). *Images of organization.* Newbury Park, CA: Sage.

Ontario Board of Examiners in Psychology (1986). *Standards of professional conduct.* Toronto, Ontario: Author.

Ryan, A.M., & Sackett, P.R. (1987). A survey of individual assessment practices by I/O psychologists. *Personnel Psychology, 40*, 455–488.

Ryan, A.M., & Sackett, P.R. (1989). Exploratory study of individual assessment practices: Interrater reliability and judgments of assessor effectiveness. *Journal of Applied Psychology, 74*, 568–579.

Sackett, P.R. (1986). I/O psychology: The state of the practice. *Professional Practice of Psychology*, 7, 15–25.

Section on Industrial and Organizational Psychology, Canadian Psychological Association (1987). Results of the I/O Section survey on specialty designation and draft recommendations. *Bulletin of the Section on I/O Psychology (Canadian Psychological Association), 3(4)*, 14–22).

Section on Industrial and Organizational Psychology, Canadian Psychological Association (1988). *I/O Section interest survey.* Old Chelsea, Quebec: Author.

Section on Industrial and Organizational Psychology, Canadian Psychological Association (1989). *Guidelines for graduate training and education in industrial and organizational psychology in Canada.* Old Chelsea, Quebec: Author.

Society for Industrial and Organizational Psychology, Inc., Education and Training Committee, American Psychological Association (1982). *Guidelines for education and training at the doctoral level in Industrial/Organizational Psychology.* Washington: Author.

Webster, E.C. (1988). I/O psychology in Canada from birth to Couchiching. *Canadian Psychology, 29*, 4–10.

15

Psychology and the Law: The Emerging Role of Forensic Psychology

A. L. Pollock
Clarke Institute of Psychology, Toronto

B. D. Webster
Clarke Institute of Psychology, Toronto

The word "forensic" derives, as is generally known, from the Latin *forensis*, meaning "of the forum". It was in the Forum that the Romans held their court proceedings. Forensic psychologists tend to centre their practice on court work, but as well are often engaged pre-trial with police and lawyers and post-trial with correctional, parole and probation authorities. A thorough explication of forensic psychology might touch on such diverse topics as police recruit evaluation, criminal profiling, lie detection, informed consent, hostage negotiation, witness interrogation, jury selection, offender classification, assessment for prison release, hypnosis, programming for community reintegration, assessment for personal injury suits, and custody and access evaluations. Moreover, a distinction can be drawn between forensic psychology *in* law, as represented by the above-mentioned subspecialties, and forensic psychology *of* law, a branch of psychological inquiry concerned primarily with the study of the legal process (Lloyd-Bostock, 1988).

It would be impossible in a brief chapter of this sort to present a exhaustive discussion of these many areas of practice and inquiry (for a comprehensive review see Bartol, 1983; Weiner & Hess, 1987). We have instead chosen to concentrate our discussion on a particularly controversial area of forensic psychological practice – the assessment and treatment of offenders. A discussion of this aspect of forensic psychology seems particularly timely. Public awareness and concern about family violence, sexual assault and the burgeoning crime rate in our urban centres has led to growing pressure on government agencies to find solutions to these serious social problems. Increasingly, the justice and correctional systems are turning to the mental health professions for guidance and forensic psychologists are finding themselves in positions of influence. It is especially important, as forensic psychology finds its footing in the legal arena, that careful consideration be given to defining an appropriate role for psychologists in the judicial and correctional processes.

In many respects forensic clinical psychologists function in much the same way as their colleagues in other branches of clinical psychology. They assess personality and intellect and they apply cognitive and behavioural principles in the treatment of psychological disorders. As they carry out these duties they must also conform to the same standards of professional conduct that guide their colleagues. Nonetheless, as with practitioners in any specialized area, forensic psychologists must contend with professional issues specific to their field of expertise.

Two related issues, in particular, set the practice of forensic psychology apart from most other areas of clinical work. First is the question of whose interests the forensic psychologist should be serving – those of the offender, the justice system or the community. Second is the matter of the implications of the forensic clinician's opinion for the rights and freedom of the offender. Of course, all clinicians should be mindful of the rights of their clients, but as Ziskin (1980) points out, in most clinical situations psychological evaluations provide tentative clinical hypotheses which are subject to revision as treatment proceeds. In the court setting, however, the psychologist's opinion can contribute to usually unalterable legal decisions by others (e.g. judges, review boards, tribunals) which may critically influence the offender's future. Forensic psychologists, in formulating their opinions, must often weigh the best interests of the offender against those of the community (Clingempeel, Mulvey & Reppucci, 1980). The task of maintaining a balanced outlook within the adversarial legal system is one of the most difficult aspects of the forensic psychologist's role.

Working within the dialectical court process, even the most skilled clinicians are apt to experience a degree of role confusion and doubt about their professional obligations. There have been numerous articles in recent years addressing the critical issue of role conflicts in forensic psychology (e.g. Arcaya, 1987; Dietz & Reese 1986; Cornell, 1987; Lloyd-Bostock, 1988; Ostrov, 1986; Rogers, 1987; Saxton, 1986). It is hard to escape the impression in reviewing this literature that next to sheer ignorance of scientific developments in the field, role distortion and confusion accounts for much of what might be considered professional incompetence in forensic psychology.

Lloyd-Bostock (1988) has pointed out that it is especially easy for psychologists to lose their professional bearings in the court room since in many respects law and psychology appear to share common interests. She observes that both disciplines are fundamentally concerned with the causes and modification of behaviour and with cognitive processes such as perception, memory and planning. This appearance of common purpose often leads forensic psychologists to stray from their designated roles as experts in criminal behaviour (Monahan, 1977). Consequently, the effect of expert opinion on criminal proceedings often has more to do with professional, political and organizational issues than with the technical skill of the practitioner. Many psychologists who find themselves drawn into legal proceedings or who willingly participate, seem oblivious to these complexities. As such, they fail to appreciate the ethical and practical quandaries arising from the conflicting role demands of the judicial process.

When clinicians overstep the bounds of their appropriate role in the legal process, their "expert" opinion may be governed as much by value judgements as by scientific considerations. But what is the appropriate role of the forensic psychologist? Curran and Pollack (1986) have forcefully argued that forensic clinicians should not stray outside the role of "fact-finder for the court" (p. 62). While most authorities would agree that psychologists should base their opinions on scientific certainty, it is perhaps unreasonable to expect that clinical judgement can ever be entirely free of personal bias, given the imprecision of the science of psychology (Lloyd-Bostock, 1988; Webster, Menzies & Jackson, 1982). In most instances, the best clinicians can do is to recognize the limitations of their science, acknowledge these shortcomings and strive for objectivity within their designated role (Arcaya, 1987; Cornell, 1987).

A prime example of role infringement among forensic clinicians is the not-uncommon practice of liberally interpreting the law to accord with the clinician's own notion of justice.

Case Illustration

Within a few days of each other, two men were referred to an inpatient psychiatric unit for pretrial assessment. In both cases the principal referral question was whether the defence of insanity applied.[1] Both men had committed violent offences against a relative. One, a man in his late forties, had beaten his mother because he believed she was subverting his efforts to find employment. The other, a man in his late twenties, shot and killed his uncle because he believed he had been spying on him.

As far as could be ascertained, at the time of their offences both men knew they were breaking the law and both appreciated the probable effect of their behaviour. In interview, both displayed psychotic symptoms including paranoia, delusions and hallucina-

1 According to Section 16 of the *Criminal Code* of Canada, "a person is insane when he is in a state of natural imbecility or has disease of the mind to the extent that renders him incapable of appreciating the nature and quality of an act or omission or of knowing that an act or omission is wrong".

tions and on psychological testing both showed signs of autistic and disordered thinking. The first man received a diagnosis of schizoaffective disorder, the other was diagnosed paranoid schizophrenic.

Although these two men seemed similarly disturbed, only in the second case did the clinical team decide there were grounds for a plea of not guilty by reason of insanity. It was generally agreed that the relatively less serious offence of the first man did not merit the lengthy period of hospitalization which typically accompanies a finding of insanity. However, because the gravity of the second man's offence raised concerns about a potential for future violence in the community, stricter security and lengthier confinement were deemed appropriate.

In fact, neither of these cases truly satisfied the standard for legal insanity. According to Rogers, Turner, Helfield & Dickens (1988), Canadian case law clearly defines the criteria for insanity as: (a) "any abnormal condition which impairs the human mind or function"; (b) a failure to understand one's "physical actions and the likely outcome of these actions"; and (c) the inability to judge "*legal* wrongfulness" (pp. 692–693). Yet, both these men appreciated the physical implications and legal wrongfulness of their offences. Furthermore, offence severity is theoretically irrelevant to the issue of legal insanity, and should have had no bearing on the clinical recommendations.

The practice of interpreting the insanity standard to suit clinical purposes or the perceived interests of the community may appear to be a relatively benign or even laudable act on the part of well-meaning clinicians. Curran and Pollack (1986), however, have argued that when personal standards are applied in place of the law "the professional forensic scientist corrupts his or her role as a legally authorized fact-finder and becomes a self-appointed social decision-maker in secret defiance of the rules of society" (p. 65). Not only does such role distortion among forensic clinicians lead to an erosion of professional identity (Dietz & Reese, 1986) but it can sometimes seriously undermine professional capabilities. For example, the survey by Rogers et al., (1988) found that in most cases experienced Canadian forensic clinicians were simply unable to define correctly the well-entrenched insanity standard. Fifty five percent of those questioned misunderstood the insanity standard as including the concept of moral wrongfulness. In the case of the insanity standard, what may have begun as a well-intentioned embellishment of the law has evidently led to a deterioration of professional competence.[2]

When the issue is legal insanity, the clinician's primary task is to explain the individual's state of mind at the time of the criminal act. That the defendant actually committed the act is generally a foregone conclusion. In other cases, however, psychological opinion is sought before blame has been established, sometimes with the hidden expectation that clinical assessment may shed some light on culpability. Under such circumstances issues of the clinician's role and competence become all the more salient.

Questions about guilt or innocence are rarely stated explicitly in court referrals. Typically, the accused is sent for a pre-trial assessment to address some general concerns about psychopathology or psychological adjustment. Often, however, the implied question is whether there is anything unusual about the defendant which might point to the increased likelihood of his having committed the offence. In some cases the psychologist may not even meet with the defendant but may be summoned as an expert witness and asked to testify on the likelihood that the offence might have been committed by an individual with the defendant's background and psychological make up. In these circumstances clinicians must be wary of attempts by prosecuting attorneys and defence counsels to cast them in the role of lie detector. To a large extent forensic psychologists can avoid this undertaking by educating the referral source about the capabilities and limits of psychological evaluation and by insuring that referral questions are explicitly stated. However, under no circumstances should clinicians allow themselves to be manoeuvred into drawing conclusions about the defendant's probable guilt or innocence.

The reliance on psychological opinion to establish guilt or innocence is commonly seen in cases of sexual assault. Psychologists may be asked, for example, whether a defendant fits the profile

---

2 Coincidentally, in December 1990 the Supreme Court of Canada handed down a ruling allowing defendants to claim insanity not only if they are incapable of understanding that their actions were legally wrong, but morally wrong as well. In effect, with this ruling, the misguided clinicians surveyed by Rogers et al. were restored to professional competence.

of a predatory rapist or whether a father accused of incest is the kind of man who might sexually assault his daughter. The Crown may have a vested interest in being able to show that a person is irresistibly attracted to children or that his sexual energy is especially apt to arise in association with situations involving physical violence. The defence deploys itself to show that such preferences, frequently established through measurement of penile erection to slides or audio tapes, do not exist.

It is true that forensic psychologists can and do offer to the Court expertise in sexology, particularly through sexual preference testing via phallometry (Abel, Blanchard, Barlow, & Mavissakalian, 1975; Barbaree, Marshall, & Lanthier, 1979; Quinsey, Chaplin, & Varney, 1981). Forensic psychologist researchers have made marked strides in our understanding of abnormal sexual functioning. They know the possible perils of phallometric findings, especially if unsubstantiated by other means, and will normally be cautious in their written and spoken representations to Court. Certainly they will understand the powerful and possibly untoward effects of their testimony. They will realize that they can easily contribute to a person being found "guilty" not so much on the grounds of the offence allegedly committed, but by virtue of being shown for all to see as a "paedophile" or a "rapist".

Phallometers can be purchased fairly cheaply and do not even seem difficult to use, judging from the accompanying manuals. Would-be forensic psychologists should realize, however, that this type of work is deeply technical and should not be attempted by those lacking appropriate knowledge in physiology and behavioural measurement. It is a subspecialty within a subspecialty and should be mastered fully or not at all. We again draw the reader's attention to the fact that obtaining assessment results is one matter and that interpreting those results to the Court is another. Both require considerable expertise and experience.

Forensic psychologists may also be asked to comment on an individual's behavioural propensities when there are concerns about dangerousness. Shah (1978) outlines fifteen points in the legal process which may be affected by clinical evaluations of an offender's potential for harmful behaviour. In Canada one such point is the application to have a convicted person declared a "dangerous offender". Such applications arise through the use of Part XXIV of the *Criminal Code*. This part of the *Code* was last revised in 1977.

Under its provisions the Crown can advance a case against a person who has committed a "serious personal injury offence" and who as a result is liable to a sentence of 10 years or more. The convicted person appears before a judge sitting alone. Part XXIV states that the court *must* hear the evidence of two psychiatrists, one nominated by the Crown and one by the defence. It also states that psychologists and criminologists may testify.

This type of testimony is especially important because of the consequences that attach to a positive Court finding. If the Court declares the individual to be a "dangerous offender" he or she may be given a fixed sentence or an indefinite sentence. It is the latter that the Crown normally seeks. Almost all of the one hundred or so cases heard since 1977 have been sentenced to indefinite detention. Psychologists often participate in these hearings. They do it either on the basis of direct psychological examination of the defendant or more generally they testify about the limits of psychiatric and psychological ability so far as predicting violent behaviour is concerned. A large literature has developed in recent years on the "prediction of dangerousness". A psychologist testifying under Part XXIV needs to be thoroughly conversant with these sources (see, for example, Monahan, 1981; Pollock, 1990; Webster, Ben-Aron, & Hucker, 1985; Webster, Dickens, & Addario, 1985).

Canadian forensic psychologists are somewhat less susceptible to the pressures and role demands of the judicial system than are their colleagues in psychiatry. This is largely because forensic psychologists are not customarily included as expert witnesses in key court deliberations. For example, although forensic psychologists in Canada have demonstrated authority in the assessment of fitness to stand trial (e.g. Menzies, 1989; Roesch & Golding, 1980; Roesch, Webster, & Eaves, 1984) and insanity (Rogers, 1988; Rogers & Ewing, in press) the *Criminal Code* of Canada still calls upon "duly qualified medical practitioners" to offer opinion in this matter.[3] Most often, when it comes to such legal issues as fitness to stand trial, the insanity defence and dangerous offender

3 Use of psychologists in pre-trial fitness examinations is routine in some jurisdictions in the United States. Psychologists are also called to court in Canada on some cases.

applications, psychologists do not represent their opinions directly to the Court but are generally relegated to the role of consultants to forensic psychiatrists.

In practice, psychologists write reports on their assessments and, often along with colleagues in other disciplines, submit their evaluations to psychiatrists. The psychiatrists then coordinate the information from various sources and send to Court a single report or letter. This arrangement can work well but it behooves the forensic psychologist to see the psychiatric report before it is transmitted to Court. The client may be badly served and the court misled if the psychological findings are inaccurately or imprecisely portrayed or if they are embedded in an inappropriate part of the report. The psychological findings, duly acknowledged to the psychologist in the psychiatric report, must be suitably represented if the psychologist's reputation is to be protected. It is important to insist on the courtesy of being able to peruse carefully the psychiatric report before it is despatched to Court.

If psychological findings are badly presented it is very probable that the psychologist will be subpoenaed to court under disadvantageous circumstances. In a way, the aim is to stay out of court at least so far as "routine" cases are concerned, to be able to do work which is beyond question or reproach and which is expressed clearly and in language that the Court can understand. It might be going too far to say that some forensic practitioners, psychiatrists as well as psychologists, write reports which are sufficiently obscure that attendance in court is made more or less necessary. Such practitioners may thrive on the "glory" of court appearances and the financial accompaniments. For some, court appearances, particularly in high profile cases, serve a largely self-promoting end. Our general point is that attendances at court need to be approached with care and a recognition that such actually needless appearances can have deleterious effects on the psychologists' reputations and on the profession as a whole. That psychologists have in Canada to date played only a restricted role in the criminal courts may in fact have been to the advantage of the profession. The opportunity now exists for forensic psychologists to construct for themselves a role governed more by scientific imperatives than by the day-to day expectations and demands of the judicial process. Our point generally is that psychologists do well to avoid becoming hired guns. They should, though, play a vital role in out-of-the ordinary cases where the courts would otherwise have difficulty in applying law.

It should be clear that forensic psychology, despite its actual long history (Münsterberg, 1909), has become a strong force only in the past 20 years. One of us has elsewhere discussed why it has taken so long for the subdiscipline to establish itself (Webster, 1984). However this may be, the important point is that there has of late been a rapid rise in interest about psychology and the law. Division 41 of the American Psychological Association is devoted to Psychology and the Law. The Division oversees the publication of *Law and Human Behavior*. It also arranges and supervises examinations for those who wish to apply for Diplomate status. Such status can be gained by psychologists who pass the required written and oral examinations. Melton (1987) has said: "Psycholegal studies may be fairly termed as psychology's new growth industry" (p. 681). The past 15 years have brought about matching increases in training in psychology and the law. In the United States this has meant the development of joint JD-PhD programmes. Five such programmes were located in a 1978–79 survey by Grisso, Sales, & Bayless (1982). As well, there have been sizeable increases in the number of APA-approved internships which include forensic psychological training (Levine, Wilson, & Sales, 1980).

In Canada there has also been a quickening of interest in forensic psychology. The Canadian Psychological Association has been developing a strong Section on Criminal Justice Systems and internship training opportunities are on the rise. Although there are as yet no joint JD-PhD programmes in Canadian universities, Simon Fraser University Psychology Department is moving in that direction in conjunction with the University of British Columbia Law School. Several Canadian universities now offer graduate-level training in specialized aspects of forensic psychology and some criminology departments encourage interest in "clinical criminology". In recent years Canadian scholars have made important contributions to knowledge within forensic psychology. For example, Rogers (1986) has written definitively on the insanity defence and on malingering and deception (1988). Quinsey's work stands out in the areas of dangerousness (1980), treatability (Quinsey & Maguire, 1983) and sexology (Quinsey & Earls, 1990). Rice has been influential in matters of the institutional management of violence (Rice, Harris, Varney, & Quinsey, 1990). Hare's work on psychopathy is widely regarded throughout the world (1980, 1986) and is complemented by the recent research of Harris (Harris, Rice, & Cormier, 1989). The country also boasts several psychologists prominent in the assessment and treatment of sexually anomalous behaviour (Langevin, 1983; Marshall & Barbaree, 1988; Laws, 1990; Stermac & Segal, 1989). Moreover, Gendreau and Ross (1979) have devoted their careers to correctional psychology arguing mainly for the development and evaluation of systematic remedial programmes. In this endeavour they have been aided by Andrews (Andrews, Kiessling, & Kominos, 1983), Bonta (Bonta & Motiuk, 1985 and Wormith (1984). These and other Canadian accomplishments have been reviewed by Rice and Quinsey (1986).

Psychological Assessment in Forensic Psychology

From the available literature we can begin to discern some distinctive qualities of the emerging role of forensic psychology. It is apparent, for example, that the traditional assessment models of clinical psychology do not serve fully the purposes of forensic psychologists. As Grisso (1987) has remarked, such models are designed to address clinical concerns about etiology and diagnosis and are ill-suited to answer forensic questions about legal constructs such as dangerousness and criminal responsibility. Instead there is a growing recognition that specialized instruments must be developed to address legal questions (Grisso, 1987) and further, that new theoretical models of criminal behaviour are required before any psychometric techniques can be applied effectively (Pollock, McBain & Webster, 1989; Quinsey & Maguire, 1986).

Psychological methods can bring a degree of precision to the judicial process which, if correctly used, could do much to minimize the sometimes arbitrary nature of judicial decision-making. For instance, as mentioned earlier, psychologists have had considerable influence in the area of fitness evaluation. Roesch, Webster, and Eaves (1984) have "Canadianized" the *Competency Assessment Instrument* (McGarry, 1973) to provide a formalized approach to the assessment of fitness according to Canadian standards. As well, recent developments in personality assessment and classification hold promise for the development of psychological typologies of criminal personality. Long an elusive goal of forensic clinicians (e.g. Greenland, 1980; Morrison, 1973), such typologies could prove invaluable in the evaluation of recidivism risk and in planning effective treatment (see especially, Rice, Harris, Quinsey, & Cyr, 1989).

One particular offender type variously referred to as "antisocial personality disorder", "psychopath" and "sociopath" has a special importance for forensic practitioners. The psychopath was described in Cleckley's classic work (1976, originally published in 1941) and in earlier times this disorder, seemingly of the will, was referred to as "moral insanity" (Prichard, 1837). While it is widely agreed that certain offenders show "a rapacious attitude toward others, a chronic insensitivity and indifference to the rights of other people that is marked by lying, stealing, cheating, and worse" (Rosenhan & Seligman, 1989, p. 493), as yet, efforts to identify reliably these individuals has met with considerable disappointment. The terms "antisocial personality" and "psychopath" continue to be applied quite freely on a day-to-day basis with little concern for the reliability or validity of these labels. Indeed there has been commentary to the effect that "such a concept is little more than a moral judgement masquerading as a clinical diagnosis" (Blackburn, 1988, p. 511).

In recent years psychological research has begun to make some impressive gains toward the reliable classification of so-called psychopaths. Samenow (1984) has applied principles of cognitive psychology in describing the underlying attitudes and thinking patterns which characterize the psychopath's world view. Hare's work (1980) in particular, has been instrumental in pinning down the concept of psychopathy. He has developed the *Psychopathy Check List* (PCL) which builds on Cleckley's basic concepts. The PCL consists of 22 items which appear to yield two main factors: selfish, callous and remorseless use of others; and chronically unstable and antisocial life style – social deviance (Harpur, Hakstian & Hare, 1988; Harpur, Hare & Hakstian, 1989). Scores from the

PCL correlate quite highly with the American Psychiatric Association's DSM-III-R (1987) diagnoses of antisocial personality disorder (Schroeder, Schroeder & Hare, 1983). Forensic psychologists can take some assurance from the work of Hare and his colleagues. It appears that psychopaths can be classified quite reliably and that the scores have predictive power. For example, Harris, Rice and Cormier (1989) found relatively high rates of violent recidivism over 10 years, among former patients who scored high on the PCL (77% against 21% of nonpsychopaths).

Still, while some advance has been made in the measurement of psychopathy, it would appear that there are presently no straightforward treatments for people so classified. Although there is suggestion, confirming widely held clinical opinion, that some psychopaths "burn out" after age 40, it remains the case that many continue their criminal way of life well into middle age (Hare, McPherson & Forth, 1988).

Treatment Programmes in Forensic Psychology

By the end of the 1970s it was becoming increasingly apparent that treatment programmes based on the disease model of criminal behaviour were largely ineffective (Gendreau, 1985). In recent years there has been growing interest in psychological approaches to offender rehabilitation. These approaches are theoretically-based, problem-focused, methods designed to assist offenders in developing the coping skills and prosocial attitudes necessary to establish productive lives in the community. The application of relapse prevention models and behavioural procedures in the treatment of sexual misconduct (Abel & Becker, 1984; Laws, 1990) and the use of cognitive-behavioural methods in treating aggressive behaviour (Goldstein & Keller, 1987) are two examples of recent developments in psychological approaches to offender rehabilitation.

If one thing has become clear after several decades of research into rehabilitation, it is that traditional psychotherapy does not effectively reduce criminal behaviour. According to Gendreau

(1985), treatment models based on social learning theory and cognitive approaches have shown the most promise particularly when they emphasize factors such as social skills and life skills development and improvement in the quality of relationships. Forensic psychologists recognize that many criminals lack the skills to lead productive lives in conventional society and require substantial guidance and direction before they can benefit from the kind of personal exploration which traditional psychotherapy treatment methods encourage.

It would be misleading to suggest, however, that the challenge of offender rehabilitation is simply a matter of treatment technique. For forensic psychologists the role of therapist is often more a question of attitude. The forensic therapist's relationship with the offender-client is rarely comparable to "free-world" therapeutic alliance (Arcaya, 1987). In everyday life, adults who enter psychotherapy do so of their own volition. They can choose not only the type of approach they wish to follow but also the therapist. They can arrange their schedules to have more or fewer sessions of therapy and are free to terminate treatment at any time. None of this holds true for forensic patients who, as often as not, view treatment quite adversely and loathe the prospect of entering therapy. They tend to see it as unnecessary, demeaning and pointless. Commonly, they attend for treatment in the institution to further requests for release on parole. Once they are released, offenders are often required to continue in treatment they neither enjoy nor want.

As a result, forensic psychologists are often confronted with hostile and unwilling clients who are compelled to attend treatment (under threat of parole denial or revocation) by a dutiful parole officer trying to enforce conditions specified by the parole board. Usually their therapeutic efforts are met with understandable resistance and guardedness. In correctional settings, psychologists encounter some of the most troublesome role demands as the goals of treatment, punishment and custodial management come into conflict (Clingempeel, Mulvey & Reppucci, 1980). Psychologists, particularly those trained in the humanistic, client-centred model, often have difficulty adjusting to the realities of enforced treatment with its implicit emphasis on behavioural control and compliance rather than personal development.

Given these limitations, forensic psychologists have to approach their therapeutic role with an attitude different from that of their colleagues in other subspecialties. Their professional conduct must in some way reconcile the inherent conflict between the offender-client's self-defined interests, the expectations of the agency and the rights of the community. Under these conditions it becomes increasingly taxing for psychologists to maintain their professional bearings. Many forensic psychologists find themselves pressured to perform a policing function in support of parole officers' efforts while trying to maintain some semblance of a therapeutic relationship with the offender-client.

Perhaps, as already mentioned, the attitude which most clearly distinguishes the forensic psychologist's approach to treatment is the tacit assumption of responsibility to people other than the identified client. Unlike most other psychotherapy clients, the offender-client typically has problems which directly threaten the well-being of others. As such, the forensic therapist has an overriding professional obligation to the offender's potential victims. Except to the extent that they contribute to criminal behaviour, the offender's personal problems are of secondary importance. This does not mean that the forensic therapist cannot also serve the interests of the offender, but those interests must be compatible with the principal goal of forensic psychological rehabilitation – stopping criminal behaviour.

The forensic therapist's expressed attitude toward the offender-client must be something like: "I am here to help you to stop victimizing other people. If this makes you feel happier about yourself and your life, all the better, but the main goal is to make it safe for you to be around other people." While this attitude may be less than ideal as a basis for establishing therapeutic rapport, it is not unworkable. It is essential that expectations between the psychologist and the referring agency be clearly specified at the outset and the same holds true between client and psychologist. Rules and consequences must be explained. The client should understand what reports on what topics are to be submitted to whom at what intervals. Limits of confidentiality, rules and consequences should be clearly laid out. The client ought to expect, for example, that the psychologist will take whatever steps are necessary to prevent him or her from committing an act of violence. Although it may be that these conditions militate against success in therapy, it also needs to be recognized that the working out of rules can, properly done, serve a decidedly positive therapeutic function.

Concluding Comment

The role of the forensic psychologist has undergone marked change over the past quarter century. Eysenck's (1964) work was widely influential at that time with its ingenious way of combining psychometric findings with the principles of conventional (Hullian) behaviourism (Keehn & Webster, 1969). It seemed entirely possible that criminal personality types could be validly identified with relative ease through the use of scales and tests and that, once established, patients and prisoners representative of the various types could be treated via conditioning and learning procedures. Another powerful point of view came to the fore with the development of radical (Skinnerian, operant) conditioning (Keehn & Webster, 1969). Token economics came to prominence (Lawson, Greene, Richardson, McClure, & Padina, 1971) as did application of social learning principles to parolees in the natural environment (Erickson, Crow, Zurcher & Connett, 1973). Over time forensic and correctional psychologists have, though, come to realize that, helpful though general psychological principles may be, it is necessary as well to have a clear understanding of how criminal law works (Yarmey, 1979), and the real as well as intended functions of prisons and penitentiaries (Megargee, 1982). Knowledge derived from laboratory and experiment is harder to apply practically than many had earlier thought or hoped. The quarter century has also seen forensic and other clinical psychologists having to contend with a decline in strength of belief in the rehabilitative ideal (Martinson, 1974). Although senior justice and correctional administrations now seem to be finding new good will for the work of psychology, psychiatry and related disciples, it becomes evident that this confidence will need to be cherished through continuing demonstrations of assessment and programme effectiveness.

The past 25 years have also been distinguished by changes in law and policy, some of which make it harder than heretofore to apply clinical knowledge and experience. Examples of such changes would include the introduction in Canada of the Charter of Rights and Freedom (which affects the way information about prisoners and patients should be handled) and the Young Offenders Act (which permits young persons much more licence in refusing treatment services than under the previous Juvenile Delinquents Act). Forensic psychologists in Canada have also been influenced by major court and coroners' rulings in the United States and at home, which have held practitioners professionally responsible for incorrect decisions (see Dickens, 1985). Psychologists are particularly apt to find themselves in uncomfortable positions when dealing with custody and access issues.

Throughout the chapter we have emphasized how difficult it is to balance professional objectives against those of the Court, the client and society generally. We have also stressed that our place as forensic psychologists rests on being astute clinicians well versed with up-to-date knowledge as it changes both in science and the law. It is an area where knowledge itself alters as a result of challenge not just in the professional periodicals but in the very Court itself (Faust & Ziskin, 1988). As Jeffrey (1964) cogently pointed out many years ago, "Courts do not greatly favour the inept".

References

Abel, G.G., Becker, J.V., Cunningham-Rathner, J., Rouleau, J.L., Kaplan, M., & Reich, J. (1984). *The treatment of child molesters.* Unpublished manual, Behavioral Medicine Laboratory, Box AF, Emory University, Atlanta, GA.

Abel, G. G., Blanchard, E. B., Barlow, D. H., & Mavissakalian, M. (1975). Identifying specific erotic cues in sexual deviations by audio-taped descriptions. *Journal of Applied Behavior Analysis, 8,* 244–260.

American Psychiatric Association. (1987). *Diagnostic and statistical manual of mental disorders* (3rd ed. revised). Washington, DC: American Psychiatric Association.

Andrews, D.A., Kiessling, J.J., & Kominos, S. (1983). *The Level of Supervision Inventory (LSI-6): Interview and scoring guide.* Toronto: Ontario Ministry of Correctional Services.

Arcaya, J. M. (1987). Role conflicts in coercive assessments: Evaluation and recommendations. *Professional Psychology: Research and Practice,18,* 422–428.

Barbaree, H. E., Marshall, W. L. & Lanthier, R. D. (1979). Deviant sexual arousal in rapists. *Behaviour Research & Therapy, 17,* 215–222.

Bartol, C. R. (1983). *Psychology and American law.* Belmont: Wadsworth.

Ben-Aron, M. H., Hucker, S. J., & Webster, C. D. (Eds.). (1985). *Clinical criminology: The assessment and treatment of criminal behaviour.* Toronto: M & M Graphics.

Blackburn, R. (1988). On moral judgements and personality disorders: The myth of psychopathic personality revisited. *British Journal of Psychiatry*, 153, 505–512.

Bonta, J., & Motiuk, L.L. (1985). Utilization of an interview-based classification instrument: A study of correctional halfway houses. *Criminal Justice and Behaviour*, *12*, 333–352.

Cleckley, H. (1976). *The mask of sanity.* St. Louis: C.V. Mosby. (Originally published 1941).

Clingempeel, W. G., Mulvey, E., & Reppucci, N. D. (1980). A national study of ethical dilemmas of psychologists in the criminal justice system. In J. Monahan (Ed.), *Who is the client: The ethics of psychological intervention in the criminal justice system.* Washington, DC: American Psychological Association.

Cornell, D. G. (1987). Role conflict in forensic clinical psychology: Reply to Arcaya. *Professional Psychology: Research and Practice*, *18*, 429–432.

Curran, W. J., & Pollack, S. (1986). Mental health and justice: Ethical issues of interdisciplinary cooperation. In W. J. Curran, A. L. McGarry, & S. A. Shah (Eds.), *Forensic psychiatry and psychology: Perspectives and standards for interdisciplinary practice* (pp. 61–74). Philadelphia: F. A. Davis.

Dickens, B. M. (1985). Prediction, professionalism, and public policy. In C. D. Webster, M. H. Ben-Aron, & S. J. Hucker (Eds.), *Dangerousness: Probability and prediction, psychiatry and public policy.* New York: Cambridge University Press.

Dietz, P. E., & Reese J. T. (1986). The perils of police psychology: 10 strategies for minimizing role conflicts when providing mental health services and consultation to law enforcement agencies. *Behavioral Science and the Law*, *4*, 385–400.

Erickson, R. J., Crow, W. J., Zurcher, L. A., & Connett, A. V. (1973). *Paroled but not free: Ex-offenders look at what they need to make it outside.* New York: Behavioural Publications.

Eysenck, H. J. (1964). *Crime and personality.* London: Routledge.

Faust, D. & Ziskin, J. (1988). The expert witness in psychology and psychiatry. *Science*, *241*, 31–35.

Gendreau, P. (1985). Critical comments on the practice of clinical criminology. In M. H. Ben-Aron, S. J. Hucker, & C. D. Webster (Eds.), *Clinical criminology: The assessment and treatment of criminal behaviour* (pp. 15–24). Toronto: Clarke Institute of Psychiatry.

Gendreau, P. & Ross, R. (1979). Effective correctional treatment: Bibliotherapy for cynics. *Crime and Delinquency*, 25, 463–489.

Goldstein, A. P., & Keller, H. (1987). *Aggressive behavior: Assessment and intervention*. New York: Pergamon Press.

Greenland, C. (1980). Psychiatry and the prediction of dangerousness. *Journal of Psychiatric Treatment and Evaluation*, 2, 97–103.

Grisso, T. (1987). The economic and scientific future of forensic psychological assessment. *American Psychologist*.

Grisso, T., Sales, B.D., & Bayless, S. (1982). Law-related courses and programs in graduate psychology departments. *American Psychologist, 37*, 267–278.

Hare, R. D., McPherson, L. M., & Forth, A. E. (1988). Male psychopaths and their criminal careers. *Journal of Consulting and Clinical Psychology, 56*, 710–714.

Hare, R.D. (1986). Twenty years of experience with the Cleckley psychopath. In W. H. Reid, D. Door, I. Walker, & J. W. Bonner (Eds.), *Unmasking the psychopath* (pp. 3–27). New York: W. W. Norton.

Hare, R. D. (1980). A research scale for the assessment of psychopathy in criminal populations. *Personality and Individual Differences*, *1*, 111–117.

Harpur, T. J., Hare, R. D., & Hakstian, A. R. (1989). Two-factor conceptualization of psychopathy: Construct validity and assessment implications. *Psychological Assessment: A Journal of Consulting and Clinical Psychology*, *1*, 6–17.

Harpur, T. J., Hakstian, A. R., & Hare, R. D. (1988). Factor structure of the psychopathy checklist. *Journal of Consulting and Clinical Psychology, 56*, 741–747.

Harris, G. T. (1989). The relationship between neuroleptic drug dose and the performance of psychiatric patients in a maximum security token economy program. *Journal of Behavior Therapy and Experimental Psychiatry*, 20, 57–67.

Harris, G. T., Rice, M. E., & Cormier, C.A. (1989). *Violent recidivism among psychopaths and nonpsychopaths treated in a therapeutic community*. Mental Health Centre, Penetanguishene: Research Report, Vol, VI, No. 1.

Jeffery, R. (1964). The psychologist as an expert witness on the issue of insanity. *American Psychologist, 19*, 838–843.

Keehn, J.D., & Webster, C.D. (1969). Behavior therapy and behavior modification. *Canadian Psychologist 10*, 68–73.

Langevin, R. (Ed.). (1983). *Sexual strands: Understanding and treating sexual anomalies in men*. Hillsdale, NJ: Erlbaum.

Laws, D. R. (1990). *Relapse prevention with sex offenders*. New York: Guilford.

Lawson, D. R., Greene R. T., Richardson J. S., McClure G., & Padina, R. J. (1971). Token economy program in a maximum security correctional hospital. *The Journal of Nervous and Mental Disease, 162,* 199–205.

Levine, D., Wilson, K., & Sales, B.D. (1980). An exploratory assessment of APA internships with legal/forensic experiences. *Professional Psychology, 12,* 400–405.

Lloyd-Bostock, S. (1988). The benefits of legal psychology: Possibilities, practice and dilemmas. *British Journal of Psychology. 79,* 417–440.

Marshall, W.L., & Barbaree, H. E. (1988). The long-term evaluation of a behavioral treatment program for child molesters. *Behavior Research and Therapy,* 26, 499–511.

Martinson, R. (1974). What works? Questions and answers about prison reform. *The Public Interest, 35,* 22–54.

McGarry, L. A. (1973). *Competency to stand trial and mental illness.* Rockville, MD: Department of Health, Education, and Welfare.

Megargee (1982). Reflections on psychology in the criminal justice system. In J. Gunn & D.P. Farrington (Eds.), *Abnormal offenders, delinquency and the criminal justice system.* London: Wiley.

Melton, G.B. (1987). Training in psychology and law. In I.B. Weiner & A.K. Hess (Eds.), *Handbook of forensic psychology.* New York: Wiley.

Menzies, R. J. (1989). *Survival of the sanest: Order and disorder in a pretrial psychiatric clinic.* Toronto: University of Toronto Press.

Monahan, J. (1981). *Predicting violent behavior. An assessment of clinical techniques.* Beverly Hills, CA: Sage.

Monahan, J. (1977). Social accountability: Preface to an integrated theory of criminal and mental health sanctions. In B. D. Sales (Ed.), *Perspectives in law and psychology: Vol. 1. The criminal justice system* (pp. 241–255). New York: Plenum Press.

Morrison, W. A. (1973). Criminal homicide and the death penalty in Canada: Time for re-assessment and new directions: Toward a typology of homicide. *Canadian Journal of Criminology and Corrections, 15,* 367–396.

Münsterberg, H. (1909). *On the witness stand.* New York: S. S. McClure.

Ostrov, J. D. (1986). Police/law enforcement and psychology. *Behavioral Science and the Law, 4,* 353–370.

Pollock, N. L. (1990) Accounting for predictions of dangerousness. *International Journal of Law and Psychiatry, 13,* 207–215.

Pollock, N., McBain I. & Webster, C. D. (1989). Clinical decision making and the assessment of dangerousness. In K. Howells & C. Hollin (Eds.), *Clinical approaches to aggression and violence* (pp. 89–115). Chichester: Wiley.

Prichard, J. C. (1837). *Treatise on insanity and other disorders affecting the mind.* Philadelphia: Harwell, Barrington & Harwell.

Quinsey, V. L. (1980). The baserate problem and the prediction of dangerousness: A reappraisal. *Journal of Psychiatry and Law*, 8, 329–340.

Quinsey, V. L., Chaplin, T., & Varney, G. A. A comparison of rapists' and non-sex offenders' sexual preferences for mutually consenting sex, rape, and sadistic acts. *Behavioral Assessment*, *3*, 127–135.

Quinsey, V. L., & Earls, C. M. (1990). The modification of sexual preferences. In W. L. Marshall, D. R. Laws, & H. E. Barbaree (Eds.), *Handbook of sexual assault*, (pp. 279–295). New York: Plenum.

Quinsey, V. L. & Maguire, A. (1983). Offenders remanded for a psychiatric examination: Perceived treatability and disposition. *International Journal of Law and Psychiatry*, 6, 193–205.

Quinsey, V. L. & Maguire, A. (1986). Maximum security psychiatric patients: Actuarial and clinical prediction of dangerousness. *Journal of Interpersonal Violence, 1,* 143–171.

Rice, M. E., Harris, G.T., Varney, G.W., & Quinsey, V. L., (1989). *Violence in institutions: Understanding, prevention, and control.* Toronto: Hans Huber.

Rice, M. E., Harris, G. T., Quinsey, V. L. & Cyr, M. (1990). Planning treatment programs in secure psychiatric facilities. In D. N. Weisstub (Ed.), *Law and Mental Health: International Perspective, 5.* New York: Pergamon Press.

Rice, M. E., & Quinsey, V. L. (1986). Contributions of Canadian applied psychological research to correctional and psychiatric institutions. *Canadian Psychology*, *27*, 1–21.

Roesch, R., Webster, C. D., & Eaves, D. (1984). *The fitness interview test: A method for examining fitness to stand trial.* Toronto: Centre of Criminology, University of Toronto Press.

Roesch, R. & Golding (1980). *Competence to stand trial.* Urbana: University of Illinois Press.

Rogers, R., Turner, R. E., Helfield, R., & Dickens, S. (Ed.). (1988). Forensic psychiatrists' and psychologists' understanding of insanity: Misguided expertise? *Canadian Journal of Psychiatry*, *33*, 691–695.

Rogers, R. (1986). *Clinical assessment of malingering and deception.* New York: Guilford.

Rogers, R. (1987). Ethical dilemmas in forensic evaluations. *Behavioral Science and the Law*, *5*, 149–160.

Rogers, R. (1988). *Conducting insanity evaluations.* New York: Van Nostrand Reinhold.

Rogers, R. & Ewing, C. P. (in press). The measurement of insanity: Debating the merits of the R-CRAS and its alternatives. *International Journal of Law and Psychiatry.*

Rosenhan, D. L., & Seligman, M. E. P. (1989). *Abnormal psychology* (2nd ed.). New York: Norton.

Samenow, S. E. (1984). *Inside the criminal mind.* New York: Times Books.

Saxton, G. H. (1986). Confidentiality dilemmas of psychologists and psychiatrists in the criminal justice system. *American Journal of Forensic Psychology, 4,* 25–32.

Schroeder, M. L., Schroeder, K. G., & Hare, R. D. (1983). Generalizability of a checklist for assessment of psychopathy. *Journal of Consulting and Clinical Psychology, 51,* 511–516.

Shah, A. S. (1978). Dangerousness: A paradigm for exploring some issues in law and psychology. *American Psychologist, 33,* 224–238.

Stermac, L. E. & Segal, Z. V. (1989). Adult sexual contact with children: An examination of cognitive factors. *Behaviour* Therapy, *20,* 573–584.

Webster, C.D. (1984). On gaining acceptance: Why the courts accept only reluctantly findings from experimental and social psychology. *International Journal of Law and Psychiatry, 7,* 407–414.

Webster, C.D., Ben-Aron, M.H., & Hucker, S.J. (1985). *Dangerousness: Probability and prediction, psychiatry and public policy.* New York: Cambridge University Press.

Webster, C. D., Dickens, B. M., & Addario, S. (1985). *Constructing dangerousness: Scientific, legal, and policy implications.* Toronto: University of Toronto, Centre of Criminology.

Webster, C. D., Menzies, R. J., & Jackson, M. A. (1982). *Clinical assessment before trial: Legal issues and mental disorder.* Toronto: Butterworths.

Weiner, I.B., & Hess, A.K. (Eds.). (1987). *Handbook of forensic psychology.* New York: Wiley.

Wormith, J. S. (1984). Attitude and behavior change of a correctional clientele: A 3-year follow-up. *Criminology,* 22, 595–618.

Yarmey, A. D. (1979). *The psychology of eyewitness testimony.* New York: Free Press.

Ziskin, J. (1980). Giving expert testimony: Pitfalls and hazards for the psychologist in court. In G. Cooke (Ed.), *The role of the forensic psychologist* (pp. 98–105). Springfield, IL: Charles C. Thomas.

16

Nontraditional Applications of Professional Psychology

R. F. Wilson
Wilson Banwell & Associates Ltd., Vancouver, B. C.

Introduction

Sixty years is not really a very long time to establish traditions against which one can write about nontraditional events. It was approximately that long ago that professional psychology made its first impact on the Canadian scene, and it was a war that turned the largely academic discipline into a "profession" (Wright, 1974). The traditional applications of psychology in Canada got their start during World War II. The skills which were developed by psychologists, as a new profession, to meet the needs of a country at war included aptitude and ability test construction, standardization and administration; career selection procedures;

and management of child development programmes through day care facilities (Wright, 1974).

In addition to the activities psychologists have practised for several decades, an understanding of nontraditional applications requires an examination of where psychologists have traditionally practised, the roles they have played, the assumptions that have supported their practices and how they have traditionally been rewarded for their activity, since each of these factors have been dramatically modified or challenged by psychologists practicing in nontraditional ways.

Psychology is still a very young profession struggling to find its identity, and thus it should come as no surprise that some of the nontraditional applications occur in the context of challenging existing standards and authority. Modern-day applied psychology is very similar to the demands of a teenage parent struggling to cope with her own maturation, while at the same time being forced to react to the needs of a demanding infant.

The present chapter attempt not only to identify nontraditional applications of psychology, but also to at least recognize the context and some of the empowering factors that have served to create the conditions allowing for the emergence of these new traditions. It is my hope that psychology will always be identified as the profession of "new" traditions.

The Context

Professional psychology in Canada emerged from university laboratories to help meet the needs of a nation at war. Thus, the skills and technologies of the laboratory became the skills and technologies of the postwar practitioners of psychology. The academicians returned to the universities and left the applied work to their students, who were generally only qualified to work as technicians. "Psychologists have been too willing to push their inadequately trained students into technical services, with the result that most 'professional' psychologists in Canada are now rated and paid as technicians." (MacLeod, p.60–61, 1955) The pattern was similar in the United States where, "... services were rendered primarily in medical settings ..., the psychologist retaining secondary responsibility for those areas in which he or she was 'technically competent'. ... This concept is essentially that of a technologist or technician, however, not of a 'practitioner-professional'. " (Rodgers, 1986, p. 143) "Traditionally" psychologists were not allowed to practise independently and were thus forced to work in the institutions of other profession, where they were defined as paraprofessionals, paid as paraprofessionals and readily adopted the self-image of paraprofessionals (Wilson, 1989). Their own discipline scorned them, leading to decades of smoldering resentment still evident on many campuses and in Canadian Psychological Association (CPA) committees; this resentment has nearly led to the demise of CPA as we know it on more than one occasion (Berry, Davidson & Gibson, 1974; Berry, 1977; Conway, 1984). The traditions of applied psychology may have had a noble start, but that quickly changed, and the profession assumed the status of second-class citizenship both on campuses and in the work environments where psychologists were employed.

The traditions of applied psychology were established under the "applied scientist" and "technologist" roles psychologists have historically served – not the "practitioner" role now rapidly developing. A practitioner-professional, as defined by Rodgers (1986), is one called upon to fill the void between what is known (scientifically validated) and what is unknown (magical): "The practitioner-professional paradoxically tends to be the steward of the cultural ignorance base more than of the cultural knowledge base in the particular area of need that is served ... " (Rodgers, 1986, p. 153). Technologists can be trained to apply the skills and techniques that have been proven to be effective in solving existential problems, and oracles and priests can, and do, attend to those elements of life that are beyond the realm of the known. A professional practitioner helps individuals and organizations seek relief from problems there is some knowledge about but no certain solution to, through application of a set of assumptions and methods generally grounded in scientific methodology. Thus, there emerges the rationale for the "scientist-practitioner" model of training applied psychologists, first espoused by Raimy (1950).

That these assumptions underlying the practitioners' *modus operandi*, and the techniques flowing from them, can be dangerous to the public seeking assistance is well documented through the history of medicine. Indeed, the history of medicine is in itself a testimony to the need for legislation governing practitioner professions. For many years physicians operated on the assumption that bleeding was an effective means of treating certain illnesses that were clearly not well understood, a practice that led to many needless deaths, including apparently that of the first president of the United States, George Washington. Medicine operates on the assumption that physiological factors account for aberrant conditions, including contemporary maladies such as depression and alcoholism. This assumption may prove to be verifiable, but today it remains an assumption. Traditional applications of psychology for many years supported the medical view, whereas contemporary nontraditional applications of applied psychology tend to rely on a wide range of behavioral assumptions. As psychologists have moved from the assumptions of other disciplines, our roles and work environments have changed.

As a discipline moves from the certainties and clear role definitions of either the scientist or technician, the need to protect the public increases. Not until the early 1960s did professional psychologists in Canada begin the struggle to establish themselves as a legislated profession, a task not completed in all provinces until 1990. Once legislation was accomplished, however, psychologists gained the confidence to establish a unique identity. The process has been gradual, with many psychologists preferring to adhere to traditional roles and procedures, while a more venturesome few have begun to create nontraditional applications of psychology.

This challenge to traditional assumptions and practices, coupled with the support of legislation, has led to the exploration of new roles, new work settings and new methods of funding. Figure 1 summarizes the relationships between three dimensions, to provide a "baseline" for the innovations to be discussed in each area. For each role–work environment–funding combination, one can contemplate (a) the history of these activities, (b) the forces shaping that history, (c) the key assumptions undergirding professional practice and (d) the trends that empower, create and characterize innovation, and the development and diffusion of nontraditional roles.

Figure 2 provides a sampling of the new options rapidly developing in Canadian psychology; these are discussed more fully below.

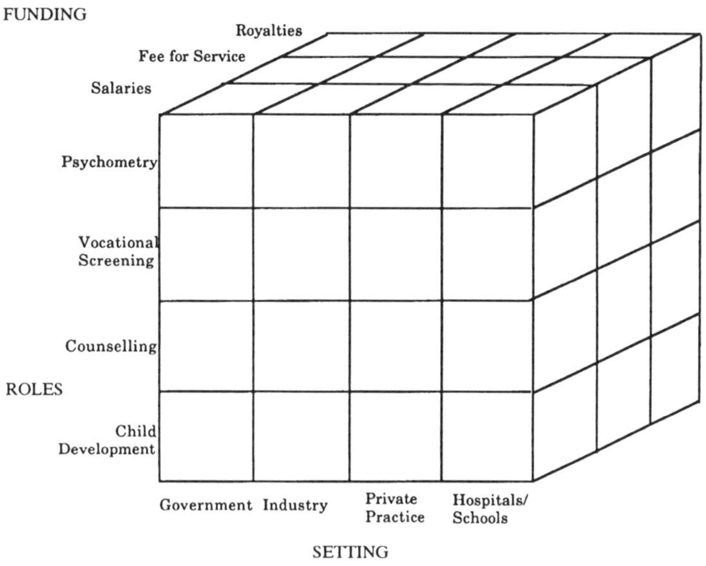

Figure 1. Traditional functions of applied psychology.

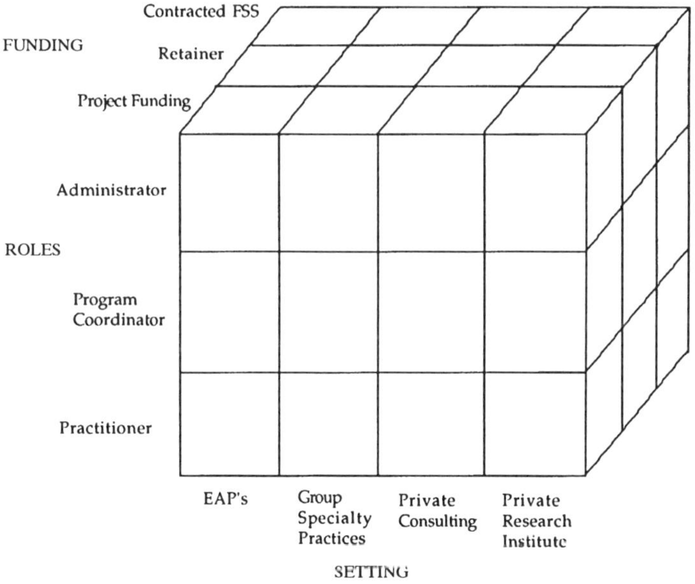

Figure 2. Examples of nontraditional functions of applied psychology.

Changing Roles and Activities

Approximately 30 years after World War II, 48.2% of applied Canadian psychologists polled still considered test construction and administration activities to be the main area of specialization, and almost 14.2% included career selection procedures among their primary duties. An additional 15.9% listed child development (education) activities as their main professional job (Ritchie, Hogan & Hogan, 1988). It would, therefore, appear safe to conclude that evaluation and assessment activities, career selection and work with children – all wartime activities – were among the "traditional" roles of contemporary Canadian psychologists.

Another skill that has achieved the status of "traditionality" is counselling or psychotherapy. Granted, these activities are more recent traditions with a life span of less than 25 years as practised by Canadian psychologists. Nevertheless, in the 1984 survey quoted above, 57.7% (figures exceed 100% because the Delphi polling method was used) of the applied psychologists reported psychotherapy as their main area of specialization (Ritchie et al., 1988). These roles, test construction and administration, vocational selection and counselling, assessment of child development and psychotherapy have become the "traditional" activities of applied Canadian psychologists. As currently practised, these activities have expanded considerably to include a wide range of psychodiagnostic skills, aptitude measurement, the evolution of programmes for special needs children and new techniques of counselling and therapy.

That new roles have been established can be seen in the labels some psychologists now use to define themselves: from psychotherapist to facilitator, from psychodiagnostician to applied researcher, from technician to practitioner, from Psychologist III to Owner. The traditional labels defining the roles of applied psychologists no longer fit the activities many perform or the functions they serve. For example, two traditional roles, psychodiagnostician and psychotherapist, have undergone major shifts from the assumptions that defined the activity to the manifestations of those activities among the very small minority of psychologists who have chosen to explore nontraditional applications.

It is important to note here that it would be quite wrong to imply that these traditional activities and functions of psychologists today no longer exist. On the contrary, the majority of psychologists in Canada continue to practise and assume roles defined following World War II, although the techniques and procedures they follow have been considerably enhanced through new technologies and advances in theory. The path followed by those who have chosen nontraditional roles and activities generally begins with challenges to traditional assumptions and reinterpretations of original data sets.

For example, traditional clinical psychodiagnostic procedures generally lead to the psychologist applying to the client a label taken from the Bible of diagnosticians, DSM III-R (1987). Many assumptions underlie the confident use of this manual, one of which is that manifest symptoms generally reflect characterological defects or poor social learning histories: Little room is left for the possibility that the environment has created circumstances to which the symptoms are an adaptive response. Thus, treatment is focused on *changing the individual* rather than changing the environment. At times this can be a very appropriate procedure; however, one of many instances where it can lead to aggravation of the problem is in the workplace. DSM-III-R (1987) allows one to have an adjustment disorder with work, although it is somewhat difficult to take the category seriously when the example of this disorder is "inability to study and to write papers or reports" (p. 301). Clearly, egocentrism is not a foreign malady to the largely academician authors of the manual.

If one operates from the premise that some individuals bring to the work environment a weaker constitution than others, then the therapist will make efforts to engage in "institutional hardening" through one of many philosophies of treatment directed at such individuals. This would be the traditional approach. If, on the other hand, one operates from the premise that the work environment itself is the problem, then the job of the therapist becomes one of helping the individual gain a new perspective, the job of the psychodiagnostician becoming one of engaging in nontraditional roles such as researcher (gathering work environment data), salesperson (convincing management that a problem exists at the work site), consultant (assisting management to create a less stressful work environment) and monitor (evaluating the effectiveness of the interventions). The activity of the nontraditional diagnostician has thus become more comprehensive. One could perhaps argue that the tasks of the new psychodiagnostician far exceed the mandate of that title, and that the new requirements demand new identities. The tools shift from an emphasis on traditional psychological tests to the use of applied research techniques appropriate to the environment being studied. "Diagnostic" labels obtained in this fashion allow for the possibility that the sources of psychological distress may include factors beyond the individual presenting with symptoms. Wilson (1986) described several nontraditional diagnoses including the "acquired entrepreneur syndrome", the "sick building syndrome", the "technostress syndrome" and the "rapid change syndrome", several of many examples of disorder resulting from environmental stressors.

Traditional approaches to psychotherapy have generally proceeded from the assumption that intrapsychic forces have gotten out of balance and can best be brought back in line through a special relationship with a trained professional. Wolberg (1954) listed 13 definitions of psychotherapy prevalent at the time, all having in common an intrapsychic "hydraulic" model of abnormal behaviour requiring a relationship with a trained professional possessing "special" skills. Eysenck (1952, 1960, 1965) challenged the traditional models of psychotherapy by suggesting that "untreated" patients did as well as those undergoing treatment. Eysenck's articles gave impetus to the growing interest in more verifiable methods of treatment, particularly those based on learning theory. Psychologists, who had long been fighting a battle to become recognized as psychotherapists, now had a powerful approach they could call their own. From would-be analysts to mental-health accountants espousing the wonders of token economies, psychologists flocked to the "new" behaviour therapies.

Common to both the analytic and behavioural methods of intervention is still the assumption that the individual expressing the problem is required to play an active role in the solution to the problem, even if the activity is relatively passive, e.g. hypnosis. This is not an assumption I wish to dispute, since the supportive evidence is overwhelming. Rather, I would offer by example evidence of a nontraditional model of "therapy", or at the least a role redefinition for the therapist, which under the right circumstances may prove to be more effective.

A number of years ago I served as a consultant, diagnostician and therapist to a native band in northern British Columbia. A common complaint referred to me (and others before I arrived on the scene) was of child neglect, ensuing largely, it was believed, through alcoholism. Efforts to understand and treat this deviant behaviour (child "abuse" neglect) on the part of the parents had consumed many hours of alcohol counselling, therapy and parenting training programmes. At one point, the RCMP had been issued instructions to arrest parents who "abandoned" their children and to have the children placed in temporary foster care. Since the village had no foster care facilities, this meant moving families of children many miles by air to a larger community where they could be placed. When the parents sobered up, they were devastated at the loss of their family and by the humiliation in front of their neighbours. Their utter sense of helplessness in the face of a controlling society they neither understood nor appreciated only further aggravated their plight and, it was believed, led to their return to alcohol.

Efforts to break the vicious cycle through therapeutic and legal methods of intervention failed to produce significant results. It seemed obvious that a new look at the problem was required. A village meeting was called where the role of the therapist changed to that of community facilitator. It was decided that the cycle of deviant behaviour could best be broken through this community process by establishing a "safe house" in the village where any children could go if their parents were "late" in coming home. Parents who had been offenders in the past were encouraged to drop their children off at the safe house prior to going "visiting". This procedure virtually stopped the arrests for neglect, the transportation of children to neighbouring communities and the loss of public face. It also increased the feeling of local control, which resulted in other spinoffs. It did not stop the alcoholism, but it did serve to isolate the substance abuse so that more traditional approaches could be attempted.

In this instance, the therapist became a facilitator, helping the community discover ways to alter the behaviour of some of its members. Examples of the utility of shifting roles abound in the files of effective contemporary therapists. Regrettably, there are few vehicles for the publishing such data, so that awareness of unique applications of therapeutic principles and shifting roles of therapists is generally discovered through informal discussions among colleagues.

A second example of a dramatic shift from traditional therapeutic roles involves the growing interest among some practitioners in becoming involved with individuals experiencing acute stages of distress. The origin of this kind of counselling began during the war with therapists responding to what was then called "battle fatigue". The modern-day euphemism describing terror and its attendant reactions is "critical incident stress" or "post-traumatic stress disorder". Until recently, psychologists did not become involved with these patients because they were usually seen in the emergency wards of hospitals or were dealt with by relatives, family doctors, police or ambulance attendants. Wilson (1984) designed a psychological intervention programme to respond to the victims of acute stress which required the therapist to go to the scene of the trauma while the victim or victims were still present. This "psychological SWAT-team" approach has been used very successfully with bank tellers or armoured car drivers who have been robbed and/or shot, and caregivers who have been traumatized by their experience at the scene of accidents. The programme has now been expanded to victims of natural disasters such as floods and earthquakes. Some of the issues confronting psychologists involved in responding to crises by going to the scene of the event are described by Jacobs (1990), who along with his students was called upon to assist in the immediate aftermath of an airline disaster in Iowa in which there miraculously were survivors.

There are many examples of psychologists stepping outside their traditional roles as therapists and providing unique services to new populations and communities, for example, developing proactive communities (Best, 1989), disaster response (Butcher & Dunn, 1989), health promotion (Best, 1989; Best, Cameron & Grant, 1986; Taylor, 1990), grief and bereavement (Wilson, 1990) and loss of personal effects trauma (Wilson, 1990).

The Setting

Everything used to be so simple. Until recently, a psychologist in Canada had basically four options to consider when looking for employment: the military, hospitals or schools and universities, industry, or private practice. Figure 3 displays the pattern of employment of psychologists in Canada over the past five decades.

Today, the above options are still available, but a psychologist may also work in an HMO (health maintenance organization), PPO (preferred provider organization), IPA (independent practice association), MHMO (mental health maintenance organization), EAP (employee assistance programme), EFAP (employee and family assistance programme), PHF (psychiatric health facility) or PSF (psychological services firm). Indeed, it is likely that by the turn of the century most psychologists will be employed in a "nontraditional" setting, and/or the traditional settings will begin to include more nontraditional options.

Cummings and Dörken (1986) describe several of the above options in the context of a rapidly changing health care delivery market in the United States driven by cost containment. "Health care is not just entering a period of change but is in the throes of a revolution. ... For psychologists, it is important to note that, for those predicting the extinction of the private practice of psychotherapy as we now know it, it is not a question of whether but when, simply because it cannot be delivered at competitive cost"

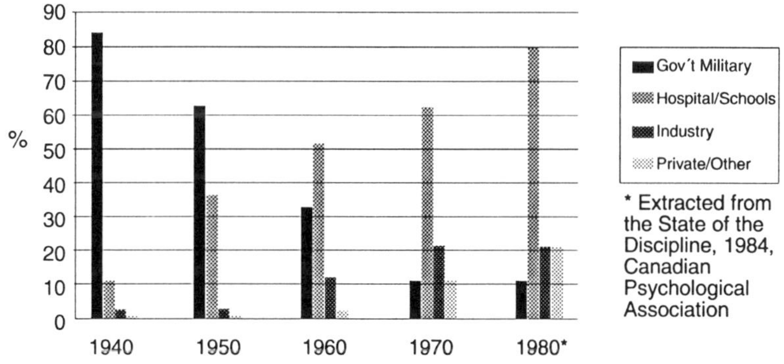

Figure 3. An estimation of sources of employment of applied psychologists in Canada.

(p. 285). These authors write about the American experience, but there is little doubt that drastic changes are coming to Canada in the near future as well.

At the time of writing this chapter Quebec has formally declared its intent to opt out of the Canada Health Act, and British Columbia has established a Royal Commission to review the health care delivery system and make recommendations for its revamping, while Ontario is examining an omnibus health care bill that would include psychology. Across the entire country large psychiatric institutions have been replaced by decentralized smaller facilities that have sought cheaper (i. e. nonpsychologist) staff to provide their services; corporations concerned with the bottom line are easily convinced that EAP programmes serviced by paraprofessionals are "good enough". What, then, can psychology in Canada do to compete in a shrinking marketplace already being serviced by "no-out-of-pocket" psychiatry and by social workers and lay therapists who cost much less? An example follows.

In 1979, Dr. Peter McLean and I established the foundation for what later became Wilson Banwell, now a large international psychological services firm. Our original task was to see if it would be possible to create a free-standing, for-profit organization of psychologists in Canada which would meet the following conditions:

1. Clients had to have access to the services at no out-of-pocket expenses. The service would have to compete with the psychiatric stranglehold on mental health services. The private-practice model was too costly for most Canadians and often added financial stress to the other burdens clients were already carrying.
2. The service had to meet the highest standards psychologists can provide in Canada. A professional service lives or dies by the quality of care provided.
3. The service had to be available within the same week people called for an appointment. Waiting for up to three months to receive psychiatric or private psychological is unreasonable.
4. The services had to be able to sustain themselves, theoretically in perpetuity, and provide a modest profit.

With these goals in mind, Canada's first, and still only, psychological health benefit was developed. The benefit is now sold by half a dozen major insurance companies in Canada, and a number of additional benefits and services have since been developed (including a unique bereavement assistance programme in which psychological counselling is included as part of the benefit of one's life insurance). The employee-owned company now employs 15 full-time psychologists and 114 part-time registered psychologists across Canada with others in various international locations. All of the above goals have been met. The company has since expanded well beyond its early aspirations, and it has remained an example of the viability of a free standing psychological services firm.

Funding Options

It is of little value to entertain unique applications of psychological skill if there is no market for the services and if no one is willing to pay for them. There must be an economy. One of the nontraditional aspects of contemporary psychology is the appreciation for this fact by a growing number of psychologists who discover that equal attention has to be paid to both marketing and providing their services (Ritchie, Wilson, Berry, Boulay, King & Sabourin, 1988). Unless efforts are placed on teaching graduate students the mechanics of the marketplace they will have to compete in, we are going to continue to force most professional psychologists into traditional environments, which today are rapidly shrinking and looking for overall cheaper ways to meet their responsibilities. Or worse still, we graduate private practitioners blinded by the riches believed to be inherent in being included in provincial health plans. (For a critique of Medicare as a source of funding see Ritchie et al., 1988 b.) At present, we are training obsolescence, not in the skills set, but in the inability of the professional psychologist of tomorrow to effectively sell those skills.

Ritchie et al. (1988 b) identified 14 different types of payment for psychological services today from 12 different sources. The resulting combinations from this contingency table yield 168 possibilities for funding psychological services. Not all combinations are available or practical. In fact, it was estimated by the authors that 95% of all psychologists in Canada earned their incomes from just eight of the possibilities: all salaried positions constituting the traditional roles and activities of psychologists described above. The authors went on to report on 24 different sources of funding psychological services they concluded will be the sources having the "greatest potential" (p. 196) for future income of psychologists in Canada: Salaries were not included in any of the 24 possibilities showing greatest promise.

Of the many nontraditional methods of funding psychological services, a "hybrid" fee for service system developed by Wilson (1979) has demonstrated considerable utility as a means of minimizing the unpredictability of the standard fee for service charged by private practicing psychologists. The funding method is called a "contracted fee for service". It is only applicable in third-party payment schemes in which the purchaser agrees to exclusive use of the services of the contractor (psychologist). In this system, the psychologist estimates the quantity of service required to service the purchaser's needs and then contracts to provide that service by spreading the payment for the service over the contract period. For example, if it is estimated that the purchaser will require 100 hours of psychological service in a given year, then 100 is multiplied by the rate per hour and the product divided by 12 to obtain the monthly fee on an annual contract. Of course, every hour of service paid for must eventually be provided. If 105 hours of service have been used at the end of the contract year, the purchaser must pay for the additional time provided; if 95 hours were used, the psychologist must refund the "underutilized" hours or provide them in a subsequent contract. In this way the psychologist has a predictable monthly income, and the purchaser has guaranteed access to timely services. A new "hybrid" method developed at Wilson Banwell is the selling of "service futures". This system only works when a fourth party buys directly from the contractor to then sell to a third-party user. The "futures" are sold much as they are in the stock market, except the price is fixed and there is thus no "trading" in the futures. The advantage to the contractor is that large quantities of service can be presold and planned for.

Conclusion

As an independent discipline, psychology is highly esteemed and has unquestionably had a significant impact on our understanding of what it is to be human. As a profession, traditional applied psychology has been viewed with less esteem and has identity problems rivaling those of the Canadian population in general. We have traditionally been servants in other people's homes – good servants, but servants nonetheless. Some have not accepted this role well and have chosen instead to seek ways of providing their skills in unique ways and in unique environments. It is my thesis that if we are to survive as a profession and enhance our identity, we must always be willing to encourage each other to choose "the road less traveled".

Acknowledgements

I wish to acknowledge with thanks the wise counsel of Dr. Allan Best in the early draft stages of this chapter.

References

American Psychiatric Association (1980). *Diagnostic and statistical manual of mental disorders* (3rd ed.) (DSM-III-R). Washington D.C.: Author.

Berry, R.G. (1977). Introduction to the report of the Vancouver Conference. In G.A. Ferguson (1977) *Report of the Vancouver Conference on the organization and representation of psychology in Canada.* Toronto: Canadian Psychological Association.

Berry, Ray, Davidson, P.O., & Gibson, David. (1974). Advisory council provincial associations of psychologists: archival comment, *Canadian Psychologist, 15,* 368–375.

Best, J.A. (1989). Intervention perspectives on school health promotion. *Health Education Quarterly, 16,* 299–306.

Best, J.A. (August, 1989). *Selling health promotion to the community: Your place or mine?* Invited presentation to the Health and Welfare Canada

St. Francis Xavier University Workshop on Approaches to Community Development and Coalition Building, Antigonish, Nova Scotia.

Best, J.A., Cameron, R., & Grant, M. (1986). Health behavior and health promotion. *American Journal of Health Promotion, 1*, 48–57.

Butcher, J.N., & Dunn, L.A. (1989). Human responses and treatment needs in airline disasters. In R. Gist & B. Lubin (Eds.), *Psychosocial aspects of disaster* (pp. 86–119). New York: Wiley.

Conway, J.B., (1984). A place for discontent and tensions in psychology, *Canadian Psychology,25,* 96–104.

Cummings, N.A., Dörken, H. (1986). Corporations, networks, and service plans: economically sound models for practice. In H. Dörken and Associates, *Professional Psychology in Transition.* San Francisco: Jossey-Bass Inc.

Eysenck H.J. (1965). The effects of psychotherapy. *International Journal of Psychiatry, 1* 99–144.

Eysenck, H.J. (1952). The effects of psychotherapy: an evaluation. *Journal of Consulting Psychology, 16.* 319–324.

Eysenck, H.J. (1960). The effects of psychotherapy. In H.J. Eysenck (Ed.), *Handbook of abnormal psychology: An experiential approach.* London: Pitman Medical Publishing.

Figley, C.R. (Ed.). (1986). *Trauma and its wake, volume II.* New York: Brunner/Mazel.

Jacobs, G.A., Quevillon, R.P., & Stricherz, M. (1990). Lessons from the aftermath of flight 232: Practical considerations for the mental health profession's response to air disasters. *American Psychologist, 45,* 1329–1335.

MacLeod, R.B. (1955). *Psychology in Canadian universities and colleges.* Ottawa: Canadian Social Science Research Council.

Raimy, V.C. (Ed.). (1950). *Training in clinical psychology.* Englewood Cliffs, NJ: Prentice-Hall.

Ritchie, P.L.J., Hogan, T.P., & Hogan, T.V. (1988). *The state of the discipline, 1984.* Ottawa: Canadian Psychological Association.

Ritchie, P.L.J., Wilson, R.F., Berry, R., Boulay, M., King, M., & Sabourin, M.E. (1988b). The funding of psychological health care services. *Canadian Psychology, 29,* 187–205.

Rodgers, D.A. (1986). Psychologists as practitioners, not technicians. In H. Dörken & Associates (Eds.), *Professional psychology in transition* (pp. 141 173). San Francisco. Jossey-Boss Inc.

Taylor, S.E. (1990). Health psychology: The science and the field. *American Psychologist, 45,* 40–50.

Wilson, R.F. (1979). *Manual for psychological health benefit.* Internal document. McLean, Wilson & Stuart, Vancouver, British Columbia.

Wilson, R.F. (1984). *Victim assistance program: A manual.* Internal document, Wilson Banwell & Associates Ltd., Vancouver, British Columbia.

Wilson, R.F. (1986). *Managing new clinical syndromes in modern industry.* Invited presentation to the International Conference on Mental Health, Expo 86, Vancouver, British Columbia.

Wilson, R.F. (1989). *Witness to an evolution.* Invited presentation to the Psychological Association of Alberta, Calgary, Alberta.

Wilson, R.F. (1990). *Grief and bereavement: enhancement to life insurance benefits.* Internal document, Wilson Banwell & Associates Ltd., Vancouver, British Columbia

Wilson, R.F. (1990). *Loss of personal effects trauma: Enhancement to homeowners insurance.* Internal document, Wilson Banwell & Associates Ltd., Vancouver, British Columbia.

Wolberg, L.R. (1954). *The technique of psychotherapy.* New York City, Grune & Stratton.

Wright, M.J. (1974) CPA: The first ten years. *Canadian Psychologist, 15,* 112–131.

V

The Future of Professional Psychology in Canada

17

Professional Psychology in Canada: Present Status and Future Promises

Keith S. Dobson
University of Calgary

Deborah J. G. Dobson
Foothills Hospital & University of Calgary

Pierre L.-J. Ritchie
University of Ottawa

As the previous chapters in this volume have demonstrated, professional psychology in Canada has produced a number of accomplishments and benefits that can be proudly claimed by its members. It has also become apparent that psychology is still a young profession, and one grappling with the developmental issues appropriate to its present level of maturity. In this chapter, we touch on themes that arise from previous chapters and from our own experiences that bear upon the present status and future possibilities of professional psychology in Canada. We have been selective in our presentation, not with the intent of implying that only the issues we discuss are important, but rather in order to highlight what we see as pivotal issues to professional psychology, and to make some predictions about the future of these issues. Obviously, such predictive exercises are open to criticism, although the most telling criticism will undoubtedly be the unfolding of the future itself.

Within the scope of identifying current trends and future issues, we have identified five major topics for discussion: (1) training and accreditation, (2) specialization, (3) public vs. private sector activity, (4) professional autonomy and (5) public policy development. Each of these topics will be discussed in turn.

Training and Accreditation

As several chapters in this volume have already addressed the issues of training and accreditation, we shall not reiterate their functions or current status. Rather, we wish to identify two critical issues in this field, one of which is historical and continuing, the other of which is more likely to emerge in the future.

One of the earliest topics confronting psychology was the level of training necessary to gain admission into the profession itself. Even though the Canadian Psychological Association for three decades steadfastly maintained that the doctoral degree is the appropriate level of training to become a psychologist and be eligible for independent practice, and even though many provinces have formally adopted the doctoral degree as the threshold credential for entry into the profession, the debate still continues about the necessary universal requirement for psychologists. Legislatures in several provinces have not adopted the doctoral requirement (see Granger, this volume). Further, within some areas of psychology (most notably, school psychology; see Holmes, this volume), the doctoral requirement has been explicitly rejected. There has been some retrenchment in British Columbia with the exemption of school psychologists from the requirements of the *Psychology Act*. In Ontario, the creation of the subdoctoral serviceprovider category of Psychological Associate also underscores the continued need to establish appropriate regulation and public protection of persons trained at the master's level, even when the doctoral standard is maintained for practice as a psychologist per se.

The level of training expected of psychologists intersects with another training issue: the type of training model used. A comparison of the American and Canadian experiences is illustrative here. The two dominant doctoral professional training models found in the United States are the scientist-practitioner degree (Ph. D. or Ed. D.) and the professional degree (Psy. D.). The critical distinction is that while graduates of the former are intended to be able to *generate* research, graduates of professional programmes are intended to be capable *consumers* of psychological research in their work as clinicians. Canada, in contrast, presently has no professional programmes.

An examination of the actual functions of practitioners (cf. Hunsley & Lefebvre, 1990) makes it clear that most professional psychologists do not engage in research, but rather provide services. Thus, while in the United States the existence of the professional training option permits the preparation of practitioners to meet service demands, an argument can be made that Canadian programmes do not graduate professionals geared to societal needs.

In Canada, there has been neither a comprehensive national assessment of personnel requirements and abilities of professional psychologists nor a recent assessment of national training needs to prompt the development of professional programmes. The State of the Discipline Review sponsored by the Canadian Psychological Association (Ritchie, Hogan & Hogan, 1988) did recognize that professional programmes were a legitimate training option. However, it fell short of actually endorsing the model, confirming only that professional programmes would be eligible for accreditation if they met the required criteria. More recently, the Report of the Task Force on Midcareer Training (Handy & Whitsett, 1991), itself an outgrowth of the State of the Discipline Review, generated renewed pressure for the development of professional model programmes in Canada as a vehicle to enable current master's-level practitioners to upgrade to the doctoral level. In part as a result of this report, the Council of Provincial/Territorial Associations of Psychologists recommended that this issue be put on the agenda for a conference on the applications of psychology which the Canadian Psychological Association may convene in late 1993.

While the current push to recognize master's-level practitioners and to generate professional training models suggest the need to re-examine the universal policy of scientist-practitioner doctoral-level training, the necessary data to make an informed decision are not available. In the absence thereof, it is not surprising that other factors, such as preferences about "usual" training models, economics, or political interest group pressure, disproportionately affect the decisions made about entry levels and training. We feel that a dispassionate review of the type and level of training needed for professional psychologists is highly warranted, much along the lines of the recent Gainesville conference on the scientist-practitioner model (Belar & Perry, 1991).

A look at the future of training in professional psychology shows that the dominant force that will continue to shape the nature of training is the accreditation process. Accreditation (see Doyle, Edwards & Robinson, this volume) is a voluntary process that evaluates training programmes for their compliance with explicit criteria. Within Canada, the Accreditation Panel on Professional Psychology now accredits doctoral programmes and internships in the areas of clinical psychology, counselling psychology and clinical neuropsychology; the Panel could be expanded to include other areas of accreditation similar to those in the United States (school psychology and industrial/organizational psychology), though to date there has been little pressure to do so.

We predict that accreditation will have two dominant effects in the future: first, to increase the rigour of programmes and the demands placed upon graduate students in professional psychology; and second, to standardize the training of neophyte professionals. Clearly, the goal of enhanced training is a worthy one that will increase not only the range of service possibilities of graduates from accredited programmes, but also the quality of service provided to the public.

Yet standardization of training is a double-edged sword. On the one hand, training becomes a more predictable process, and graduates can be assumed to have basic core knowledge in their respective fields. On the other hand, standardization may lead to rigid definitions of training, to a lack of innovation in training procedures and to a form of stultification in the entire profession. Since a gap between training programmes and societal or service requirements may not become obvious for as long as a decade, it will be important in the future that there continues to be some degree of exploration of diverse and innovative training models and procedures.

In summary, although training models and curricula have been developed considerably over the past decade, pressure will continue for the assessment and modification of training programmes. This includes the movement away from discipline-oriented work toward more interdisciplinary models (e.g. cognitive sciences, neurosciences; Scott, 1991), controversy over training models within the discipline, an effort by legislatures to provide services to the largest number of citizens at the least cost and the development and assessment of the professional aspects of psychology. Thus, it is hardly surprising that every State of the Discipline Review to date has included a component related to training; this need for review will continue in the future.

Specialization

An ongoing debate in our field is whether psychology is a single discipline with many applications (cf. Matarazzo, 1987) or rather a loosely federated group of specialties (Conway, 1991; Hall, 1988). This debate is fuelled, in part, by continuing discussions over the nature of specialties and proficiencies. Typically, a specialty is considered a subset of knowledge and skills that can be differentiated sufficiently from other areas along four dimensions to justify receiving a separate identity and individual labelling. The four dimensions are *client populations, problems addressed, techniques and technologies, and service settings* (Sales, Bricklin, & Hall, 1983; Service, Sabourin, Catano, Day, Hayes, & MacDonald, 1989). In contrast, proficiencies are areas of knowledge and skills beyond a generic core in one or more (but not all four) of these dimensions.

Whether any areas of professional psychology possess the complete set of attributes to qualify as a specialty according to the above criteria is a matter of discussion, although some professional areas certainly qualify as proficiencies. Most graduate programmes in psychology do not train generalist professionals, though many do attempt to have their graduates capable of career flexibility, with skills that can be adapted to different areas of practice or enhancement over time. Rather, Canadian graduate programmes in professional psychology are developing proficiencies in their graduates (see Dobson & Dobson, this volume). The accreditation of doctoral programmes and internships further implies that professional psychology has identifiable proficiencies. Finally, some provinces (e.g. Quebec, British Columbia) have adopted a *de facto* system of specialties, with registered psychologists being permitted to self-declare areas of special training and expertise. The establishment of the Canadian Register of Health Service Providers in Psychology by the CPA and the provincial associations and regulatory bodies in 1985 also delineated "health service" as an area of practice different from others, based on public and private sector need for a credible and reliable system to identify such psychologists.

A critic of the trend toward specialization in professional psychology could argue that we have moved to a point where the centrifugal forces have left no room in the middle of the profession for a common core of knowledge (Scott, 1991), and that further development of specialties will create artificial boundaries to practice, role inflexibility, inordinately lengthy training programmes, increased costs to consumers and a reduction of general service providers in favour of more lucrative specialties (Schaps & Sales, 1983; Service et al., 1989). Yet the potential advantages of formalizing a system of specialization include recognition of the fact that psychology has developed to the extent that specialization has occurred, resulting in improved quality of care in specialized areas of practice, cost-effectiveness of special services, and enhanced professional prestige and job satisfaction.

Despite the important arguments opposing specialization, organized psychology appears to have accepted that the arguments in favour of specialization outweigh the risks. The CPA/CPAP Task Force on Specialty Designation (Service et al., 1989), created at the wish of the 1984 State of the Discipline Review (Ritchie, et al, 1988), recommended development of a Canadian system for specialty designation. This suggestion was adopted by both the Canadian Psychological Association and the Council of Provincial Associations of Psychology. The CPA/CPAP Task Force report contains a number of optionsfor the formal recognition of specialties, ranging from self-declared areas of proficiency (where practitioner self-limit themselves to areas of practice where they can practise ethically), through a national register of proficiencies (somewhat analogous to the Canadian Register of Health Service Providers in Psychology), to nationally credentialed specialties – or even to legislatively established and enforced mandatory specialties.

Before any degree of consensus begins to emerge on the topic of specialties in Canada, several critical steps will be required:

1. First, criteria must be established for recognizing the existence of a proficiency or specialty.
2. Second, the value of a voluntary vs. a mandatory system of designation must be set, as mandatory systems can only be implemented by provincial regulatory bodies, while voluntary systems may be implemented by national or provincial organizations.
3. Third, there must be a review of the training and practice in potential proficiencies or specialties to determine whether the identified areas satisfy the criteria established.
4. Finally, a system must be established by recognized organizations to review the credentials of psychologists who wish to be granted status of possessing a proficiency or specialty.

In our view Canadian psychology has grown to a sufficiently differentiated state that the formal recognition of specialties is only a matter of time and effort. The profession will initially move from a system in which individuals self-declare "specializations" to a model in which organizations undertake a voluntary review of proficiencies on application by psychologists. A recent development in American psychology could have an important impact on the evolution of proficiency certification in Canada. Under the auspices of the American Psychological Association's Practice Directorate, a system for creating and delivering focused postdoctoral proficiency training is presently being established. The intended consumers are licensed and practicing professional psychologists. The potential for operating the system on a continental basis has already been recognized, and much like the joint accreditation agreement between the APA and the CPA (see Doyle et al., this volume), an analogous collaborative venture in this regard might arise.

As the definitional processes associated with specializations become more clear, a mandatory model of specialization will occur, though likely not in the near future. Finally, some organization or coalition of organizations will need to embrace the idea of proficiencies and specialties, and to work diligently to create the policies and procedures for credentialing this type work. To date, no organization within Canada has stepped forward to assume this mantle.

Public Versus Private Funding

One of the unfortunate omissions in the literature on professional psychology relates to the economics of the profession. For example, we do not know how may psychologists work in public vs. privately funded positions, nor the gross incomes of Canadian psychologists in these settings (although such data might exist with Revenue Canada). Despite the lack of definitive data for tracking the rate of change, there has been a gradual shift in funding sources from public to private funding, which, not surprisingly, mirrors that experienced in other professions.

An examination of the traditional means of funding professional psychology, even 20 years ago, shows that almost all positions were in public institutions: universities, colleges, hospitals, mental health clinics, schools, government and the military. Even though there was some limited amount of private counselling and clinical psychology services and some consultation in industry, the public purse paid for the vast majority of psychology positions. This situation has changed considerably over the past two decades. As provincial health-care plans steadily moved toward providing *basic* universal coverage, a market niche was created for the provision of privately insured supplementary health services, including psychology. Today, most major health-care insurance companies offer psychological services as a basic or optional component of their extended health plans. In the last decade, a growing number of employers have purchased or created employee assistance plans for their employees, many of which also offer time-limited psychological services (see Wilson, this volume). The exemption won for psychologists from the Goods and Services Tax (described in detail below) has further enhanced the ability of psychologists to operate in a financially sound manner in the private market.

Psychology has also gained advantages in the private economy through legislative changes and new legal procedures that have created other niches for the provision of services. The *Young Offenders Act* specifically designates psychologists for the assessment and treatment of young offenders, thereby creating a role for psychologists in this service sector. As well, recent no-fault insurance in Ontario permits the assessment and treatment of the victims of motor vehicle accidents by qualified psychologists. Also, the courts have begun routinely to turn to psychologists for assessment services related to custody and access disputes. Finally, these expanded roles and the credibility accorded psychology by the general public have progressively increased the demand for all applied psychological services, especially diagnosis, counselling and psychotherapy. The corporate world also continues to pursue its utilization of psychological knowledge and expertise.

The above does not mean that the range of income sources for psychology has found its logical limits. As Ritchie, Wilson, Berry, Boulay, King and Sabourin (1988) note, contemporary psychologists only use 12 of 168 hypothetical sources and methods of payment with any regularity. They suggest there is considerable market opportunity for the expansion of income models and sources, many of which are in the private sector (agency or corporate).

The effects on the profession of a shift from public to private funding is difficult to predict. Consequences for consumers of psychological services would likely be increased competition for funding and some cost containment as well as an increase in the consumer orientation of psychologists. This also creates the need to make services more understandable and marketable to a larger range of potential service purchasers. Other potential benefits –

assuming no erosion of current sources of income – would be an enhancement of the range of service opportunities for professionals and an increased overall range of services, with professional innovation meeting the needs of new markets.

There are, however, some risks involved in shifting to the private market. As private sources increasingly fund psychological services, the perception may arise that public funds are less needed. For example, as employee assistance programmes and private insurance carriers offer psychological services, provincially funded health-care programmes may feel less need to maintain their commitment to this activity. Given the well-known pressure on governments to trim health-care expenses, professional psychologists may in fact find themselves in a decreasing public market. If public funds for psychology do erode, unemployed or economically disadvantaged Canadians may find themselves unable to obtain adequate psychological services. Another problem concerns quality assurance: Although all psychologists have an ethical duty to provide competent service, in the private market psychologists get paid for the services they provide, regardless of their training to provide such services. The economics of survival in a private market may begin to dictate the types of services offered. Though there are checks and balances on quality control (e.g. individuals or groups with poor service reputations typically find they are not able to find work, the procedures for complaint and discipline in place regulatory body for psychology of each province), are these safeguards sufficient to ensure consistent quality control? On a positive note, Ontario's new Regulated Health Professions Acts, which includes psychology, introduced a 'Continuing Competence' requirement.

Recent fiscal pressures on all levels of government as well as on the private sector have affected every aspect of Canadian life including the health-care system. Since most professional psychologists will continue to be trained in the provision and delivery of health services, the future of Canada's health-care system will be of vital importance to the profession and to individual psychologists. Efforts at cost containment will continue. Experiences in the United States with managed care suggest that Canadians need to pay careful attention to similar developments in Canada.

In summary, there is little doubt that a shift away from public funding of psychological services and toward private funding is under way. We predict that the current balance will persist, and that the shift will likely continue into the foreseeable future. Professional psychology must position itself to provide competent services that meet the emerging market demands. It must not abandon its historic commitment to high-quality, publicly funded services.

Professional Autonomy

As the preceding chapters in this volume have amply demonstrated, there has been a remarkable expansion in the scope of professional psychology over the last decade, much of it into areas where a service has been needed and where psychological expertise has been one of the few or only means of addressing the service demand. Examples of this type of expansion include court-related assessments, employee assistance programmes, neuropsychological services, family assessment and therapy and a variety of services for the business world. Here, the steady development of services has often been limited less by competing professions or oppositional forces than by the number of trained psychologists and the proclivities of most psychologists not to venture into new practice areas. Inadequate funding has further affected the public's accessibility to most psychological services.

In contrast, there are areas of sustained problems of autonomy and resistance to the expansion of services. Nowhere have these phenomena been more in evidence than in institutional health-care facilities with their clear limitations to the autonomy of psychologists. For example, in some hospitals in Canada psychologists do not have autonomous departmental status, but rather function in divisions of Departments of Psychiatry. There are limits to a psychologist's functional scope of practice in the hospital, including admiting and discharging patients, and serving as their primary 'care-giver', even if the primary treatment consists of psychological 'care'.

The CPA, in collaboration with provincial associations, recently lobbied successfully to achieve greater recognition for autonomy of psychology in the accreditation standards of the Canadian

Council of Health Facilities Accreditation (CCHFA). The CCHFA has also asked psychology to be one of five professions to develop prototype standards for Quality Assurance. With the support of several provincial associations, the CPA has struck a Task Force to create such a proposal.

Even such well-established limits to autonomous practice as those just listed are coming under increased scrutiny and discussion within professional psychology. A recent court case in California (CAPP vs Rank) lead to a ruling that psychologists are capable of independent diagnosis and treatment of hospital inpatients (Youngstrom, 1990). Several other American states either already have similar legislation (e.g. North Carolina, Georgia), or are working toward this type of independent practice model within hospitals (e.g. New York, Massachusetts, Ohio). Such changes, however, do not assume a shift in payment mechanisms; privileges are available to both salaried and private practice psychologists.

Another area in which increased professional autonomy is presently being considered in the United States is prescription privileges. Several authors have argued that psychologists should be able to provide a more comprehensive and parsimonious treatment than is currently available by prescribing psychoactive drugs to patients (Brentar & McNamara, 1991a; 1991b; DeLeon, 1986; Fox, 1988). Obtaining these privileges would have several positive effects beyond enhanced patient care, including promotion of the image of psychology as a profession, increased financial opportunities and enhanced job satisfaction.

Resistance to such an expanded scope comes from both within and without the profession. Physicians have argued that medical training is required for the safe administration of medication (Staff, 1989a; 1989b). Others contend that obtaining prescription privileges would distort the nature of the profession as well as have a negative effect on and lengthen professional psychologists' already demanding training; it would cause marketing difficulties and lead to a major struggle between professional psychology and medicine (DeNelsky, 1991). Whether these potential problems justify the effort to obtain prescription privileges is a matter of continuing debate.

In Canada, arguments for hospital and prescription privileges for psychologists are less often heard. Also, there has been a traditional lag in efforts to enhance the professional autonomy of psychologists in Canada compared to their advent in the United States. Hence, current battles for autonomy being fought there are likely harbingers for the next decade in Canada. While not all changes will ultimately be adopted, American gains in professional autonomy have usually followed in Canada. There will be continued efforts on the part of organized psychology to gain autonomy and professional freedom, and we believe that the ability of professional psychology to organize itself to support sustained lobbying efforts will be a determining factor in whether these efforts succeed.

Public Policy Advocacy

In contrast to the situation in the United States, where organized professional lobbying and advocacy for public policy has long been a central activity of the national and state psychological associations, the Canadian experience with advocacy has been rather limited. Despite the examples of individuals who have been involved in public advocacy and some initial forays into the realm of public policy (typically to secure initial regulatory legislation in all provinces), there has emerged neither a true national strategy nor a plan on how to engage in advocacy, nor have the means to enact that strategy developed. Recently, some progress has been made toward making advocacy an ongoing component of national and provincial psychological organizations.

Several factors have worked against active political advocacy within Canadian psychology. From the earliest introduction to the profession onwards, exposure to the process of advocacy remains sparse. The training of psychologists in Canada is relatively conservative, with a large emphasis given research training and a small emphasis given public policy and social advocacy. The socialization of graduate students into the profession has therefore been limited. The organization of the Canadian political and constitutional worlds, with the powers affecting psychology being variously distributed and/or shared between federal and provincial governments, has caused a sporadic patchwork of lobbying efforts to evolve with little cohesion and frequent duplication of efforts supported by only marginal resources. Also, the economies of scale in a country with a relatively low population such as Canada has meant that in most areas of the country it has taken longer to gather a sufficient critical mass of psychologists available to advocate. Finally – and largely as a result of these factors – there were not even basic internal structures within the profession to organize and conduct lobbying strategies until the recent past.

Paradoxically, the coming of age of professional psychology occurs at a time in Canadian culture when all professions are undergoing a process of devaluation. What little data exists, however, suggests that psychologists are generally relatively well regarded by the public. While psychology has earned a reasonable degree of credit and trust (see Granger, this volume), there remains the ongoing challenge to maintain and build upon this positive perception while enhancing our advocacy efforts. The challenge should not deter the profession from assuming this task; indeed, from the perspective of the *Code of Ethics*, adopted by the Canadian Psychological Association and eight of the ten provincial regulatory bodies, the value statement accompanying the principle on Responsibility to Society demands social action and advocacy. Two aspects of this value statement are cited to highlight this injunction to psychologists:

> Psychologists, both as professionals and as private citizens, have responsibilities to the societies in which they live and work, such as the neighbourhood to city and to the welfare of all human beings in those societies.

> In order to be responsible to society and to contribute constructively to it's ongoing evolution, psychology as a whole needs to be self reflective about its place in society and about the ways in which it might be contributing to or detracting from beneficial societal changes. ... individual psychologists must decide for themselves the most appropriate and beneficial use of their time and talents in helping to meet this collective responsibility.

The *Code of Ethics* makes explicit that psychologists have an ethical responsibility to advocate change in societal values, practices and policies where such change is to the benefit of society. The transition from an individual ethical duty to the claim that professional psychology has an organizational duty to advocate social policies and positions is not difficult. Whether psychologists' advocacy in the public forum is ethical will be largely contingent upon whether their political behaviour and their advocacy choices meet the same standards as the other professional behaviours of psychologists. Fundamentally, the choices professional psychology makes with respect to advocacy do not require any different decision making or action than ethical conduct for individuals. This leaves much room for legitimate differences of opinion and informed debate while eschewing a stance of moral superiority.

While there are a number of examples demonstrating advocacy within psychology of specific legislation and social policy, Canadian psychologists have been reluctant to commit themselves or their resources to lobbying for either their own interests or for broader social change. These efforts have been irregular and reflect the absence of a general strategy. Clearly, psychologists have been involved in advocacy related to the establishment of psychology acts in all ten provinces as well as the North West Territories. The development of such legislation serves a social utility by ensuring certain standards of training, ethical conduct and public protection. It also serves the legitimate guild interests of psychology to create a viable profession, to limit unqualified access to service provision and to create employment and service roles for psychologists in the marketplace.

There are other examples of political advocacy, much of it also at the provincial level (see Granger, this volume, for Quebec examples). Among several noteworthy examples are the innovative collaboration of the Corporation professionnelle du Quebec with their pharmacist counterparts to mount a large public information campaign on psychological alternatives to medication as a means of coping with distress; the pioneering development by the Ontario Psychological Association of a political network instrumental in helping to secure psychologists' inclusion in "no-fault" insurance benefits; the licensed act of diagnosis in the new Regulated Health Professions legislation; the sustained work of the Psychologists Association of Manitoba with their Ministry of Health on expanding access to psychological services and the involvement of B. C. psychologists in the delivery of mental-health services to aboriginal Canadians. While provincially based advocacy initially developed in the provinces with larger numbers of psychologists, the attention given in the early 1990s to sustaining advocacy in all provincial associations is one of the most hopeful indicators for psychology's future. The information sharing and collaboration afforded by the Council of Provincial Associations of Psychology and the emerging support of CPA increase the probability that the profession is at a watershed in its commitment to respond more consistently to its responsibility to society.

One of the best national examples is the advocacy surrounding the introduction of the Goods and Services Tax legislation by the federal government in the fall of 1989. When the legislation was first tabled in draft form by the Minister of Finance, the intent was to tax all goods and services in Canada, with certain few exemptions. While health care was designated as exempt from taxation, psychological services were not included as part of the health-care exemption because of the narrow criterion adopted (i. e. public funding under provincial Medicare plans on a fee for service basis).

The absence of an exemption for psychologists' services from the Goods and Services Tax (GST) prompted a strong response from organized psychology. Persons requiring psychological services had experienced artificial barriers of various sorts (e.g. third-party gatekeepers, exclusions from certain payment mechanisms). As a result, psychologists had already begun advocating increased accessibility to psychological services in several provinces. The new federal legislation would have effectively created an additional barrier. The lack of an exemption also implied that psychological services did not constitute an essential component of health care. At the urging of several provincial associations, the CPA quickly made the decision to seek inclusion of health-care psychologists as exempt practitioners from the GST provisions.

The response of organized psychology to the GST was historic in its intensity and magnitude of effort. The CPA coordinated the joint advocacy campaign of the national and provincial associations of psychology, with the Council of Provincial Associations of Psychology playing a pivotal role. Funds were gathered on a voluntary basis to support the mail, telephone, travel and other costs related to a national advocacy campaign, and a small network of individuals across the country provided information to the several thousand psychologists who eventually participated in the campaign about what and when to advocate. So when the Finance Committee hearings on the GST bill were held across the country, professional psychology was well represented.

There is no doubt that the GST campaign was not uniformly smooth and successful. Indeed, after the Finance Committee hearings, the Minister announced to the House of Commons a few amendments to the bill, thereby rejecting most of the recommendations of the Finance Committee, one of which included the exemption of psychologists' health services. Additional focused lobbying in the winter and early spring of 1990, however, resulted in the inclusion of psychologists in the third and final reading of the bill.

One of the lessons to be learned from the GST campaign is that professional psychology can organize itself and effectively lobby on issues of national importance. Indeed, the GST campaign stands as a major achievement in national lobbying among all health-care professions. Another lesson lies in the reason psychologists were ultimately exempted from the legislation: In the final analysis, psychologists were perceived as advocating a position that was fundamentally in the public interest, rather than from a self-interested perspective. Further, psychologists did not attack the political philosophy behind the bill; rather, they limited their comment and lobbying efforts to the impact of the legislation on those who need psychological services. In essence, they spoke up vigorously on behalf of their patients. Legislators and bureaucratic policymakers serve the public to whom they are accountable. While large groups can sometimes generate sufficient pressure to achieve measures that support their narrow interests at the expense of the public, most efforts to advocate policies inconsistent with what is perceived as the public good are likely to be unsuccessful.

Another lesson from the GST campaign is that effective advocacy is expensive. The financial costs as well as the utilization of paid and volunteer human resources were greater than had ever been mounted for any other such campaign in Canada. In the short term, it would have been difficult to mount so quickly another major advocacy effort if a similar public policy issue had been forthcoming. Fortunately, active consideration is currently being given by the CPA, the CPAP, the Canadian Register and several provincial associations to establishing a sustained national advocacy program.

The long-term value of the GST campaign remains to be determined. Was it an exception to historic passivity in Canadian psychology or rather an early example of a more activist orientation? What is clear is that members of the public who use psychological health services already benefit from the exemption. The success of the GST campaign has also been noted by other health disciplines, so that professional psychology is obtaining opportunities for collaborative efforts it would not otherwise have had. One of the more important outcomes is that psychology has been specifically recognized and named in federal tax legislation as a profession providing basic health services on a basis similar to the more established health professions. While the immediate implications of this recognition are limited, judicial or statutory recognition in one instance can serve as the precedent for such recognition in other arenas.

But there are other notable areas in which professional psychology has been either ineffective or even silent. Perhaps no better example exists than the recent attempt by the federal government to establish legislation related to abortion. Irrespective of one's individual moral position on this issue, one criterion the federal government considered for legally sanctioned abortion was maternal psychological distress. Had this legislation been passed into law, there would have been abortion decisions based upon this circumstance.

Given the implications of the proposed legislation for professional psychologists, some response might have been expected. It could have paralleled the clear opposition to the Bill by the Canadian Medical Association as an inappropriate intrusion into the delivery of health care or it could have addressed the difficulty of developing a valid set of criteria for establishing the necessary condition of such psychological distress, or it even could have offered an evaluation strategy based upon sound psychological research. Yet no word came from psychology to influence the debate or the ultimate implementation of the abortion bill. The silence of organized psychology on this issue is perhaps understandable, given the affect that it engenders. Nonetheless, such a lack of action is at best paradoxical and contradictory to the ethical decision-making process adopted by the CPA, psychology being implicated in the legislation regardless of its consent.

Other areas amenable to social policy advocacy will no doubt continue to emerge in areas in which professional psychology has gained expertise. If current trends prevail, the profession will be in an enhanced position to address these areas. We share a vision in which professional psychology will not simply react to emerging issues, but will help proactively to shape the debate and the social fabric of the country. An issue on which there has been considerable discussion and general agreement over the years (though not universal agreement – see Wilson, this volume) is the inclusion of psychologists in Medicare. There have even been efforts at the provincial levels, most notably in Ontario, Manitoba and British Columbia, to seek inclusion in provincial health-care plans.

Serious consideration of reforms to the system that has largely been in place since the creation of Medicare 25 years ago is now beginning. The Canadian Psychological Association, in collaboration with six partners (Canadian Hospital Association, Canadian Long-term Care Association, Canadian Medical Association, Canadian Nurses Association, Canadian Public Health Association, Consumers Association of Canada), has created the Health Action Lobby (HEAL) to promote the preservation and careful reform of the Canadian health-care system. In addition to supporting the five historic principles of accessibility, comprehensiveness, portability, public administration and universality, HEAL also endorses illness prevention, health promotion and health public policy as cornerstones for reform. The advent of HEAL and role of psychology within it have the potential to influence the balance of public and private funding of psychological services over the next decade.

In summary, sustained advocacy by professional psychology on a range of issues linking psychological knowledge, expertise and practice with the public good is both an ethical requirement, particularly from the perspective of social responsibility, as well as a matter of enlightened self-interest. Although there have been some examples of effective political advocacy, there are other areas in which psychology has been either mute or passively acquiescent. The profession requires a system to derive clear and defensible social policy positions as well as the ability to then act upon these positions. Various models for such structures exist to some extent already; all provincial societal organizations as well as the Canadian Psychological Association (CPA) have Professional Affairs Committees (or their analogue). Another option is to pool financial resources to develop a commonly shared advocacy agency, either ancillary to an existing organizational structure such as the CPA or in some other manner. Until a coherent stable structure exists, professional psychology will not realize its maximal social utility nor its optimal potential to render effective professional services.

Summary and Conclusions

This chapter distills from the many areas in which professional psychology has grown several critical issues for continued development. The areas of training and accreditation, specialization, public vs. private sector funding, professional autonomy and advocacy will be among the major determinants for the future of professional psychology in Canada. Within each of these areas, we have highlighted current trends and made some predictions about the future.

Concurrent with the publication of this book is the latest period of doubt about the future of Canada as a federal state. While the specifics of constitutional debate are beyond our scope, the outcomes of the current debate have important implications for the future of our profession on the upper half of the North American continent. Whether to remain a single nation or create new forms of economic union or establish asymmetrical federalism or sovereignty-association, even with varying options for the distribution of powers, are only a few of the options presently being considered. The choices made will determine the larger political and social systems that will define the challenges and opportunities we face in our profession. They will also strongly influence the structures and procedures we need to support the continued evolution of our profession and its contribution to society.

Perhaps the most heartening short-term development for professional psychologists is that psychology has chosen to play an active role in the overall process. Through the Health Action Lobby (HEAL) described earlier, the CPA and the provincial associations have developed proposals to safeguard the integrity of the health-care system and to enhance its capacity to respond to the needs of citizens under whatever new constitutional arrangement. The inclusion of "healthy public policy", illness prevention and health promotion as well as more traditional direct patient services in HEAL's framework for reform covers the large majority of psychological services. Those not included, largely in the domain of industrial-organizational psychology, will likely be untroubled since the corporate world with whom they usually work closely prefers to remain unfettered by public policy intrusions into the private sector.

On balance, our estimation is that professional psychology's future is bright, but there will undoubtedly be growing pains in such a diverse and complex profession. We trust that psychologists will show the ethical and impassioned efforts for the enhancement of professional psychology that have characterized its growth in the past half-century.

References

Belar, C., & Perry, N.W. (1991). *National Conference on Scientist-Practitioner Education and Training for the Professional Practice of Psychology*. Sarasota, FL: Professional Resource Press.

Brentar, J., & McNamara, J.R. (1991 a). The right to prescribe medication: Considerations for professional psychology, *Professional Psychology: Research and Practice*, 22, 179–187.

Brentar, J., & McNamara, J.R. (1991 b). Prescription privileges for psychology: The next step in its evolution as a profession. *Professional Psychology: Research and Practice*, 22, 194–195.

Conway, J.B. (1991). Not cognitivism, but professionalism and clinicalism will prevail in clinical psychology: The worst dreams of Hebb and Tulving. *Canadian Psychology*, 32, 451–460.

DeLeon, P.H. (1986). Increasing the societal contribution of organized psychology. *American Psychologist*, 41, 466–474.

DeNelsky, G.Y. (1991). Prescription privileges for psychologists: The case against. *Professional Psychology: Research and Practice*, 22, 188–193.

Fox, R.E. (1988). Prescription privileges: Their implications for the practice of psychology. *Psychotherapy*, 25, 501–507.

Hall, J.E. (1988). The role of the state. In G. Stricker & A.R. Rodriguez (Eds.), *Handbook of quality assurance in mental health*. New York: Plenum Press.

Handy, L., & Whitsett, S. (1991). *Report of the CPA-CPAP Task Force on Midcareer Training for Psychologists.* Old Chelsea, Quebec: Canadian Psychological Association.

Hunsley, J., & Lefebvre, M. (1990). A survey of the practices and activities of Canadian clinical psychologists. *Canadian Psychology, 31*, 350–358.

Matarazzo, J.D. (1987). There is only one psychology, no specialties, but may applications. *American Psychologist*, 42, 893–902.

Ritchie, P., Hogan, T., & Hogan, T. (1988). *State of the Discipline Review: Opinicon II.* Old Chelsea, Quebec: Canadian Psychological Association.

Ritchie, P., Wilson, R., Berry, R., Boulay, M., King, M., & Sabourin, M. (1988). The funding of psychological health care services. *Canadian Psychology*, 29, 187–205.

Sales, B. D., Bricklin, P., & Hall, J. (1983). *Manual for the identification and continued recognition of proficiencies and new specialties in psychology (Draft Report of the Subcommittee on Specialization).* Washington, D.C.: American Psychological Association.

Schaps, L.S., & Sales, B.D. (1983). Specialization in psychology: Lessons from other professions. In B.D. Sales, P. Bricklin & J. Hall (Eds.), *Manual for the Identification and continued recognition of proficiencies and new specialties in psychology.* Washington, D.C.: American Psychological Association.

Scott, T.R. (1991). A personal view of the future of psychology departments. *American Psychologist*, 46, 975–976.

Service, J., Sabourin, M., Catano, V., Day, H., Hayes, C., & MacDonald, G.W. (1989). *Report of the CPA-CPAP Task Force on Specialty Designation.* Old Chelsea, Quebec: Canadian Psychological Association.

Staff (1989 a, June). Psychotropic medications. *Registrar Report*, p. 11–12.

Staff (1989 b, September). Psychiatrists oppose prescription privileges and direct medicare reimbursement for psychologists. *Registrar Report*, p. 8.

Youngstrom, N. (1990). CAPP v. Rank is overturned. *The APA Monitor.* Washington, D.C.: American Psychological Association.

Appendix 1

Universities Providing Graduate Training in Professional Psychology

Alberta

The University of Alberta, Edmonton, Alberta, T6G 2E1
The University of Calgary, Calgary, Alberta, T2N 1N4
The University of Lethbridge, Lethbridge, Alberta, T1K 3M4

British Columbia

The University of B. C., Vancouver, B. C., V6T 1W5
Simon Fraser University, Burnaby, B. C., V5A 1S6
University of Victoria, Victoria, B. C., V8W 2Y2

Manitoba

The University of Manitoba, Winnipeg, Manitoba, R3T 2N2
The University of Winnipeg, Winnipeg, Manitoba R3B 2E9

New Brunswick

Université de Moncton, Moncton, New Brunswick, E1A 3E9
Mount Allison University, Sackville, N. B., EOA 3C0
University of New Brunswick, Fredericton, N. B., E3B 5A3
St. Thomas University, Fredericton, N. B., E3B 5G3

Newfoundland

Memorial University of NFLD, St. John's, NFLD, A1C 5S7

Nova Scotia

Acadia University, Wolfville, Nova Scotia, BOP 1XO
Dalhousie University, Halifax, Nova Scotia, B3H 3J5
Mount Saint Vincent University, Halifax, Nova Scotia, B3M 2J6
St. Francis Xavier University, Antigonish, Nova Scotia, B2G 1CO
Saint Mary's University, Halifax, Nova Scotia, B3H 3C3

Ontario

Brock University, St. Catherine's, Ontario, L2S 3A1
Carlton University, Ottawa, Ontario, KlS 5B6
University of Guelph, Guelph, Ontario, N1G 2W1
Lakehead University, Thunder Bay, Ontario, P7B 5E1
Laurentian University of Sudbury Sudbury, Ontario, P3E 2C6
McMaster University, Hamilton, Ontario, L8S 4L8
Ontario Institute for Studies in Education, Toronto, Ontario, M5S 1V6
University of Ottawa, Ottawa, Ontario, KlN 6N5
Queen's University, Kingston, Ontario, K7L 3N6
University of Toronto, Toronto, Ontario, M5S 1A1
Trent University, Peterborough, Ontario, K9J 7B8
University of Waterloo, Waterloo, Ontario, N2L 3G1
The University of Western Ontario, London, Ontario, N6A 3K7
Wilfred Laurier University, Waterloo, Ontario, N2L 3C5
University of Windsor, Windsor, Ontario, N9B 3P4
York University, North York, Ontario, M3J 1P3

Prince Edward Island

University of P.E.I., Charlottetown, P.E.I., C1A 4P3

Quebec

Bishop's University, Lennoxville, Quebec, JlM 1Z7
Concordia University, Montreal, Quebec, H3G 1M8
Université de Laval, Quebec City, Quebec, G1K 7P4
McGill University, Montreal, Quebec, H3A 2T5
Université de Montreal, Montreal, Quebec, H3C 3J7
Université de Quebec, Sainte-Foy, Quebec, G1V 2M3
Université de Quebec
  en Abitibi-Temiscamingue, Rouyn, Quebec, J9X 5E4
  à Chicoutimi, Chicoutimi, Quebec, G7H 2B1
  à Hull, Hull, Quebec, J8X 3X7
  à Montreal, Montreal, Quebec, H3C 3P8
  à Rimouski, Rimouski, Quebec, G5L 3A1
  à Trois-Rivieres, Trois-Rivieres, Quebec, G9A 5H7
Université de Sherbrooke, Sherbrooke, Quebec, J1K 2R1

Saskatchewan

University of Regina, Regina, Saskatchewan, S4S OA2
University of Saskatchewan, Saskatoon, Saskatchewan, S7N OWO

Appendix 2

Graduate Programs in Professional Psychology in Canada 1993

British Columbia:

University of British Columbia

1. Department of Psychology: Clinical (Ph.D. — APA and CPA accredited), Environmental (Ph.D), Forensic (Ph.D.)
2. Department of Educational Psychology: Educational Psychology (Ed.D.)
3. Department of Counselling Psychology: Counselling Psychology (Ed.D.)

Simon Fraser University

1. Department of Psychology: Clinical (Ph.D. — APA and CPA accredited)

2. Department of Educational Psychology: Educational Psychology (M.Ed.)

University of Victoria

1. Department of Psychology: Clinical neuropsychology (Ph.D), Clinical (Ph.D)
2. Department of Educational Psychology: Educational Psychology (M.Ed.), Counselling Psychology (M.Ed.)

Alberta:

University of Alberta

1. Department of Psychology: Personality and psychopathology (Ph.D)
2. Department of Educational Psychology: Educational psychology (Ph.D.), Counselling psychology (Ph.D.)

University of Calgary

1. Department of Psychology: Clinical (Ph.D.), Industrial/Organizational/Ergonomics (Ph.D.)
2. Department of Educational Psychology: Counselling psychology (Ph.D.), Special education (Ph.D.), Rehabilitation (Ph.D.), School and Community-Clinical (Ph.D.)
3. Faculty of Graduate Studies: Clinical (Ph.D.)

Saskatchewan:

University of Regina

1. Department of Psychology: Clinical (Ph.D)
2. Department of Educational Psychology: Counselling psychology (M.Ed.)

University of Saskatchewan

1. Department of Psychology: Clinical (Ph.D — APA and CPA accredited), Applied social (Ph.D)
2. Department of Educational Psychology: Educational psychology (M.Ed.)

Manitoba:

University of Manitoba

1. Department of Psychology: Behaviour modification (Ph.D), Clinical (Ph.D. — APA and CPA accredited)
2. Department of Educational Psychology: Educational psychology (M.Ed.)

St. Boniface University

1. Department of Educational Psychology: Educational psychology (M.Ed.)

Ontario:

Lakehead University

1. Department of Psychology: Clinical (M.A)

University of Windsor

1. Department of Psychology: Clinical (Ph.D. — APA and CPA accredited), clinical respecialization diploma

University of Western Ontario

1. Department of Psychology: Clinical (Ph.D. — APA and CPA accredited), Clinical neuropsychology (Ph.D), Personality, interpersonal behaviour, and applied measurement (Ph.D), Industrial/organizational (Ph.D)

2. Department of Educational Psychology: Counselling psychology (M.Ed.), Educational psychology (M.Ed.), Guidance counselling (M.Ed.)

University of Waterloo

1. Department of Psychology: Applied (M.Sc.), Clinical (Ph.D. — APA and CPA accredited)

Wilfred Laurier University

1. Department of Psychology: Applied Community (M.A.)

University of Guelph

1. Department of Psychology: Applied Child (M.A.), Industrial/Organizational (M.A.)

York University

1. Department of Psychology: Clinical (Ph.D. — CPA accredited), Clinical — developmental (Ph.D)

University of Toronto

1. Department of Psychology: Human neuropsychology (Ph.D.). 2. Institute of Child Studies: Child Assessment and Counselling (Diploma)

Ontario Institute for Studies in Education, University of Toronto

1. Department of Psychology: Educational psychology (Ph.D, Ed.D), Counselling psychology (Ed.D), School psychology (Ph.D, Ed.D)

Queen's University

1. Department of Psychology: Clinical (Ph.D. — APA and CPA accredited), Basic and applied (Ph.D)

Carleton University

1. Department of Psychology: Neuropsychology (Ph.D)

University of Ottawa (CPA & APA accreditation)

1. School of Psychology: Clinical (Ph.D. — APA and CPA accredited)
2. Department of Educational Psychology: Educational psychology (Ph.D.), School psychology (Ph.D.)

Quebec:

Concordia University

1. Department of Psychology: Applied (M.A), Clinical psychology (Ph.D. — APA and CPA accredited)
2. Faculty of Education: Art Therapy (Diploma)

McGill University

1. Department of Psychology: Clinical (Ph.D. — APA and CPA accredited), Neuropsychology (Ph.D)
2. Department of Educational Psychology: Counselling psychology (Ph.D.), Educational Psychology (Ph.D.)

Université de Montreal

1. Department of Psychology: Clinical (Ph.D), Counselling (Ph.D.), School (Ph.D.), Community (Ph.D.), Industrial/organizational (Ph.D), Behaviour Therapy (D.Ps.)

Universite de Laval

1. Ecole de Psychologie: Clinical (Ph.D), School and development (Ph.D), Social and community (Ph.D)

Université du Quebec à Quebec

1. Department of Psychology: Clinical (Ph.D.)

Université du Quebec à Chicoutimi

1. Department of Psychology: Clinical (M.Ps. — coordinated with UQ-Trois Rivieres)

Université du Quebec à Trois-Rivieres

1. Department of Psychology: Clinical (M.Ps. — coordinated with UQ-Chicoutimi)

Université de Sherbrooke

1. Department of Psychology: Human Relations (M.Ps.), Industrial/Organizational (M.Ps.)

New Brunswick:

University of New Brunswick

1. Department of Psychology: Applied (Ph.D)
2. Department of Educational Psychology: Educational psychology (M.Ed.), Counselling psychology (M.Ed.)

Nova Scotia:

Acadia University

1. Department of Psychology: Community — Clinical (Ph.D.)
2. Department of Educational Psychology: Counselling psychology (M.Ed.)

Dalhousie University

1. Department of Psychology: Clinical (Ph.D. — collaborative with Mount Saint Vincent, Acadia and Saint Mary's universities)
2. Department of Educational Psychology: Educational psychology (Ph.D.)

Mount Saint Vincent University

1. Department of Psychology: Clinical (see Dalhousie University)
2. Department of Educational Psychology: Educational psychology (M.A), School psychology (M.A)

St. Francis Xavier University

1. Department of Psychology: Clinical (see Dalhousie University)

Saint Mary's University

1. Department of Psychology: Clinical (see Dalhousie University), Applied (M.Sc)

Prince Edward Island:

None

Newfoundland:

Memorial University of Newfoundland

1. Department of Psychology: Clinical (M.Sc)
2. Department of Educational Psychology: Educational psychology (M.Ed.), Counselling psychology (M.Ed.)

Note: The sources of this table are the *Directory of Canadian Universities*, Association of Universities and Colleges of Canada, 1986, and *Graduate Study in Psychology and Related Fields*, American Psychological Association, 1992, as well as library work conducted by the author and ably assisted by Todd Willoughby. All listed degrees are the *highest* potential degree; generally doctoral programs also provide Masters level training. All errors, of which there are likely several, are the authors.

Appendix 3

Regulatory Bodies of Psychology in Canada

Alberta	Psychologists Association of Alberta[1] Suite 400, 10123–99 St., Edmonton, Alberta, T5J 3H1 (403) 424–5070
British Columbia	College of Psychologists of B.C.[2] Suite 10, 865 West 10th Avenue, Vancouver, B.C., V5Z 1L7 (604) 877–1454
Manitoba	Psychological Association of Manitoba 18th Floor – 155 Carleton,

1 These associations provide both regulatory and societal functions in these provinces.

2 In addition to the College of Psychologists of B.C., a societal organization is currently being formed, called the B.C. Psychological Association.

	Winnipeg, Manitoba, R3C 3H8 (204) 947–3698
New Brunswick	College des psychologues du Nouveau Brunswick[1] C.P. 1194, Succursale A, Fredericton, N.B., E3B 1BO (506) 459–1994
Newfoundland	Newfoundland Board of Examiners in Psychology P.O. Box 5666, Station C, St John's, Newfoundland, A1C 5W8 (709) 737–8874
Northwest Territories	Dept. of Safety & Public Services, Government of Northwest Territories, Yellowknife, N.W.T., X1A 2L9, (403) 920–8058
Nova Scotia	Nova Scotia Board of Examiners in Psychology P.O. Box 27124, Halifax, N.S., B3H 4M8, (902) 423–2238
Ontario	Ontario Board of Examiners in Psychology 101 Davenport Road, Toronto, Ontario, M5R 1H5 (416) 961–8817
Prince Edward Island	P.E.I. Psychologists Registration Board Richmond Centre, P.O. Box 2000, Charlottetown, P.E.I.. C1A 7N8 (902) 368–4430

Quebec	Corporation Professionelle des psychologues du Quebec[1] 1100, avenue Beaumont, Ville Mont Royal, Montreal, Quebec, H3P 3E5 (514) 738–1881
Saskatchewan	Saskatchewan Psychological Association Mental Health Centre, P. O. Box 1056, Weyburn, Saskatchewan, S4H 2L4 (306) 848–2800

Societal Bodies of Psychology in Canada

Manitoba	Manitoba Psychological Society 1000 – 363 Broadway Ave., Winnipeg, Manitoba, R3C 3N9 (204) 947–3698
Newfoundland	Association of Newfoundland Psychologists[3]
Nova Scotia	Association of Psychologists of Nova Scotia P. O. Box 594, Stn. M, Halifax, N. S. B3J 2R7 (902) 428–8454
Ontario	Ontario Psychological Association Suite 221, 730 Yonge St., Toronto, Ontario, M4Y 2B7 (416) 961–5552
Prince Edward Island	Psychological Association of P.E.I.[3]
Saskatchewan	Psychological Society of Saskatchewan[3]

3 These associations have no permanent address. To obtain the name of a current contact person, please call the Canadian Psychological Association office at (819) 827–3927.

Appendix 4

National and International Psychological Organizations

National

Canadian Psychological Association
Chemin Vincent,
Old Chelsea, Quebec,
J0X 2N0
(819) 827–3927

Canadian Register of Health Service Providers in Psychology
37 Clarence St., Suite #4,
Ottawa, Ontario,
K1P 5P4
(613) 562–0900

International

American Psychological Association
750 First St., N. E.,
Washington, D.C. 20002–4242
(202) 336–5500

American Board of Professional Psychology
180 Broad St. East,
Rochester, N.Y. 14604

Association of State & Provincial Psychology Boards
P. O. Box 4389,
Montgomery, Alabama 36103

European Federation of Professional Psychologists Associations
c/o Dr. Ype Poortinga, President (1992–1993)
Norsk Psyckologforening
Prof. Dahlsgt. 18
N-0353 Oslo Norway